The Longest Winter

The Longest Winter

Scott's Other Heroes

MEREDITH HOOPER

JOHN MURRAY

First published in Great Britain in 2010 by John Murray (Publishers)
An Hachette UK Company

I

A CIP catalogue record for this title is available from the British Library

Hardback ISBN 978-0-7195-9580-6
Trade paperback ISBN 978-1-84854-306-5

Typeset in 11.5/14 Monotype Bembo by Servis Filmsetting Ltd, Stockport, Cheshire

Printed and bound by Clays Ltd, St Ives plc

John Murray policy is to use papers that are natural, renewable and recyclable products and made from wood grown in sustainable forests. The logging and manufacturing processes are expected to conform to the environmental regulations of the country of origin.

John Murray (Publishers)
338 Euston Road
London NW1 3BH

www.johnmurray.co.uk

For Michael and Rachel

Contents

List of maps and illustrations ix
The British Antarctic Expedition 1910–13: characters and
    locations xix
Antarctic expeditions relevant to this account xxiii
Measurements and place-names xxv

Introduction I
1   It *must* be an Englishman 7
2   Leaving London: 1 June–30 September 1910 29
3   The home run: 1 October–31 December 1910 40
4   The little village at our cape: 1–28 January 1911 58
5   In search of our home: 29 January–9 February 1911 ... 75
6   Coal will decide: 12–20 February 1911 93
7   The unknown coast: 20 February–10 April 1911 103
8   Living at Cape Adare: 10 April–21 July 1911 121
9   The uncertainty of the ice: 27 July–16 August
    1911 139
10 The damnedest luck: 21 August–20 October 1911 151
11 Penguin summer: 21 October 1911–1 January
    1912 165
12 At last science!: 3 January–17 February 1912 182
13 Hope deferred maketh the heart sick: 18 February–
    7 March 1912 197
14 Marooned: 10 March–1 April 1912 211
15 Icy isolation: 1 April–31 May 1912 225
16 Igloo winter: 1 June–31 July 1912 242
17 Dismal misery: 1 August–30 September 1912 253
18 Drygalski past: 1–27 October 1912 266

CONTENTS

19 Saving themselves: 28 October–7 November 1912   280

20 Homewards: 8 November 1912–26 January 1913   295

Acknowledgements   308

Bibliography   311

Notes   317

Index   348

List of maps and illustrations

MAPS

Antarctica and the Southern Hemisphere   xi
The Ross Sea region of Antarctica   xii
Victoria Land, Antarctica   xiii
Evans Coves and Inexpressible Island, Antarctica   xiv
Ross Island, Antarctica   xv

ILLUSTRATIONS

Campbell and his men relax, safe at last   front cover
Browning's Midwinter Day menu card   132
A plan of the ice-cave   220

PLATE SECTIONS

Campbell and his men outside the Cape Adare hut
Terra Nova departing New Zealand
Relaxing in the sunshine on the deck of *Terra Nova*
Man-hauling stores from *Terra Nova* to Cape Evans
Equipment and ponies on the Cape Evans beach
Hauling ballast below Mount Erebus
Unloading one of Campbell's ponies at Cape Evans
Levick skinning an Adélie penguin
Campbell and Levick gutting a seal at Cape Adare
Searching for biological specimens at Cape Adare

A specimen at last – Priestley with seaweed at Cape Adare
Abbott wearing the noseguard he invented
Priestley searching for specimens near Mount Melbourne
Winter quarters hut at Cape Adare
Carsten Borchgrevink's hut at Cape Adare
Browning and Dickason cooking at Cape Adare
Dickason on his bed in the hut
Campbell working at his chart table
Priestley typing at the central table
Abbott on his bed by the galley
Levick starting a post-mortem on a crabeater seal
Midwinter dinner at Cape Adare
Dickason with slops bucket and ice axe
Priestley and Campbell summer sledging near Evans Coves
Two loaded sledges during summer sledging
Browning and Abbott on the Boomerang Glacier
Levick, Browning and Abbott in their tent
Abbott and Browning at the entrance to the ice-cave
The interior of the ice-cave
Dickason Campbell and Abbott emerging from the ice-cave
Priestley, Levick and Browning outside the ice-cave

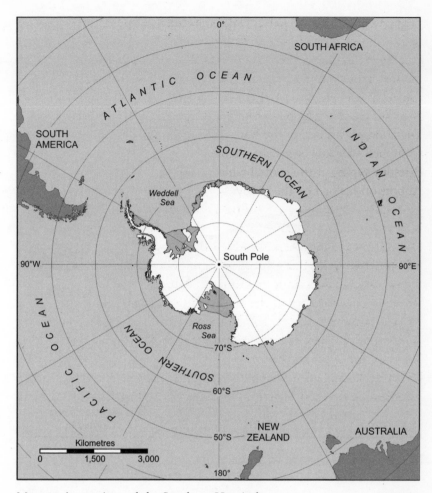

Map 1   Antarctica and the Southern Hemisphere

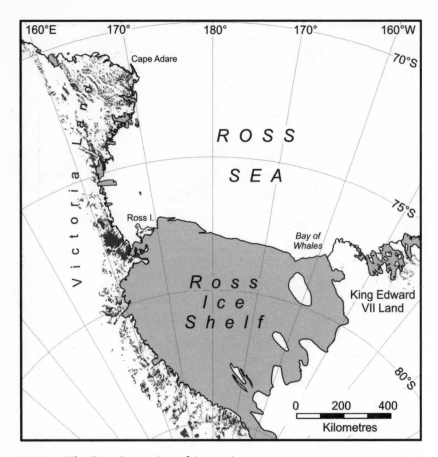

Map 2   The Ross Sea region of Antarctica

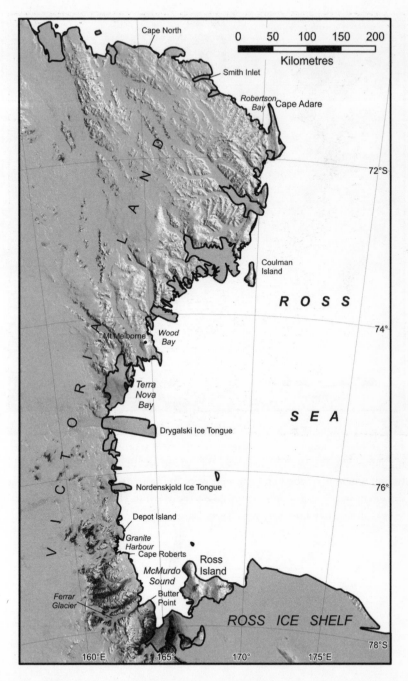

Map 3   Victoria Land, Antarctica, with locations mentioned in the text

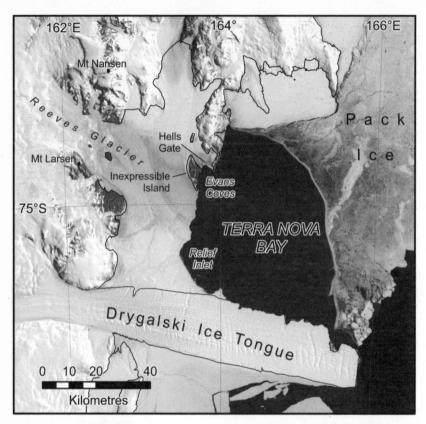

Map 4   The area of Evans Coves where Campbell's party landed on 8 January 1912 to begin exploring. In autumn unexpected, intense winds began sweeping down the Reeves Glacier from the inland ice sheet, across Inexpressible Island, where Campbell and his men were living in an ice-cave. The satellite image on which this map is based shows these winds clearing the pack ice out to sea, almost blocking access to Terra Nova Bay, as occurred in 1912.

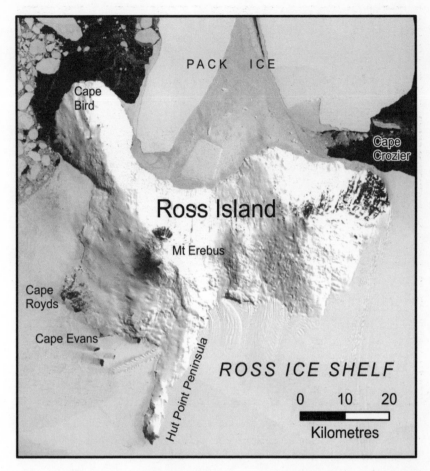

Map 5　A satellite image of Ross Island, showing its relationship to the Ross Ice Shelf ('the Barrier'), and extensive sea ice in McMurdo Sound

A for Antarctica, all frost, ice and snow
    the place where half witted explorers all go
B for the word they most frequently use
    though not, we admit, without frequent excuse.

Murray Levick, written inside the cover of his ice-cave diary,
1912

The British Antarctic Expedition 1910–13
Characters and locations

CAPTAIN ROBERT FALCON Scott listed everyone on his British Antarctic Expedition under two headings: ship and shore. Departing New Zealand for Antarctica in November 1910, his expedition vessel *Terra Nova* had fifty-nine people on board. Thirty-one moved on shore when the ship anchored against the ice in January 1911, leaving twenty-eight in the ship's party to take *Terra Nova* exploring and then return to New Zealand. Scott set up his winter quarters hut at Cape Evans on Ross Island (see Maps 2 and 5), in the angle of ice-filled ocean where the massive ice shelf men called 'the Barrier' met the mountain ranges of Victoria Land. Scott's aim was to try and achieve the South Pole, and almost everyone in the shore party contributed to that goal in one way or another.

In line with Scott's long-planned objectives, the shore party was divided into an Eastern party and a Western party. The great majority, designated as the Western party, used the hut on Ross Island as their base. Those whom Scott selected to travel towards the Pole, in various supporting roles, became known as the Southern party, with the five who finally made the assault on the Pole being the Polar party. A small group of men detailed off to do geology on the Victoria Land coast (see Map 3), in the summer of 1911 and the summer of 1912, were designated Far West.

The Eastern party, consisting of six members, formed Scott's 'other expedition', with the task of establishing a second base to explore and do science while Scott concentrated on the Pole. Within three weeks of arriving at Cape Evans the party left, supplied for one or two years' isolation with their own equipment, hut, food and two ponies to pull sledges. Their long-planned goal was to discover the nature of the land terminating the eastern end of the Barrier ice shelf, discovered by

Scott in 1902, during his first Antarctic expedition (see Map 2). Scott had named his discovery King Edward VII Land, after the son of Queen Victoria, but no one had yet managed to get ashore.

The Eastern party's adventures and travels, in particular the long winter they spent at Evans Coves (see Maps 3 and 4), are the subject of this book. To everyone on Scott's expedition in Antarctica, the Eastern party was always called the Eastern party, whatever happened to them, wherever they were, even when their plans changed and they were sent north. However, unknown to anyone in Antarctica, the Eastern party was re-designated in London as the 'Northern party'. Perhaps a letter from Wilfred Bruce, Kathleen Scott's bluff jovial brother, who served as a lieutenant on *Terra Nova*, initiated the change: 'alas, no longer "Eastern!"', he wrote to Kathleen, as *Terra Nova* took the Eastern party north. *Terra Nova* removed all the remaining members of Scott's expedition from Antarctica in January 1913. The Eastern party now found that back in London they had been re-designated as the 'Northern party'. The new name replaced the old in all published documents, reports and accounts of the expedition.

This book tells the story of the Eastern party, as it happened, drawing on the participants' diaries and journals. It therefore uses the name 'Eastern party'. As far as Lieutenant Victor Campbell, Dr Murray Levick, Raymond Priestley, Petty Officer George Abbott, Petty Officer Frank Browning and Seaman Harry Dickason were concerned, they were, as they sang in their Eastern party sledging song:

'Captain Scott his Eastern Party & we're going strong'.

Details of the Shore party, with their ages on the day of landing in Antarctica, Wednesday 4 January 1911, follow:

The Western party
Taken from the ship's complement

Leader Captain Robert Falcon Scott CVO RN, known as 'The Owner', aged forty-two

Lieutenant Edward R. G. R. Evans RN, known as 'Teddy', aged twenty-nine

Lieutenant Henry R. Bowers RIM, known as 'Birdie', aged twenty-seven

Dr Edward L. Atkinson, Surgeon, RN, known as 'Atch', aged twenty-nine

Captain Lawrence E. G. Oates, 6th Inniskilling Dragoons, known as 'Titus', in charge of ponies, aged thirty

William Lashly, Chief Stoker, RN, aged forty-two

Robert Forde, Petty Officer, RN, aged thirty-five

Edgar Evans, Petty Officer, RN, aged thirty-four

Thomas Crean, Petty Officer, RN, aged thirty-three

Patrick Keohane, Petty Officer, RN, aged thirty-one

Thomas Clissold, Cook, RN, aged twenty-four

Frederick Hooper, Steward, RN, aged nineteen.

Scientists were led by the chief of the scientific staff, Dr Edward Adrian Wilson, zoologist, known as 'Uncle Bill', aged thirty-eight. They included:

Dr George C. Simpson, meteorologist, known as 'Sunny Jim', aged thirty-two

Charles S. Wright, physicist, known as 'Silas', aged twenty-three

Edward W. Nelson, biologist, known as 'Marie', aged twenty-seven

Apsley Cherry-Garrard, assistant zoologist, known as 'Cherry', aged twenty-five.

In addition, there were:

Cecil H. Meares, in charge of dogs, aged thirty-three

Herbert G. Ponting, camera artist, aged forty

Tryggve Gran, ski expert, aged twenty-one

Bernard C. Day, motor engineer, aged twenty-six

Demetri Gerof, dog-driver, aged twenty-two

Anton L. Omelchenko, assisting with ponies, aged twenty-seven.

The Far Western party at this stage consisted of:

Thomas Griffith Taylor, geologist, known as 'Griff', aged thirty

Frank Debenham, geologist, known as 'Deb', aged twenty-seven.

The Eastern party was made up of:

Lieutenant Victor L. Arbuthnot Campbell, RN, known as 'the wicked mate', aged thirty-five

Dr George Murray Levick, Surgeon, RN, known as 'the Old Sport' or 'Tofferino', aged thirty-three

Raymond E. Priestley, geologist, aged twenty-four

George Percy Abbott, Petty Officer, RN, nickname 'Tiny', aged thirty

Frank V. Browning, Petty Officer, RN, nickname 'Rings', aged twenty-eight

Harry Dickason, Able Seaman, RN, nickname 'Dick', aged twenty-five.

The ship's party comprised three lieutenants – Harry L. L. Pennell RN, who took over the command of *Terra Nova*; Henry E. deP. Rennick RN; and Wilfred M. Bruce RNR, a brother of Scott's wife, Kathleen. It also included Francis Drake RN, Assistant Paymaster.

There was one scientist: Dennis G. Lillie, biologist. Alfred B. Cheetham RNR was Boatswain.

Francis Davies, Leading Shipwright, RN, worked at key moments ashore. Walter William Archer, chief cook, RN, and Thomas S. Williamson, Petty Officer, RN, both joined the shore party for the 1912–13 season.

A further nineteen men were separately listed, as engineers, stokers, firemen, petty officers, able seamen and a steward. Leading Stoker Robert Brissenden drowned in New Zealand in 1911. Several men left the ship, to be replaced by others.

Antarctic expeditions
relevant to this account

British Naval Expedition 1839–43
Captain James Clark Ross RN
HMS *Erebus*, HMS *Terror*

Belgian Antarctic Expedition 1897–9
Lieutenant Adrien de Gerlache
Belgica

British Antarctic Expedition 1898–1900
Carsten Borchgrevink
Southern Cross

British National Antarctic Expedition 1901–4
Lieutenant Robert Falcon Scott RN
Discovery

German Antarctic Expedition 1901–3
Professor Eric von Drygalski
Gauss

British Antarctic Expedition 1907–9
Lieutenant Ernest Shackleton
Nimrod

British Antarctic Expedition 1910–13
Captain Robert Falcon Scott
Terra Nova

Norwegian Antarctic Expedition 1910–12
Roald Amundsen
Fram

Japanese South Polar Expedition 1910–12
Lieutenant Nobu Shirase
Kainan-maru

Australasian Antarctic Expedition 1911–14
Dr Douglas Mawson
Aurora

Measurements and place-names

DISTANCES IN THIS book are given in the way they were used, and understood, by the men concerned: that is, in nautical, or geographic, miles. One hundred nautical miles equals approximately 115 statute miles, or 185 kilometres. A nautical mile relates to latitude.

Latitude is measured from the equator in degrees: from 0 degrees at the equator to 90 degrees north or south at each pole. Each degree is divided into sixty parts, called minutes. Each minute equals one nautical mile, so each degree of latitude equals 60 nautical miles.

To stay consistent with the measurements used at the time, this book uses feet and inches, gives weights in pounds, and temperature in Fahrenheit.

Place-names are those used by the people concerned: for example, 'the Barrier' for the Ross Ice Shelf. The maps in this book, specially prepared by the British Antarctic Survey, include only those places mentioned in the text, for ease of reference. However, several names – for example, 'Terra Nova Bay' for the bay north of the Drygalski Ice Tongue – are included to help with locating the areas concerned on current maps. All the specially prepared maps are based on satellite imagery. Two of them include pack ice, to give a sense of this all-important dimension to negotiating journeys.

Introduction

RAYMOND PRIESTLEY, TWENTY-FOUR years old but a veteran of Antarctic exploring, with the usual run of extreme experiences and side-stepping death that seems part of being in Antarctica, stands watching Captain Scott set off across the sea ice, accompanied by eleven men, twenty-six excited dogs and eight ponies – restive, passive, surly or pig-headed awful, depending on their already sorely revealed characteristics. Scott's aim, to lay a depot of provisions as far south as manageable in the time available, is a key first step in his plans to achieve the South Pole the following summer.

Having grown up in the tight little cathedral town of Tewkesbury, Gloucestershire, Priestley thinks that the straggle of well-wishers is like a small town out for an airing. Earlier on this day, Thursday 26 January 1911, Priestley knocked off work in order to have a 'general goodbye & good luck party'. All hands were called aft on the expedition ship *Terra Nova* for Captain Scott to say farewell, with the camera artist Herbert Ponting cinematographing Scott's speech-making to the men lined up respectfully on the deck.

Now most of the ship's company has filed out to see the depot party leave. Ponting, here to portray Scott's expedition on film and glass plate negatives for audiences back home, is recording the departure. But theatrical moment turns to farce as Oates's pony, Christopher, takes charge of his loaded sledge and overturns another. The chief of the scientific staff, Dr Edward Wilson, driving one of the two dog teams, with Scott, suffers a chaotic false start, with a dog being dragged along some distance under their sledge. Scott's first Antarctic expedition, in 1901–4, and Ernest Shackleton's in 1907–9, had both included sledge dogs, but neither leader trusted these unfamiliar animals. Scott is trying dogs again, in addition to ponies, which were considered to have been successful during Shackleton's expedition. Priestley rather enjoys watching everyone trying to cope with the dog teams, especially the 'amateurs'. He worked with ponies when he was here in Antarctica with Shackleton, and he liked exercising Shackleton's under-used dogs.

'Today has seen our first real separation when we saw the Depot Party off finally', Priestley writes in his journal on the evening of the 26th, describing the mishaps of the departure with amused detachment, then getting on with his usual straightforward daily account of actions achieved. The morning was spent in the tedious task of watering the ship, collecting ice from the glacier for the ship's freshwater tanks. Yesterday, Wednesday, he hauled sledge-loads of dog biscuits and pony fodder to make a depot for Scott's party, while Captain Scott stayed on board *Terra Nova* writing letters. Last night Priestley spent chatting with Edgar 'Taff' Evans and Thomas Williamson, Petty Officers, who had been on Scott's first Antarctic expedition. Priestley has generally kept quiet about his experiences on Shackleton's expedition. It doesn't do to talk about it. But, relaxing with the seamen in their quarters, he tells them what it was like being in the support party when Shackleton set out from this place in October 1908 on his attempt to reach the South Pole, with the ponies struggling through deep snow. Several of the men who had hoped to be chosen for the shore party but are staying on the ship gave Priestley presents of clothing they had brought in case of need. They like him. He's quiet and straightforward.

Then Priestley has a good grumble in his journal. He is here in Antarctica as the Eastern party's geologist, to explore King Edward VII Land, 500 miles to the east. The Eastern party will set up Scott's second base, exploring and doing science while Scott tackles the South Pole. But Priestley and the other five members of the Eastern party have been working on behalf of Scott and the Pole attempt ever since they arrived, and they are still working. Priestley can't wait to get away. Tomorrow, at last, *Terra Nova* will start taking them and their 30 tons of stores and equipment east. Finally, the Eastern party will be on their own.

★

Raymond Priestley used his detailed daily journals as the source for his book, published in 1914, about the adventures of the Eastern party; by then, however, the Eastern party had become known as the Northern party, so Priestley had changed the name. Chapter 1 of Priestley's book, *Antarctic Adventure*, opened with two paragraphs that welded start and final ending. A thoughtful, appropriately moving farewell scene now graced the departure of Scott and his depot party, because – unknown, of course, to anyone at the time – this had turned out to be a final farewell. No one in the Eastern party ever saw Captain Scott again.

Priestley's *Antarctic Adventure* was invested and shaped from the first words with perpetual hindsight. The tragedy that was to befall Scott and his four companions in the final Polar party was established from the beginning as the defining event, the lens through which the whole expedition was to be perceived.

On the 26th of January, 1911, a little group of men stood together on the sea ice . . . Six, at any rate, of those who are alive today are destined to have that scene engraved on their memories for the remainder of their lives . . . and though no forebodings disturbed the serenity of the parting, it was ordained that we should never set eyes again on five of the men whom we were proud to number among our friends . . . The scene of the start was indeed a lively one . . . Captain Scott himself is saying good-bye to Campbell, the leader of the Northern Party, and giving him parting advice, discussing with him the prospect of securing good winter quarters . . . The time given for leave-taking soon passes, and we stand cheering, hat in hand, while the cavalcade files off southward across the sea ice, while in the hearts of all of us must ring, as they do still in mine, the words of our leader as he wished each of us good fortune and thanked us for what we had done already towards making the expedition a success.

An air of nostalgia and poignancy hangs over 'the words of our leader' – words that Priestley did not record in his diary at the time. Nor were they recorded by Lieutenant Victor Campbell, sparsely built and spare with words, outwardly martinet, inwardly thoughtful, whose brief career in the Navy had been replaced by the pleasures of summers in Norway, fishing and sketching; nor by Dr Murray Levick, the Eastern party's large ex-rugby-playing naval surgeon, devoted to competitive sport, and writing at the least a novel during the months ahead. Perhaps it was because, according to Levick, Scott's 'little speech' was 'made [to] the men of the ship'. The Eastern party's three naval ratings – handsome, upright Petty Officer George Abbott, Petty Officer Frank Browning, a torpedo expert raised on a Devon farm, and the alert young Londoner Able Seaman Harry Dickason – did give brief matter-of-fact summaries in their journals. But by definition no one knew what lay ahead. Current, and previous, experience was all.

Absent from Priestley's book are his wry amusement at the rather chaotic departure, his feelings of frustration about the way the Eastern party's work was being subordinated to the requirements of the attempt on the Pole, the references to his experiences as one of Shackleton's men. Missing too is any mention of his companionable conversations with Petty Officer Evans, one of the five men to die, who did not in fact depart with the depot party but stayed on the ship another day, to accompany the geological party as guide and instructor on their first summer expedition to Victoria Land. Instead, the ultimate tragedy established the criteria, layers of *post hoc* significance anointing events previously innocent of emotional loading, editing away now inappropriate detail of semi-confusion and humdrum reality.

The death of Captain Scott on the return from the Pole, with the deaths of his companions Dr Wilson, Captain Oates, Lieutenant Bowers and Petty Officer Evans, reset the clock of the entire expedition. Once the tent, almost buried by snow, was discovered with the bodies inside, skin yellow and glassy, frozen with the kind of brutal finality that meant Scott's arm, when it was moved to retrieve his journal, cracked with a gunshot report as the bone snapped; once the last brave, poignant letters were read, and the journals and diaries, with their complex layering of things said, things left out; and once Scott's telling of the journey, that extraordinary, painful, powerful piece of writing, began to work: once what had happened became known, then accounts of the expedition ran to a different beat. The deaths wrenched perspectives from their moorings. Increasingly, the story focused on the single narrative that ended in tragedy and heroism. It became a drama with a central cast, a one-track setting, a reduced timeline.

The tragedy came to overshadow everything that occurred to the other members of Scott's British Antarctic Expedition 1910–13, or the *Terra Nova* Expedition – the two names were used interchangeably. The expedition became known as 'Scott's Last Expedition', the finality of that title all-defining, casting its shadow backwards, gripping events, narrowing and sharpening the plot. Accounts of what happened shifted to take account of what was to happen. Writing, and thinking, accreted 'hindsight bias': understandable, unavoidable but insidious. No one wished to challenge the overriding narrative, to dislodge the tone and beat of the powerful and moving story that had swept into the imaginations of a world audience.

At the heart of Scott's expedition is a tragedy. But alongside it there is also positive, life-affirming success. The five men of the final Polar party died. But the six men of Scott's other expedition, the Eastern party, 'Campbell & Co.', as Scott's lively brother-in-law Lieutenant Wilfred Bruce called them, got through extraordinary adventures and hardship. Theirs is one of the great tales of survival. It runs parallel to Scott and the Polar party, an essential part of Scott's expedition, woven into the very fabric of the planning and the outcome.

The story of Campbell and his men is told here as the events happen, in real time. Staying with the moment, the participants, by definition, only know what they can know. They plan, worry, speculate, make decisions, according to their understanding, as each day unfolds. Enough of the diaries and journals, sledging and field notebooks, lists, instructions and letters, photographs and drawings, survive to be able to create a sense of what it was like for Campbell and his men to be there, exploring and coping, on Scott's expedition; to let the participants tell the story themselves. My aim has been to avoid hindsight and, as far as I can, judgements. To let the expedition rebalance. Freed from the burden of the tragedy that descended on the Polar party, released from the *post hoc* grip that tightened around the narrative, the story of six of Scott's other heroes assumes its proper place.

Most of my research for this book was done at the Scott Polar

Research Institute in Cambridge, immersed in the primary source material month after privileged month, smelling the bitter smoke absorbed from the blubber fires still infusing the pages of Levick's ice-cave diaries, seeing the dirty whorls of thumbprints holding down the pages, reading the complete run of Priestley's rough diaries – the unedited words, written on the day. Comparing unedited versions with later fair copies, looking always for the reality of time and place. Finding that, the more I read, the more intimately the accounts inter-leaved, and discovering how, unexpectedly, various parts of the expedition kept coming together and informing each other. 'Anyone', Nelson Mandela has said, 'who has explored the world of archives will know that it is a treasure house, one that is full of sur-prises, crossing paths, dead ends, painful reminders and unanswered questions.'

History is writing about what is, fiction about what is not. Fiction can be more doctrinal than history, because the historian is weighed down by facts: the 'sticky clay of history'. Part of the 'sticky clay' is the range of participants. 'Numerous voices need to be heard': essen-tial to listen to but not always easy to find. The Eastern party, made up half of 'officers' and half of 'men', has a particular draw. The voices of all six members can be heard.

This story also has another element. Antarctica, the place, is central. I have added my voice to descriptions of the landscape, ani-mals, events and circumstances, drawing on my own experience of working on the continent, and on board polar research ships, selected as a writer on a range of Antarctic Artists and Writers programmes. Travelling from beyond Cape North, in the west, to beyond the Bay of Whales, in the east - that great right-angle of coast discovered by Captain James Clark Ross RN in 1841 – I have visited the precise landscapes that held the Eastern party.

I

It *must* be an Englishman

It is one of the symptoms of this age of nerves and hysteria
that we magnify everything, that our boasts are frantic
and our scares pitiable, that we call a man who plays well
in a football match a hero, and that all successes are triumphs . . . but . . . when we are all feeling a little down-
hearted at seeing our supremacy in sport and in more
serious matters slipping away from us, it is a moral tonic
to find that in exploration we are still the kings of the
world.

The Sketch (26 March 1909)

IN 1771 SAMUEL Hearne, a young Hudson Bay official, described
being guided across the snows and frozen lakes of northern
Canada by a group led by a Chipewyan chief he called Matonabbee.
Women, Matonabbee told Hearne, were the only way to get loads
moved in this kind of country. One woman could carry, or haul, as
much as two men, and travelling any considerable distance, or for any
length of time, without their help was not possible. Women also
dressed the meat, prepared it for eating, pitched the tents, made and
mended the clothing, found fuel and kept the men warm at night.
And the expense of maintaining them was trifling. They cooked, so
they could subsist in scarce times by licking their fingers. Matonabbee
used seven wives to drag his sledges during the seven-month journey.
When the terrain made sledges unusable, the women shifted the loads
on to their backs. Hearne noted in his journal that Matonabbee's
wives were selected for strength. The men, he wrote, looked
for wives to be broad of shoulder, sturdy of leg.

The requirements for travelling in the southern polar regions were substantially the same as those for Matonabbee and his wives in the north: tents for camping, food and cooking utensils, fuel, bedding, warm clothing, adequate footwear, axes, knives and weapons. Like Hearne, travellers in Antarctica also needed to carry navigating instruments, diaries, books, maps and writing implements. In the Canadian north the land yielded much of what was required for a journey. In the Antarctic there was no timber to make tent-poles and sledges and frames for snowshoes, no birch bark and wood for canoes, no dry moss to burn as fuel. Animals for food, fuel and skins could be found only along the coasts, and most were summer visitors. There were none inland, where men yearned to go.

But women as beasts of burden were not an option in the southern polar regions. There were no indigenous people at all, and never had been: no one to coerce, flatter or persuade with trade goods or newly acquired Christianity, no one to act as porter or bearer and carry the necessities of survival. There were not even any local animals to capture and use as burden carriers, although Japanese explorers, on seeing emperor penguins, did briefly joke about using them instead of sledge dogs. The largest land-living all-the-year-round animal in Antarctica turned out to be a 2-millimetre-long mite. The largest plants were thumb-high.

Explorers travelling to Antarctica had to transport from their metropolitan centres, or collect from colonial outposts *en route*, every single thing they needed or might need. The necessities for survival had first to be loaded into ships, transported south across the world's stormiest ocean, then unloaded on to ice or land. Logistics were central to all plans, and the issue demanded constant attention. Expedition ships as carriers plus containers were ideal bases from which to explore. But once men landed ashore, the intractable problem was moving away from base. However pruned down, however fretted over, enough basic supplies to maintain life, and efficient work, had to be carried. Man in Antarctica was a snail creeping along with his house on his back. Either he introduced animals to drag and carry or he looked to the industrial leadership of the Western world – the remarkable innovations in transport – and tried adapting them to ice and snow: motorized sledges, a tracked motor car, even an aeroplane. Or man became the pack animal, carrying his load or dragging it behind him on a sledge.

The absence of indigenous people had other impacts. Explorers had always, where possible, used local informants, reluctant or willing, to assist as pilots for sea journeys or guides over land: key moments in the transfer of knowledge, the gaining of those 'hard won fragments' to fit on to the map of the world. In Antarctica explorers could not draw on oral traditions: there were no tales of mountain passes, no insider knowledge to fillet out concerning seasonal variation and animal behaviour or the vagaries of weather and climate. There was no chance to observe local survival techniques: ways of living off the land or management of wind, water and ice. Antarctica was *tabula rasa*. This unknown land demanded no understanding of foreign ways or languages. It required no money, passports or negotiations with officials. There were no police, no laws, no armies, no rules and regulations. No markets or bazaars, no roads, no foreign diseases to catch or avoid. No children or old people. No females at all. Explorers were on their own. They had to make decisions, and act, according to their understanding of the appropriate ways to solve problems. Exclusively male, they arrived carrying their sense of themselves, their sense of their nationalities, and their place in society, in their minds. Confident that challenges were there to be met and overcome, their only points of comparison were each other.

Captain Robert Falcon Scott listed his latest thinking about ways to shift loads in an eight-page illustrated pamphlet published on 15 September 1909, setting out the objectives of his new expedition to Antarctica. The startling news had just been released that two Americans had separately and competitively claimed the achievement of being first at the North Pole. The main object of his expedition, Scott stated, was 'to reach the South Pole and to secure for the British Empire the honour of that achievement'. A serving naval officer specializing in torpedo warfare, broad chest, trim figure, and ambition like permanent sandpaper rasping at his inner thoughts, Scott had been grappling for many months with the problems of transport. Now he proposed three solutions. Ponies, Scott wrote, had delivered 'brilliant results' hauling sledges over the ice in the first stage of Ernest

Shackleton's recent attempt on the South Pole, and he intended using them as draught animals, along with dogs. But the best hope lay in technical innovation. Shackleton had taken one motor car, but its performance had been limited. Scott had been trialling a prototype of a motor sledge in Norway. Motors had the advantage of requiring no food when not in use. Ponies and dogs ate whether working or not.

A fourth option was not listed because it was taken for granted. British explorers in the northern polar regions had a long tradition of pulling their own sledges. No load-carrying wives capable of carrying 200 lb of weight, but the noble joy of harnessing up and swinging along, a team of men pulling together. The British Arctic tradition had been transferred south with Scott on his first expedition. For Scott, regardless of the other possible means of transport, there was always man-hauling.

The desire did not need restating, or the ambition justifying. To get south, to the Pole. To stand where the earth spun on its axis. But crucially, to be the first. 'You <u>shall</u> go to the S Pole', the sculptor Kathleen Bruce wrote in her big, vigorous handwriting in thick blue ink on a single sheet of notepaper in July 1908, in the exciting months after Robert Falcon Scott asked her to marry him, 'oh dear whats the use of having energy & enterprize if a little thing like that cant be done'.

Scott had made an initial, halting, trek south across the ice in the direction of the South Pole in the summer of 1902–3, as a 34-year-old Royal Navy lieutenant leading his first expedition. In company with Ernest Shackleton, a 29-year-old Irish-born Merchant Navy lieutenant who in deep, husky tones, dark eyes flashing, could quote poetry by the half-hour, and Edward Wilson, thirty, a physician from the comfortable town of Cheltenham with a preference for zoology, watercolour painting and ascetic Christianity, Scott had discovered a range of mountains with glaciers mighty beyond belief spilling their loads on to the seemingly endless ice plain. Standing at their farthest south, the three men had no way of knowing whether the magnificent mountains continued on or even whether the Pole, still another 400 miles away, was situated on land. The South Pole might in fact be in an ice-covered sea, like the North Pole in the Arctic. Yet, in spite of exhaustion, despite semi-starvation and suffering symptoms of scurvy, the three men were captured. Antarctica was almost totally unknown, untouched, but they had experienced its beauty and mystery, its ferocity and challenge. Antarctica drew them in, attached itself to their very beings. It was harsh, unforgiving, careless. But it became an integral part of their desires and their ambitions.

Scott had established his expedition in the great right-angle of ocean, ice and rock discovered sixty years earlier by Captain James Clark Ross RN. Ross, an experienced navigator in Arctic waters and the first to reach the North Magnetic Pole, found a sea here in the south unexpectedly free from pack ice, its western edge a mountain-rimmed coast he named Victoria Land, after the young Queen Victoria. Sailing further south than anyone had ever managed, Ross saw a glaring white line across his route that became an extraordinary wall – 'Britannia's Barrier', he called it – sheer continuous cliffs of ice rising high above his ships' masts. Where the Victoria Land coast met the wall of ice, an island with two volcanoes was discovered: one extinct, one exotically alive. Ross called the live volcano spewing fire and smoke into the frigid white world Mount Erebus, after his sturdy wooden ship, built to bombard harbours with fiery destruction from its heavy guns, and the elegant cone of the other volcano Mount Terror, after his second ship. The southernmost stretch of water bounded by the island and by Victoria Land, Ross named McMurdo Bay, after the first lieutenant on *Terror*. Then he took his two ships east along the wall of ice cliffs until, glimpsing the possibility of land ahead, he was stopped by heavy pack ice from exploring any further. Returning to the northern entrance to his sea, Ross tried sailing west along a mountainous coast, naming a wide scoop of bay after the surgeon on *Terror*, John Robertson, an inlet in the harsh coast after the mate of *Erebus*, Alexander Smith, and – thick pack blocking his ships – a snow-capped bluff, the furthest west feature he could see, Cape North. Marking the entrance to his sea, Ross had found a bold cape like a northward-pointing limb, with plunging cliffs of dark rock, which he named Cape Adare. Where so much in the south polar regions was speculation, Ross had achieved a magnificent sweep of known coast.

In 1899 the explorer Carsten Borchgrevink, whose father was Norwegian and whose mother was English, landed with nine men on a beach at Cape Adare and built a hut. He and his men became the first to winter on the Antarctic continent and the first to use dogs and skis. Next summer they sailed south down the Victoria Land coast, made the first landing on Ross's mighty Barrier and achieved the first (short) journeys south across the ice. 'To my mind', Borchgrevink wrote in his book *First on the Antarctic Continent*, 'the big barrier . . . is nothing more than the northern extremity of a great ice sheet sloping northwards from land near the South Pole . . . With a sufficient number of reindeer, sledges and dogs, and a very small party of scientific men, I believe that a great southern latitude may be reached on this ice-sheet.' Borchgrevink, funded by a British newspaper proprietor, driven and determined to explore the unknown continent of Antarctica, infuriated members of the British establishment. They considered that he was using resources that ought to have been available for the expedition about to set out under Lieutenant Scott, and Borchgrevink's achievements were minimized.

Scott openly took his expedition ship *Discovery* where others had been. Arriving at Ross's Barrier in January 1902, he worked east, discovering – where Ross had indicated the possibility – low, snow-covered hills and several patches of bare rock. Scott named the new territory King Edward VII Land, then turned back to an inlet in the Barrier face, perhaps where Borchgrevink had come ashore and made his brief dash to the south. Here, on 4 February, Scott climbed into the wicker basket slung beneath a gas balloon and ascended, to gaze across an apparently level surface of ice. Shackleton went up even higher, before the balloon was declared unsafe and abandoned.

Ross's McMurdo Bay turned out to be a sound, and here, on the southern tip of the island Ross had discovered, with smoke streaming from the crater of Mount Erebus, Scott established his expedition base. Small parties of men were sent out to start tackling the mountains and glaciers of Victoria Land while Scott, Wilson and Shackleton made the first three-month-long attempt to travel south over the exhausting expanse of the Barrier.

Scott considered the long sweep and curve of coast first discovered by his naval predecessor Ross to be a peculiarly British preserve. Extend Ross's vast quadrant of sea, ice and rock to its logical conclusion – fix its point on the South Pole – and the Pole, it seemed obvious, although not to all, must be achieved by an Englishman. But for Scott a kind of visceral possessiveness grew. During his first expedition he had explored swathes of territory, a remarkable achievement, although he had planned to encompass even more. Now he considered that it was all his to continue exploring. He had, he thought, a 'sort of right' to the entire region, a natural priority, a 'prior claim'. Privately, but unshakeably, he staked out the details in his mind's eye. There was work still to do, and, emphatically, it was his to do. In particular, the Pole waited, the route begun by him, the journey uncompleted.

But the pull of Antarctica could not be confined. The very emotions that captured Scott also captured others. The mix of passions and desires, the indefinable seductions, the mark on the soul, differed from man to man. In each person they touched, the ambition to achieve, for self, or country, or loved ones, to pit oneself against all that Antarctica could do, grew and grew. Whatever the dream – to discover land or untapped resources, new life forms or evidence of ancient life and climates; to climb untouched mountains, or understand the workings of ice. To lead an expedition and not be led. To get to the South Pole first.

Scott's sense of shock when Ernest Shackleton exhibited the Antarctic passion in 1907 was deep. Shackleton, invalided back to Britain after that terrible first journey across the Barrier with Scott and Wilson, had devoted himself to raising sufficient financial backing to announce his own expedition, with the explicit intention of reaching the South Geographic Pole from a base on Ross Island. A party would also try to achieve the South Magnetic Pole. A third party, according to the plans published in the journal of the Royal Geographical Society, would travel east across the Barrier to explore King Edward VII Land (where an authorized post office would be opened to sell stamps), while a winter party would observe the breeding of the emperor penguins. Finally Shackleton proposed to explore by ship the unknown coast west of Cape North, where Ross had turned back. The long-established business of 'scientific voyaging', which had sent ships and men across the seas to every part of the world, was well understood. Science and geographical discovery were appropriate and expected components of expedition objectives, and Shackleton had included a respectable quantity – generally similar to Scott's aspirations on the *Discovery* expedition – as well as the hope of finding mineral resources. But above all, and openly, Shackleton was driven by the desire to get to the Pole.

Scott – his personal space so crudely invaded, as he saw it, by a man whom he considered his subordinate officer, his physical space under threat – brought to bear the powerful weapons of gentlemanly conduct: the sense of honour and fairness. Scott had not made any declaration in public that he wished, or intended, to return to Antarctica. He had set no date and made very few plans. Shackleton protested that he had had no inkling of Scott's desires. He, Shackleton, would be departing within months, and the backing he had achieved depended on his attempt on the Pole.

Using Dr Edward Wilson, their mutual friend, as mediator, Scott deployed a restrained moral outrage, couched in polite but increasingly non-negotiable phrases, overlaid by reminders of the duty owed to a former commander. Scott defined his sphere in a series of letters. He claimed not only the right to complete the journey he had started towards the Pole, and turned back from, in 1903, but much more: 'of course . . . I want to clear up all the other parts we left in doubt – the geology of Victoria Land and its extension beyond C. North.' A private promise was agreed that Shackleton would leave McMurdo Sound to Scott. Yielding to months of pressure, Shackleton acknowledged a territorial claim of significant proportions and signed a letter of agreement on 17 May 1907, only weeks before his expedition was due to depart: 'I shall not touch the coast of Victoria land at all.' He would, in the phrases drafted for him to sign, 'rigidly adhere to' what had been agreed. Scott had achieved what he considered only his due.

But the realities of exploring in this harshest of environments forced Shackleton to break his promise to establish his winter quarters either on the Barrier, at the inlet where the balloon ascents had been made, or on King Edward VII Land, as agreed. His ship and men at risk from further delay and his resources of time and coal stretched to the limit, Shackleton with heavy heart turned to the forbidden space, Ross Island. The alternative – failing his backers, letting down each man on his expedition, returning to Britain without even landing –

was unthinkable. Having unloaded everything ashore on a rocky cape 20 miles further north than Scott's old base, Shackleton's ship *Nimrod* departed north for the winter.

Scott was incensed when news of Shackleton's 'unanswerable breach of faith' reached him. He declared his contempt for Shackleton as a professed liar. Key people were sent a copy of the letter of agreement. But in March 1909 news cabled through from the southern hemisphere brought an astonishing revelation: exploring on from the furthest south reached under Scott's command, Shackleton, it was announced, had got within 97 miles of the South Pole. The journey pioneered a route up a vast glacier on to a high cold plateau, with four men dragging their barest necessities on a wooden sledge, struggling for breath at the unexpected altitude, shivering in their thin tent, bitterly hungry. After all the speculation, this awful anonymity of emptiness, the glaring, relentless whiteness, the surface sculpted into sharp-edged ridges by chilling, debilitating winds, seemed to be a heart-diminishing location for the South Pole. Exhausted, short of their goal, Shackleton and his companions had barely managed to stagger back to safety. Suffering and yet surviving, having had the courage to turn away and give up.

Shackleton's near-miss turned the imaginary but nevertheless real point where every direction pointed north, where the sun never set for six months and never rose for the next six, where nothing lived and no one had ever been, into a graspable goal. The South Pole could be achieved. Getting there first mattered. Desire could no longer be corralled as one man's prerogative. Pole-getting had moved beyond privately nursed ambitions or personal rivalries kept to the inner circle of controlled and controlling players. Technological revolutions in the speed and means of communicating turned Pole-attaining into public performances, the stuff of popular news with high consumer appeal, no longer confined to discussions in key societies, strategically placed articles and speeches to certain institutions but dangerous and splendid, glamorous and heroic, the stuff of the penny press, the illustrated weeklies, of news cabled around the world.

'Darling do you know what haunts me – haunts me – never altogether leaves me', Kathleen Scott wrote, much later. 'It is your little grey face . . . that I met at the Station the day you came up from your

ship after the Shackleton news came.' Shackleton returned home in
June 1909 a national, and imperial, hero, swept up in waves of emotional and patriotic fervour, with the public eager to follow his every
move. Genial, restlessly energetic, a racy raconteur, attracting
schemes and ideas, Shackleton's presence added a dimension of
uncertainty for Scott, who had still made no public announcement
that he intended leading a new Antarctic expedition. Shackleton
claimed that he had no immediate plans, but could he be trusted not
to return to Antarctica and complete the Pole journey? Scott felt the
need once again to protect his clearly enunciated rights to territory:
Shackleton must acknowledge that he, Scott, had unfinished
Antarctic business.

The 'Scott–Shackleton difficulty' exercised the Council of the
Royal Geographical Society. Admiral Sir Lewis Beaumont, the Vice-
President, reminded the President, Major Leonard Darwin, of the
self-evident truth that expeditions to Antarctica should be, and
remain part of, the important business of geographical discovery. The
Society 'would not encourage or support an expedition merely
intended to reach the Pole', he wrote on 19 June 1909. Shackleton
would probably go for it again, but Scott should not 'try to compete
with Shackleton on a Pole-hunting expedition'. If Scott wanted to
return to Antarctica, let him lead a 'scientific expedition into new
regions . . . with exploration and the Pole as secondary objects'.
Anyone going over Shackleton's old route would make no new discoveries, and Scott would be making 'a very great mistake' if he
competed with Shackleton 'merely to do that 97 miles'.

Once more Wilson tackled Shackleton on Scott's behalf, remind-
ing him of the miserable business of his broken promise in going to
McMurdo Sound.

My opinion as you know was that you ought to have thrown up
the whole show . . . You took Scott's job practically out of his
hands against his wish & knowing that he was hoping to finish
it. Frankly admit that you have had your turn . . . No one but
you can at the present moment clear the way for Scott. But *you
can*, & what's more to the point, *you should*. Play the game now
by him as he has played the game by you.

Scott and Shackleton maintained a visibly polite relationship. On 1 July Scott wrote a precise formal letter to Shackleton:

> If, as I understand, it does not cut across any future plan of yours, I propose to organize the Expedition to the Ross Sea, which, as you know, I have had so long in preparation so as to start next year . . . My plan is to establish a base in King Edward Land and to push South and East . . . I should be glad to have your assurance that I am not disconcerting any plan of your own.

'I understand that you have already your expedition in preparation,' replied Shackleton on 6 July,

> and it will not interfere with any plans of mine . . . I wish you every success in your endeavour to penetrate the ice and to land on King Edward VII Land and attain a high latitude from that base. I quite agree with you that good geographical work can be done from that quarter, and it will have a newer interest than McMurdo Sound.

The focus of the correspondence was on King Edward VII Land, but Shackleton by acquiescing was in effect renouncing any claim to return to that redolent corner of the Ross Sea where Barrier ice met the Victoria Land coast in the dramatic evocative landscape of Ross Island and the smoking Mount Erebus.

Privately, Wilson was contemptuous of Shackleton, unable to forgive the man who had been his close companion. 'I am afraid that he has become a regular wrong'un', he wrote to a friend in August 1909. 'I have broken with him completely and for good, having told him in a somewhat detailed letter exactly what I thought of him and his whole business. I consider he has dragged Polar Exploration generally in the mud of his own limited and rather low down ambitions.'

Needing to present 'a more scientific expedition than Pole hunting', Scott had assembled a raft of ideas, which he presented in a letter to Darwin: 'the plan. . . provides . . . for the scientific exploration of a considerable extent of the Antarctic continent and will therefore I hope commend itself to the Royal Geographical Society.' Scott's interest in geographical discovery and science was deep and genuine. But getting to the Pole was the overriding objective. In the pamphlet formally announcing his expedition, in September 1909, Scott listed a range of 'scientific objectives', at the same time adroitly folding in achieving the Pole with discovery and exploration. He would establish two bases: one at McMurdo Sound, the other 'breaking new ground' far to the east, in King Edward VII Land. The proposed sledge journey to the Pole could start from either, but the map he included showed a straight line from the unknown region of King Edward VII Land to the Pole, obstacles unknown, so discounted.

Initial euphoria about quick dashes was leavened with reality when, in early November 1909, Shackleton's account of his Pole attempt was published, revealing the desperate details of an immensely hard journey. But despite appeals to patriotism, Scott's fund-raising continued to be sluggish. Geographical discovery and the doing of science were resource-hungry, and reaching the Pole in the most efficient way became paramount. Scott decided to make his attempt on the Pole from Ross Island, using Shackleton's route. The exploration of King Edward VII Land – a key move in the visible doing of discovery and science – was now transferred to an independent party, separately equipped, under its own commander. A central piece of delegating, this exploring party would depart soon after the shore party had landed in Antarctica, to establish a second base in King Edward VII Land. Operating in parallel with the polar push, the independent party could not be large. Scott's plans for his 'attack on the Pole' would use a lot of men. But that end-point of Scott's right-angle of coast, the eastern marker of his domain, would be secured by what Scott now called the Eastern party, in anticipation, and proof of intent.

But these were heated times. The Antarctic passion bred plans for the remaining Pole with audacious aims and uncertain funding. Contenders announced schemes in bursts of publicity: American challenges, a possible Belgian expedition, a Japanese attempt. 'It would be deeply regrettable', stated a *Times* leader on 13 September 1909, the day Scott's new expedition was made public, 'if . . . the brilliant record of British Antarctic exploration were . . . to be checked, with the inevitable probability . . . that the Pole would first be reached by an explorer of another nation.' The *Daily Mail* wrote the same day: 'The people of this country have not been accustomed to take second place in any field of human endeavour . . . the South Pole alone remains our sphere of action. A race for it is certain in the immediate future.' The New York correspondent of the *Daily Telegraph*, describing a craze for polar enterprise, warned that an American expedition could at any moment 'be quietly organised and be under way before the world at large is taken into America's confidence'. Everyone realized, he reported, that such an expedition, 'secretly planned', was possible.

The Antarctic passion delivered to Captain Scott, unexpectedly, a tall and coolly handsome young man who walked one January morning in 1910 into the crowded offices of the British Antarctic Expedition in Victoria Street, just along from the Army & Navy Stores, those purveyors of imperial necessities, and said that, no, he wasn't there to enlist as a member of Scott's expedition, nor was he interested in a large salary. He would even turn down the offer Scott immediately made, of being one of three to form the final Pole party for the final dash. The young man was tanned with the Australian summer he had just been enjoying. He was confident, having only eleven months previously completed the longest unsupported Antarctic sledging journey so far, when, as part of Shackleton's expedition, he and two companions achieved the South Magnetic Pole, or at least got as close to it as was possible to calculate. He was tough, hard and immensely strong: all the qualities Scott looked for. He was also a scientist. He was even that useful thing, given the expedition's intention to raise funds in the colonies, a colonial. Douglas Mawson's parents had taken him from Yorkshire to Australia as a two-year-old; but, as Raymond Priestley, who had shared Shackleton's hut with him in Antarctica, said, Mawson was 'first, last and all the time' Australian.

What Mawson did want was for Scott to listen to an idea. Antarctica, as so far understood, was represented on maps as a roundish blob, a presumed – though unverified – continent. The map as challenge and mystery: a dotted line indicating what was guessed, a solid line what was known. Evidence of action, proof of achievement. Each fragment of filled-in coast represented long ocean voyages from northern hemisphere to southern, from metropolitan centre to the outer limits, from civilization to utter lack. Then, once arrived, critical journeys, on foot, from local bases, temporary structures in the empty immensity, out into the unknown. Each success represented the essential phase still to come, news brought back from the periphery to the centre, to committees and societies, newspaper accounts and lecture audiences, to books published, charts examined, scientific collections studied, measurements checked, articles and reports written. Data in place. Both Scott and Mawson had intimate experience of some of the lines on the map. Both had added to them.

For three hours Mawson talked to Scott about the advantages of exploring the unknown 'northern' coast that lay directly south of Australia: glimpses achieved seventy-odd years earlier from one landing only, in 1840, for a few hours. Otherwise 2,000 miles of not knowing stretched from Cape North, the farthest west that James Clark Ross had reached in 1841, to Gaussberg, discovered by a German expedition in 1902. Mawson was enthusiastic, serious, finger-jabbing: 'I ask him, has he thought of the coast W of Cape Adare. He said that he had not.' Only a year earlier Mawson had got within 100 miles of this unknown coast, sledge-hauling up from the south-east across the high icy plateau, to the site of the South Magnetic Pole. If Scott would land him and a party of three carefully picked men at Cape Adare, or wherever it was convenient to land him further to the west, then, said Mawson, he would sign up to his expedition. Valuable scientific data could be obtained in the Cape Adare area, with the possibility of mineral resources. Mawson proposed to lead a party exploring from what would be a second base for Scott, contributing to the results of the main expedition. Scott, noted Mawson, 'was much interested in it, and said he would go into the matter'.

Scott prided himself on his strength and fitness. A little less than average height, at forty-one his face might smudge with tiredness, but his eyes, extraordinarily violet-blue, could challenge and hold. Capable of immense charm, Scott was at the top of his game. Douglas Mawson, 'six feet three in his socks', at twenty-seven a lecturer in mineralogy at the University of Adelaide, with intense blue eyes that could warm, or coolly assess, was openly ambitious: the newcomer, beginning to mount an assault. Scott pressed Mawson, putting him down as a member of his expedition, to be confirmed in three weeks.

On his return Mawson found Scott sitting with his trusted confidant Dr Edward Wilson, now head of the expedition's scientific staff. 'I did not like Dr Wilson', Mawson noted flatly in his log. The expedition's resources, said Scott, were tied up with achieving the South Pole and with a second expedition to King Edward VII Land, already being organized by its leader, Lieutenant Victor Campbell. Scott therefore turned down Mawson's proposal to explore the unknown northern coast of Antarctica with a small landing party. Mawson countered that he would do it himself. Scott 'now took up a defensive attitude . . . He stated that it had always been his intention to do what he could around the north coast but could promise nothing.'

Mawson thought that Scott had listened to his ideas and then decided to incorporate them into his own plans: 'picking the plums out of the north coast by a boat reconnaissance' when his ship left at the end of summer, scooping up discoveries by sea. But this was disingenuous. Exploring the northern coast was an established ambition. Mawson had been with Shackleton when *Nimrod* tried but failed to achieve it on the way out from Antarctica less than a year earlier. Scott himself had tried and failed in *Discovery* in 1904. Claiming priority of ideas was an arbitrary business in this continent, where vast ambitions, stated with sweeping confidence, were part of the game. Ideas were picked up, left aside. Or, if attempted, nipped by the constraints of reality.

Scott took Mawson home to meet his attractive, persuasive, strong-minded wife, Kathleen, on 26 January, hoping to convince Mawson to change his mind and enlist on his expedition. Scott's technique with young men who had plans for their own Antarctic expeditions was, if relevant, to incorporate them and their ideas. Lieutenant Teddy Evans had given up a scheme to establish winter quarters in King Edward VII Land and explore south, to become at the age of twenty-eight Scott's high-energy, enthusiastic second-in-command, bringing with him his fund-raising contacts. Evans had already travelled to Antarctica as second officer on one of the ships sent south to help relieve Scott on his first expedition.

Mawson explained his ideas to his former leader, Shackleton, drawing a map of Antarctica with proposed routes and bases marked

in for discovery, exploration and science. There was also the powerful pull of resources, that long-acknowledged hope of minerals in this
last undiscovered land mass. Mawson had been instructed by
Shackleton to search for minerals after achieving the Magnetic Pole,
but there had not been time. Now, encouraged by Shackleton, and
using the *Nimrod* office in Regent Street, Mawson planned an independent expedition along the unknown coast. One day Shackleton
'came in early to the office . . . and said to me: "I have decided to go
to the coast west of Cape Adare and you are to be Chief Scientist. I
hope you will agree to this".' Although taken aback, Mawson said he
thought Shackleton had 'fully realised the value of the expedition and
now wished to run it'. Shackleton claimed 'he could lay his hands on
about £70,000' and took Mawson to meet an old friend and sup-
porter, the steel magnate Gerald Lysaght, in Somerset. Mawson, all
infectious grin and sharp intellect, talked to the industrialist for five
hours, after which Lysaght promised £10,000 to the expedition.
Shackleton had embarked on a complex dance with old steps, linking
Mawson into existing rivalries and polar ambitions, mixed with
Shackleton's search for financial security and fame.

'What do you think of this news. Does it matter – Is it a hoax to
keep Mawson', Kathleen wrote in agitation to Scott, 'What is at the
bottom of it.' She had met Mawson again by chance in a telegraph
office and had a long talk with him. 'I asked whether it was an absolute certainty, and Mawson said that Shackleton had said he could not
draw back now he'd got too much money.' But things were not as
bad as they might be. The idea was to go the following year. 'My
little heart aches for my dear . . . worrier. Still the more there is to
strive against the more worth while succeeding. Damn Shackleton.
God bless you K.'

Shackleton informed Scott, the Royal Geographical Society and
the Royal Society about his new expedition on 21 February 1910. It
was a 'purely *Scientific*' proposal. There was no intention to go near
the Pole. 'I am particularly anxious', Shackleton wrote to Scott,
'not to clash with your Expedition, nor in any way to hinder your
pecuniary activities.' His expedition would do only science, and geographical exploration of the unknown north coast of Antarctica, from
the most easterly, Cape Adare, to the farthest west, Gaussberg, and

would not leave 'until about a year after you have sailed for the South'. After releasing an outline in the *Daily Mail* on 18 March 1910, Shackleton left on an American lecture tour to raise sorely needed funds to pay off debts outstanding from his previous expedition.

To Scott both ends of Ross's long sweep of coastline were his to deal with, if he wished: *lebensraum* of the mind. The more geographical and scientific work he could say he was aiming to achieve, the better. A good run of discoveries would bring credit to his expedition. They could counter negative comments in the geographical world, and sometimes the press, that a proper balance had not been achieved between geographical discoveries, with the massive amount of unexplored territory waiting in Antarctica, and what was perceived as an 'arid' push for the Pole, which would result in less than 100 miles of new land. Campbell's party, exploring King Edward VII Land to the east, would add a strong piece of geographical work to the British Antarctic Expedition's balance sheet. But exploring to the west along the unknown coast should happen as well. There was in addition the real, by definition unrepeatable, pleasure of filling in blanks on the chart, of solving geographical problems, as expressed so passionately by Douglas Mawson. But Mawson was now, it appeared, allied to Shackleton.

Scott and Shackleton had argued over the uncharted north coast to the west of Ross's discoveries three years earlier, during the difficult discussions limiting Shackleton's movements. 'I . . . consider that the unknown land . . . is free to anybody who wishes to explore that part', Shackleton had written. 'I do not look upon either Wood Bay or the land to the West of Cape North as being within the Province of any particular previous expedition.' Scott now turned Shackleton's argument to his advantage. On 29 March 1910 he wrote to the President of the Royal Geographical Society, Major Leonard Darwin, seeking to clear the way for his actions: there should be open access, irrespective of any prior proposals to send expeditions or explore, he proposed.

I think Shackleton wants the coast from Cape North to Gaussberg left alone for him in 1911, I have no objection to his going there but I don't want any objection from him to my going there. I have always wished to retreat round Cape North for a second season and possibly to establish meteorological stations on that coast . . . I want it so settled before I leave that I am free to go where I please without the reproach that I am trespassing on his ground. Will you give the matter some thought from this point of view?'

The Royal Geographical Society had just distributed a non-official letter to 3,250 Fellows asking for contributions to fund Scott in his 'primary object to complete the work of penetrating the Antarctic Regions to the South Pole, which he had begun and which had been so well advanced by Sir Ernest Shackleton'. Since it was now known that American and German expeditions were competing for the same prize, 'this gives Captain Scott's Expedition a more distinctly national character than it had before, and should stimulate British contributors.'

As requested, Major Darwin gave some thought to the matter Scott raised. He sent his conclusions to Shackleton in a letter dated 29 April 1910.

My dear Shackleton

As I know from both you and Scott that some correspondence has taken place between you with reference to the regions which you propose to explore, perhaps I may be allowed to make one or two brief observations thereon before either of you are hidden in the ice.

In my opinion, every explorer should in future be at liberty to go exactly where he likes, without, at all events, any liability to an accusation of breach of faith. This being adopted as a general principle, then in addition to this it would be no doubt very advantageous if explorers would discuss how best to partition the work amongst themselves so as to avoid overlapping as far as possible. But the result of such negotiations should not involve more than a statement of what each <u>intends</u> to adopt, but which each <u>can</u> abandon <u>at any time</u> at all.

These are my views, which though uncalled for by either party, perhaps I may be permitted to mention.

Yours sincerely,
Leonard Darwin

Darwin's letter took account of the current reality. Exclusion zones were not internationally practicable, and the Royal Geographical Society had a significant international standing. But Darwin went further. The principle he enunciated was stated in such a way as to apply not only to the area Scott had raised in his letter but in all cases, and to every explorer. An explorer could choose to go anywhere and to discuss it, or not, with other explorers with similar desires. If, having discussed it, he stated an intention, the intention could be abandoned at any point.

In truth, landing in Antarctica was proving exceptionally difficult; there was pressure on the few usable landing places so far discovered, and repetitive use was unavoidable. A known and proven landing place was more than just a given point on a chart. In the great uncertainties of Antarctica a landing place represented an archive of existing knowledge: routes, resources, reliability. But it also represented the experiences of those who had used it, and, as such, carried emotional content; hence powerful feelings of competitiveness and possessiveness were aroused.

Scott was about to describe his expedition plans in a speech to the Fellows of the Royal Geographical Society. Shackleton's intentions, however, were still far from clear. Mawson tracked him to the middle of America in the middle of May 1910. Late one night in a hotel room in Omaha, Nebraska, Mawson drafted a letter of agreement and intention, using both sides of a single sheet of paper, corrected it and then wrote it out and got Shackleton to sign that he would pay Mawson the salary and expenses he owed him for work already undertaken, that he intended to proceed with the expedition to explore west of Cape Adare, and that Mawson would be in charge if he decided not to command it, but that Shackleton would still help to raise the necessary funds for equipment.

In London, Scott's expedition ship *Terra Nova* was due to depart in two weeks' time. An old Dundee whaler, three-masted, refitted at speed, with auxiliary engines and expedition experience, grease scraped out, paint slapped on, holds disinfected, bunks added and an icehouse built, she had been loaded with as many of the necessary stores and equipment as men, working immensely long hours, had been able to assemble. Lieutenant Evans would command the ship as far as Australia. Scott needed to stay behind, raising money and dealing with the almost crushing mass of details still requiring his attention.

For Scott, getting south was a series of objectives, of tasks to be dealt with. There was a relentlessness to his task-oriented, task-driven approach, of tension constantly replenished, of release constantly deferred. As each task was finished, so the next pressed. Each one was embedded in varying degrees of analysis but also in assumptions, hopes and, as Scott saw it, his luck. Some tasks depended on the performance of individuals. Here judgement was central. Some could be delegated. Some depended utterly on the physical world: on the chances of weather, temperature, seasonal variation, on how much snow, how little, what type, on quantities and quality of sea ice, on blizzards and how long they lasted. But the Antarctic world was barely known, the physical realities still only fleetingly experienced, with no way yet of establishing suitable or reliable parameters. Scott was renowned for hard work, but he was also impatient. The Antarctic world was uncertain and by definition unpredictable.

On his first expedition all had been new, the options unknown. Now the objectives were clear and unyielding. Before, he had had everything to learn. With little preparation, still less any long-held or hidden desire to explore, least of all in the polar regions, Scott had been catapulted into his first command and success. Now he was experienced. He had studied widely and thought long before committing himself to key decisions. Transport, equipment, clothing, food, numbers of men, numbers of depots, weights and quantities, time-frames – these were the keys. But if the Pole was not achieved first time, another attempt had to be made, because to Scott, and to those involved in the planning and funding of the expedition, it seemed clear that without the Pole all other achievements, including the science, would be reckoned at a discount. With the Pole they would gain lustre and *gravitas*.

Scott stood before his audience at the Royal Geographical Society. In appropriately thoughtful but elevated language he presented the task of aiming for the Pole as a new national enterprise. 'There is something more than mere sentiment, something more than an appeal to our sporting instinct in its attainment; it appeals to our national pride and the maintenance of great traditions, and its quest becomes an outward visible sign that we are still a nation able and willing to undertake difficult enterprises.' The task was hard, the outcome uncertain; the Pole might well not be achieved in the first year.

Talk of the 'mere last 97 miles' – the repetitive nature of a known route – had entirely disappeared. Discreet but inevitably damaging questioning of Shackleton's statement about the final distances achieved on the polar plateau had been initiated. Scott was privately sceptical. His only reference, for those in the know, was the merest glancing prod: 'The general public, whose knowledge . . . is derived from the sensational press, can count success only in degrees of latitude, and hitherto it has been content to accept little more than bare assertion in support of such claims.' The expedition that had immediately preceded his was not otherwise alluded to.

The Eastern party, Scott told his audience, was a key part of his expedition strategy. Exploring King Edward VII Land justified 'a great effort in the attempt'. But the announcement was hedged around with verbal provisos. The small Eastern party would 'have to face the unknown severity of a winter in one of the most inhospitable parts of the Antarctic regions' and 'unknown difficulties and dangers in the journeys they undertake'. 'I realize', said Scott, 'that this part of my plan is beset with difficulties.' The Eastern party would be landed 'if open seas are to be found', but even then 'a suitable wintering-place may not be found, and even if found, the difficulty of landing stores remains'.

In contrast, only one proviso constrained the announcement of a second strand of exploring. Once the Eastern party had been landed, the expedition ship *Terra Nova* would 'reconnoitre' the coastline west of Cape North as far as Adélie Land 'with a view to landing parties upon it on a future occasion'. Scott had rejected Mawson's proposal to be landed with a small party on this coast, citing lack of resources. Shackleton had picked up the plans, publicly announcing his intention to lead the expedition. Scott now stated his intention to examine – a year ahead of Shackleton and Mawson – a thousand miles of this unknown coast.

Scott concluded his speech by outlining the dates and details of the attempt on the Pole, and the science he hoped to achieve. The difficulties, the struggles, the likelihood of changes of plan, the possibility of unpredictable, unexpected results, the importance of the science – all had been fixed in his listeners' minds. An overarching narrative, laid out in advance of the action.

The three great qualities leading to success, Major Darwin informed the guests at a farewell luncheon in London the day before *Terra Nova* left, were experience, the determination to win the prize sought for, and absolute confidence between leader and led. Captain Scott had all three. He had obtained all the information he possibly could from other Arctic and Antarctic travellers. He and his staff meant 'to do or die'. But as to how far south the expedition would reach, the difficulties were 'simply immense'.

'Captain Scott is going to prove once again that the manhood of the nation is not dead, and that the characteristics of our ancestors, who won this great empire, still flourish amongst us', Darwin said. And everyone stood, to drink a toast to 'Success to the Antarctic Expedition, and good luck to its leader'.

2

Leaving London

1 June–30 September 1910

Captain Scott, with the experience of three centuries to draw upon, and a complete knowledge of the arduous nature of the task, will have the best equipment that science and forethought can provide.

Travel & Exploration (March 1910)

D URING THE FIRST two weeks of June, Scott's expedition ship, *Terra Nova*, pottered along the southern coast of England from London round to final farewells at Cardiff, in Wales. A succession of last chances to get ashore and have a night's enjoyment, shop, say farewell to friends and family. More seriously, as Captain Scott reminded all hands at a meeting aft, this was the last chance for every man to make his will. 'The will was a big item for me,' commented Petty Officer George Percy Abbott cheerfully, 'my sum totum being three shillings and four pence in the Bank, & a Bike.' All Petty Officers had signed on as Able Seamen, at £6 a month. Abbott, with Petty Officer Frank Browning and Able Seaman Harry Dickason, already friends, missed the last boat off to the ship at Stokes Bay but boarded next morning with a small black kitten scooped up from The Anchor public house, as *Terra Nova* got under way, towards Cowes.

Everyone agreed that good-natured Abbott, 'Tiny' to his friends, perhaps the tallest man on the ship, was strikingly handsome. Well-built, his muscles toned by regular Swedish exercises, qualified as a physical instructor 1st class, he was also a champion wrestler. But Abbott's strength came with a shining straightforwardness and innate manners, qualities already being noted by the wardroom officers. Just thirty, his hair had already turned grey.

The kitten was too young to feed itself and squawled all day, and the men didn't want it in their crowded quarters under the forecastle. Browning took pity and fed it, and the kitten slept in the foot of his hammock and purred when he came off watch. Browning's fine dark eyes and slim build made him ideal to play Neptune's wife in the Crossing the Line ceremonies – that and his tendency to glance away, or look down, unassertively. Having grown up on a farm in Devon, at twenty-nine he was a qualified torpedo instructor. Everybody liked him. He and the Londoner Harry Dickason, twenty-five, also a torpedo man, 'old chums and inseparables', had been brought over to *Terra Nova* by Lieutenant Teddy Evans from a former ship, as had Abbott.

Departing from Cardiff, *Terra Nova* shed a swirling trail of sodden tracts and periodicals pushed on board by the well-meaning and religiously inclined. The crowds lining the banks reminded Apsley Cherry-Garrard of the Oxford and Cambridge boat race. 'Cherry Garrard is accompanying us without any special vocation', noted Dr George Simpson, the expedition's dapper and precise meteorologist, on leave from the Indian Meteorological Office. Scott called Cherry-Garrard 'an adaptable helper'. His most useful attribute had been to donate £1,000 to the expedition, enough to pay the first year's salary of five Simpsons. With inherited estates, reasonable wealth, at a bit of a loose end but desperately keen to join, a tense, likeable, generous and sensitive young man, Cherry-Garrard had been included five weeks before departure as assistant zoologist to his friend Dr Wilson. Cherry's degree at Oxford was in Modern History – without his spectacles people across the street were out-of-focus blurs – but now his name swelled the list of expedition scientists. As did the name of Captain Lawrence Oates, Inniskilling Dragoons, an officer with a distaste for army life and a deep understanding of horses. A survivor not only of being shot at – Oates had been wounded in the Boer War, leaving his left leg slightly shorter than the right – but also of typhoid, smallpox and numerous childhood illnesses, Oates, an independent man, of independent means, tall, strong, and silent, had also contributed £1,000 to expedition funds. As Scott's other 'adaptable helper', Oates would take over charge of the expedition ponies in New Zealand. Exploration, men said, was a game. If so, Oates was playing it, except that his rule-book was seamed through by a sense of duty.

Oates, nicknamed Titus, had made a further contribution to funds by signing on as a midshipman for a nominal sum, joining 21-year-old Tryggve Gran, who had commissioned a vessel to be built for his own Norwegian expedition to Antarctica but had accepted Scott's offer of a place as a ski instructor, and a small, wiry but sturdily built Royal Navy surgeon called Edward Atkinson, a quiet, kind man who specialized in parasites. All three jumped to the command of every officer, but in particular First Officer Lieutenant Victor Arbuthnot Campbell. Campbell, Merchant Navy and Royal Navy (retired), and serving on an 'honorary footing' – that is, costing the expedition nothing – ran the ship with tight discipline and an unshakeable belief in the virtues of routine. His raucous voice shouting orders penetrated, despite his trim frame and neat small mouth, to every corner. Men regarded him with respect and a degree of fear. He was the 'wicked mate', according to Gran. To Charles Wright, a 23-year-old Canadian physicist part-way through postgraduate work in Cambridge, Campbell was supposed to be 'a martinet and tries to live up to it', but Wright observed that Campbell always had a fat head when wakened at 4 a.m. for his watch. Otherwise Campbell was courteous, reserved, deeply shy and capable of exercising real charm to get what he wanted. As Mr Mate he was also known as 'No. 1' or 'Father', which he happened to be, because his private life included an eight-year-old son. But it also included a wife still grieving deeply over the drowning of her sister during a summer in Norway. Campbell's passions were fishing and shooting, preferably in Norway. His skills included skiing and speaking Norwegian. Off duty he sketched, wrote the minimum required in his journal and occasionally listened to music, as long as it wasn't sad.

When they were off duty, the three midshipmen – Oates and Atkinson, now firm friends and both keen boxers, and the confident, enthusiastic Gran – gave as good as they got. Scraps and fights and general rowdy foolery ricocheted through the cramped cabins and over and under the wardroom table. Oates, in particular, went for Campbell. Both had been at Eton, but Campbell was five years older.

Terra Nova was a wooden sailing ship when many of her sailors had never worked sail. She was under-powered, and her engines were greedy users of coal, that bulky, dirty but on this trip most essential of cargoes. Twenty-six years' work had left structural scars and deep-seated inadequacies as a carrier of up to sixty men plus an enormous quantity and complexity of stores and equipment. She leaked continually – through the decks and on to the bunks when it rained, and through a so far untracked hole in her stern. Two feet of water needed to be pumped out every watch, a continuous and tiring task. As Captain Scott's chosen expedition vessel, *Terra Nova* carried the Royal Yacht Squadron ensign, which freed her from the loading constraints of the Board of Trade regulations. She rolled. Affable Murray Levick, the second of the two Royal Navy surgeons released by the Navy Board for the expedition, earned respect for getting up from a meal, going out to be seasick and then ambling his sizeable presence back to continue eating. Levick, a specialist in physical training and diet, had served under Scott on HMS *Essex* in 1908. A letter from Scott informing him that the Admiralty had been requested to allocate his services to the expedition had arrived nine weeks before *Terra Nova* was due to depart.

Abbott, doing his Swedish exercises up on deck, enjoyed talking to the scientists. Dr Simpson had strung wires around the ship and across the bridge, to the annoyance of the officers, in order to measure amounts of penetrating radiation (cosmic rays). Simpson assumed that Wright would be his assistant in his large, instrument-led programme of research. The Canadian Wright was beginning to realize that he would need to negotiate opportunities to pursue his own research. Wright fitted everyone's idea of the colonial, with his vivid language, strength, toughness and independence of mind. But he came with added advantages: a backwoodsman, he was used to camping, ice and snow.

All expedition members had to join in the naval routines. Simpson, who preferred to get on with his science, had nevertheless to 'turn up in spotless (more or less) white clothes for Church each Sunday morning'. He also had to join in pumping – 'objectionable work & blisters the hands badly'. Without it ever being made explicit, expedition members were expected to join in the work of the ship.

Volunteers were called for, and, as Cherry noted, you volunteered: shovelling coal, feeding the fiery furnace down in the engine room or going aloft to reef or furl sails. When squalls struck, men clung to the yards, heavy sails flapping in the screeching wind, straining to hear the shouted orders, each roll swinging them through seventy feet of arc, faces and hands stung by hard rain or driving hail. They lined up to the pump handle and pumped, and pumped again, learning the repetitive sea shanties of the Merchant Navy, sung, to Scott's ear 'in a flat and throaty style', roaring them out until their hands roughened and the daily hosing down with seawater couldn't dislodge ingrained sweat and dirt. Most took turn on watch and did whatever unpleasant job was going; they were tired, their bodies toughened; and they got to know each other, to work together, to find out each other's strengths and weaknesses. The mood was generally one of persistent cheerfulness, the ethos one of no complaining and silence about perceived risks. 'I noticed the sharks swimming round along the short stretch we had to swim to reach the boat', Wright informed his father about their one, difficult landing, on the deserted island of South Trinidad in the Indian Ocean. 'I was very pleased with myself later for saying nothing about them till we were all off.'

Browning taught his black cat tricks, climbing a rope, going aloft. 'All hands were amused, considering him quite a sailor.' He taught him to eat biscuits and cheese with his sardines, and not to mind a bath in warm water when tar from the rigging stuck on his fur. He made him a little hammock with two small blankets and a pillow, all correct. It was sport, wrote Browning, to see the cat getting in when the hammock was slung up and the ship rolling. There were other pets on the ship, but the little cat lying with his head on his pillow, with his beautiful sleek black fur and his one white whisker on the port side, was the favourite, and everyone called him Nigger.

Approaching Cape Town, Teddy Evans asked Abbott who on the mess deck could cut hair, and the ever-helpful Abbott volunteered his services. Evans commanded a generally happy ship with verve and energy, mixed with a taste for skylarking and being rowdy: his most dramatic party trick was picking a man up by the seat of his trousers with his teeth. However, Scott, in South Africa with his wife,

33

Kathleen, had unexpectedly decided to take over command of *Terra Nova*. Abbott, a suitably splendid representative of navy manhood to display in the colonies, accompanied the respectably shorn Evans ashore on 1 August to collect Scott. In the privacy of the whale boat Evans asked Abbott if he was keen on landing in the Antarctic. 'I said yes, and thought everyone aboard was. He said I should probably land with the Eastern Party as Lieut Campbell wanted me; so I was mightily pleased, but had to keep it a secret.' Scott had announced that he would assess the men and make his selection on the run to Australia. Campbell had moved quickly to get Abbott first, but insiders could have guessed. Wilson had already 'demonstrated the art of bird skinning' to Abbott, and Abbott had vowed in his diary to 'do my best to pursue the art'.

'My dearest V', Victor Campbell wrote to his cousin Vera, in London, on 17 August, 'I wish you were here to talk to me. You could smoke a cigarette & we could discuss all sorts of things.' *Terra Nova* was making extensive and free use of the naval facilities at Simonstown, and Campbell was on board, almost alone. Those who could had escaped up country – Atkinson and Oates had invited Abbott and five other men from below decks to 'stay in a beautiful hotel', for dinner and billiards. Abbott was also given permission to go ashore and give an exhibition of club-swinging, sword drill and dancing the hornpipe. Campbell drew Vera three land crabs, called Clarence, Fred and José, and enclosed a photo of Lieutenant Rennick, Tryggve Gran and himself after working in the hold in the tropics: three smiling young men relaxing on board, handsome Gran with bare legs. 'I wanted to cut off Gran's legs (in the photo) as it is immodest but I can't find my nail scissors – so you can cut them off before showing them', Campbell wrote. Then 'about my landing' – and Campbell drew Vera a small map of King Edward VII Land, the ocean-facing edge of the great Barrier, and an inlet.

Scott had arrived in South Africa with a new theory and a revised plan. Exploring King Edward VII Land was integral to expedition rhetoric, a key objective announced in speeches. Now reality loomed. Little was known about King Edward VII Land, and thick pack ice appeared to clog the approaches, so Campbell might never be able to get his party ashore. No one had ever managed to land there. Scott informed Campbell that he should not attempt it. Instead, he should land on the Barrier and walk east, getting on to King Edward VII Land from the Barrier surface.

Landing on the Barrier was also a problem, but Scott had a solution. King Edward VII Land, he thought, would turn out to be a range of mountains, forming the eastern boundary to the Barrier. These mountains, Scott argued, continued on under the ice of the Barrier, causing an obstruction, resulting in stresses that, in turn, caused the seaward-facing edge of the Barrier to break away. Scott explained that he knew where this happened: at the deep branching bight he'd found near the eastern end of the Barrier in February 1902, which had been named Balloon Bight, after the balloon in which he and Shackleton made their ascents. The very existence of Balloon Bight, clearly marked on maps, proved his hypothesis. Scott thought that a line ran south from the head of Balloon Bight. To the east, towards King Edward VII Land, the ice of the Barrier surface would be stable because it rested on land. To the west the ice was afloat and thus unstable. Campbell should now land at Balloon Bight and build his winter quarters hut to the east of Scott's hypothetical line, on the stable ice, then walk in spring with his party to King Edward VII Land in safety.

In Campbell's little map for Vera, complete with ice cliffs, ice floes and a scale showing distance, 'land' 'fast ice barrier' and 'floating barrier' marked in, Scott's hypothetical line emerged from the top of the inlet like a long crack. 'I am to be landed at balloon bight on the barrier', Campbell wrote to Vera,

> as we cant get near the land owing to ice floes – Scotts idea is one side of the bight is resting on land the other afloat so that ice aground is safe, I sincerely hope it is I am sure it must be – our leak is still there but gives us all good exercise . . . Good night dear V. take care of yourself and write often.
>
> Your loving Coz Vic

Scott's new plan had obvious advantages. Additional gains would come from it, however, that were not necessary to share with Campbell. In January 1908, trying to set up his winter quarters according to the terms of the agreement made with Scott, Shackleton stated that he could find no trace of Balloon Bight or Balloon Inlet, as it was sometimes called. Instead, south of where it should have been, Shackleton claimed that he found a wide bay, which he called the Bay of Whales. Convinced that a large mass of the Barrier had recently broken away, thus removing the inlets used by Borchgrevink and Scott, Shackleton decided that he could not risk building his winter quarters on the ice shelf. The disappearance of Balloon Bight was at the centre of Shackleton's decision to break his agreement with Scott and go to Ross Island. Scott considered these reasons merely a construct, but it was awkward stuff. The Royal Geographical Society wanted its two leading polar explorers to be seen to be co-operating. Darwin had written to Scott in June 1909, suggesting that he amend a draft letter Scott had written to Shackleton 'so as to make it absolutely clear that you do not think he really could have landed'. The two men maintained a visibly polite relationship with each other. But to Scott, Balloon Bight existed. Scott's theories about why it must exist, and how it related to the structure of the Barrier, shored up his conviction that Shackleton was casual about the truth. Scott's disdain for Shackleton's probity had a firm footing in the inlet's presence, and Campbell had been instructed to land in it. Given Scott's new theory, the Eastern party could winter on the ice at Balloon Bight in safety. And by approaching King Edward VII Land from Balloon Bight, Campell would be carrying through the plan that Shackleton had failed to initiate.

But beyond this, Scott's primary intention was to get *Terra Nova* heading north as quickly as possible to begin exploring west, along the unknown coast. He wanted the ship to stay in the ice until the end of March 1911, maximizing the chances for discovery during the first summer season, a year ahead of Shackleton and Mawson's proposed expedition. By delivering the Eastern party to Balloon Bight, by side-stepping trying to reach King Edward VII Land from the sea, two valuable resources – time and coal – would be saved.

Scott's desire to keep *Terra Nova* exploring along the north coast until the close of autumn carried a real risk. The decision when to head north, away from the ice spreading over the surface of the sea as winter approached, was a severe responsibility for a ship's commander, central to the safety of his vessel and crew, and by setting a date Scott risked *Terra Nova* being trapped in the ice. But Scott considered the consequences of the ship spending the winter in the ice entirely manageable and minimal. Such a situation, he wrote, 'would not be dangerous'. The winter would 'probably be passed very comfortably'. However, 'public and private anxiety' would need to be allayed if *Terra Nova* failed to return from the ice, and certain actions taken. Scott had already dealt with the implications. Before leaving London, he had asked Admiral Sir Lewis Beaumont to undertake the responsibility, putting into his safe hands five days before he left for Cape Town a statement dated 11 July 1910, to act as a supplementary to the 'authorised programme of the Expedition'. Beaumont was to select 'the most opportune time' to bring it to public notice, in part or in whole, to prevent, if the occasion arose, 'public speculation and useless foreboding'.

Above all else Scott wanted to avoid the débâcle of government-funded rescue ships that had soured his first expedition. He took Beaumont through the timings. If *Terra Nova* became trapped exploring for new land in March 1911, no relief ship would be needed. *Terra Nova* could escape in time to return to New Zealand for coal, then get back south again to McMurdo Sound probably at the very end of the next summer, early March 1912. All the shore party programmes could still be carried out as arranged. Even if *Terra Nova* remained caught until mid-summer, and therefore unable to reach Antarctica at all, 'no anxiety need be felt' by anyone. His men – at least, all those near the coast – could live entirely off the land.

> In McMurdo Sound there exists, as is well known, an ample supply of seals and penguins from which fuel, food and clothing can be drawn for an indefinite number of years. In the event of the non-arrival of the ship in 1912, the supplies of civilised products will naturally be consumed with economy, so that these also can be made to cover a number of years. There is no reason why whole shore Parties should not continue to live in comparative comfort until the arrival of the relief Expedition.
>
> The fate of those who remain in the *Terra Nova* would be more problematic, but it must always be remembered that good

food is plentiful everywhere on the seaboard of the Antarctic Regions.

Douglas Mawson, with the redoubtable fifty-year-old geologist Professor Edgeworth David and Dr Mackay, all Antarctic novices, had achieved their long, difficult trek to the South Magnetic Pole in 1908–9 man-hauling an astonishing 1,260 miles, relaying two sledges for half of the five months travelled, with no support parties. Mawson and Mackay had killed Weddell seals hauled up on the sea ice, using their meat for food and their blubber for cooking, thus extending the time they could be out. A journey like this had the capacity to set a template in Scott's mind. Campbell and the Eastern party had similar conditions to manage, surely, exploring along the coast of King Edward VII Land, with a push up through the mountains to the probable plateau beyond. Scott became an enthusiastic proponent of the assumption that his men – as long as they lived on or near the coast – would need nothing other than local resources to survive, thus reducing his logistical worries in one swoop. So confident had Scott become that he extended, for the purposes of planning, the capacity of his men to survive to 'an indefinite number of years'.

Terra Nova left Simonstown on Friday 2 September 1910 with every-one back to their usual ship-board tasks, except that Abbott now spent part of every day in the main hold working on sledging gear and overhauling scientific instruments, instructed by Edgar Evans, who was also instructing Frank Browning. Cutting Scott's hair on the 20th, Abbott discussed sailing ships dying out in the navy – he had served in a full-rigged ship. But preparing for the expeditions to come pressed, and it was obvious that Scott needed to announce his choice for the shore parties earlier than he had intended. Four weeks after departing, on Friday 30 September, Captain Scott 'called Ship's Company aft and made known his selection for landing party', noted Browning, who 'was very pleased to hear my name among them, I was to form one of the Eastern Party under Lieu V Campbell and try to get to King Edward VII Land'.

Campbell had already been allocated Murray Levick as his doctor. A geologist would join the Eastern party in Australia. Allowed the 'pick of the blue-jackets', Campbell added Harry Dickason to his choice of Abbott and Browning. The only able seaman in the shore party, Dickason, was included as cook, but he didn't know how to cook and so was detailed off to the galley to learn. Given the isolation to come, three men who were established friends made sense. A number of men on the mess deck with previous Antarctic experience had signed on to *Terra Nova* in the hope of being in the shore party. But Scott had selected only Chief Stoker Lashly and Petty Officers Tom Crean and Edgar Evans, all powerfully built men who had sledged with Scott and knew his ways. Campbell had selected three men from the lower deck with no experience at all of polar life or conditions.

3

The home run

1 October–31 December 1910

> Whether you are bound for tropical deserts or Arctic
> snows, stick to the clothes you habitually wear at home,
> and, when you get on the ground, dress as much as pos-
> sible like the natives.
> Harry de Windt, 'Hints for Travellers in Arctic Regions'
> (March 1910)

SITTING AT THE wardroom table *en route* to Australia, Oates was
explaining to Campbell how to kill a pony. You want to do it
first time. Get it to face you, head dropped. And Oates drew a horse's
head from the front, with an equilateral triangle marking the spot.
Two of Scott's precious ponies, a central component of his transport
strategy, were being allocated to the Eastern party. But two or ten,
the same essential care and maintenance needed to be understood.
Ailments and injuries: recognize the symptoms, said Oates, listing
what to do for thrush, choking, fits, constipation. Care of ponies, on
the march and in camp: 'sponge out nostrils and hocks (stern) with a
damp sponge or rag after a day's work'. Campbell filled page after
page of careful notes. How to feed the ponies, and how to deal with
the constant problem of watering, which required precious fuel to
melt ice or snow. Ponies added hugely to the logistical burden, and
the skills needed to be acquired. How, for example, could they be
stabled through the winter in King Edward VII Land? There was
only timber for a hut. Humans, by contrast, took up exactly two
pages of Campbell's notebook.

The Eastern party carried a heavy responsibility. Getting to the
Pole would take major resources: the necessity was acknowledged.

In the meantime, the Eastern party were to be geographical achievers, exploring unknown territory. But they were also in the vanguard for the achieving of science. Why was the pack ice so heavy at the entrance to the Ross Sea? Wilson hoped that the Eastern party would solve the riddle. Was King Edward VII Land the start of a mountain range running south? What route did it offer to the Pole? Surveying, magnetic work, geology, zoology, biology – the Eastern party was to be a subset of the main party, a mini-version of its skills and expertise. Each scientist drew up instructions in his own special department, to guide the Eastern party in taking observations. Campbell made more headings in his notebook. Meteorology: lists of equipment, with notes on how to use the barometers (two supplied) and method of mounting them, how to use the thermometer and Stevenson screen, with a drawing of the box that would need building. How to measure amount of snow. How to work a hypsometer and tide gauge. The importance of carrying out magnetic observations and measurements for variation of the compass. Weddell seals, Campbell noted, were 'almost fearless', easily killed for food, palatable 'and a preventative, and even an actual cure for scurvy'.

Campbell's expertise was surveying, and he had the added advantage of experience of snow and ice acquired in Norway. His three seamen were by definition all-purpose handymen, and strong. But they were polar novices. George Murray Levick, by virtue of his medical training, was expected to be the Eastern party zoologist. He had also been appointed the party's photographer, exercising that relatively new technique for scientists, detailing in photographs the appearance and form of objects: rocks with locations, seaweeds, land plants, animals – both habits and habitat – as well as recording physical locations. Levick practised taking photographs in the difficult Antarctic conditions, assiduously, to the annoyance of those he asked to stop what they were doing and pose; he also had to learn how to develop film, given minimal facilities. Levick had been struggling to master the elements of navigation ever since leaving London. 'He has not succeeded and will not', commented Charles Wright, but he is 'learning to bake bread'.

Expedition supplies and equipment loaded into the holds in London were the bank vaults, the department store, the total of their household goods, along with anything extra that could be squeezed on board in Australia and New Zealand. But the Eastern party – about to be isolated, unable to correct what had been forgotten or was discovered to be needed – had to acquire, now, and that meant raiding the ship. Every member of the Eastern party was adept at a different kind of finding and keeping. Stores 'disappeared,' equipment was 'borrowed' – established naval practice that had equipped *Terra Nova* from various sources reapplied now to equip the Eastern party.

Lieutenant Henry Robertson Bowers, Royal Indian Marine, a 'little square block of a man', red-headed and white skinned, who got sunburnt even when it rained yet appeared oblivious to the cold, had taken on that most thankless of tasks, ship's storekeeper. His large beaky nose earned him the immediate nickname Birdie, and nothing escaped his indefatigable, efficient eye or memory, or seemed to shake his constant state of cheerfulness. Campbell had hoped to get Birdie for the Eastern party, but Scott had taken one look and secured 'the perfect treasure' for the Polar party. Birdie, however, was helpful to the Eastern party's needs, Campbell was polite and persuasive, and Campbell's cabin reputedly hid a mine of useful things, regularly raided to re-establish ownership. Levick was accused of being so relaxed that he acquired and then forgot where he had hidden the booty.

Coming in to Melbourne through rough seas and rain on 12 October, Scott found a telegram waiting: 'Beg leave to inform you *Fram* proceeding Antarctica. Amundsen.' The heated atmosphere of competing expeditions had seemed a distant memory. Tryggve Gran was summoned to Scott's cabin in the hope that he could provide elucidation about his fellow countryman. Roald Amundsen, the renowned Norwegian polar explorer, had been planning to spend four or five years drifting across the northern polar regions in the famous Arctic ship *Fram*, doing scientific and oceanographic research. But Gran couldn't help. Astonished, mystified, and unenlightened, Scott kept the news from his officers. Gran, however, did tell Campbell, whom he had known previously in Norway. Campbell was equally amazed. Busy with official engagements and fund-raising on shore, Scott then heard that the Japanese were also about to depart for the Ross Sea in the *Kainan-maru*, intending to make a dash for the Pole.

Professor Edgeworth David, head of science on Shackleton's expedition and ever helpful to Antarctic aspirations, persuaded the government of Australia to contribute a large grant to Scott, who had been relying on it. Scott had asked Edgeworth David to find him geologists, those interpreters of the structure of undiscovered lands, who would also look for exploitable minerals: valuable men. The Australian Thomas Griffith Taylor had already been recruited from Cambridge. Now a second geologist, Frank Debenham, was waiting to join the ship, but a third highly qualified man failed his medical at the last moment. Edgeworth David generously suggested a replacement – his assistant, the 24-year-old Raymond Priestley, who was currently working long hours in the University of Sydney geology department helping write the Shackleton expedition's Antarctic geology volumes, having been a very junior member of Shackleton's science staff. Shackleton was cabled for permission. Priestley sent a quick letter to his father at the Abbey House School, Tewkesbury, a modest establishment and his home, which offered 'a thoroughly Modern Education . . . with Special Care of Delicate Boys . . . and a large Playground', and left to pick up the ship in New Zealand.

While in Melbourne, Scott received a letter from Douglas Mawson courteously expressing his regret that he had not joined him. Mawson explained he had taken no steps to raise funds for his proposed expedition to explore the coast of Antarctica directly south of Australia, 'so that you may never regard me as a usurper of funds which might otherwise have gone towards your enterprise'. Scott replied asking to see the details of the proposed expedition and inquiring whether Shackleton would still lead it. But Mawson was now away, prospecting astride a camel for radium and sapphires in the Australian outback.

By the time Mawson was able to reply with the details Scott asked for, *Terra Nova* was at Lyttelton, New Zealand, undergoing a final refit in the fine protected harbour over the hills from Christchurch. Recognizing in Scott 'an ideal of generosity and true humaness', Mawson wrote that currently his plans involved embarking in a year's time, leaving four men at Cape Adare, another batch as near the

Magnetic Pole as possible and two more parties with luck to 'knit up the coastlines' as far as Gaussberg. With regard to Shackleton, 'he may or may not be in charge – when I last saw him he fairly definitely stated that he could not get away.' 'Should the expedition fall through', Mawson wrote, 'I . . . would like to make some arrangement with you for continuing, as a corollary to your expedition, with scientific work to the west of Cape Adare. I have strong and well formed plans for doing work in that direction.' Mawson was sure Scott would be happy with Priestley, who would be able to bring him up to date on all that had happened in the McMurdo Sound area since *Discovery* departed.

Scott's plans for exploring the coast west of Cape Adare overlapped directly with Mawson's. Scott had foreseen this possibility and dealt with the implications in his concept of open access irrespective of prior proposals, as set out in his letter of March 1910 to Major Darwin: 'I want it so settled before I leave that I am free to go where I please without the reproach that I am trespassing on his [Shackleton's] ground.' According to the concept as expounded by Darwin in his response to Shackleton of 29 April, this doubling up of objectives was acceptable. 'In my opinion, every explorer should in future be at liberty to go exactly where he likes, without, at all events, any liability to an accusation of breach of faith.'

But doubling up, and competition, it was suddenly evident, could come from more than one direction. Amid rumours and confused messages Scott now heard that Amundsen and *Fram* were headed for 'a spot on the coast of West Antarctica', intending to try for the Pole. Few remembered that Amundsen had been in Antarctica before any of the current crop of explorers, having spent thirteen months in 1898–9 trapped in the ice in the Belgian expedition ship *Belgica*. Scott chose to say very little about Amundsen's planned arrival in Antarctica or attempt on the Pole. Darwin's April letter of suggested principles provided for general application. Gran described a New Zealand journalist telling him Scott's reply to a question about Amundsen: 'if the rumour is true . . . then I wish him good luck.' Given Scott's letter to Darwin, and the Darwin principles, it was an understandable response.

At Lyttelton another attempt was being made to repair the leak on

Terra Nova. Everything in the ship, Abbott explained to a friend, 'had to be got out, and put in store'. In the meantime Abbott was helping the ship's carpenter, Davies, erect the framework of the expedition's two winter quarters huts on some open ground, then bundling up all the timber. But on a warm Sunday Abbott switched roles, attending on Captain Scott and the Governor of Australasia on an excursion to view the expedition's ponies and dogs, held in quarantine on Quail Island, out in the bay. Scott had instructed Cecil Meares, the enigmatic Far Eastern traveller he had hired to journey to Siberia and choose his expedition animals, to obtain only white-coloured ponies, on the assumption (based on Shackleton's experience) that they would survive longer in the Antarctic cold.

Scott was in genial mood. Soon *Terra Nova* would steam out of Lyttelton Harbour, and the horrible business of trying to raise enough money to cover the ever mounting expedition expenses would no longer be his to deal with. He would still have to worry about them, yes, but there would be no more speech-making or humiliating begging. With his beloved Kathleen by his side he watched while Anton Omelchenko, a diminutive jockey from Vladivostok who had been hired to help bring the animals on the long, tiring journey to New Zealand, drove selected teams of small, shaggy, whitish ponies along a level road close to the water's edge, wooden sledge clattering along behind. Wavelets clicked up the beach, the air smelt of lush woods and early summer. The visitors were especially pleased with the dogs, a 'fine fierce lot', according to Abbott. A team harnessed to a sledge and driven by Demetri Gerof, a Russian dog-driver recruited by Meares as his assistant, 'simply tore up and down the hills'. The dogs had been trained to take the mail from post to post along a well-defined route crossing the frozen Sea of Okhotsk. They were going to a place of no routes or posts. But no matter.

Under instruction from Oates, Abbott started learning to manage the two ponies selected for the Eastern party, although the dogs appealed to him more. But these were happy days in a beautiful place, relaxed lunches with Oates and Meares, and swimming in the sea. Responding to the social freedom of New Zealand, Abbott was enjoying himself hugely, going on 'glorious' outings, performing the hornpipe to entertain visitors, accepting the challenge to wrestle at the Agricultural Fair in Canterbury – where he won a gold medal ('I have not received it yet, consider it doubtful I ever shall') – and dancing with the local beauties.

Raymond Priestley arrived from Sydney and began working on *Terra Nova* dressed in a black shirt with coloured silk handkerchief knotted around his neck, a scarlet tasselled cap and old cricketing trousers held up by a leather belt wide enough to tether an angry bull, with a sheath and sheath-knife. His Shackleton credentials were signalled with Professor Edgeworth David's Antarctic fur coat and Shackleton's dress boots, dignifying the increasingly grubby and torn cricket trousers. Priestley had joined Shackleton's expedition while still an undergraduate at Bristol University College because, he claimed, his older brother happened to talk to the right person at the right time. Now being in the right place had worked again.

Priestley was glad to find his friend Bernard Day on board. Day, with his long, lanky legs and lugubrious face, had been Shackleton's patient motor mechanic who'd coaxed the air-cooled Arrol-Johnston motor car some miles across the Antarctic ice before it broke down irretrievably. Scott had hired Day to take charge of the three expensive motor sledges, the expedition's third strand of transport, with all that hung on their performance. Despite his rather rakish clothes, Priestley enjoyed only a brief spate of nicknames. Nelson, the sophisticated intellectual biologist – who shared with Priestley the distinction of having left university without completing a degree – called him 'Hogarth' or 'the Rake' because the cap and fur coat reminded him of Hogarth's *The Rake's Progress*. An alternative, 'the Pirate', lasted a bit longer. But none stuck, and Priestley subsided into the largely untenanted ranks of those with no nickname, and was universally known as Raymond. Thorough and practical, Priestley had managed in the rush of departure to go out and spend some of his minimal spare cash on an ice axe and crampons to make the Eastern party 'more comfortable'. The Eastern party had – in its last, and youngest, member – someone with Antarctic experience.

Cargo was being restowed on board *Terra Nova*. Eastern party stores were marked with a broad green stripe, while red was used for everything else. By 26 November everyone was on board. The eight last expedition members had squeezed in with their possessions, along with another lieutenant, one of Kathleen Scott's many brothers. An easy-going, cheerful Merchant Navy man, taken on at a token wage, Wilfred Bruce was older than his fellow lieutenants. He had helped Cecil Meares bring the dogs and ponies from China to New Zealand. Now he and Meares were hardly on speaking terms, but it couldn't be helped. And the fact that he was Scott's brother-in-law would need to be carefully managed. A committed diary-keeper, Bruce had bought a local diary for 1911, preliminary pages dense with useful information: a list of 'His Majesty's Ministers', the royal family, names of colonial governors under 'The British Empire', lessons for Sundays, total populations – that of Tasmania, 186,860 (with mail from London to the capital, Hobart, taking thirty-two days), that of New Zealand, 1,042,994 (with mail taking thirty-nine days).

The last night in Lyttelton, 25 November, given all the confusion of final loading, Browning had hidden his black cat in the Harbour Board shed. So many people wanted the cat that Browning feared he'd be stolen. Back on board, said Browning, the little cat 'was surprised to find his old quarters occupied by ponies'. *Terra Nova* was grossly overloaded. The tobacco presented to the expedition alone weighed a ton. Fuel in all its forms clogged the decks: sacks of coal wedged between cases of petrol, paraffin and oil drums lashed over hatch spaces, bales of compressed hay and forage piled high. Additional fodder for the ponies, insisted on by Oates, had been stacked in two of the water tanks, meaning a further dire reduction in fresh water.

Supplying the motive force to the various means of transport was always going to be a bulky business, but the means of transport themselves – finally all on board – pushed space to the limit. Three enormous wooden cases containing the experimental motor sledges were lashed on deck. Four ponies stood tethered in stalls near the galley, while the others were under shelter in stalls on the forecastle deck, displacing the seamen. The seamen had agreed to sleep one deck down, but space was so crowded that there wasn't room even for Nigger's small hammock, and the muck from the ponies' stalls had begun dribbling through the decking. The dogs were chained to stanchions, exposed to winds and salt sprays. Browning left behind a large magpie, a present from a lady, but three rabbits, a guinea pig and another kitten had found their way on board as gifts.

Seamen, officers, scientists – everyone had to get on with it. This was the essential prerequisite for joining. Humans were by every reckoning the expedition's fundamental means of transport. Toughness proved fitness for purpose, to Scott. Humans could do without. Ponies – with a grim sea voyage ahead – had priority.

After one more stop for a last grasp at coal, a last loading of fresh butter and mutton carcasses and a welcome gift of two grey woollen jerseys per man there was a final sad farewell for Scott, Wilson and Evans as a tug stood alongside and took their wives off. The three women had a tumble of memories. Intense, happy holiday days with their husbands. A whirl of official engagements and being entertained. Tensions, and some jealousies. For Kathleen Scott, a complex involvement with the expedition. She had sewed 432 name-tags on to the clothes of certain favoured young men. But she also knew more of the expedition's planning than most participants. And she knew the most about its leader. Dr Wilson, that enigmatic, deeply admired, spiritual man, would now take the responsibility of being her husband's friend and support.

The distant shore flattened, the swell took over and *Terra Nova* finally departed New Zealand on 29 November 1910. From now on there would be no contact, no news, until, all going well, the ship arrived back out of the south next March or April.

The overloading was manageable, if only the weather was reasonable. It wasn't. Two days out, *Terra Nova* met the kind of storm the latitudes south of New Zealand deliver with relentless frequency. Huge swells built up, and steep-sided hills of cold green water swept over the decks. The two main pumps choked. In the dark and the howling wind the handpump was rigged, and the seamen worked in shifts. Browning: 'we were pumping in water up to our waist and at times when the ship rolled heavily it would be up to our armpits.' Abbott: 'one of us would get washed off our feet . . . somebody would grab you, or by luck we would bring up against something solid.' The upper deck cargo broke adrift. Browning: 'cases of petrol were washed overboard . . . the cases being swept across . . . by the heavy seas would knock you off your feet.'

The handpump choked. Down in the engine room the water rose, the fires went out and baling began with two teams, two hours on, two hours off, three iron buckets, one man on the floor waist-deep in bilge water handing up bucketload after bucketload to the first man on the vertical iron ladder and so on up, contents slopping as the ship rolled sluggishly, men singing anything that came into their heads as long as they were singing. Priestley's team put him in the open so he could vomit directly into the raging sea, along with the contents of each bucket, rather than over the heads of the men on the ladder. One pony died, another had to be shot. The dogs, chained by the necks, were swept from side to side by the heavy seas, and one drowned. Coal, petrol and fodder were lost overboard – vital resources irrevocably reduced.

The gale eased on 3 December. Atkinson: 'we damn nearly foundered.' According to Abbott, 'The Ponies & Dogs suffered the most, poor beasts, it was pitiful to see their dumb agony.' Atkinson helped Scott, Oates and some others hoist the dead ponies out of the forecastle, through the skylight and over the side – a dirty job. The skylight space was so small it stretched out the ponies like dead rabbits, said Teddy Evans. Priestley collapsed with his perennial seasickness back into his bunk, his foot gashed and bleeding where he'd stepped on broken glass in the chaos. Privately, Priestley thought the seas that Shackleton's ship *Nimrod* met on her departure from New Zealand had been worse. But it didn't do to mention Shackleton's expedition.

Four days after the great storm, air and sea temperatures dropped suddenly; spray froze on the deck, and leather mitts were served out to the seamen for rough work. Whenever the watch sang a shanty, the dogs chained on the decks set up a long miserable howl. Gran had already claimed an iceberg, which turned out to be the spout of a whale, and Campbell had seen one, but only from the crow's nest through a telescope. But the next day there were two, travellers in the empty ocean, swells breaking against their cliffs, spray bursting upwards.

Ahead lay the inherently unknowable. The pack ice, that frustrating, unreadable white blockade, straddled the entrance to the Ross Sea. A wide band of floating ice, sections of last winter's frozen surface of the sea, and the winter's before, mixed with thick chunks of hard glacier ice riding low in the water, shuffling and rubbing together, moving north, herded by wind and currents into loose conglomerations or tight impenetrable knots, slices of ice pressured into ridges and contorted heaps, with leads of black water winding through the glittering white, closing, then opening. How thick would the pack be this season? How far would it extend this year? Scott had studied where previous vessels had entered and left the pack, and he opted for the course he thought would give the best chance of a fast passage. All he wanted was to be out the other side as speedily as possible.

But for most of the men on *Terra Nova* everything ahead was new and wondrous. At 7.00 a.m. on Friday 9 December the ship entered the ice, the swells calmed and they saw their first penguins. The day after, they saw the first seals. 'Everybody got rifles and revolvers and knives, and there was a great and horrible slaughter', wrote Cherry-Garrard. Wilson and Cherry put on overalls and began skinning. Cherry was still learning how, but the flensing knife slipped and he cut his hand badly. Everyone ate their first seal steaks and liver. Abbott was trying to learn some Russian from 'the Boys', Demetri and Anton, hired by Meares to help with the animals.

On Sunday the 12th Ponting's ever-inquisitive eye noticed Gran producing from the hold 'great bundles of the Scandinavian snow-shoes, called *ski*'. All hands were ordered on to the sea ice, despite wind and snow, and Gran gave the first lessons in skiing with the latest idea, two sticks. Everyone was intoxicated by that curious sense of invulnerability, of walking on a solid surface where there should be water, until the ice suddenly gave way to reveal the deep black ocean just beneath, into which two ship's officers plus one Petty Officer all fell. So too, noted Campbell, did Nigger the cat. Officers and scientists were issued with skis, then the ratings, and instruction continued, with Gran having first adjusted the bindings – a tough job, without the right tools or a workshop. It wasn't much fun learning on ice floes scarred with ridges and cracks, hard lumps and sudden snow-filled holes. Shackleton had taken a few pairs of skis but didn't use them on the sledging journeys. Bernard Day was so impressed by skis that he reckoned all expeditions from now on would use them.

Terra Nova butted and charged. High up on the main mast an officer stood on a heap of hay in the crow's nest among cigarette ends, watching for open water and shouting instructions through a megaphone to the steersman and on down to the engine room via the midshipman on the bridge. It was a cold and private world, where the wind sang, and delicately beautiful snow petrels, the pure white birds of the pack ice, fluttered and swooped. And it was pleasant, as long as there were no acrid fumes from the furnaces. The ocean's frozen surface lay in expanses of flat whiteness, vast fields of ice, or it was cracked into slabs, or shoved together into jumbled heaps. Massive icebergs ploughed their own routes. Sometimes, with sails set, *Terra Nova* worked through mush or through alleyways of ice as high as a church tower. With engines silent the officers could hear the sound of music from the men's quarters, the mandolin and violin. At other times, engines labouring, *Terra Nova* made only a mile or two a day, shoving and ramming at the ice. Stopping on the 13th to collect fresh water ice to melt for water (there was an allowance of only one cup of water a day per man for washing), Priestley thought the heavy pack very similar to the pack that turned Shackleton back from King Edward VII Land in January 1908. Soon he would be experiencing his second attempt to land in this difficult place. On the 16th he and Campbell, during an Eastern party council meeting, went through a list of two weeks' sledging food they planned to have packed and ready for a prospecting trip at Balloon Bight. There wouldn't be much time to organize stores between the shore party landing and the Eastern party's departure.

Apart from anything else, they weren't getting through the pack ice, which never seemed to end. The frustration affected some more than others. Levick, apparently sociable – he enjoyed his bridge four, with Scott – was minding some of the constraints, in particular the one cup of water only per day for washing, cleaning teeth etc. Considered easy-going, beneath the apparently bland exterior he was not an obvious fit. He was fed up with ship life. 'I hate it,' he wrote on 18 December. The waste of the scientists' expertise was deeply annoying to Scott. This 'very poor showing' of our 'tremendous experts', as Scott called them, was a problem, although in all other ways, as he wrote to Kathleen, the scientists had had to take their share of the jobs with 'no hesitation or distinction' – and it would be the same when it came to unloading cargo or any other hard manual labour.

But the worst of the pack ice – even worse than the delay – was the waste of coal. Every attempt to move used precious coal, and *Terra Nova* ate it. The furnaces used 2 tons of coal to get steam up, and by that time the opening in the ice might have closed. The reiterating decision for Scott, inherently difficult but increasing in stress as days passed with minimal progress, was when to draw fires, when to put them out, when to raise steam again. All plans involving *Terra Nova* came down in the end to this one simple measure: lumps of black coal, and the hungry mouths of her inefficient furnaces.

Coal was the bulkiest of cargoes. The amount carried defined what could be achieved. Despite the best efforts of Bowers to load the maximum on board, the sums were unarguable. They were burning 8 tons a day, and under 300 tons remained. Enough must be left for the ship's exploring trip to the west beyond Cape Adare, then for the journey back to New Zealand. What to do was the problem. Any delay used coal, but delays were caused by the unknowables – the state of the ice, the weather, storms, wind direction – all the physical realities of this complex place. The further south the heavy pack extended, the more coal was used, but guessing the boundary of the pack was impossible.

On 23 December, after days of trying sails and then raising steam, then drawing fires, of starting and then stopping, a long discussion began in the wardroom about the implications of the diminishing coal supply. Participants noted the options in their journals. If the pack lasted much longer, something would have to go. Delay, measured in coal, meant choices would have to be made. Scott had committed to two exploring expeditions using the ship in opposite directions. Resources were stretched, and the end-points of Scott's long right-angle of coast – both springboards for discoveries – were in conflict.

Priorities were now exposed. The Eastern party, it turned out, would take the impact. *Terra Nova*'s voyage of discovery to the north, it was revealed, had precedence over the exploring of King Edward VII Land. Given this priority, the logic was simple. The rationale was timing. Scott wanted *Terra Nova* to explore the unknown coast west of Cape Adare this season. The amount of coal remaining defined the number of days the ship could spend exploring, and there might not be enough coal to take the Eastern party to King Edward VII Land as well. The long-nurtured plans for tackling the eastern end of the Barrier could be shelved. Since the ship was heading north in any case, the Eastern party could instead be dropped off by *Terra Nova* somewhere suitable beyond Cape Adare. Scott suggested Robertson Bay, avoiding using the emotive 'Cape Adare' associated with Borchgrevink's expedition. Cape Adare's steep eastern flank bordered the Ross Sea, and its western flank formed the boundary of Robertson Bay. But, as Scott knew well, having landed during the *Discovery* expedition on the shingly spit of beach near the tip of the cape's inner coastline where Borchgrevink had built his hut, this was the only place so far discovered in the area where a ship could unload stores. Everyone agreed that the failure to put the Eastern party ashore at King Edward VII Land would be a hard blow for Campbell and his men. The alternative – getting them to explore the unknown northern coast – seemed to be nothing more than a compromise.

Mawson's and Shackleton's expedition to explore this northern coast had been announced in British newspapers, but there was no mention in anyone's journal during these difficult days on *Terra Nova* of other expeditions, or of the pre-empting of Mawson's plans if the Eastern party was put ashore in Robertson Bay. Priestley, who had worked in Sydney with Professor Edgeworth David on Shackleton's geological results, would have known the outline, but the expeditioners in the wardroom of *Terra Nova* had a lot to occupy their minds.

Harry Pennell, the ship's immensely hard-working, popular Navigator, turned twenty-eight on the 23rd and was hoisted in celebration up through the forecastle skylight, an honour so far only given to two dead ponies. Next day, Christmas Eve, the sun shone, and the ice glowed lavender and rose pink. Pools of water between the floes were still as mercury, reflecting the ice above like identical pages in an open book. The sky, in an infinite delicacy of shading from blue to green to pale yellow to orange to red, lay mirrored in the still water. After days of dull, overcast light the beauty was transforming. In Campbell's cabin a battle erupted so intense that Campbell was later found hanging over the rail feeling extremely sick, having been attacked by Oates and Atkinson for taking twenty matches for the Eastern party. 'Campbell, Priestley & I have been laying our hands onto everything we can get that might come in handy for the Eastern party, & are accumulating little secret stores about the ship', Levick admitted. The fight degenerated, with Oates dragging Wilson's clothes off and the chief scientist bursting naked into the wardroom, dragging Oates along on his back. *Terra Nova* had been forcing a slow way through the ice, engine at full steam, shoving her weight against the solid blocks, the ice scraping and grinding along her sides, but they'd had to stop, again, in thick tight pack and once again let the fires go out. The letting off of steam was happening in engine room and wardroom. Frustration was showing.

For days the decks had been flecked red with the slaughter of sufficient Adélie penguins, caught by a variety of risible means, to provide Christmas lunch. Now, ice and sky merging in the strange, chilling featureless white-grey light that denied shadows, the ship fast in the pack, the seamen ate their Christmas lunch (there was a slice of penguin breast for Nigger) with cigars, a bottle of stout and chocolate served out to each man. Tom Crean's rabbit, one of the three that came aboard at Lyttelton, gave birth in a nest in the ponies' hay, and Crean promised a sample of offspring to everyone who asked.

Christmas dinner for the officers in the wardroom was subdued. Afterwards everyone had to sing or tell a story. Meares, absolutely tuneless, delivered his own composition in a cracked, metallic voice:

> I'll sing a little ditty about our expedition
> And many of the members that south would go
> But if it isn't pretty I hope that you'll forgive me
> It's hard to be a poet when youre tightly in a floe
>
> *Chorus:*
> Then give three cheers
> For all aboard our Steamer

The Skipper & the officers the engineers & crew
And may we all sit round again some other jolly Christmas
And drink to those that think of us and love us too.

The first four verses were followed by:

The last verse, alas! is a much more serious topic,
  About the Eastern Party I don't quite know what to say
The wicked mate, the doctor fat, the dapper little Priestley –
  Well! we hope that we'll all meet again another day.

'It's a libel', protested Priestley 'as I am the biggest officer of the Eastern party . . . and the poem was written by a man smaller than myself.' But on that rather sober thought they sang 'Auld Lang Syne' and 'God Save the King'. Outside, the white and frozen world, the occasional call of penguins. Inside, uncertainty and more talk. There were another 450 miles still to go before landing.

The day after Christmas everyone in the shore party busily wrote letters. Wilfred Bruce could not see why they were bothering. The ship was still fast in the pack. Even the plans to explore the unknown northern coast west of Cape North now seemed at risk. Their captivity weighed heavily on Scott's mind. 'It is a very, very trying time', he wrote.

A month after *Terra Nova* left New Zealand, on 29 December, they began to move forward, steadily. Bruce made a list in his diary of the entire ship's company, each name followed by occupation and destination, 'ship' (S) or 'shore', with 'shore' divided into 'Eastern' (E) or 'Western' (W), and a subset 'Far W' for those who would be going west to do geology in Victoria Land.

TERRA NOVA's crew. December 29th

Officers	Scott	Leader & Owner	Western Party
	Evans	Captain	"
	Campbell	No. 1	Eastern
	Pennell	Navigator	Ship's
	Rennick	Watch keepers	"
	Bowers	"	Western
	Bruce	"	Ship's

Surgeons	Levick		Eastern
	Atkinson		Western
A. P.	Drake		Ship's
	Wilson	Leader Scientific Staff	Zoologist
	Simpson	Meteorologist	W
	Nelson	Biologist	W
	Cherry-Garrard	assistant Zoologist	W
	Debenham	Geologist	Far W
	Griffith Taylor	"	Far W
	Lillie	Biologist	(Ship)
	Wright	Geologist	Far W
	Priestley	"	E
	C. H. Meares	Charge of dogs	W
	H. I. Ponting	Photographer	W
	Capt. E. L. Oates	Charge of ponies	W
	A. L. Day	Charge of sledges	W
	T. Gran	Ski-runner	W

<u>The above are all ward room</u>

Williams	Chief Eng.	A. Cheetham	Boatswain
Lashly	2nd " W	Archer	Chief cook
Webb	3rd "	Davies	Carpenter

<u>Petty Officers</u>

Evans W	Crean W	Williamson S	Heald S	Paton S
Ford W	Leese S	Browning E	Mather S	
Parsons S	Abbott E	Keohane W	Baily S	
Dickason E	McCarthy S	Williams S	Knowles S	
Burton S	McGillion S	McDonald S	Brissenden S	
McKenzie S	Copp S	MacLeod S		
Servants	Hooper W	Neale S	Clissold W	
Anton W	Dimitri W			

Terra Nova finally cleared the pack on 30 December, well to the east and a little north of Cape Adare. With the ice lid removed, the swell regained possession and the 'old Bug Trap', as Lieutenant Rennick called her, immediately resumed rolling, then pitching heavily in a fierce gale. 'Owner worried & fidgety,' wrote Bruce, 'small wonder, as we are burning coal & drifting N.W.' All the susceptible were immediately seasick, and *Terra Nova* had to run for shelter in the pack. For Priestley, with the ship 'up on her hind legs dancing', it was quite the worst night he had ever spent at sea.

On New Year's Eve Cherry-Garrard lay in his bunk, too seasick even to write his diary. The cut on his right hand from learning to skin crabeater seals after the first slaughter in early December still had not healed. Someone shook his shoulder, whispering to wrap his blanket around him and come and see the land. It was Atkinson. Cherry stood, shivering. He could see nothing. Atkinson told him to look to the horizon. 'All the highlights are snow lit up by the sun.' And Cherry saw 'the peaks appearing, as it were over the clouds, like white satin, the only white in a dark horizon'. The first glimpse of Victoria Land. Antarctica, in the last hours of the last day of the year.

4

The little village at our cape

1–28 January 1911

We know all about things down here now. Exactly how
to feed and clothe ourselves and how to set to work. It is
a simple life and therefore very healthy.

Scott to his mother, from Cape Evans

ON NEW YEAR'S Day 1911 Scott was writing Kathleen a
32-page letter that she would be able to show to significant
people about the doings of the expedition. He was also writing her a
private letter, to which he added paragraphs over the weeks. Sitting
with his comforting pipe held between his fingers, he thought about
the Sunday service that morning. The hymn had been 'Rock of
Ages', gloriously appropriate with land finally visible, the words rolling stoutly out into the vast distances, familiar rituals in the face of
geographic magnificence. He had lectured the assembled company
after prayers about keeping all expedition news secret. Bernard Day
noted the instructions: be very careful when sending photographs or
diary reports home with the ship to family and friends, or vital
publishing contracts could be at risk.

Scott hadn't been able to stop smoking. Kathleen was worried by
his cough and 'that horrid little noise in yr throat'. Abstaining was so
difficult, but he could reassure her that she wasn't to worry about his
'gloomy' moods being infectious in this present company – 'it would
take a lot to cool them down'. In fact, they buoyed him up.

He told her his immediate plans. As soon as they had landed, the
next move would be the depot journey, transporting a load of supplies a good way south on the Barrier. The ponies had to get as fit as
possible first, but the short wait would allow everyone to 'settle down

comfortably' in their hut; also the ship needed to choose 'the best time' to get to King Edward VII Land. With the uncertainty of the pack ice over, the Eastern party's plans were back in place.

The sun shone with intense brightness, the wind had dropped to a calm, and men lay heaped like lizards on the deck of *Terra Nova* absorbing the warmth of a beautiful day. Scott joined them, sitting a little apart, the sun beating down on his balding head. He couldn't do anything about balding either, but he knew himself to be fit – the equal to anyone, he was convinced. Soon the famous sights would appear: Ross Island and Mount Erebus, with its trail of fiery smoke, the glaring straight white line of the ice barrier, McMurdo Sound, all frozen over. Soon they would choose where to come ashore and build their winter quarters hut. Everything was about to start.

After breakfast on Tuesday 3 January the bold black bulk of Cape Crozier at the eastern end of Ross Island came into view. Here, where the ice of the Barrier met immovable land, the pressure squeezed the surface of the ice into contorted parallel ridges. Emperor penguins guarded their eggs in the dark and bitter cold of winter on the edge of the pressure ice, and Adélie penguins came in spring in their thousands to build their nests on a pebbly beach to the west of the cape's abrupt cliffs.

Ross Island, stuck to the Barrier like a fly permanently gripped by flypaper, was etched with memories and emotional associations. For Scott, Wilson and a handful of men on board from Scott's first expedition, this was a long-awaited return. Nine years earlier Scott had been able to work his ship *Discovery* right down to the south-west corner of Ross Island, where a prefabricated hut of Australian outback design with wide sloping verandas – used almost exclusively for storage – was built close to the shore where *Discovery* lay frozen in for the winter. From Hut Point men could get by one route or another across the sea ice and up on to the Barrier. But this was also redolent territory for Day and Priestley, here so recently with Shackleton. Unable to land on the Barrier or King Edward VII Land, Shackleton had tried but failed to get his ship through the sea ice to Hut Point and had come ashore instead 20 miles to the north, on a rocky promontory named Cape Royds. Glaciers streaming off Mount Erebus, with treacherous ice falls and crevasses, blocked all attempts to get via the land from Cape Royds to the Barrier. The only possible route involved travelling across the sea ice that covered McMurdo Sound. The ice broke up and moved north in late summer, but not always. No one knew when the ice would be solid enough to trust, when it would silently disappear. The *Discovery* hut at Hut Point had become a vital refuge and staging post for Shackleton and his men. The bare, previously untenanted hut saved the lives of stranded travellers, trapped by unpredictable sea ice and unable to get back home to Cape Royds.

Scott didn't expect to be lucky enough to get as far south as Hut Point this time, but he and Wilson had a plan, keenly anticipated. If they could establish their winter quarters at Cape Crozier, the dangers and frustrations of having to travel across the sea ice suffered by Shackleton could be avoided. From Cape Crozier Scott could get straight on to the ice of the Barrier and set out direct for the Pole. Wilson could study the emperor penguins. He longed to get hold of some eggs and examine the embryos, believing he might discover the ancient link between birds and lizards hidden in the delicate structures of the incipient bird folded inside its shell. Wilson had drawn an enticing map, a narrative of desire, with a hut built on the edge of a snowdrift, a road for sledges leading on to the Barrier and a blue ice glacier, 'where we shall cut a cave for an ice house – & from which we shall get all our drinking water'. One arrow pointed east 'to King Edward VII's Land, about 500 miles'; another pointed west, '30 miles . . . to Hut Point'. As though marking on the details could make the dream happen.

But in his private letter to Kathleen, Scott told her of a reason for wanting to establish his expedition winter quarters at Cape Crozier, a reason 'which I have not written in any other account but which I think you will readily understand. There is no trail of Shackleton there. Always I have had a feeling that Cape Royds has been permanently vulgarized.'

The search began at 1 p.m., on Tuesday 3 January, with what Priestley called Option 1. *Terra Nova* moved along the final 5 miles of Barrier before the ice met Cape Crozier, with everyone staring out, searching the ice cliffs for signs of a place where the surface dipped low enough to allow ponies and the motor sledges to be landed.

Their Antarctic ark required above all a safe anchorage and a firm ice platform on which to unload. But the ice cliffs rose 60 feet or more, white as chalk. Option 1 failed.

For Option 2, Priestley had a participating role, a seat in the whale boat examining the coast of Cape Crozier itself for a landing place. A nasty lumpy swell was running. Getting ashore was out of the question, and Option 2 died before it began. But they examined the ice foot used by the emperors – Priestley thought it very scrappy, and too high to land on – and rowed west under the cape's precipitous cliffs of rock, dwarfed by their height. On board again, they made a final attempt, steaming along to the Adélie penguin rookery, where a red tubular canister fixed on a pole for messages during Scott's first expedition was still intact, a forlorn vertical in a waste of penguin guano. An ugly swell was breaking on the steep shore, and small grounded bergs were an added hazard. 'Another disappointment today . . . but . . . It would have been madness to attempt to land our stores there', Scott wrote to Kathleen. 'Its no use repining so we're off to Cape Royds and darling I love you still.'

Priestley was happy that the Western party was going to winter at Cape Royds after all: 'It will be like home going back to the old place again.' But there was sadness too, because he had found out how Shackleton's hut was going to be used. Priestley tried to be philosophical.

> I am very glad that Armytage & I spent our last few hours putting the old hut straight for I would like it to appear fairly neat even if it is going to be used as a pony stables. It seems rather a sacrilege that it should be used as but everything has to give way to expediency down here & any way if the ponies are as comfortable in the Hut as we were they ought to be pretty fit by the time they go South.

At least the landing should be pretty easy, and 'we should be able to get away fairly early & try to establish ourselves at King Edward's Land'.

Much of the light night *Terra Nova* worked along the ice-bound north coast of Ross Island making a running survey, with eleven men taking sights and noting results. One black cape was named after Campbell, 'as all the capes on Ross Island are 1st lieutenants,' he told his cousin Vera, happily, 'except Crozier who was Ross's 2nd in command'. But, unknown to the men surveying, Carsten Borchgrevink, who had landed at its base, had already named the cape after the English poet Tennyson.

Early the next morning, Wednesday the 4th, *Terra Nova* rounded the north-western corner of Ross Island and began steaming south, finding clear water to everyone's 'tremendous surprise'. So, after all, Cape Royds was left alone, and they got 7 miles closer to Hut Point before being stopped by ice. High on the upper crosstrees Scott, Wilson and Evans looked across to the coast, then out to small islands, trying to gauge the sea ice to the south, debating where to settle. Priestley was invited up to add his local knowledge and by 7.30 a.m. it was decided, according to Priestley, 'that we should go to the Skuary', a gently sloping black beach beside a smallish blunt cape, where skua gulls nested. 'We rammed the Ice three times going full speed ahead,' reported Abbott, 'getting through as far as possible, then stopped Engines & got out Ice anchors and made the Ship fast.' Campbell immediately started preparations to unload cargo.

Scott, Evans and Wilson walked across the sea and up on to solid land to choose the site for their new hut. They were closer to the Barrier than Shackleton had been, with the joy of coarse volcanic grit beneath their boots. Scott renamed the place Cape Evans, after Teddy.

The sun shone. Sea-groggy ponies were hoisted out on to the ice, weak legs dangling, and deck-cooped dogs were let loose to race in a frenzy, the bloodied bodies of slaughtered penguins scattered in their tracks. From 5 a.m. until midnight, day after day, men worked, lifting and shifting cargo off the ship and on to sledges, getting stores and equipment across to the beach at Cape Evans. Scott deployed all his transport options to drag the loads: two motor sledges, two teams of dogs, two teams of men, with ponies added as they recovered. Campbell and Levick were being initiated into the rites of man-hauling a sledge by Priestley, who had composed an 'Eastern Party song'.

> We're Captain Scott his Eastern Party & we're going strong
> We've got a sledging song
> And now we won't be long . . .

Sledging immediately turned into a competition: the 'Eastern Party team' against all-comers. Browning was in the opposing team and got so worn out competing that he went on the sick list with blistered feet. Priestley reckoned that the first Saturday he, Campbell and Levick walked 25 miles in ten trips, dragging a total of 5 tons.

Here's the Western winter quarters
& we're landing on the floe
Ah long we've got to go
We ache from top to toe
And every blessed officer comes up and says we're slow.

Them and us, workers versus authority.

Campbell was in charge of transport from the ship, while Teddy Evans managed everything on shore. The number and range of jobs that needed doing were almost overwhelming, but Scott wanted no delays in setting up winter quarters. All those left on board were still in their damp, cold berths, but the shore party slept in tents, with Scott supervising and planning from his own, known as the Holy of Holies, according to Teddy Evans. Heaps of provisions were being sorted by Bowers, then moved on by parties of men, their faces burnt and blistered, lips cracked so it hurt to smile. Levick and Browning, suffering the agonies of snow-blindness, had been given jobs in the dim light of the ship's hold. Abbott was on shore, as one of three hands helping Davies the carpenter build the hut, getting his introduction to Antarctica – 'a frozen sleeping bag is not an ideal place to rest one's weary bones'. Large skuas with strong, hooked bills tugged at the entrails of penguins dismembered by the excited dogs, and Nigger the cat, happily off the ship, chased the skuas. Imported animals delivering their small whirlpools of havoc.

Scott commandeered every resource to the current necessity. The business of science – zoology, biology, bacteriology, geology, much of it summer-dependent – had to wait. The only exception was Ponting, who was free to film and compose pictures, a unique resource designed to define and promote the expedition. Scott hoped that Ponting's film, to be shown in that rapidly growing form of public entertainment the cinema, would help raise funds badly needed for a second year in Antarctica.

'There's twenty-four of them go West & only six go East', sang
Priestley,

> But though in numbers least
> We really won't be fleeced . . .

The twenty-four would live here at Cape Evans in their comfortable
hut. The six of the Eastern party were, of necessity, toiling every
hour on the larger party's behalf, their search for their own winter
quarters not yet begun. But bending to the weight, pulling in step,
they bellowed out the chorus:

> For we've got canvas on our bellies & spikes on our boots
> Sledges to pull along for Western party brutes
> They call us thieves and scavengers but we don't care a hang
> We're callous and case hardened sons of Ham
> Oh! Damn

At 8.00 a.m. on Sunday the 8th sufficient acknowledgment of the
deteriorating state of the ice road after days of sunshine came too late
to save the third and newest motor sledge, and a tranche of Scott's
transport planning. Scott had ordered Bernard Day to get the motor
off the ship on Saturday evening. Early on Sunday morning
Campbell, according to his journal, 'went out to look at the ice and
found a crack running parallel with the ship with rotten ice on each
side of it' – so bad that one of the men fell through. 'I told Capt.
Scott, who gave orders, that the ponies should not cross the bad bit
but that the stores should be drawn out over the crack by men on ski.
The motor sledge he thought could be pulled safely across owing to
its big bearing surface, so . . . I put all hands on and tried to rush it
across.' But coming up to the bad place, Petty Officer Williamson
went through, followed immediately by the heavy rear of the motor,
dangling vertically in the water, the rope holding it cutting into the
thin ice as man after man was forced to let go, hands squeezed against
the surface. Only Priestley and four others were left, bracing
against the impossible weight. Suddenly the motor took charge, at a
gallop, and sank to the bottom, everyone running to firmer ice.
Priestley and Pennell worked their way cautiously back across the
rotten ice towards the ship, to get a lifeline for the stranded men. But

Priestley fell through, sinking over his head into the shock of freezing water. Swept under the ice lid by the current, he managed to grip the floating rope, made of sisal, which Campbell had ordered to be used as a safety precaution, and to jerk himself up while Pennell, stretched out flat, hooked an arm under his armpit and heaved him out, unable to speak, barely able to move.

Back on ship, in spite of his teetotaller inhibitions Priestley drank a glass of medicinal brandy and tried to warm his shivering body in the sun. Communications with shore stopped, and there was some grateful pottering around a generally empty ship. Archer the cook announced he had melted enough water in the galley for everyone aft to have a wash. Then Priestley helped Alf Cheetham, the much-loved and respected boatswain to unship the wooden case of the now deceased motor sledge. Diminutive Cheetham, squeaky-voiced and a father of thirteen, had been to Antarctica more times than anyone on board. He understood sailing ships and the ice, but he had no desire to land and go sledging. He'd heard enough about that from the men who had.

By Thursday the 12th the stores were unloaded and ashore, and the hut was finished externally, all in record time. Astonishing quantities of work had been got through. 'Of course the elements are going to be troublesome,' Scott was writing in his private letter to Kathleen, 'but it is good to know them as the only adversary and to feel that there is so small a chance of internal friction.' The 'little village' at 'our Cape' was a happy place.

On Saturday the 14th, working on the interior of the hut, Abbott noticed a difference in Captain Scott, who 'has been away from us the last couple of days, he turned up this afternoon looking quite young: he had shaved and washed; it is very noticeable among such a motley crowd'. 'Our Cape was passed undisturbed by Shackletons people,' Scott was writing to Kathleen, 'and so one feels no touch of profanity – I cannot tell you what a relief this is.' But on this Saturday Priestley was recording in his diary his knowledge of the place from Shackleton's expedition. 'It is very hard for me to remember Winter Quarters as Cape Evans, since I knew it so well as "The Skuary".'

Oates had allocated two of the better ponies to the Eastern party, and Browning and Dickason were busy breaking one of them in,

Browning driving it with loads between ship and shore. But the inadequate quality of many of the ponies was increasingly visible. Oates listed their manifest defects in his diary. For Scott, given how much depended on the ponies, this was a matter of real anxiety, and he decided that he must 'alter the arrangement'. Campbell must give up his good animals and hand them back, getting two inferior animals in return. The journey to the Pole must take precedence. Campbell was informed of the decision after Sunday service on the 15th: 'he took it like the gentleman he is.' The Eastern party got Hackenschmidt, a vicious kicker, intractable temper, an endless source of trouble and the most difficult to handle, and Jehu, considered by Scott a 'very weedily built animal'.

Campbell, Levick and Priestley had been working hard helping prise 30 tons of volcanic rocks out of the moraine behind the hut as ballast for *Terra Nova*'s holds. Priestley thought the rock-collecting very dangerous work; but then last Sunday he'd been lucky not to drown. Campbell wanted to take his two officers on a trip to Cape Royds. He and Levick needed an opportunity to have at least tried travelling overland and camping in Antarctica before they left on their expedition. And they could kill seals for the Eastern party's stores while Priestley geologized. On Monday 16 January, permission granted, the three men crossed over the glacier and scrambled down towards Shackleton's hut.

For Priestley – coming at last through the porch of his old home, opening the inner door – the memories were almost too much. Everything was exactly as they'd left it in those last days of rush and crisis getting on board *Nimrod* at the beginning of March 1909. A tray of scones was still balanced on a box, saucepans still on the Mrs Sam stove, clothes drying on the rope slung above, personal baggage everywhere, ready to go but no chance to take it, boots under beds. Fifteen of them had lived here in Shackleton's 'Portable House', complex lives jammed together, each man taking turns with the domestic chores, the table slung overhead when not in use.

Priestley stood at the entrance to the corner cubicle shared by Edgeworth David and Mawson, no space to move in the confused squalor of over-crammed lives, equipment and papers piled on every surface, clothes bulging off hooks. He looked into the cubicle where

Frank Wild and Joyce had squeezed themselves next to the printing press, laboriously setting the first book printed in Antarctica; then into his own, shared with James Murray, the Glasgow biologist, who had suffered much of the winter with enteritis. He ran his finger over small possessions, still coated with dust and smuts from the stove. But the smells had gone. All the odours of cooking, the pall of tobacco smoke, the reek of acetylene from the lighting plant, the whiff of men's bodies – all leeched away by the intense cold that preserves, and allows small quarter for change, or decay.

Priestley had arrived in Antarctica aged twenty-one, two years through his undergraduate course at Bristol, and used to shared living. His family were close, he had brothers and sisters. But he was also used to institutional lack of privacy; his father was headmaster of a boarding-school and they lived as part of it. Middle-class English, middle income, middle England. Wesleyan Methodist, strictly bought up, no alcohol, no smoking, no swearing, no whistling on Sunday. With almost no time to prepare he had boarded an emigrant ship, sharing a cabin with seven men from the expedition, cheapest fare, London to New Zealand, to join *Nimrod*; then here, to the most extraordinary experiences.

As he came out of the larder, Priestley's Burberry blouse caught the top of the copper tank and turned the tap on, like it always used to. And suddenly he could hear Bob the cook's raucous voice cursing him for his clumsiness. 'Nothing is changed at all except the company. It is almost dismal. I expect to see people come in through the door from a walk.' There were well-defined hoof marks on several of the drifts, so new-looking that 'we could have sworn someone must have been down here this year . . . The whole place is very eerie, there is such a feeling of life about it. Not only do I feel it but the others also.'

The hut with all its contents was so immediate, so part of other lives, that somehow Priestley did not want to touch things. But he took an old pair of his Burberry trousers to wear, and some jam, a plum pudding and gingerbread for their tent; they'd fed very well during Shackleton's expedition. And he scavenged along the shore, finding a case of Garibaldi biscuits and bottles of beer.

The first night – 'my first time writing a diary in a sleeping bag in a tent in the snow', Levick noted happily – Priestley was sure he heard people shouting: 'I thought I had got an attack of nerves.' Campbell heard it too. 'It must have been the seals but we are getting so worked up that we should not be a bit surprised to see a settlement of Japanese or some such people.'

Levick had killed his first seal. 'It is most horrible butchery but being a necessity it is no good flinching at it.' The Weddell seals were lying on the ice, hauled out in companionable groups of twos and threes. They gazed with big brown eyes, heads swivelling, bodies still, flippers folded against their thick, torpedo-shaped sides. Their coats were dappled greys, fawns and creamy browns, mottled tones. Levick and Campbell killed three more, then skinned them, skins rolled with blubber inside, as instructed by Priestley. Priestley had already cut a grotto into a snowdrift to store the carcasses.

Levick was growing a beard, but being here wasn't like being in other places. There were no windows to see your reflection in, no shiny surfaces to catch your image, not even the still water of a pool. None of the visual self-regarding and checking that are part of living in houses, of walking down a street. A little later, 'my beard is coming on well by the feel of it'. He thought the colour was fair, then possibly reddish-brown, 'but Priestley says it is like burnished gold'. The two of them strolled through the Adélie penguin rookery just beyond Shackleton's hut. It was nearly the end of the third week in January, and the adults were hurrying between nest sites and sea, feeding their growing chicks, ungainly bottom-heavy triangles of grey down, fronts matted with spilt food, stomachs sagging with their most recent meal. Wilson had described the Adélies thoroughly, Levick decided, but he would write about them in his zoology notes next summer. They were really having 'a grand little holiday'.

The weather hadn't been good enough for the geology trip Priestley had planned, but he collected a box of coloured rocks for the seamen on *Terra Nova* – souvenirs of Antarctica for them to take home. It was time to work their way back to Cape Evans across the glacier, although Levick 'required a strong yank with the rope delivered just as the right moment' to get him over the crevasses. Levick took little pleasure: it was his first encounter with these unpredictable cracks where the ice, under stress, had fractured apart, some cracks bridged, some horribly visible, dark deep frightening splits. Back at Cape Evans – with Levick and Campbell both suffering from snow-blindness – they found that Dr Atkinson had discovered a new kind of tapeworm, and Gran had knocked himself unconscious executing a ski-jump for Ponting and his continuous demand for photographs.

In their absence Scott had been visiting his old hut at Hut Point, which had not been lived in during the *Discovery* expedition but was redolent with memories. Situated so close to the Barrier, its existence had been crucial to Shackleton's expedition. Now Scott found the hut filled with snow and in a mess ('dreadfully heartrending') and had to camp outside with Meares and the dog team. For Scott the 'barbarous' neglect of a simple duty by their 'immediate predecessors', including to his disgust, human faeces, was the ultimate profanity. It 'oppressed me horribly'. He'd already thought through the detail of such matters at their new hut, writing a memo on 'Sanitary Arrangements' in advance: the landing party must be warned to pay strict attention to the 'cleanly regulation' of bodily functions from the moment of landing. A temporary latrine would be replaced once the hut was erected by three regular latrines. Scott laid down the design and the means of disposal – in addition specifying 'a space slightly removed from hut and clear of gangways . . . set apart as general urinal and for night use and during blizzards'. Discipline in these matters was sensible good practice.

A month had passed since the longest day of the southern summer. The hours of light had begun their inexorable shrinking, temperatures would start dropping. More importantly, the sea ice, their essential road south from their position here on Cape Evans, was unpredictable and could start breaking up any time. The ponies and drivers chosen for the all-important depot journey across the Barrier were assembling to depart. The Eastern party's two ponies were slung back on board *Terra Nova*. '<u>Not</u> the two we expected', said Dickason. He and Browning had not been told that the ponies they'd worked to break in had been replaced. Priestley acknowledged the inevitable. 'I suppose it is only right that we should suffer to advance the chances of the Pole party good luck to them.'

Suddenly the ice began breaking out in earnest. How long could the remaining ice be trusted? Their winter quarters hut at Cape Evans was closer to the Barrier than Shackleton's at Cape Royds, but the gnawing anxiety was the same as it had been for Shackleton. Unpredictable, seductive sea ice: threat and promise, hope and denial. Inherent in its blue-white smoothness, its ability to lull and lure, was the sense that, despite the dark, waiting ocean just below, apparent security remained, that walking on water would, somehow, not be denied. There was no comfort. There could never be. Sledges and fodder for the depot party were loaded on board *Terra Nova*, Captain Scott came aboard, and the ship moved south, 6 miles, to Glacier Tongue, a narrow outpouring of glacial ice jutting into the sea between Cape Evans and Hut Point.

The Eastern party were officially on their way. Sufficient time and coal had been allocated for Campbell to have a try for reaching King Edward VII Land – although within strictly confined limits. But the Eastern party's energies were still being totally absorbed by the needs of the main expedition. 'My dearest V.', Campbell wrote to his London cousin, 'I've so much to write to you about & so little time to write in.' The depot party's gear had to be unloaded and sledged across the ice of Glacier Tongue. Abbott fell awkwardly as ice caved in, 'nearly cooking one of our party. Narrow escape', commented Dickason. Campbell and Priestley had to prepare a route for the ponies to cross over the Tongue in safety. The gap where the sea ice rubbed up and down against the edge of the Tongue was bridged, as always, by a treacherous snow lid. Priestley, knowing where this tide-crack was located, warned the pony party. But they insisted, Priestley remarked sadly, on taking the ponies over the snow lid. Two got over safely 'and they were beginning to laugh at us but the third went in up to his neck'. The poor animal had a great fright and had to be hauled out with ropes 'looking very weak and miserable and trembling much', Scott wrote, with sympathy at its suffering.

'I shall be glad to get away in search of our own home', Priestley wrote forcefully. 'We seem at present to be doing a lot of work without any material advantage occurring to ourselves.' But the next day, Thursday 26 January, Scott and Wilson came to the ship for lunch and farewells. According to Browning, Captain Scott said 'he was very pleased how every one had worked to get the stores ashore so quickly'. Dickason noted that Scott gave a short speech and 'wished our party success in King Edward VII land and shook hands all round'. All the ship's company filed out to Glacier Tongue to see the depot party off. 'One of the ponies bolted', wrote Browning, '. . . we watched them until they were little specks on the snow.' Wilson, as the expedition's busy head of science, described bidding a 'final goodbye to our friends on board and the Eastern Party who are to attempt to establish a station on King Edward's Land', and he listed their names, with Browning as a seaman and Dickason not included. The focus was on the brutally demanding task of the Pole. The Eastern party was in effect a limb, about to be severed.

Scott had been critical of Shackleton for making his attempt to get through the pack to King Edward VII Land too early in the season, the best time being late in the summer, when the pack was at its loosest. But the jostling of priorities pressed. Decisions, as always, depended on a shifting tranche of options, on newly emerging factors in the complex business of running an expedition. Scott had always planned for *Terra Nova* to stay out exploring to the latest date in the season, even at the risk of being frozen in the ice. Now he had changed his mind. Now the last thing he wanted was to risk his ship being caught, because *Terra Nova* was carrying mail that needed to be delivered without delay. If his first attempt to reach the South Pole failed, Scott had declared that he would make a second. But that second attempt required a replacement set of animals. 'You will perhaps . . . know that we are here with the hope of reaching the South Pole', Scott had just written, on 22 January, to Major-General Sir Douglas Haig, Chief of Staff of the British Army in India. Oates thought that Indian Transport mules trained to work in the Himalayas would be more effective than the inadequate Siberian ponies. Emphasizing the urgency of the case, and the altogether exceptional circumstances, Scott requested the gift of seven Indian mules: 'We . . . feel that it *must* be an Englishman who first gets to the Pole. Pray help us if you can.' Oates had written to a friend in his regiment at Simla, a nephew of Haig. Almost certainly the mules would be forthcoming.

Campbell had been given command of *Terra Nova*, and been issued by Scott with detailed orders: command would be transferred to Pennell once the Eastern party had landed. 'I'm awfully pleased',

Campbell wrote to Vera. He could attempt to get ashore at King Edward VII Land, or 'an inlet in the Barrier' – Campbell had his own hopes for an inlet marked on the *Discovery* chart – but the utmost time that could be spent in trying to find winter quarters was seven days, counted from reaching the position of Balloon Bight. If the ship was unsuccessful, she should proceed to Robertson Bay and land the Eastern party there. The Eastern party was increasingly last year's scheme, pressed by the new reality. The bagging of the Pole had always been paramount. But achieving the necessary logistics for a second attempt, if the first failed, had moved in as a key objective for Scott. *Terra Nova*, as bearer of letters to facilitate the next attempt at the Pole, must leave polar waters before running any risk of being iced in. Dates were therefore screwed back. The Eastern party was being dispatched promptly and allocated a finite time to get ashore for the purpose of exploring King Edward VII Land. The sooner the attempt was made to land them, the sooner *Terra Nova* could head north and start exploring the coast west of Cape North and the longer the time that could be spent achieving results before it was necessary to turn for New Zealand, to deliver the all-important mail.

But first Campbell had to take *Terra Nova* across to Victoria Land to deposit a four-man party with their stores for a six-week geological expedition at a place called Butter Point. Priestley devoutly hoped they'd be able to get the ship alongside and not have to sledge the food and fuel across the sea ice. He had painful memories of Butter Point: waiting weeks to be picked up here during Shackleton's expedition, he'd woken early one morning to find the sea ice that he and his companions Brocklehurst and Armytage were camped on breaking up and the three of them adrift on a large floe. They'd drifted helpless and frightened until, around midnight, by chance their raft of ice bumped a snout of fast ice. Racing across the floe, they'd scrambled up, desperately pulling their sledge after them, gear tumbling off, as their floe swivelled and then moved on, to the open sea. The memory of being adrift had never left him.

Fortunately *Terra Nova* managed to come alongside at Butter Point, and on Friday the 27th the stores were unloaded. Levick with some of the men went to kill six seals to leave in a depot somewhere on the Barrier, 'in case', said Dickason, 'of the ship not being able to reach us next year and we have to sledge it back'. Priestley searched for the black flag marking the Butter Point depot that he'd helped build in the spring of 1908, with supplies for Mawson, Edgeworth David and Mackay at the start of their sledge journey to the South Magnetic Pole. He found it, the flag bleached by the sun, shredded by the winds. Looking inside the milk tin they'd used as a post box, Priestley found a letter that Armytage had written: another terrible memory. Five months ago Armytage, depressed, unable to find his place back in humdrum life after Shackleton's expedition, had lain down on the floor of his club in Melbourne, in his evening clothes, with all his medals, and shot himself through the head.

Priestley divided the food and oil in the depot between themselves, the geological party and the ship. The sailors bagged the cigarettes supplied by a company that Shackleton had an interest in (one of his many attempts to make a fortune). Bruce took a small box of thermometers as a souvenir. Priestley made arrangements for poor Armytage's letter to get to Australia. He took some of Mawson's unexposed photographic plates for Levick. Then he selected a pair of new ski boots, fur mitts and woollen mitts, and a bundle of Jaeger clothing, for himself. Fuel, food, clothes – three necessities for survival in Antarctica: Priestley knew the priorities. One snow-covered heap demolished, contents reallocated. Memories, perhaps, shelved.

The geological party set off up the glacier so fast that they didn't even say goodbye, with Griffith Taylor carrying a jumble of objects, geological hammers hanging off his belt and specimen bags hanging out of his pockets, Frank Debenham happy to be experiencing his first Antarctic field trip, Wright keen to have a chance to do glaciology, and Petty Officer Evans content to look after them. 'If it were all new it would be wildly exciting,' observed Lieutenant Bruce, Kathleen Scott's brother, 'but it has been partly explored before.' Priestley, one of those previous explorers, gazed wistfully after them.

Three men, including Ponting with his camera gear, were returned to Cape Evans. Campbell and Priestley went ashore at 2.30 a.m. and collected a big tent to keep their supplies protected while their winter quarters hut was being built, and iron runners with instructions how to fit to fit them on to their sledge for glacier travel. Runners and instructions had been provided by Bernard Day, and Priestley woke him to say goodbye: they'd miss each other. Simpson the meteorologist, in charge of the Cape Evans hut during Scott's absence, took Campbell and Priestley to see the ice-cave he and the knowledgeable Wright had created in a drift of compacted snow: four days' burrowing, with the result a light-excluding, controlled environment for their delicate magnetic variation work. Searching through the bookshelf in the library, in Scott's den, Carsten Borchgrevink's book on his Southern Cross expedition at Cape Adare turned up, and Priestley took it 'in case we should be compelled to winter on Victoria Land after all. However Campbell has already read a considerable deal of it & says that it is utterly useless for conveying accurate and definite information.'

The Eastern party was finally on its way. Pausing briefly at Cape Royds, they collected the seals they had killed ten days earlier for a Barrier depot, adding twenty newly slaughtered Adélie penguins. A motley collection of last-minute things were scooped up from Shackleton's old hut. Priestley suffered fewer inhibitions on this visit and took geological hammers and chisels, candlesticks, Brocklehurst's folding chair and a pemmican cutter. Pemmican, that staple of sledging food, dried and pounded pre-cooked meat with melted fat, had to be sliced into carefully judged portions when preparing and weighing out sledging food. A pemmican cutter speeded up this tedious job. Priestley collected some illustrated magazines for the ship and retrieved his box of rocks for the crew. Abbott and Browning came to the hut with one of the sailors. The men 'no doubt' took, commented Priestley primly, but he had their word they'd take nothing of value. Abbott thought it a very nice, comfortable-looking hut, and picked up a few mementoes. Browning merely noted in his journal that he thought the hut in 'very poor condition' and that 'Mr Priestley took away some things he had left behind'.

Back on board, Campbell headed the ship north, then east. 'Whereas the main party have landed on land which has been partially explored before', wrote Levick, 'we are now entering on an entirely new arena, and do not know what we shall find. May it be land!'

5

In search of our home
29 January–9 February 1911

To the Great Barrier
We have sailed from your farthest West, that is bounded
by fire and snow,
We have pierced to your farthest east, till stopped by the
hard, set floe.

'Nemo' (Shackleton), 1902

CAMPBELL HAD TWO depot sledges packed and ready to go, on Scott's orders, stored directly under the main hatch of *Terra Nova* so they could be accessed easily. One was to be left, if possible, as a depot on the Barrier as the ship went east, while the other was to go ashore with the Eastern party. The seals and penguins, stacked frozen and stiff in heaps, were Campbell's own precautionary back-up. Careful and thorough, Campbell was naturally a forward planner. At last, his expedition was truly under way.

Sledges and men could generally be got ashore without much difficulty. Campbell's major problem would be finding a place where two ponies could be landed, with fifty bales of fodder, and the bulky building materials for their hut, along with iron bedsteads and mattresses, chairs and a table, the boxes filled with tinned carrots, dried spinach, curry sauce, ham loaf, bloater paste, bottled gooseberries and the boxes of housekeeping equipment: 12 soup plates, 1 weighing machine and weights, 1 mincing machine, 18 meat hooks, 2 dustpans, 2 saucepans and 1 steamer 'not quite fitting either' – columns and columns of necessary items listed by Bowers in blue pencil in his notebooks. It was an imposing pile, everything collected and hoarded for the Eastern party's icy isolation, with care, graft and some cunning. When it came to 'looting' the 'Steamer' – Meares's mocking name for *Terra Nova* – Campbell and his men were generally believed to have taken everything they could lay their hands on.

A month earlier, Scott had faced the same challenge of finding somewhere to unload stores and animals. But he was landing on the known quantity of Ross Island, with its beaches and rocky coves. King Edward VII Land, as far as anyone knew, had only ice cliffs. 'It should always be remembered that the difficulties encountered in reaching a landing place may be insurmountable when it is desired to relieve the party landed', Scott wrote in his orders to Campbell as commander of *Terra Nova*. 'I regard the chance of being able to find a suitable wintering station in King Edward Land as being wholly problematical and I am quite prepared to learn that it was deemed inexpedient to attempt a landing.'

Scott's instructions to Campbell as leader of the Eastern party were brief: 'Should you succeed in landing', his object was 'to discover the nature and extent' of King Edward VII Land. Instructions for the end of the expedition were specific about dates, then confidently general. They must be ready to embark on 1 February 1912 but, if after a fortnight *Terra Nova* had not turned up, start walking back, 'if circumstances permit'. Keep near the edge of the Barrier in case the ship was passing. If a convenient inlet in the Barrier was found as they travelled east, establish a depot of food and fuel, in advance. A party from Cape Evans would lay a depot on the Barrier the following summer, 30 miles to the east of Cape Crozier.

No one had ever walked along that wall of ice. The surface of the ice shelf terminated, precipitously, with no warning or indication, sliced off as though by a sharp cleaver. Walking anywhere near that vertical drop into the sea could be done only in good visibility.

Taking *Terra Nova* along the Barrier, Campbell made a running survey, dodging the debris as huge sections of cliff sliced away from the mother lode, spray and ice particles shooting up, the sharp bang at the creation of each iceberg loud and peremptory. 'A fine sight to see one long wall of ice', thought Dickason. On the last day of January, a good breeze getting up, Campbell left the Barrier's edge and sailed directly for King Edward VII Land, but the straight run turned into an unpleasant ride as the wind changed to a strong headwind and *Terra Nova* bucketed along into heavy headseas, spray freezing over every surface, doing just over 1 knot with a horrible twisting motion. 'Good old tub,' said Dickason, 'shall never be caught exceeding the speed limit.' Priestley disappeared into his usual miserable seasickness.

On the morning of Thursday 2 February, just after 8.00 a.m., King Edward VII Land was sighted, a kind of rolling hill of ice and snow. To Priestley, emerging wanly, it looked 'uncommonly like common or garden Barrier'. But hopes were high. After all, thick pack hadn't stopped them. The sky was clear and visibility good. Campbell climbed with Pennell to the crow's nest to find somewhere to get ashore.

By 6 p.m. it was all over. Hopes had been dashed to the ground. Ahead lay a wide bay with solid, unbroken ice to a line of distant ice cliffs. Heavy pack strewn with icebergs blocked their way north. South, the land – or what they assumed was land – rose white and smooth behind a line of high, sheer-sided ice cliffs. There was no sign of a mountain, not even the glimpse of a rock. 'Of all the desolate places in the world', wrote Bruce to his sister Kathleen Scott, 'none can compare with this.' 'Campbell & Co.' couldn't be put on 100-foot-high cliffs. 'We looked everywhere for a place to land, and were quite prepared to do so in this desolate spot,' recorded Levick, 'but could find no possible place . . . so reluctantly . . . started back Westward, with the object of finding "Balloon Inlet" discovered by Capt. Scott.'

But Campbell had a private hope, a place where he thought he could enter King Edward VII Land from an unregarded side-door. In the early hours of Friday morning, 3 February, as *Terra Nova* headed back along the Barrier edge, a Force 8 gale blowing thick with drift, Campbell found what he was looking for: the entrance to a small opening marked on the *Discovery* chart. Eagerly, he took *Terra Nova* inside, examining the ice cliffs for weathering, scanning their heights for possible landing places, peering cautiously along narrow, winding inlets. The ice walls were grey, veiled with seams and the faint horizontal lines of each year's snow accumulation, ancient snowfalls stacked up, squeezed into thin parallel bands. They were surrounded by a kind of waiting silence, the extraordinary watchful, listening silence of the ice. But there was nowhere to get ashore, and Campbell's hope for a landing withered.

The rest of the day, with the gale continuing, they worked on preparations for landing at Balloon Bight, or Balloon Inlet, or Barrier Inlet, that many-named break in the Barrier's face. Campbell planned to land a four-man team – himself, Levick, Priestley and Abbott – to reconnoitre on skis. The emergency sledge, in case the ship should be blown off while they were on the Barrier, was loaded with six weeks' provisions plus Campbell's invaluable Primus stove and 8 gallons of paraffin. Abbott had prepared wind clothes, attaching their mittens in approved style to lengths of lamp wick to prevent them blowing away. Scott, in his orders to Campbell as commanding officer, had emphasized that 'every precaution possible should be taken to avoid a situation on ice which may break away from the Barrier or Land'. Campbell had taken Levick, his second-in-command, aside 'and asked me if I was willing to land here. Of course I said I didn't care twopence where I went.' But Levick thought that 'Priestley seems to rather kick at landing on the Barrier, chiefly I suspect because there doesn't seem much chance of our ever seeing anything but flat expanse of snow and consequently there wouldn't be much for a geologist to do.'

But for Priestley it was all a ghastly replay. He had faced this issue three years earlier, at the start of Shackleton's expedition. Shackleton planned to establish his winter quarters at the inlet in the Barrier, where he had landed with Scott on the *Discovery* expedition in 1902. While Shackleton attempted to reach the South Pole, a party including Priestley would travel across the ice shelf to King Edward VII Land. It was the strategy for approaching King Edward VII Land that Scott had explained to Campbell in South Africa five months earlier.

More to the point, Priestley knew that none of the inlets – whatever their names – now existed. But he didn't say much. He was now one of Scott's men, the most junior of the Eastern party's three officers, and the youngest. However, Priestley's frustration ran deep. He had been with Shackleton. He had lived through the anxieties and decisions as *Nimrod* sailed along the Barrier edge in January 1908 and failed to find the opening to Scott's Balloon Bight. He had seen Shackleton search also for a second inlet, where Borchgrevink had made his dash south with dogs. Neither could be found. Instead, to general confusion, a broad opening had been discovered where hundreds of whales were feeding. *Nimrod* had worked further east, still searching. Then as Shackleton turned back retracing the ship's tracks what must have happened became clear. The edge of the Barrier must have broken away dramatically, taking the two small bights with it. The current Barrier edge was now much further south, indented by the big new bay Shackleton had discovered. The ice was obviously frighteningly unstable. If the ice front had broken away so dramatically, so recently, it could continue doing so. Fearing the Barrier's instability, Shackleton had decided against building his winter quarters in the new broad bay which he named the Bay of Whales, even though it provided the longed-for access to the ice shelf. Reluctantly, Shackleton had turned towards Ross Island, in spite of his promise to Scott, with all the stress and misery that decision aroused. Priestley had actually been in the Bay of Whales. Despite this, 'Everybody has always been doubtful about this Bay of Whales we reported.'

Around nine in the evening of this long Friday 3 February 1911, in clear weather, the Balloon Bight dispute – at least on *Terra Nova* – was resolved, very simply. 'Off the place Balloon Bight should have been,' Campbell noted in his journal, 'but there was no sign of it. Our sights showed we were south of the old Barrier edge in 1902.' 'About ten o'clock tonight', reported Priestley, happily, before climbing into his bunk for a quick sleep, 'we steamed into a deep bay in the Barrier which proved to be Shackleton's Bay of Whales' – his loyalties briefly reverting, then eliding – 'and our observations have been wonderfully upheld by our present sights & angles . . . but our traverse along the Barrier has set the matter at rest finally.' Water-fretted lumps of ice peeled from the ice cliffs dipped and bobbed, the rippled surface of the water reflecting the golds and rosy pinks of the sky. Short wedges of misty spray indicated whales blowing – glimpses of triangular fins, the curve of black backs rising above the surface, the hiss of fishy breath expelling. There was no doubt now that the small inlets in the Barrier face had become merged into one, and the resulting Bight had broken back considerably further. 'Otherwise it is the same', wrote Priestley, 'the same deceptive caves & shadows having the appearance from the distance of rock exposures, the same pressure ridged cliffs, the same undulations behind . . . It was satisfactory to find all our observations coming right & everybody backing up the Shackleton Expedition'.

Around midnight Bruce came on to *Terra Nova*'s bridge, Lilley the biologist with him. Suddenly, to their wild excitement, they saw a ship tied up to the ice: three masts, with no funnel. On the deck of *Terra Nova* there was confusion, shouting, everyone rushing up, pulling on clothes. The men forward were sure they could see a hut, perhaps even a party approaching: 'curses loud and deep were heard everywhere.' The stranger ship was the *Fram*. Amundsen wasn't somewhere on the other side of Antarctica. He was here, in the Bay of Whales. *Terra Nova* ran close by *Fram*, then made fast to the ice a couple of hundred yards ahead. Lilley woke Priestley up with the 'astounding news'. Campbell, with Levick and Priestley, were lowered over the side with their skis, then set off towards a dark spot, which turned out to be not a hut but an abandoned depot.

Far to the west this midnight, on the Barrier, Scott and his depot party were just crossing their first crevasses, not having achieved much of a distance. The ponies were being driven at night in the hope that would ease the work. But the animals plunged and snorted whenever they sank into soft snow, exhausting themselves, the weight of the loaded sledges bumping along behind. Early on the morning of Saturday 4 February, Scott, his men, the ponies and the two dog teams halted. They named their camp 'Corner Camp', because here their route would turn and head due south.

During the early hours of Saturday 4 February, Campbell talked to the commander of *Fram*, Lieutenant Nilsen, and heard that everybody was off settling Amundsen in his winter quarters. Amundsen would be at the ship early in the morning. The casual but careful interchange of information began, reported back on board by Campbell. *Fram* had got through the pack in only four days. Amundsen would make his 'descent' on the Pole next season. 'This is encouraging as it means a fair race', noted Priestley. The news for the Western party would keep them all 'on tenter hooks of excitement all the Winter'. By now it was 4.00 a.m. on Saturday the 4th.

Campbell had arrived at a place where it was possible to get his supplies and animals ashore. There was plenty of room to build his hut, and he and his men could sledge across to King Edward VII Land over the Barrier, as Scott wanted. He was here to explore the new land at the eastern end of the Barrier, an objective entirely separate from the Norwegians. The Bay of Whales was the last chance to survey King Edward VII Land, the purpose of the Eastern Party. But Campbell was argued against. His desire to land was denied. Bruce: 'we dissuaded him, as the feeling between the two expeditions must be strained.' In line with the general consensus Priestley considered that 'Our plans have of course been decided for us, we cannot according to etiquette trench on their country for Winter Quarters but must first return to McMurdo Sound & then go off towards Robertson's Bay & settle ourselves as best we can.' All the doubts, all the discussions about where to be for the winter, had been settled, finally – but in the most startling, unexpected fashion.

In effect, Amundsen's action was in line with the general principle suggested by Darwin in his interchange with Scott last year, transmitted to Shackleton: 'every explorer should in future be at liberty to go exactly where he likes, without, at all events, any liability to an accusation of breach of faith.' Scott, by deciding to send *Terra Nova* to explore the unknown coast west from Robertson Bay, despite the declared intentions of Mawson and Shackleton's new expedition, and to direct the Eastern party to explore the same coast if a landing at King Edward VII Land failed, was acting within the terms of Darwin's suggested principle. But there was a difference. 'It would be no doubt, very advantageous', added Darwin, 'if explorers would discuss how best to partition the work amongst themselves so as to avoid overlapping as far as possible.' Not imperative, but certainly preferable.

Scott had been public about his plans for exploring the unknown coast, although he had not discussed partitioning the work, or attempted to avoid overlapping. Scott's plans to achieve the South Pole were clearly stated, whereas Amundsen, immersed in the labyrinthine requirements of ensuring funds for his expedition, had kept his change of destination from the Arctic to the Antarctic a secret. Amundsen's ambition to be first at the North Pole had been shattered when two Americans separately claimed it. So he had switched south, to try for the remaining Pole.

The men in the wardroom of *Terra Nova*, in those exciting hours after discovering Amundsen, knew none of the manoeuvrings and thinking behind the suggested framework for action set out in the letters between Scott, Darwin and Shackleton. Leaving the Bay of Whales to Amundsen, not sharing the space, seemed to be in accord with Scott's attitudes to territory insofar as past experience had revealed them. Withdrawal seemed the appropriate action. At this key moment the Eastern party's role as a separate expedition – 'Scott's second shore party', as Lieutenant Nilsen called them – was made subordinate to Scott's objective of attaining the Pole.

The morning of Saturday the 4th was spent in visits, unexpected sociability inserted into isolation. 'Several of us went aboard the *Fram*', wrote Abbott; 'Amundsen shook hands with us & had a yarn about the ship, his dogs etc. He is a fine looking man & looks a typical leader; . . . about 40 years of age, very weather beaten & had nearly white hair.' Amundsen, Browning wrote, 'asked me if we had any newspapers later than September on board as he had not seen any, and . . . I collected all the newspapers I could get also a few Magazines and took them on board the Fram and gave them to Capt Amundsen he was very pleased.' The Norwegians knew that *Terra Nova* planned to go to King Edward VII Land and had thought they might see the ship.

Amundsen's hut, built about 2 miles in from the ice edge on a sloping site, had foundations dug through the snow down to the underlying blue ice. Along one of the hut's lengths the two carpenters needed to hack down 9 feet to reach the rock-hard ice; nevertheless the building had been completed in ten days. Fourteen large military bell tents surrounded the hut, to protect the stores and the 115 Greenland dogs. Campbell, Pennell and Levick visited for breakfast, drinking coffee and eating the cook Lindstrom's delicious hot cakes, inspecting everything in detail and taking photographs. Campbell thought Amundsen had selected 'not a very good place' for his hut, and noted what he considered a better one.

Campbell, Pennell and Levick inspected *Fram* with her diesel engines, which had required no additional fuel since leaving Europe. Levick was excited, positive, absorbing all he could – 'this has been a wonderful day'. Priestley entertained several officers and men from the *Fram* on board *Terra Nova*, where science was being energetically and visibly pursued: sounding, water sampling, hauling a plankton net. Each side let slip more information. The Norwegians heard that Campbell was bound for Cape North. The Eastern party heard how Amundsen had told his crew the night before leaving Madeira that 'they <u>were</u> going to the North Pole but were going South first'. The Norwegians, it turned out, had also been unsure about the configuration of the Barrier edge. Priestley thought they'd aimed for Borchgrevink's Bight. To Campbell, *Fram* 'shaped course direct for Balloon Bight but of course found it gone so decided to winter in the Bay of Whales'. Lieutenant Nilsen, commanding *Fram* and new to Antarctica, explained that he'd used photographs of Balloon Bight to help find its narrow opening in the Barrier but discovered instead a great break in the wall.

Terra Nova let go at 2 p.m. on Saturday afternoon, dredged for two hours, then left to continue surveying the Barrier edge to the point they had reached on the way east. 'Amundsen suggested my wintering there', wrote Campbell, committing the barest minimum of a complex, highly charged and painful fourteen hours to his journal. Having spent his summers in Norway and speaking Norwegian, Campbell did not feel uncomfortable with his temporary hosts. There'd been discussions about Campbell having the area to the east of Amundsen to explore. Could a decision like this be taken without first checking with Scott? But checking was impossible. Giving up the chance to be the explorer of King Edward VII Land was terribly hard. To the safety-conscious, two huts in the same general area had obvious advantages. Campbell listed terse, inadequate little reasons for saying no: 'it would not do . . . it would have taken too long to get my hut and stores to a safe place and coal was running short.' 'Very disappointed about K.E. Land', he wrote to Vera. Scott in his orders to the commanding officer had allowed seven days to find winter quarters between Balloon Bight and King Edward VII Land. The ship had arrived at King Edward VII Land on Thursday, and now it was only Saturday. In all the hundreds of miles of imposing ice cliffs fronting the great ice Barrier, and in spite of a coast of an unknown length fronting the unexplored King Edward VII Land, Campbell had found only this one location, the Bay of Whales, where he could bring an expedition ashore. Shackleton had discovered it and not dared to use it. Scott had rejected the information that it existed. Amundsen, finding it, had dared to use it. Campbell desperately wanted to.

Priestley wrote a set-piece in his journal.

> Well! We have left the Norwegians & our thoughts are full, too full, of them at present. The impressions they have left with us is that of a set of men of distinctive personality, hard & evidently inured to hardship, good goers & pleasant good-humoured men: – All these qualities combine to render them very dangerous rivals but one cannot help liking them individually, in spite of the rivalry. We have news which will make the Western Party as uneasy as ourselves & the World will watch with interest the race for the Pole next year, a race which may go any way & may be decided by sheer luck or by dogged perseverance on either side.

'The Eastern Party', summarized Abbott, 'would have landed in the Bay of Whales, as it was the only possible place to land stores etc along the Barrier; but of course as the Norwegians are there we are leaving them a clear field.' 'No science, no nothing just the Pole!!' Bruce reported in a letter to Kathleen several weeks later, at the end of February. 'We learnt all we could, though really very few questions were asked either side. Individually . . . they all seemed charming men, even the perfidious Amundsen.'

At Corner Camp, Scott planned to start marching south on the evening of Saturday the 4th. But during the afternoon a blizzard began: powder-fine snow crystals scooped off the Barrier surface by the rising wind, flowing like a fast grey-white river, knee-high, then rising, as the wind speed increased into a full gale, until everyone and everything inside it was lost to sight. A white maze, a frightening blank, denying any sense of direction, a roaring, driving confusion. So they stayed in their tents.

Headwinds prevented *Terra Nova* making progress on Sunday the 5th. According to Scott's orders, the ship was to call at Cape Evans to report where Campbell had been landed, before heading north to Robertson Bay. So fires were banked, and *Terra Nova* hove to. Campbell conducted a service in the wardroom in an execrable manner, according to Levick, 'but he did his best'. Heavy arguments continued, with Bruce listing the themes: the changes to the Barrier edge, and why; the rights and wrongs of Amundsen; and 'the chances of our being able to beat them'. Everyone accepted that Amundsen's plans for a five-year science cruise in the Arctic had been made point-less by the achieving of the North Pole in April 1910: but why had he kept his landing place a secret? Some thought Amundsen's hut, a short way inland on the Barrier, was in a most dangerous position. The ice could break away, 'in which case, it would be all up with them', according to Levick. But if not, 'it is going to be one of the finest races next summer that the world has even seen' – especially because the routes of the two leaders would meet at the Beardmore Glacier, and 'they might actually see each other'. The general feeling in the wardroom on *Terra Nova* – and Priestley agreed – was that the Norwegians were in dangerous winter quarters, but

> if they get through the Winter safely, and they are aware of their danger, they have unlimited dogs, the energy of a race as Northern as ourselves & experience with snow-travelling that could be beaten by no collection of men in the world. There remains the Beardmore glacier. Can their dogs face it & if so who will get there first? One thing I feel & that is our Southern Party will go far before they permit themselves to be beaten by any-one, & I think that two parties will reach the Pole next year but God only knows which will get there first.

At the other end of the ship, the lower deck had not been informed that Amundsen was in the Antarctic. Finding him 'came as a surprise to us all', said Browning. Abbott couldn't help thinking about the striking difference in clothing between the Norwegians, dressed in sealskins, and 'our fellows . . . wearing ordinary clothing, very few of us wearing winter clothing yet'. Abbott hadn't rated ponies since working with them at Quail Island, although at least they would be useful as meat. He was convinced that 'dogs are by far the swiftest & safest animals that can be used for transporting food supplies etc.' and so was impressed by the Norwegian dog teams. Writing to a friend, he explained that pack ice had stopped them landing at King Edward VII Land and that the Norwegians were in the next landing place 'so we were done out of that', but 'we are now in search of another place to land on & I will put at the top of this letter, just where it is, when we get there'.

Priestley was up on deck washing rocks. The dredging carried out in the Bay of Whales had brought up random pieces of Antarctica's inland geology, imprisoned in the great ice sheet and transported, over millennia, until released at the Barrier's edge to fall through the ocean: ice-rounded pebbles, small smoothed chips, reddish-brown and grey-black. Priestley was happy. At last he could do some geology.

Next day, Monday the 6th, the Eastern party were back to ship's work. Their stores had been piled ready to go on top of fuel that was now needed to fire the furnaces, so they humped the boxes to a new place, and on Tuesday the 7th moved them again because the metal on the boxes affected the compass. The ship was beginning to settle into a new pattern, with a reduced crew. Nigger, turned out of his quarters for bullying a blue Persian kitten, was shifted to the mess. The wind freshened, the sea got up. Everyone sat around darning socks. No other excitement. Campbell decided he would put his two ponies ashore when they reached Cape Evans, with their fodder. Ponies would be of no use to the Eastern party on the Victoria Land coast, but very useful to Scott on 'their attempt to beat Amundsen' (as Priestley put it). The language had changed, for good. There was now a race. Amundsen had known that from the start: a race came with his decision to switch directions and poles. But so far nobody on Scott's side knew, only those on the *Terra Nova*. If the Eastern party had managed to establish their base at King Edward VII Land, maybe no one would ever have found out: a very strange thought. But to Bruce there could be nothing as exciting as discovering *Fram*. Even an eruption of Erebus would fall flat after that.

At the Bay of Whales the Norwegians found that they still had visitors. They developed colds, although the symptoms lasted only a few hours, which was lucky, because there were only nine men in the shore party. Amundsen, like Scott, had thought about the reasons for the narrow bays and bights in the Barrier face; he, too, assumed that Balloon Bight was caused by an obstruction below the ice, which altered the flow and caused stresses and breaks: an illustration from Ross's 1841 expedition seemed to corroborate that assumption, showing a break in the ice face in roughly the same place as Balloon Bight. Amundsen thought that the Barrier – or at least this part of it – rested on underlying land. But unlike Scott, who thought the obstruction was an extension of King Edward VII Land, Amundsen considered it 'subjacent land, banks etc.' Shackleton's Bay of Whales – 350 miles, Amundsen estimated, from McMurdo Sound and 100 miles from King Edward VII Land – could, he assumed, be 'sufficient distance from the English sphere'. Taking the chance offered of being a whole degree of latitude (60 nautical miles) closer to the Pole, Amundsen had therefore built his hut, now named Framheim, on the Barrier. *Fram* would soon leave them for the winter, first to go east to have a brief try at discovering more of the King Edward VII Land coast, then to do oceanographic work in the South Atlantic.

At Corner Camp, on the Barrier, the blizzard lasted three days, from Saturday the 4th until Tuesday the 7th. 'Personally,' wrote Cherry-Garrard, after they had been lying in their bags for thirty-six hours, 'I have slept about 24 of them.' Everyone had started on the depot journey tired, having worked long hours from the moment they arrived at Cape Evans, and then left in a terrible hurry, practically a panic, Cherry thought. But lying here inside the tent, he was warm, though hungry, 'just bursting out once or twice a day for the ponies etc . . . Ponies seem v. wretched but v keen on grub'. His pony Guts was the unlucky animal that had fallen into the tide crack at the edge of the ice tongue.

At 10.00 p.m. on Tuesday 7th February the line of men leading ponies pulling sledges set off south. The blizzard seemed to have affected the ponies badly – two of them especially – although Oates had worked hard in the wind and blinding snow to help them. 'One supposes they did not sleep', Scott wrote; 'all look listless and two or three visibly thinner than before.' There was no denying that some were poor-quality animals. Only 10 miles were achieved. Scott wrote on Wednesday the 8th: 'I'm afraid we shall not get very far.'

But whatever the costs, they had to keep as many ponies as possible alive.

Off Cape Evans on Wednesday the 8th, Campbell sent a whale boat in to the few men left at the winter quarters hut, with their startling news. We 'astonished the natives', said Priestley with satisfaction, 'and learnt their small adventures'. The ice at Cape Evans had broken out, so the two ponies were lowered, struggling and frightened, into the sea and pulled behind the whaler 500 yards to the beach, where Anton waited with towels, and whisky to pour down their throats. Hackenschmidt was dragged, supine, but Jehu swam gamely. Campbell wrote his report for Scott, listing everything observed and achieved: the Barrier surveyed, the non-existence of Balloon Bight, the existence of the Bay of Whales, finding *Fram* and the Norwegians, Amundsen's plans to go to the Pole using dogs, and his plans to send *Fram* north for the winter. The Norwegians had the only possible landing place along the Barrier. He was sorry not to have seen Scott, in case the instructions for the Eastern party might have been altered, given Amundsen's offer at the Bay of Whales.

The Eastern party was now fully detached, getting jobs done, then on its way again as quickly as possible. Campbell moved *Terra Nova* south to Glacier Tongue to water the ship, setting off at midnight with Priestley and Abbott to ski across the sea ice with his all-important report to be left as 'ship's mail' at Hut Point. After scribbling a message on the hut door – 'mail for Capt. Scott in bag inside South door' – they turned back, but the 8 miles seemed very long. 'We would look at the Ship & then go on for about ¼ of an hour without looking at her', wrote Abbott, less practised on skis, so slower; 'then have another look & she appeared just as far off as ever.' On board again at 4.30 a.m., muscles aching, 'Mr C. sent me a bottle of stout for'rard when we got back to the ship, it was simply glorious.'

Priestley felt so tired he didn't get up until lunchtime on Thursday, and even then it was only because of Bruce's 'piteous appeals' for help, to off-load the redundant pony fodder into a new depot on Glacier Tongue, and water the ship. Two men were excavating ice out of an ever-deepening hole on the Tongue, while Abbott carried

the pieces to the ship. Suddenly the end Abbott was on broke away
with a sharp bang, splitting in two, throwing him into the sea. The
massive lumps rolled over, hauling their hidden depths into the air,
water and ice fragments streaming off, then heaved in the backwash
of the impact. Abbott, desperately treading water between the jostling lumps, was saved from being crushed only by the quick action
of Bruce. Back on board with the same treatment as the ponies, a
good tot of whisky and a good rub down, Abbott reckoned he felt
'up to date' again. Just this morning, at Hut Point, he'd looked at
the cross erected to remember Vince, a young seaman who had
slipped to his death in a blizzard on Scott's first expedition. 'The
sight of this cross in such a desolate spot is very sad', he reflected.
Now, this afternoon, it could have been him. Abbott 'was lucky not
to get squashed', noted Bruce, making no mention of rescuing him.
Doing something and saying nothing about it was part of what one
did.

But two more members of the Eastern party appeared to be in
trouble. Scott had sent back requests from the Barrier for items to
be brought to Hut Point: 'marmalade, tobacco, jam', commented
Priestley tartly, and the ponies' snowshoes. Levick and Browning had
set off early in the morning for the hut, with rucksacks weighing 60
lb. They hadn't returned. 'Much anxiety', said Bruce. Campbell
'knocked us off at tea time', said Priestley, 'to rest ready to form a
search party'.

The two men finally appeared after twelve hours, Browning desperately thirsty: they'd drunk nothing all day. Levick was furious and
humiliated. He'd taken so long because Browning, 'absolutely useless
on ski', had lagged behind from the beginning. Levick had made
Browning take off his skis, but he couldn't walk efficiently, or climb.
'I now had a fair example of the uselessness of the average bluejacket
in using his feet.' The return journey was worse. A heavy wind got
up, leaving the surface of the sea ice like glass. Browning fell, Levick
couldn't see the ship in the drift and went ahead, then took pity and
waited, but progress was painfully slow. Levick admitted in his journal that he was in 'rather a funk' but Browning, 'whom I now classed
as a gutless swab', had failed, and 'it was all I could do to keep my
temper'. 'Our journey was a rather hard one', Browning was writing

at the other end of the ship, 'as we were both new to skiing . . . at times we had to go down on our knees to prevent our being blown backwards.' The surface was like glass, 'and I came down a cropper'. Levick and Browning were novices, and both were new to Antarctica. Levick had never tried the tricky route to Hut Point, he had never led, and this was the first experience for either man of a longish journey over sea ice.

Everyone who came south was expected to manage by doing, to learn by finding out. Suffer snow-blindness, then learn to wear goggles. Get frostbitten, then learn to put on a windproof jacket and helmet. Trip over each other in a tent, then learn a proper tent discipline. Several men had already cut a hand badly, butchering seals. Learn a way of holding the knife, or make adjustments to the handle so it didn't slip. But there was also the seductive pleasure of the hierarchy of knowing, with its own useful tension of competitiveness. Combined with an established tradition of distrust and distaste for overt 'professionalism', and a delight in the business of being an amateur, it was a potent mix. The practice of amateurism amused; it engaged the energies. And it implied, by definition, inherent superiority. Only the superior could afford to be amateurs. Underlying everything was the assumption that simply being British was enough, an idea reinforced, for the naval men, by a tradition and training that assumed and expected an ability to cope in all circumstances. The assumption was further reinforced by the complacent, satisfying sense that the system appeared to work. Britain ruled a mighty empire, and young men, educated in her public schools, hardened by the daily playing of team games, went out to the far corners of the earth to govern, maintain order and legislate.

It was a difficult set of assumptions for foreigners to manage. The two Russians didn't attempt it; Wright, Debenham and Griffith Taylor were used to being categorized as colonials. Tryggve Gran had a more difficult time. He was considered cocky. Although the youngest, as a Norwegian he had obvious expertise. The hierarchy was nevertheless complicated. In the arcane business of sledge flags – each officer sporting his pennant, the symbols subtly marking territory (Oxford or Cambridge college, or the absence of), identity and social standing (mottoes, coats of arms of various provenance) – Gran had unbeatable status. His sledge flag, a silk pennant, had been presented to him at Buckingham Palace by King Haakon of Norway, the gift of Queen Maud, a daughter of Queen Victoria.

But at the heart of this expedition, as he had on his first, Scott was drawing on the professional skills of men trained within the Royal Navy and the Merchant Navy, providing him not only a solid base to draw on but also the advantage of operating within established hierarchies. The Captain's word was all. Officers functioned according to rank. Above all, ratings brought up within the hard training of the Royal Navy were expected to be able to do whatever was required of them, to the best of their abilities. To obey orders, and to turn their hands to anything. To be, in Scott's words, devoted, able and loyal.

The Eastern party were about to be isolated: six men living in the same small space, eating at the same table. At Cape Evans a wall of boxes filled with stores had been built as a bulkhead in the new winter quarters, dividing the galley and the men from everyone else beyond, mess room from wardroom. According to Scott, the officers (sixteen) had two-thirds, the men (nine) the remaining third. Outside, one of the wooden crates housing a motor sledge had been converted to a three-seat latrine with an entrance at either end. The internal organization of the Eastern party's hut was yet to be decided. The three officers had been working together at Cape Evans and had shared a week's camping. The three crew men were old friends. But the six were untried as a team. This first pairing of Levick and Browning had been a failure, and that was unsettling.

Levick calmed down, had a bath (only the second chance since 6 December), washed his clothes and listened to the gramophone. His motto, according to the others, was *Festina lente*. Hasten slowly. Known on occasion as Toffers, Tofferino or The Old Sport, inclined to be overweight and to make resolutions to do something about it, Levick was generally easy-going. Priestley noted that the 'only alternative he is ever known by is "Mother" the reason for which . . . is obvious when you have known him a few weeks'.

Lieutenant Wilfred Bruce, an insider yet an outsider on this expedition, having arrived on the scene only in New Zealand, a 'volunteer' but with a central role on *Terra Nova* now that Lieutenant

Evans had joined the shore party and Campbell was about to depart on his own expedition, was keeping a full journal. He was also writing a long letter to his sister Kathleen, to send when they arrived in New Zealand. She wanted to know exactly what had happened and what he thought about everyone.

Priestley and Levick with Campbell were a queer trio, according to Bruce. Priestley was 'wildly energetic'. Levick was, Bruce thought, 'the slowest man I've ever met, but persistent, & when he wants a thing, though he'll fiddle about horribly – generally gets it.' Campbell 'is a queer bird. Awfully full of his own importance, he was quite sure that his King Edward VII Land show was going to be <u>the</u> thing of the whole expedition. His disappointment when he failed to land anywhere in the east was almost pitiful.'

With Levick and Browning safely back on board, the Eastern party departed on Thursday evening, 9 February, north to Robertson Bay and points west. Campbell recorded this final departure of his exploring party with minimal brevity. Partly this was his style. He'd sent his wife, Lil, extracts from his journal, 'appallingly dry reading & still worse to write, but it is a record of our doings'. But he had no desire to go to Robertson Bay. King Edward VII Land had been his chance. As leader of his own expedition, he would have discovered new ground, been an explorer. He still mourned the lost opportunity of the Bay of Whales.

Campbell kept his emotions tight. He did not talk or write about what might have driven him to take on the task of leading the Eastern party – the dreams, or ambitions. But his misery was visible. '8 P.M. We shoved off and after calling at Cape Evans proceeded north. Wind E thick with snow.'

For Wilfred Bruce a line was drawn: 'Finish with McMurdo Sound for this year!'

6

Coal will decide

12–20 February 1911

We have had the worst of luck with the pack, weather, & absence of landing places & now we have to be dumped in the first possible place regardless of chances of sledging or of science or else return home.

Priestley, February 1911

THE STARTLING SOUND of a woman's voice filled the wardroom of *Terra Nova*, the lovely faces of debutantes in the midst of the 1907 London season gazed up from the table. The expedition gramophone was out, playing records, and everyone was appreciating the pictures in the magazines Priestley had brought back from Shackleton's hut. The journey north had been straightforward, and now, Sunday 12 February, only three days from Cape Evans, they were within 20 miles of Cape Adare.

The wind began to blow hard from the south-east, thick with snow: not what they wanted. If they overran Cape Adare, they would need to use coal to get back. So they stopped engines, furled sails and hove to. But the wind freshened into a heavy gale. The lightly laden *Terra Nova* was driven on north through terrific snow squalls, with blinding snow and lurching heavy seas, everything movable moving. Priestley was incapacitated, Levick sick and Campbell worried because the coal problem was so serious that losing days to the gale threatened even their plans for landing. By Wednesday 15 February, over 100 miles north of Cape Adare, with the gale still Force 7, they got up steam and started 'jogging back', managing about 4 knots, tumbling uncomfortably, swells still huge. Next day, Thursday the 16th, they sighted land, glimpses of grey and black through the spray and freezing drift. It was still blowing hard. 'We're all dead sick of this gale . . . four whole days now, and it's wasting a lot of coal', wrote Bruce, 'and the ship tumbles about so much that any sleep is out of the question. All we can do to stay in our bunks.'

Scott's hope was that Campbell would find a suitable place to build his hut and winter in the vicinity of Smith's Inlet, discovered by Ross in 1841. From here it should be possible to work west along the coast to Cape North, Ross's furthest point, then start discovering the unknown coast beyond: the 'main object of your exploration in this region'. But Campbell couldn't even bring *Terra Nova* near the coast until he was already east of Smith's Inlet. As the ship steamed on east, back towards the entrance to the Ross Sea, through lumpy weathered bergs and heavy open pack, Campbell stared bleakly at the unfolding coast. They would land anywhere there was a chance. But there was nowhere.

Priestley was hauled out of his bunk to give his opinion. The mountains were dark, bony rock, pared to their rib cages, peaks streaked with ice. The glaciers were steep, tremendously crevassed and tumbled about, and appeared to turn acute corners before reaching the sea, terminating abruptly in ice walls 40 to 50 feet high. Between the ice walls precipitous cliffs of rock rose sheer out of the water. There was no ice foot, or piedmont. Broken pack lay close in under the cliffs, grinding in the big swell. Sledging along this coast would be impossible. The place seemed to repel all boarders. The western journey Scott wanted could not be achieved.

The coal problem exacerbated the issue: there was simply no contingency for bad weather or pack ice, or for the reality of this harsh coastline, fronting the full onslaught of the southern ocean. Priestley worried through the coal calculations in his diary:

> We have only another day or two's grace & either must land in the neighbourhood of Robertson's Bay or we must confess ourselves failures & return with the ship to Lyttelton . . . We are all praying for a few day's fine weather & I believe the ship's party are every bit as anxious to get rid of us & get home as we are to get off. It would break me up pretty considerably to have to go back to Lyttelton . . . there is still plenty of chance of that happening.

But the Antarctic would not conform to desires. It delivered what it did because that is what it was. For men struggling to achieve what they wanted, it was the fates, or luck, or Providence, or the gods, or God. The schedules they set themselves to keep were so – apparently – carelessly thwarted. But schedules based on assumptions were particularly vulnerable in Antarctica. The place was not enigmatic or heartless. It was, by definition, indifferent.

Somewhere had to be been found to establish their winter quarters, and the tonnage of coal allocated to get them ashore was fast disappearing. Pennell would take over command of *Terra Nova* once Campbell and his men had landed. Scott's orders to Pennell were 'for the ship to explore to the west of North Cape as far as the coal supply allowed'. A dedicated quantity of coal had been set aside for *Terra Nova*'s voyage of exploration. Its existence – let alone the amount – was never mentioned in the current miserable calculations: it could not be accessed. But the general shortage of coal was shrivelling Campbell's options, the hopes of achieving something. The Eastern party – Scott's declared strand of exploring, the geographical discovery and science planned to take place in parallel to the attempt on the Pole – was failing to find even a foothold to work.

Late on Friday the 17th *Terra Nova* entered the deep scoop of Robertson Bay. Campbell had studied the charts and read the accounts, but every feature that he hoped would deliver a solution to his need to land failed to provide a footing. 'We are well in Robertson Bay', wrote Dickason, 'glacier ice and ice-bergs and not a square yard of beach to be seen; we intend going right round the bay so we ought to pick up somewhere!'

That 'somewhere' was increasingly Cape Adare, the 20-mile-long mountainous marker at the head of the Ross Sea. Campbell was deeply against it. Cape Adare was the furthest point possible from the direction they wanted to travel. They would be jammed in on the east when they needed to be going west. The only known landing place, the pebbly spit near the northern tip like a wart sticking out from a finger, was, as everyone knew, where Borchgrevink had built his two huts and spent a winter. Sledging from the cape was difficult, as was clearly revealed in Borchgrevink's account. Most painful, it was old, well-trampled ground.

Campbell's frustration was all the more intense because they had had an opportunity to land, in the Bay of Whales, and turned away. Cape Adare – which they were now having to strive to achieve – was in reality far from what they wanted. It was a last resort, meeting no criteria that the Eastern party had been set or that they had set themselves. It seemed incredible that in all this vast expanse of coast they, as Scott's second shore party, had to end up on the same beach as the only other explorers who had landed in the area, to live through an Antarctic winter in the shadow of the first expedition to achieve that distinction.

But proved landing places in these vast untenanted spaces were few. Places where it was possible to get ashore, to unload equipment – and, equally important, to be collected again, predictably and in safety – were turning out to be rare. The pressures on such places were multiple. They offered the possibility of continuity in scientific data-gathering, a kicking-off point for further exploring, the potential of embedded resources – a hut, or food, clothing, fuel, necessities that could define life or death. Landing places, in their rarity, were competed for. Mawson, in proposing to Scott that he should be put ashore at Cape Adare with a small team, had planned to actively use Borchgrevink's resources to look for economic minerals, do biology and possibly even work south, approaching the Magnetic Pole from the cape. But thinking like this was not currently uppermost in Campbell's mind. He wanted to explore new lands, to discover, to push back the unknown.

In the litany of Antarctic landing places, the Eastern party had been dealt poor options. Campbell had been given a territory to explore with no known landing place, directed to land at an inlet that had been shown no longer to exist, arrived at a bay whose existence had been denied, directed again to explore a territory with no known landing place and was about to end up at the only known landing place, which had already been thoroughly explored. Having just experienced the double-booking of the Bay of Whales, he was having to move in after the previous tenants at Cape Adare.

Early on Saturday 18 February, at a little past 3.00 a.m., *Terra Nova* stopped off the spit at Cape Adare. An almost full moon, golden-coloured, was reflected as agitated segments in the water. The rising sun touched the peaks of the massive range of the Admiralty Mountains far to the south. Campbell and Davies, the carpenter, came ashore through the cluck and clatter of brash ice to prospect for a site for the hut. They were wet to their waists with freezing water. But they were walking on pebbles and rocks. Penguins stood in small groups on the beach uttering single harsh squawks.

The place was much bigger than Campbell had thought, the scale large and the distances substantial. Closing off the view, terminating the depth of the beach, foreclosing its width, was a monumental curved-sided steep wall of black basalt like a colossal elongated boulder, a thousand feet high, streaked down its front with the white of drifted snow. Across the gravelly surface Borchgrevink's living hut looked small and hunched, boxes and rubbish scattered outside forlornly, but it was still here. The second hut was partly dismantled but standing. Human occupation, in this vast, untenanted Antarctic space.

Campbell came back on board. Still in command of *Terra Nova*, he tried one last throw. He could, he suggested to Levick and Priestley, steam out around the top of Cape Adare, travel part-way down the Victoria Land coast and try to land at Wood Bay, north of Mount Melbourne or, he was desperate enough to suggest, even on Coulman Island. Good work could be achieved, exploring and science, their two objectives. There would be precious little of that if they stayed here. It was one last chance. But there was a risk. If they experienced any trouble with the pack, or with gales, they would have to return immediately to New Zealand. The choice was between making one more attempt, with the possibility of failure, or disembarking immediately.

Levick wanted to stay. The risk of returning to New Zealand seemed too great, 'and I said so decidedly'. Priestley agreed, preferring certainty over probability. Campbell, a consensus-seeker, bowed to the majority, as he had done at the Bay of Whales. On the Barrier the deciding point, this pivot for all that will be, or might have been, had passed more slowly; here it was over in minutes. The landing was resumed, and the three Eastern party officers left for the beach with Campbell's talisman, a load of emergency stores. An hour later they were relieved by Abbott, Browning and Dickason. For the three seamen the event revealed the decision. 'Early in the morning of the 18th Feb 1911 the ship tied up off Cape Adare about ½ a mile from the shore,' wrote Abbott, '& we knew at least that this was the destination for the Eastern Party.' To Dickason the 'whole place . . . smells rather strong, but still it is solid rock beneath us and not glacier ice'.

Moving all their stuff ashore had to be done quickly. The beach was a risky landing. Whaler and cutter worked between ship and shore, bringing three-quarters of a ton or more a time. A big swell dumped on the beach, there was a strong tide, and Levick and Priestley unloaded up to their thighs in cold water, drenched whenever a swell broke awkwardly and shoved them against the unyielding ice of the ice foot, or a stranded floe. They were in constant danger of being jammed between a boat as it broached and the ice, but the only accidents were broken oars and the whaler filling and capsizing. Lengths of timber for the hut roof, boxes of provisions, bags of patent fuel, personal gear – all the possessions were lifted off, got ashore and pushed up out of the tide's reach. The bay swilled with rafts of pack ice moving silently in with the flood tide, then carried out again with the ebb tide. While the pack was in, the men cleared the congestion on the beach, stacking what they could out of reach of the swell. With the ebb tide, unloading started again. Abbott and Browning, under the guidance of Davies, prepared the foundations for the hut, placed near to Borchgrevink's, then started getting the framework up, a slender skeleton against the sky. Everyone turned in at 1.30 a.m. on Sunday the 19th, with Campbell openly despondent. But 30 tons of stores and equipment had been got on shore.

First thing on Sunday morning a party of ten willing men came over from the ship. They carried gear up to Borchgrevink's huts, stacked provisions in depots and worked on the new building so that, by the time it was dark, the skeleton was clothed with match boarding. And the first Adélie penguins had been killed.

After dinner Levick and Priestley took an introductory walk around their estate, 'admiring the poultry etc.'. 'The scent here is very strong,' Abbott wrote carefully, 'it's like being in the bottom of a large aviary.' Adélie penguins require suitable landing places. The urgency of an immutable biological clock propels them to a place ashore where they can build their nests, lay their eggs and raise their chicks. Having found it, Adélies return to the same place generation after generation. But the attributes sought by Adélies – ease of landing, rocks or pebbles, a surface clear of snow – are precisely those prized by humans. Their rarity can bring conflict of use. Here at Cape Adare the pungent smell of meals regurgitated to feed hungry chicks, of excreta deposited, was the very essence of the site, where hundreds of thousands of individual lives were lived every year. Nothing decays in the cold. Dead chicks, eyes pecked out by skuas lay scattered, a skua larder. Dead adults, bodies partly dismembered by leopard seals or battered by the ocean, lay embedded in the pebbles. All the detritus of living and breeding, of struggling and failing, scattered over this vast city of Adélie life, this intense metropolis of struggling and renewal. But now it was mid-February, the brief summer was coming to an end and the spaces were emptying. This season's chicks had fledged, and many of the adults had gone. Some, choosing to moult here, stood, as they must, conserving their body mass because they could not go to sea to feed until they grew their new feathers.

But for the men who had just arrived the place smelt, and that would have to be dealt with. As there weren't many penguins around, they had better get on with stocking the winter larder. 'Nothing like having a good supply of fresh meat in hand', said Dickason. All the amusement of watching these funny little birds would have to wait until next spring.

On the other hand, being next door to departed human neighbours had immediate advantages. Borchgrevink's living hut, interlocked Baltic pine of Norwegian construction, simple and solid, was filled with snow but also with stores, and was usable. His roofless stores hut was sound. Dickason installed himself in the living hut, got a stove going, and that essential for labouring men and their spirits, a hot drink, started appearing. Dickason had a reputation for being able to conjure a fire out of a block of ice.

In the evening the pack drifted in again, preventing the ship's party from returning to *Terra Nova*. Spare sleeping-bags and blankets were found, and everyone somehow crowded companionably into Borchgrevink's little hut, the first building on the Antarctic continent;

but no one thought about that as they wrote their last letters home or enjoyed talking. They would not see each other for nearly a year. 'We had a jolly time', said Abbott, putting his sleeping-bag on Borchgrevink's table near the window. Bruce, spending his first night in a sleeping-bag ('beastly!'), reckoned Campbell had bucked up a bit. Priestley insisted on staying on watch and carried on lumping cases. At 4.00 a.m. on Monday the 20th *Terra Nova* steamed into sight, sounded her siren and Priestley turned all hands out.

Campbell had handed Scott's orders to Harry Pennell, who was taking over the command. Levick photographed the final departure, *Terra Nova*, steam up, mid-distance across a quiet sea, with smoke coming from her tall stack, the last boatload going out across the water and two figures standing awkwardly on the shore. 'The hands went on board early this morning taking our mail with them', wrote Browning: 'the ship left for NZ Mr Pennell who is in charge of the ship came ashore and wishes us all goodbye before leaving, we watched the ship go out and returned to our beds again as it was quite early.' But Abbott stayed in his sleeping-bag on the table, watching through the window 'the ship steam away out of sight en route for Lyttleton once more'. Priestley did not see the send-off, as he was 'frantically searching for a piece of stove-piping I was accused of having been seen last with & which had disappeared'. Nobody mentioned the actual destination of *Terra Nova*. Campbell's entry in his journal was typical: 'When the pack cleared out the ship party re-embarked and after saying goodbye proceeded North to New Zealand.' It was as though the intention to explore was not happening, or at least left unacknowledged.

They were here. But when could they leave? Scott's instructions about their departure were explicit. Campbell would not be relieved until March 1912, over twelve months away, as *Terra Nova* headed north at the end of next summer. His party should be ready to embark by 25 February, but if the ship had not come by 25 March, he and his men would have to prepare for a second winter. They might find some useful stores remaining at Cape Adare, from Borchgrevink's expedition, but they shouldn't rely on any. Scott thought that 'Seals and penguins should be plentiful', but 'in no case would it be advisable to attempt to retreat along the coast'.

Campbell wanted to leave earlier. Having seen the conditions along the coast from the ship, he did not hold out much hope of fulfilling Scott's objective of exploring to the west. Any sledging the Eastern party did achieve, he feared, would be decidedly local. His particular work, surveying, would be terribly reduced, if not impossible. Campbell wanted to get away at the very first opportunity, to go somewhere he and his men could achieve real work. He'd come to Antarctica to lead an expedition to explore new land – to 'break new ground'. In the event, the Eastern party, a piece on Scott's chessboard of expedition objectives, had been shunted down the list as other pieces on the board took precedence.

Quietly stubborn, Campbell was determined to try and do a modicum of what he had come to do. Unable now to have any communication with Scott, he was on his own. As such, he and Pennell agreed new orders for *Terra Nova*. The ship would relieve Campbell not at the end of next summer but at the beginning, on arrival from New Zealand, and would put the Eastern party down on the Victoria Land coast as it went south. In the time they had available – five or six weeks – they would sledge through the mountains, exploring, reaching the high plateau if possible, doing real geographical work and science. It would be a compensation for their major disappointment at missing out on King Edward VII Land and being landed here at Cape Adare, where their chances of achieving substantial exploring were slight.

Terra Nova would therefore pick them up in early January 1912, putting them ashore, if possible, at Wood Bay, just north of Mount Melbourne. Pennell would then collect them again on 20 February 1912, in exactly a year's time. Campbell had quietly and resolutely clawed back the chance of an opportunity.

Campbell wrote a quick letter to Vera:

Cape Adare Feb 18th 1911,
Dearest V.
'L'homme propose' etc. . . . .
    we just reached here & bundled ashore – not bad winter quarters but hopeless for sledging mountains over 12,000 feet sheer from the sea . . .
    but when the ship comes down early in the next year I hope

she will pick me up and put me in Wood Bay on her way down
for Scott calling for me on her way up –

Goodby dearest V

Your loving Coz

Vic

Wilfred Bruce described Campbell as *Terra Nova* sailed north:
'when we eventually landed him at C Adare he was in the depths of
misery at first, thinking he could do nothing out of the way. But we
talked cheerfully to him of his plans & before we left he had bucked
up immensely.'

Campbell and his men pose beside their hut at Cape Adare after church, 17 December 1911.
Seated, from left: Raymond Priestley, Victor Campbell, Murray Levick. Standing behind:
George Abbott (in the clean white pyjama jacket), Harry Dickason, Frank Browning.
Levick's hand pulling the string to release the camera shutter is hidden under his hat

Left: Preparing to depart New Zealand for Antarctica, November 1910. Black smoke pours from the single funnel of *Terra Nova*

Below: Officers and scientists lie around on the deck of *Terra Nova* in brilliant sunshine, afternoon of 28 December 1910. Captain Scott smokes his pipe

party man-hauls a sledge-load of stores from *Terra Nova* across the sea ice to Cape Evans, oss Island, January 1911

he beach at Cape Evans with tents, stores, ponies and partly built winter quarters hut. hree men haul an empty sledge back to *Terra Nova*, anchored at the ice-edge, January 1911

Above: Boulders piled on the sea ice in front of Mount Erebus. Campbell and his men use ponies to haul volcanic rock across to *Terra Nova* for ballast, 13 January 1911

Left: One of Campbell's two expedition ponies being lowered into the sea off Cape Evans. It will have to swim for the shore, dragged behind the waiting rowing boat, 8 February 1911

Levick, wearing his rabbitskin hat, on the deck of *Terra Nova*, skinning an Adélie penguin. Levick was always happy to pose for Herbert Ponting, the expedition's camera artist

Campbell and Levick with a freshly slaughtered Weddell seal at Cape Adare. In the first months seals were shot. Later they were clubbed or stabbed. Levick guts the seal while Campbell, rifle under his arm, watches, 1911

Above: Priestley, Browning and Dickason pushing through slush and pancake ice in the Norwegian pram trying to collect biological specimens in Robertson Bay, 28 March 1911

Left: A specimen at last! Priestley holds up a length of seaweed washed up at Cape Adare, 1911

Above: Abbott dressed ready for sledging, wearing the nose-guard he invented. Lying on the snow are two man-hauling harnesses, Cape Adare, winter 1911

Right: Searching for specimens in a freshwater lake beside a moraine during the summer expedition, January 1912. Priestley, as always, seems oblivious to the cold

Browning unloads ice from a sledge to melt into fresh water, outside the hut at Cape Adare, 1911. Everyone reckoned the hut wouldn't last many winters

Levick clears snow from a window of Carsten Borchgrevink's hut at Cape Adare, which was lived in by ten men during 1899 and was the first building on the Antarctic continent

7

The unknown coast

20 February–10 April 1911

Ship dodging about like a rat in a trap . . . Ice all round,
we want some change, or we shall be caught.

Wilfred Bruce, February 1911

TERRA NOVA NEARLY rammed an iceberg in a thick gale the
day after leaving Cape Adare, Tuesday 21 February. The ship
passed along its solid length in eerie silence close enough to see the
long, fringing icicles, to feel the chill from its rock-hard wall. The
men were very tired; it had been a long, hard voyage and they were
short-handed. Ahead were waters filled with polar uncertainties and
hazards. Boatswain Cheetham's experience, as well as the knowledge
of a few men in the crew who had been south before, would be
invaluable.

But Harry Pennell was enjoying himself. Just twenty-eight, this
was his first command. The way *Terra Nova* rode the waves in a
heavy sea like a living being, not like the 'half-submerged rock' of the
iron ships he was used to, gave him real pleasure. Always on the
bridge in the severest cold and roughest weather, he slept only four
to six hours out of every twenty-four, on the bridge, or under the
chart table. If you had a turn at the wheel, Atkinson said of the trip
from England, and you were half a point off for half a minute, Pennell
would be out of his chart-room in the deck-house checking the
compass. On that trip he'd done all the meteorological work and
recorded all sightings of sea birds and whales. He was quick to learn,
happy to teach, modest yet highly capable, and his daily entries in the
ship's log were meticulous and informative. 'He's a thoroughly good
sort', thought Bruce. Everything was 'smooth as clockwork'.

A little before midnight the weather cleared, they altered course and headed towards the unknown coast. Scott wanted Pennell to get as far west as Adélie Land, traversing 30° of latitude. But he cautioned due care. The time spent exploring depended entirely on Pennell's judgement about coal reserves; also, the summer season was closing fast. Scott's orders to the commander now reflected an entirely different mind-set from the instructions he had left with Beaumont. The ship should not try to penetrate any large body of pack ice or approach any coast under pack ice conditions. *Terra Nova's* role as postman, and as provider of essential transport to a second polar attempt, should that be needed, dominated.

On the beach at Cape Adare the newly alone six turned in with misgivings as *Terra Nova* left early on Monday the 20th, then turned out again three hours later, very reluctantly, into a regular gale and the pressing necessity to finish building their hut. Abbott, as the expedition carpenter, reckoned he'd better get on with it, but it was not easy in a strong wind, hands clumsy with cold. Campbell and Levick had decided to sleep in Borchgrevink's roofless store hut, so Campbell rigged up a tarpaulin. Priestley bedded down with the three men in Borchgrevink's living hut, but he was relieved because the missing piece of stove-piping had turned up, 'so I am absolved from the imputation of having lost it'.

And Priestley faced up to killing penguins. He'd managed to avoid it on Shackleton's expedition, so now he just started, by massacring thirty. He reckoned 120 were needed as food for the winter, so there was plenty more killing to do.

> Now I am as murderous as anyone . . . They are such friendly brutes; they come round to inspect our tent and stores & seeing us they come up for a yarn & are promptly smitten on the head with a large club & then beaten until the shape of their heads is utterly changed. This is necessary for less drastic treatment only results in our coming back to them in a few minutes time to carry them off & finding them staggering about.

A group of giant petrels sat companionably on the spit, like geese, large-bodied birds with golden eyes and strong yellow bills hooked to tear apart flesh. Levick and Priestley shot a selection as spoil for the table, and then Priestley fetched the hand-barrow to carry two white-plumaged, two grey-headed and three fawn-feathered mixed with grey and white. Southern giant petrels, circumnavigating the globe in these southern latitudes, returning to breed in the same small portion of rocky land, could mate for life, but they were fresh meat, so worth trying. As a final bit of local hunting Levick and Priestley shot a skua on the wing, and the next day they bagged a couple more.

Priestley began to feel optimistic. Even at his unhappiest the previous week he'd decided that they should be able to get some good work out of the winter and spring, although summer sledging would be a failure. By Wednesday the 22nd he reckoned the winter – barring, of course, bad luck, and at least until sledging started – would be a 'marvel of comfort'. Dickason had baked his first batch of bread on Borchgrevink's stove. Apart from the problem of their work, they couldn't be better off. After all, no party had ever set up winter quarters in Antarctica next door to two huts ready built, with a supply of random equipment to scavenge and use.

On Wednesday 22nd February, at a camp they named Safety Camp on the edge of the Barrier, Scott read Campbell's report, and found out that Amundsen was at the Bay of Whales and, in addition, that Balloon Bight did not exist.

Depot-laying hadn't been much joy. They hadn't got quite as far south on the Barrier as Scott had hoped, and had established their supplies of fodder, dog food and fuel on February the 17th a bit short of the hoped-for 80° south, in a 'gigantic' depot cairn as tall as a man, with tea tins tied to sledges planted upright in the snow acting as reflectors. The cold hit them: early autumn was sterner out here on the Barrier, and there was frostbite all round. 'I have been wondering how I shall stick the summit again, this cold spell gives ideas', Scott wrote at what he called One Ton Camp. 'I think I shall be all right, but one must be prepared for a pretty good doing.' The three weakest ponies had been sent back early with Teddy Evans. On Saturday the 18th Oates, Gran and Bowers set out from the depot at One Ton to get the remaining five weary animals back to Hut Point, while Scott, impatient to find out the news from *Terra Nova*, raced ahead with both dog teams, taking Wilson, Meares and Cherry-Garrard. The first night, with everyone exhilarated by the distance covered by the dogs, Cherry as cook concocted a 'kind of hurrah party'. Having moved earlier into Scott and Wilson's tent, he had been astonished at how an efficient, well-run tent improved the quality of the sledging experience. Eager to shorten the journey, Scott cut out the corner of Corner Camp, and the dog team tumbled in a tangle of harnesses down a crevasse; Scott then insisted on being lowered 60 feet to rescue two animals from a ledge. But they'd achieved the distance fast, with Scott running beside the sledge much of the way 'most untiringly – wonderful for a man of 42', wrote Cherry, with the unknowingness of youth. The dogs were now ravenous, thin and tired.

On arriving at Safety Camp at 4.30 a.m. on the 22nd, they were met by Teddy Evans with the bad news that only one of the three ponies he'd been asked to coax back had survived. Scott, Wilson and Cherry with several others walked on to Hut Point but found the hut empty and no mail bag, although they hunted everywhere, putting forward all kinds of wild theories, increasingly anxious. Very tired, they slogged back to Safety Camp, where they discovered the mail bag, which had been brought over independently by Dr Atkinson, who had hoped to meet Scott on the way.

Cherry described what happened after Campbell's unexpected, unsettling news had been read. '[L]ast night & for many hours Scott cd think of nothing else nor talk of anything else. Evidently a great shock to him – he thinks it very unsporting since our plans of landing a party there were known.' Scott, in fact, had suggested the Eastern party land in Balloon Bight since, in his view, the Bay of Whales did not exist. There was much discussion of the detail in Campbell's letter – the Norwegians as a 'tough looking lot', the Greenland dogs 'bigger than ours', the fact that Amundsen could start a good deal further south, and earlier, than Scott. 'Scott thinks he will get to the Pole – said so in as many words . . . Scott said anyway we wont hurry – mentioned possibility of trying a nearer glacier than the Beardmore.'

Wilson doubted that Amundsen understood 'how bad an effect the monotony and the hard travelling surface of the Barrier is to animals'. Amundsen's prospects of reaching the Pole were not very good – however, were he to be fortunate and his dogs a success, 'he will probably reach the Pole this year, earlier than we can'. Then, with the prospects of Campbell and his party coming to mind, he assumed that Campbell would have landed at Cape Adare, and he approved, as chief of the scientific staff, 'as it would give him a fine field for work which Borchgrevink never touched.'

On Wednesday the 22nd, just twelve hours after starting to search for the unknown coast, *Terra Nova* sighted snow-capped mountains to the south-west. Pennell wrote happily: 'so the luck of the *Terra Nova* was in this season.' '[M]ade land, new land, at 3.pm', crowed Bruce. There was another discovery, almost as though in celebration, certainly a fortuitous incentive. 'We find we have more coal than we expected to – much jubilation! And probably some really good work for the world in general, and the Expedition in particular.' Bruce had a personal celebration, shaving, bathing and changing into clean clothes. The weather was lovely. More peaks appeared above the horizon, then a range of hills and an enormous glacier tongue. Pennell steamed towards the new land until darkness and the pack stopped them.

Next morning, Thursday the 23rd, they tried to penetrate the ice, bumping in to within 4 miles of the glacier tongue. But the sea was an impenetrable white plain of ice, studded with the angled slopes and lopsided tops of grounded icebergs: forty-seven of them were countable from the place where, with huge reluctance, they had to give up. Land and ice seemed all one, a white frozen unreachable world, with clouds now hiding everything except the lowest level. So they bumped their way out again through lumpy, difficult ice and continued steaming to the west, outside the edge of the pack, sounding and watching. The pack, however, kept pushing them north. Grey, glaring light distorted distance; then the weather changed, blowing hard, thick with snow.

On Saturday the 25th the sun broke through, and they saw what they thought was an archipelago of islands, except they turned out to be icebergs. Then – land again: a 'cliffy coast-line', steep and rugged, with glaciers and rock, except that the view was frustratingly truncated by a line of cloud, like enticing scenery at the start of a play with the curtain half-up. Pennell was producing results as Scott wanted, when he wanted them. One end of his desired wedge of discovering was delivering new marks on the chart. But Scott himself wouldn't be able to know of the success until he arrived back from his attempt at the South Pole, in more than a year's time. The estimated schedule had the Polar party at the Pole on, 'as an ideal day', 22 December 1911, Midsummer Day, the longest of the year, with the sun at its maximum altitude.

Hopes ran high for reaching this latest land. Pennell put *Terra Nova* at the pack. But they stuck, unpleasantly, for twelve hours, until they managed to get free. Bruce: 'Everyone breathed easier, for it would have been a bad place to spend one or more winters in. I think we won't do it again!' Next day, Monday 27 February, with ice surrounding the ship, they worked hard to keep free of the insidiously freezing sea. The spaces between floes were filled with slush or frozen over with new ice, viscous, thin, but impossible to push through.

Pennell tried to deal with what he found. He could not know the complexity of the sea ice, the seasonal play of locality. This late season pack was a jumble of broken pieces of old floe mixed with lumps of hard glacier ice, bits and pieces filling the spaces, rubbing and clogging. Dangerous, unpredictable stuff. It could not be tackled in the dark, and darkness closed down perceptibly earlier every day. Their route was a zigzag of attempts to get back south followed by retreats north. Determined to try continuing west, they were driven back east. By the beginning of March, try as they might to continue exploring, *Terra Nova* had discovered no more coast.

At Cape Adare the beat of approaching winter meant doing essential jobs first. Everything was being sacrificed to finishing their hut, a complicated design a bit like a puzzle, with layers – external, internal, insulation – needing to be assembled correctly, in the right order. Ten men had fitted into Borchgrevink's living hut. Campbell's hut would be much bigger, but it was looking a bit like the house that Jack built.

Penetrating below the surface – as Priestley was doing, digging a drainage trench around the hut, or Levick, trying to level the floor

inside – had unleashed an overpowering smell. They were unwit-
tingly disturbing the accumulated evidence of centuries of penguin
lives. Tiny squid beaks, the bones of fish, partly digested krill, moulted
feathers, caught in layers of the once ingested, now rejected, formed
a pinkish paste that filled the spaces between the layers of pebbles.
Levick attempted to get rid of the smell with calcium chloride, and
temporarily blinded himself; he had to retire to his bag with a streaming nose and agonizing throat. 'At least no one is offering to take my
job over', Priestley commented with grim humour, shovelling more
guano-embedded pebbles out of his trench. 'An unsavoury mess.'

Outside, the hut had been tied down with wire cables, like
anchoring a haystack, and a porch had been started on the side facing
the wind. Inside, the cooking stove had to be assembled, a labyrinthine task, and dark green linoleum laid – a very tasteful colour,
Priestley reckoned. The six beds were placed in position, officers on
the side with the windows, and the men on the other. Campbell was
in the corner farthest from the door, between the chronometer box
and the chart table; Levick as second-in-command was in the other
corner, with Priestley between them. Each officer had 6 feet by 6 feet
of space as his own property, with pencil marks on the wall demar-
cating the boundaries. On the other side of the hut the two Petty
Officers had the corners, Abbott nearest the door and Browning in
the far corner. Dickason's bed was close to Browning's, but their
space was compromised by the need to fit the galley, stove and
acetylene plant along the same wall. Material striped in two shades of
green to make privacy curtains had been supplied, all colours having
almost certainly been selected by Kathleen Scott's artistic eye. Now
they were here, no one bothered with privacy.

Enough fresh ice had to be carried daily to the hut to melt into
water, but finding ice not polluted by penguins was a real problem.
Campbell, examining the mutton carried from New Zealand, found
it covered in mould and so condemned it. Skuas found feasting on
this unexpected addition to their diet were shot and added to the
larder. Priestley burrowed an ice-cave in to a piece of stranded iceberg on the beach, but a high tide swilled around inside it and the
inmates, forty stiff little corpses, were rehoused in a new icehouse
built of wood lined with ice blocks. More penguins were required for

winter. Priestley and Levick did the horrible work, a 'ghastly business . . . they are possessed of perfectly extraordinary vitality'. Priestley dreamed of having a sharp, heavy sword, or a scythe. 'It is only the necessity for our having animal food which can excuse these slaughters . . . I was very nearly sick this morning & even Levick who as a doctor is used to blood felt pretty bad.' For Levick, 'Penguins and Seals are our only antidote from the dread scurvy.' Atkinson, based at Cape Evans, adhered to currently fashionable theories about possible factors in the causation of scurvy: darkness, excessive cold, dirt, the absorption of food with any decomposing material. Levick had a robust attitude: he was concerned with prevention, and that meant, as far as he was concerned, fresh meat. But the penguins were 'dear little things, and I hate having to kill them'.

The meteorological screen was set up (the bleakest-looking spot within reach of the hut, according to Campbell), and meteorological observations begun. Campbell started surveying, Levick was busy taking photographs, and everyone collected a few rocks. They climbed to the top of Cape Adare, following the penguin paths up, and found to their astonishment nest sites covering the steepest slopes. The ascent wasn't difficult, except for snowdrifts and loose black basalt rubble.

Walking the perimeters of their space, they were already getting to the edges of what they could do, where they could go. Dickason, still thinking as a sailor, looked out to sea every day, noting the winds and the movement of the pack ice in the bay. For Levick, gazing across at the distant range of snow-covered mountains with their mighty glaciers delivering their ice loads into the ocean, the unknown country beyond was the challenge; but the mountains were impassable for sledging. They were stuck on a triangle of gravel attached like a plaster to the limb of the cape. The cape, with its sheer precipices where it fronted the Ross Sea, offered no way, as far as they could see, of getting from it on to the inland plateau. In the midst of these distant views and unsurpassed grandeur the six of them were – at least until the sea ice became thick and firm enough to let them try travelling along the unknown coast that Scott wished them to explore – 'absolute prisoners'. Having noted what Borchgrevink and his men had tried to do, they already knew this.

On the evening of Saturday 4 March they celebrated a house-warming with a concert of gramophone records and a toast in whisky to sweethearts and wives. Priestley had long wondered where the Eastern party would lay their heads. Well, it was here, and an anti-climax. Then it was on with the work. Borchgrevink's uninsulated second hut was cleared for storage and his living hut set up to use as a workshop. The first night in their own hut Levick put his photographic plates in water and found them stuck fast in ice next morning. Campbell decided that Levick would have to do the tedious, messy business of developing films in Borchgrevink's hut, but Abbott wanted to set up a gym in there as well and had already installed a punching ball.

The same day, 4 March, to the north-west, *Terra Nova* just escaped being trapped. The weather was calm and there was no pack, yet the surface of the sea suddenly froze. '[T]hough we kept going', Bruce wrote,

> our thud got slower & slower as the ice froze thicker, & eventually we stopped. Then the wind changed & blew, & the ice broke up. But we had drifted, & were shut in by the pack. For several days we've seen nothing but ice from the crow's-nest, heavy pack without a break, but we kept her moving, under sail generally, & we've found blue water, several lanes of it, & we are jubilant.

On 7 March, with no prospect of getting further south, *Terra Nova* gave up the search for new land and began attempting to get clear of the pack, to start the run back to New Zealand.

Abbott worked outside all of his thirty-first birthday, 10 March, in a gale, without wearing his windproofs, building an emergency 'roundhouse' of snow; a latrine had been constructed against the side of Borchgrevink's hut, but in a blizzard men could lose their way and needed something closer. At his birthday dinner, after everyone had made themselves tidy for the meal, as always, 'Mr Priestley gave me a present, Pope's Odyssy of Homer, a very nice little volume. We had Penguin & Bacon, Plum pudding & Champagne at 7.00 p.m. The Eastern Party drank my health . . . I drank health to my mother & all the Party.' But the next day Abbott was ill, 'probably with a chill', noted Levick. 'I have put him in bed and given him some medicine which I hope will not do him any harm. He is quite one of the most splendid men I have had the chance to know, and I am quite fond of him.'

They were settling into a winter routine. This meant Priestley was free for scientific work 'if I want to be'. He could always collect specimens – that is, whatever he could find – the first, most basic stage of scientific work. On Wednesday the 15th he collected seaweed, algae and rocks. Abbott noted that this was the day *Terra Nova* was due to arrive at Stewart Island, south of New Zealand. 'We have been talking about them a good deal & picture the merry times they will have on their arrival at Lyttelton.' A poignant memory, given the happy weeks he had spent in New Zealand. Abbott, ever equable, was still labouring to finish building the roundhouse in the lee of their hut: 'it turned out quite a comfortable place.'

Terra Nova, driven in the opposite direction to the one wanted, was running short of key necessities. On 14 March, 'Water, kerosene, oil, matches, rapidly running out', noted Bruce. 'Another week's head wind will be serious.' On Sunday the 19th they got a fierce gale, losing part of their bulwarks, he wrote to Kathleen: 'tremendous battles with the sails . . . people coming down from the yards quite exhausted . . . nearly everyone was damaged somewhere.' On the Monday night the wind dropped, and the ship absolutely wallowed in a terrific cross-swell: 'Still going backwards, nearly due South in afternoon.'

At Cape Adare this same Sunday the 19th brought their first real gale, with winds reaching 84 m.p.h. before the anenometer broke. A tent used as protection while doing magnetic observations was an early victim, gone for ever, the only evidence of its bounding route being gouges in the shingle. They'd thought their stores of coal were safe from the sea, but the next day, with an enormous roaring surf pounding up the spit, they had to rescue the precious supplies and haul them to the hut. The great waves carried huge balls of ice on their crests. As the waves curled over and crashed down, they flung the ice far beyond the high-water mark, fist-thick fragments shooting up from the impact like missiles. This first Cape Adare blizzard shook the hut so forcefully that books, bottles and plates tumbled off the shelves. Levick celebrated the event with a poem, and Priestley copied the lines into his diary: Levick has 'blossomed forth into a poet & here is his first spasm . . . we still want a chorus'.

Here's to the Blizzard of sweet seventeen
   Here's to the calm minus forty
The lower degrees that are still & serene
   The blizzard so boisterous and rorty
Wrapped up in your windproof your body's all right
   With your hand lying snug in your mitten
But your beautiful nose is exposed to frostbite
   And as often as not is frostbitten
Whatever you wear in the wind, there remains
   The ever insoluble puzzle
Of how to be happy though blue in the face
   With the icicles stuck to your muzzle.

But by Tuesday the 21st the weather was so fine that Campbell could do surveying work, and Priestley began teaching Browning and Dickason how to read the barometer and thermometer. He needed assistants and found them 'very apt pupils'. Levick, as official expedition photographer, struggled with the tedious but extremely difficult business of developing and fixing his photographic plates with primitive and makeshift equipment, and unreasonably cold conditions. 'For an amateur it is full of trials.'

On Thursday the 23rd *Terra Nova* continued to battle headwinds. Bruce wrote: 'Things have gone so hardly for us we hardly hope to do it . . . We're still pretty cheerful, but sometimes we're all inclined to scream . . . and we curse her & pray for a few hours spell.' Then on Sunday the 26th the wind came from the right quarter, and they could start racing home before a south-west gale under steam and sail. More bulwarks had been washed away, and the wretched pumps had choked again. Davies the carpenter kept the ship going by punching holes in an enamel jug and holding it as a filter over the bilge-pump intakes. The following day, Monday 27 March 1911, *Terra Nova* arrived at the shelter of a lushly wooded sub-Antarctic island with green trees for ice-tired eyes and the wonderful, affirmative smells of things growing, and of wet earth.

Bruce observed with a poignant jolt that the child of the postmaster at Patterson's Inlet, Stewart Island, was 'sweetly pretty'. The other world was here, waiting. Pennell and Drake went ashore to send telegrams, and the news carried out of Antartica by *Terra Nova* was on its way to the wide world. 'Got a letter from you', wrote Bruce on 28 March, still adding notes to his long letter to Kathleen '. . . telling me to tell you everything. Well, I've done pretty well, haven't I? I'll try & tell you a little more about people, though.' Discovering that she intended making extracts from all her letters, to keep Admiral Beaumont up to date with the expedition, Bruce responded that 'if he takes any interest in the ship's movements', she could quote from his long letter to her: 'We've done a little, & we're rather pleased with ourselves.'

Kathleen, as well as writing to her brother, had been writing to her husband, knowing that her letters could not be carried to him until *Terra Nova* left on its second trip south to Antarctica, towards the end of the year. Her letters accumulated – descriptions of her life, of what their small son Peter was doing, responses to things he had written to her – loving letters, caring deeply for his plans and hopes. She was worrying so much because she knew how low he had been. The discontinuity was hard. By the time the ship reached Cape Evans again, some time early in 1912, her 'dear Con', as he was known in his family, would have been to the Pole. But at least, now that *Terra Nova* has reached New Zealand, she would get the first news, and would know how the first months had gone.

On *Terra Nova* officers and men read the newspapers, including reports of the Japanese expedition departing for Antarctica: 'They'll probably go to the Bay of Whales, find Amundsen there, be too late to go anywhere else, and camp beside him', Bruce wrote. 'What a scramble there's going to be.' Beards were shaved off, and underneath people looked quite strange. It had taken a hard three weeks from the northern edge of the sea ice to reach this island haven. But at least they were not trapped, somewhere to the south. The sea ice and the Southern Ocean both delivered a casual brutality, and predicting either was not possible.

The worst thing that happened at the Cape Adare hut on Sunday 26 March was Campbell choosing a hymn that only he and Levick knew, and the ordeal of them droning, then grimly chanting, through all the verses with no one joining in. After church they all went outside for a group photograph, taken by Levick, posed against Borchgrevink's hut, Priestley wearing his talisman fur coat from Edgeworth David and sitting on Brocklehurst's folding stool from Shackleton's hut, Campbell on a kitchen chair, wearing full fur mitts rather formally, the three men standing behind.

'We have plenty to do,' summarized Campbell on Monday 27 March, 'and our time is passing wonderfully quickly.' He was surveying and doing the magnetic observations, Levick was taking photographs; Priestley did geology, as well as meteorology and biology. 'We turn to at 7 A.M., breakfast 8, lunch 1, tea 4.30. After tea we knock off work and wash or mend clothes etc. Dinner at 7 and then gramophones, chess or games. We are usually asleep by 11 P.M.'

Campbell's account itemized the activities of the three officers: the three key members on an expedition, navigator, medical man and scientist. In fact, Levick spent much of the 27th trying to find the expedition matches: his ability to lose things was becoming a joke, but also a bit of a worry. Priestley spent the morning helping Campbell survey, the afternoon typing and the evening getting the meteorological log up to date, as well as planning to dredge and fish the following day, the 28th, from the pram, their small Norwegian boat. This turned out to be a fruitless exercise. Priestley took Browning and Dickason: one man hung over the bow of the pram with Borchgrevink's wooden snow-shovel trying to push the fast-forming ice out of the way, one sculled and one tried to fish. Their desire to achieve the first specimens of marine biology resulted in a catch of seaweed and one polychete worm.

The three seamen were busy doing the things they were there for. Everyone shared the same spaces, but in a real sense the men were the staff. Listing the activities of the staff was not something one would generally do: at least, not someone from Campbell's world. On the day that Campbell described the officers' activities Abbott spread sealskins over the roof of the lean-to he was building on the windward side of the hut, as well as spending some hours in the workshop – 'Borchy's hut' – where, responsible for all sewing, he bent his long back over the heavy-duty sewing-machine donated by the Singer Company, capable of sewing anything from silk to thin metal. Browning fixed netting on to the dredge net. In general, Dickason's duties kept him inside, like any housewife or cook. As the expedition's handymen, Abbott, Browning and Dickason performed the many domestic tasks, which included collecting ice for water, bringing up the coal, fixing the stove, throwing the washing-up water and rubbish outside, and fetching food. Each Saturday morning they performed the Saturday scrub-out: 'Lt C, the Dr, and Mr P ', as Abbott always listed them in order of rank in his journal, were pushed out of the door, whatever the weather, having first lifted everything from under their beds on to their beds, while Abbott, Browning and Dickason – the 'scrubbers' – cleaned and washed the hut. For Priestley the weekly task of heaving his boxes of rocks, ice axes and hammers on to his bed was a chore. But the naval tradition, insisted on by Campbell, of a weekly clean kept standards up.

Every evening Abbott had been climbing Cape Adare for the exercise. Once, setting off, he found Campbell driving two penguins towards the hut, so he joined in killing and skinning them instead. Once he slipped on the snow slopes, having dropped his ski stick, but luckily he was with his pal Dick: 'I would have been in an awkward position if by myself.' 'There is a place I go to,' he wrote on the last day of March, 'high up amongst the rocks – I sit down & just feast myself on the glorious scenery until I begin to feel cold – then make my way down.' For Abbott it was 'simply grand'.

In London the news from Antarctica, cabled through by *Terra Nova* from Stewart Island, unleashed shock, disappointment and surprise: Amundsen was in the Bay of Whales; Scott's second base was not at King Edward VII Land but, instead, at Cape Adare.

'Everybody wants to know about Amundsen and to say "Isn't it dreadful?" but I refuse to be worried', Kathleen wrote in her ongoing letter to her husband; 'it is evident there is nothing to be done . . . if the Gods decide agin us, there will be compensations – Bless you my darling one, I have <u>such </u>confidence in you – not that you will necessarily beat Everyone else but that if you lose you will lose with dignity – whatever happens you will do it all<u> right</u>!'

But for Douglas Mawson, in London to raise money for his new expedition from wealthy Australians visiting for the coronation of George V, there was cold fury. The news that Campbell had been inserted exactly where Mawson had informed Scott he intended to put a detachment of his own expedition arrived a week before Mawson was due to speak at the Royal Geographical Society to present his plans. Scott had requested Mawson's plans when *Terra Nova* was in Australia, and Mawson had willingly given them to him. It was a second blow. A few days earlier he had received a polite but regretful letter from Mrs Lysaght in reply to his, concerning the £10,000 donation from her husband that Shackleton had on various occasions assured Mawson was available for the new expedition. 'My husband is ill in a Nursing home . . . I am afraid he would not in any case have been able to support your Expedition, as all that he could afford – indeed more – he did for Sir Ernest Shackleton this time last year. Sir Ernest can, and will no doubt, tell you what that was.' The money had been swallowed up, Mawson had to presume, by Shackleton's various schemes. Although Shackleton had continued to publish his plans to lead an expedition along the northern Antarctic coast during 1910, he had withdrawn in December 1910 as priorities shifted, leaving Mawson as the combined leader and head of science of what was now known as the Australasian Antarctic Expedition.

Kathleen Scott entertained the deeply angry Mawson to lunch on 8 April and found him in 'in a rather bad frame of mind', convinced that Scott had always intended to land a party at Cape Adare and 'hadn't really made a fair try for King E. Land, and so on galore'. Mawson had 'persuaded himself that you had "done him in the eye"', she wrote to her husband. She explained to Mawson how absurd his thinking was and won him round, preventing him from saying 'anything foolish' at his presentation to the Royal Geographical Society; and they had parted 'excellent good friends'. 'I told him I wanted to champion him, but he must play the game better.'

Mawson, addressing the Fellows on Monday 10 April, emphasized the scientific nature of his forthcoming expedition by summarizing current thinking about the shape and form of Antarctica, with its history of past warmth and land connections to Australia, South Africa, South America and New Zealand. Standing tall, speaking incisively, he reminded his audience that his plans were the same as those published the previous year. Now, he explained, owing to unforeseen circumstances there was a change: the intention to drop a few men at Cape Adare must 'in the light of recent events . . . be eliminated from our programme'. He then made clear his views about the ability of men to survive in Antarctica by using seal meat and blubber as food; as far as he, Mawson, was concerned, it was only applicable in a specific context – that is, when sledging over sea ice in early spring.

Major Darwin needed to frame his Presidential response to Mawson's address with care. Darwin's letter to Shackleton of 29 April 1910, stating his understanding of some principles of exploration, was presumably known to Mawson. Shackleton himself was in the audience. Scott had applied the principles to the journey of discovery that *Terra Nova* had just completed along the north coast of Antarctica, having instigated the letter precisely to clear that objective. *Terra Nova* had discovered new land on the coast Mawson had planned to explore: an achievement but, under the circumstances, a little awkward. Darwin's principles also covered Scott's decision to send the Eastern party north, resulting in their establishing themselves at Cape Adare. But now the unexpected, unlooked-for issue of Amundsen had arisen. Amundsen could be considered to have acted within the principles, although obviously unaware of them.

Darwin dealt with the difficulty by shifting his ground. He was glad, he said, addressing the audience, to express 'my own personal opinion that no explorer attains any vested rights merely by exploration, and that we should therefore welcome all foreign scientific competition on the Antarctic continent, wherever it may appear, as long as information is given in good time in advance'. Darwin's letter of 29 April listed neither the doing of science nor the necessity to inform in advance, stating only that 'it would no doubt be very advantageous if explorers would discuss how best to partition the work amongst themselves so as to avoid overlapping as far as possible'.

Exploration, it now appeared, needed two extra characteristics to qualify for Darwin's approval: to be 'scientific' and to be signalled in advance. Mawson's proposed expedition clearly qualified on both grounds, as did Scott's current expedition. They both thus belonged in a different category from Amundsen's. 'I cannot refrain from expressing my regret,' Darwin summarized, 'that Captain Amundsen did not give an opportunity of discussing his Antarctic proposals before he left Europe for the south.' The distinctions had been established; the grounds for objecting to Amundsen's action were in place.

The Royal Geographical Society voted Mawson a contribution of £500 for his newly truncated plans – the same as their grant to Scott, except Scott's had been boosted by more than three times that amount through other ways. Kathleen Scott, attending the meeting, shook hands with Shackleton, but didn't speak to him. However, she invited Mawson to stay, should he wish, and she helped him with finding that latest hope for a technological enabler, an aeroplane. Given the indignation over Amundsen poaching on Scott, Scott apparently poaching on Mawson's long-stated plans risked seeming unattractive. Pennell had held a press conference in Christchurch on 1 April at which he described the new land *Terra Nova* had discovered, but the achievement remained low-key. Scott's expedition was desperately in need of funds to cover a second year, the competition from Amundsen was ominous, and positive publicity was essential. Shackleton, honouring his written obligation to help with fundraising, made a public appeal on behalf of Mawson's Australasian Antarctic Expedition through the *Daily Mail* on 8 May. The resentment expressed by the 'Scottites', who considered that all fundraising should be focused on the needs of Scott's expedition, fanned the flames of old rivalries and competing factions. 'Sir Lewis Beaumont seems rather against Mawson', Kathleen wrote in her ongoing diary for her husband, recording details of the heated London gossip circuit, 'but, curiously enough, doesn't seem much against Shackleton and <u>doesn't know</u> Shackleton dislikes you.' That inveterate old defender of Scott and arch-factionalist Sir Clements Markham, reporting the achievements of Scott's expedition in the Royal Geographical Society journal, set the agenda crudely but clearly. Scott's expedition (unlike, by implication, Amundsen's) 'is a scientific one' which 'includes the south pole in its contemplated work': money is required to support the 'men who are risking their lives for science'. Lieutenant Pennell had had 'a most interesting cruise', discovering new land to the westward in two places. Campbell, 'an expert ski runner, and a man of expedients', is set to make discoveries west of Robertson Bay – a 'region . . . assigned to Scott by agreement . . . Other explorers are of course welcome to co-operate in this or any other direction.'

For Mawson the whole of his stay in London had been 'about as distressing a time as could be imagined'.

8

Living at Cape Adare

10 April–21 July 1911

We worked & ate & read
Did science, went to bed
Priestley, sledging song, April 1911

THE PENGUINS HAD gone from the beach. Pebbles lay in heaps and ridges, future homes and past homes untenanted. Giant petrels no longer sat on the spit. The shallow ponds in their long parallel scoops had frozen over. Darkness came quickly now: the generous, lingering sunsets of late summer were at an end. The place looked bleak when the wind blew from the south, driving fine white drift off the top of Cape Adare, colours draining to greys and blacks and dirty whites. The bitter southerlies sweeping across the three small huts scoured the beach, chiselling out all snow, leaving it icy hard and bare.

Every morning Priestley took the 6.00 meteorological readings, walked along the ice foot for a couple of hours before breakfast, examining it for changes, then spent another couple of hours practising cutting steps in ice and climbing on snow slopes. He was 'as hard as nails', noted Levick admiringly. He never seemed to mind the cold. But Priestley was bored: responsible for a range of sciences, he couldn't get on with any of them except meteorology, a tedious, time-consuming activity that he hadn't been trained in. The geology he could achieve was 'infinitesimal'. His notes on changes in ice formation probably only confirmed work already done. The subject of sea ice needed proper apparatus and technical training, and he had neither. His biological work so far was nil. He was noting everything to do with the weather, but he didn't know what was important. He planned to describe and draw auroras, but that was meagre work, a basic accumulating of information in a haphazard manner. And Priestley was facing his second Antarctic winter in four years. From 19 May the sun would disappear until the end of July: 'if I were a heathen I should be a sun-worshipper & very devout.' Sometimes he walked with others, but mostly he was on his own, a solitary figure beating the bounds of his limitations.

The only civilian and only scientist, joining the expedition late, and a Shackleton man, Priestley was an outsider on many levels. Ten years younger than the other two officers, Levick and Campbell, he even lacked the officer's unofficial badge, a sledging flag. 'Will some kind friend . . . make me a sledge flag', he'd written home urgently, from Cape Evans enclosing a drawing and specifications: he wanted it bright green, 3 feet long, right quarter 3 sharks, left quarter crossed geological hammers, right low 'skull & crossbones', left low 'finger pointing E'. This may be some trouble but I'd be awfully pleased.' There were other layers of tension. He was the only one of the six who didn't smoke. Strong navy tobacco smelt horrible to him, and the smoke could make him feel ill or even vomit. There was no escaping it inside the hut, even less inside a tent, when sledging. Campbell and Levick smoked their pipes together in ritualized ways. Moreover, in the precisely understood but unstated discomfort of social status Priestley was the clear outsider, having been to a grammar school, whereas Campbell, at Eton, and Levick, at St Paul's, had an easy superiority. Priestley had been an undergraduate at Bristol and hadn't finished his degree. On the other hand, he was the only one with Antarctic experience.

During a reasonably friendly argument over lunch about whether girls ought to play hockey with boys, in April Campbell had suddenly 'lost his temper and was exceedingly rude to Priestley in front of the men, and P. replied in the same strain'. As 'no 2 of the party', Levick considered his role was to be a buffer between Campbell and the others, acting for both sides 'in case of unpleasantness arising.' Now he tackled Priestley, 'as I felt sure, knowing Priestley's temper, that he would lose it still further if Campbell spoke to him, and probably create a most uncomfortable situation'. Priestley 'had put himself absolutely in the wrong'. Levick made him promise that 'if ever he was going to have trouble with Campbell, over complaints or any-thing else he would do it privately and not in the presence of the men'. Campbell 'means to be a decent chap,' Levick summarized in his journal, 'and is, on the whole . . .'

Emotions were a privilege. Abbott, Browning and Dickason, like good servants in a household, expressed none in public or were not thought to have any; or if they did have emotions, they were not of significance. Dickason especially, as an able seaman and cook, had an extra layer of anonymity. He tended to be left off lists of expedition members. Here at Cape Adare the three seamen were 'living and messing' with officers. No physical barrier divided the hut, but Levick, as doctor, and second-in-command, did not think there would be trouble. Training was deep: the men knew how to show due respect to, and keep the correct distance from, all officers. Levick considered Abbott a fine man. The navy hierarchy would function down the line, and Abbott, as senior Petty Officer, would keep the two other men in their place, watching that no over-familiarity occurred, even though living was shared. 'We ought to get on all right, and there isn't much chance of their losing their heads.'

But Priestley's experience of Antarctica had been at Cape Royds, under Shackleton as leader, with groupings shifting and realigning, and people falling out but generally getting on. At Cape Adare he had a leader in Campbell who was still feeling his way and adjusting to blighted hopes. Priestley had little experience of operating within the naval code. And he knew what was to come. Sledging meant shared intimacy: pulling together in harness, sleeping and cooking in a small tent, were a very different business from the way they were living in the hut.

Levick had a companion, an unwavering, trusted friend: his dia-ries, good-sized books where he could say what he thought as he thought it, make judgements as freely as he wished. His pen had broken on the voyage out, but he'd managed to get another by swapping his double-barrel 12-bore gun with Bruce for a fountain pen, noting that the relative value of articles in Antarctica changed according to their owners' requirements. Levick enjoyed setting out dialogue. He wasn't yet sure of the subject for the novel he planned to write, but it would be 'good employment for the winter months'.

For Priestley his diaries were part of his plan of work, a record of actions, events and observations of the physical world. Occasionally he described what happened between people, but he was guarded: a copy was being sent to his family. Priestley used shorthand for some of his scientific note-taking. When shorthand appeared in his diary, that was the ultimate privacy. After the argument during lunch on 6 April Priestley wrote one line only, describing Campbell fixing up a tide stake, and concluding 'quiet day'. The days that followed were treated equally sparsely. Campbell had made no entry in his journal since the end of March, then on Sunday 9 April summarized the week as 'calm, snowy and dull', with the time simply flying.

Campbell in his role as leader was isolated. He insisted on naval discipline, with misdemeanours written in the log-book – that is, marked down for future reference in a man's service career. Levick understood the system and worked to it. Close in age, the two officers tended to gravitate to each other, and being paired with Campbell was to Levick's advantage. But Campbell had the frustration of having his job curtailed, by place and time: the little he had to survey needed reasonable weather and daylight, both of which were rapidly diminishing. His opportunities at Cape Adare were limited, as he knew would be the case – not that this made it any easier to bear. For Levick his role as doctor was currently no more than a sensible insurance policy. He'd instituted various procedures, such as testing the hand-grip of each man (he headed the list by a good deal, he noted) and a weekly weighing. His allotted scientific work in zoology was currently non-existent, but as official expedition photographer he could roam at will, and developing and fixing the glass plates kept him busy and engaged.

Mealtimes, those hazardous repositories of individual rituals and personal characteristics, continued vulnerable. Priestley sulked. Campbell was irritable, and rude to Levick. Levick thought Campbell stiff and unimaginative, and his carefulness and caution 'small minded and lacking in guts'. He found his leader's 'uncertain temper' difficult to put up with. After a particularly unpleasant bout one breakfast Levick followed Campbell outside and 'as soon as we were alone fairly let him know he had overstepped the mark'.

All personal space inside the hut was by definition public. Any private conversation had to happen outside, carefully stage-managed, so the intention was not visible; otherwise speculation about what might be being said could flourish, emotional growths in the aridity. Having cleared the air, Levick considered that things were very different, that he and Campbell were that necessary thing, excellent friends. But he could tackle Campbell directly; Priestley, as junior, had to have his annoyance mediated. In the important matter of a harmonious hut Levick was an interventionist.

Levick now decided to tackle Priestley, whom he considered sulky, certainly short-tempered and definitely 'moping'. Levick had to admit Priestley was dedicated and worked with a kind of intense ferocity, but he needed to be jumped out of his miserable mood.

Round 1 took place when Levick and Campbell told Priestley one Sunday how much they liked the girls' faces on the covers of his 'sixpenny novels', discussing which ones they wanted to decorate the spaces by their own beds. Priestley primly noted that 'my rights as purchaser and owner of the books are left out of the question altogether'. The two older men tore the covers off and pinned them up, playing games, drawing on them, turning them over – all harmless enough, big boys teasing the younger boy, except that Priestley didn't understand. Priestley was painfully conscious of the choices he'd made about which photographs to stick on the wall by his bed, the small indications of inner life, his 'gallery' of pictures visible for all to see. He described every one else's gallery: Campbell, being married, had Mrs Campbell and the boy; Levick had his dog; Abbott had a 'perfect galaxy of beauty. He must certainly be a favourite with the ladies.' Browning had 'quite a decent gallery', and Dickason's was 'as small as it can be'. But Priestley, in these few but significant decorations of the hearth that the six feet of personal space in the hut allowed, was far too shy 'to put up those I most care about'. Instead, he had a photograph of Nebuchadnezzar the pet penguin from Shackleton's expedition, a portrait of 'Sir Ernest himself' and a large map of Antarctica. Awkward stuff.

Round 2 involved Priestley having his leg pulled continuously at mealtimes, which Levick decided 'bucked him up quite a lot & he has now started to pull mine in return and is altogether quite another person'. Mutual leg-pulling, with all its shared language and allusions, was one way of being included. Keep someone out of the game, then let them in. Abbott, Browning and Dickason had an unavoidable role, as audience: leg-pulling of officers was not a privilege to be shared by the men. Abbott leaned far in the other direction – always attentive, polite, alert to ways in which he could be helpful, anticipating moods and needs. Browning was his own man. Dickason was an unknown quantity; none of the officers made any assumptions about him. And he was young – only a year older than Priestley.

Round 3, involving Levick pretending after breakfast that his and Campbell's post-breakfast pipes had personalities, provoked a walkout by Priestley. There were limits.

On one of his many days outside, too dark to see much, with 'little to do', Priestley thought up another verse of his 'Sledging Song'. He called it the 'Eastern Party's song 4th verse'.

We then took ship & ventured East with luck more foul than
    fair,
    Tracked the Norski to his lair
    Then turned North to Cape Adare.
Then built our hut & lit our pipes & hibernated there
The winter quickly sped
We worked & ate & read
Did science, went to bed
Dreamt dreams that curled our hair.

For Priestley, their luck had been foul. He was a reluctant hibernator, but the dreams that curled his hair were all about the action to come. He worried about sledging over sea ice: the experience of being adrift on Shackleton's expedition went deep. 'I can't help wishing that half our sledging work was well done & behind us.' Thinking about geology on Cape Adare, 'I hope to put in some days work up there next summer', he noted, 'if we return alive from the coast journey.' Mentioning the possibility of disaster could be a kind of insurance policy, or a sad, poignant leitmotif for future readers of the diary of the deceased, or an outlet for real worries.

The sledging to come rumbled in the background of all their activities. Campbell had announced the plan of campaign soon after arriving. Their reason for being here had to be tackled. They had to try exploring to the west, to achieve what they had come to do. The party would be divided into two teams, Campbell decided. He would take Priestley's experience and Abbott's strength, leaving Levick with Browning, and the advantage of Dickason as cook. But even getting off their beach, let alone travelling along the edge of Robertson Bay, depended on the sea freezing hard enough to trust. Campbell reckoned that the powerful currents sweeping around Cape Adare weakened the ice, while the strong tides in their bay broke it up. The result was unstable, unpredictable sea ice conditions. The inescapable conclusion was that they had to sledge in winter and spring, while the ice was still solid. Two separate sledging parties would therefore leave for the west in mid-August, returning at the end of October. As a precaution Abbott was making various versions of a canoe, or canvas boat, to take with them. Borchgrevink had used a kayak, and Campbell wanted several, so Abbott experimented with a cover of canvas, oiled with melted blubber to make it waterproof, fitted over a sledge; then he tried another, made from the unused curtain material. Both floated very satisfactorily. The boats would add considerably to the weight they had to carry, but if the sea ice did break up, they could escape.

Borchgrevink had made the decision in 1899 that, in general, crossing the sea ice was an unjustifiable risk. The Eastern party would now have the satisfaction of attempting it. Borchgrevink had been criticized in England for failing to break out of the wider prison – for never trying to get beyond Cape North, for failing to penetrate the interior. The Eastern party would now do it. But sea ice was key. With it they could move; without it they were stuck. But even if sea ice formed, the real danger they faced was its stability.

The first of the violent winter storms hit in early May. Pebbles hurled by the wind pounded the wooden sides of the hut, frozen spray drove across the beach, beating against the windows, the roar of the wind, mixed with the din of grinding, screwing pack ice, deafened them. Borchgrevink's descriptions of the ferocity of the Cape Adare storms had been mocked as 'fairy tales'. Now, experiencing hurricane-strength winds, thrown to the ground, blown along on their backs, crawling against the terrific gusts, lost and disoriented in whirling drift only yards from the hut, the six men admitted that, after all, the Norwegian had not exaggerated.

One day in late May they stood amazed, watching as the pressure lifted large pieces of ice bodily up, piling one on to another to create a frozen white wall 150 yards long, with pieces balancing, teetering, then slowly toppling, to push up again and again: the power of ice, the power of the ocean. And always, with anxiety, they watched the ice out in the bay. Unless it built up and then held to become a firm road, they would not be able to start exploring. But always the ice formed, only to be driven out by a hurricane; and the bay was black again, and the sea ran free.

Browning and Dickason had taken over some of the meteorological readings: routine work, requiring attention to detail, well within their capacity, in Priestley's view. Priestley had decided to match Borchgrevink's two-hourly readings, involving a punishing schedule and uncivil hours. But it was difficult, because among all their things they had no alarm clock. Campbell solved the problem by offering a prize for the best invention, which was won immediately by Browning, with an ingenious three-foot-long apparatus involving a bamboo under tension, a burning candle and a pre-wound gramophone. Caruso singing the 'Flower Song' from *Carmen* at full volume became indelibly imprinted on every man's mind as, every night, Browning's 'Carusophone' broke their sleep. But Priestley still fidgeted, reluctant to lose control and delegate: 'To do our men justice they are all jolly keen & the trouble is not to make them take observations but to prevent them from taking them when I am about myself as I wish to get all possible ones myself since I am responsible.'

With opportunity and practice the boundaries between the six men were easing. As the ice at last began spreading across the bay, they could extend their walks out over the frozen ocean, and excursions were made, with different pairings, to photograph a spectacular ice-cave in a trapped iceberg or to the 'two sisters' – pinnacles of rock rising near the tip of the cape, now accessible on foot. Levick was teaching Abbott how to take photographs, and Priestley taught Browning. They were beginning to work through each other's ideas. 'We are having terrific arguments on all sorts of subjects', Priestley reported on 18 May. 'Yesterday the subject for debate was "The Elimination of the Unfit from future generations of Englishmen", today we got on to . . . "The Soul, what is it? & its future existence?"'

In the hut one evening, doing his usual night watch stint, Priestley enjoyed a surprise present, a slice of blackberry tart specially cooked by Dickason for Abbott. Private food. The secret lives of the men. Abbott, Browning and Dickason – Tiny, Rings and Dick to each other – were used to crowded quarters: 'captured young', as Priestley put it. Levick had decided that Dickason, a 'fine chap', should have outside work to get fit for sledging, so Abbott and Browning were taking turns in the galley. Levick now considered Browning clever and useful, although the dire journey across the ice to Hut Point in February had not been forgotten. But the three seamen knew how to watch out for each other. One dark winter morning Dickason overslept.

> I very near caused a sensation in camp this morning, instead of turning out when called I lay on and dropped off to sleep again, when next I woke it was a quarter past eight and I had to have breakfast ready by half past, so by flying around and putting the clock back twenty minutes I had things ready when the others turned out. Of course I readjusted the clock at the first opportunity, or at least 'Rings' did the trick whilst I screened him, very narrow shave. 'You blighter!'

Ice in the bay brought the first seals looking for clear water to haul out and rest on the floes. Campbell shot two of them, and Levick and the men skinned and cut them up, which was cold work. Next day the meat had to be hacked out of the floe, where the bodies had frozen to the surface: a lesson learned. But the sea ice required constant alert attention. One afternoon in fine calm weather, walking out alone across the sea ice, Abbott stopped to admire an ice formation. He took a step forward, his foot broke straight through and he only saved himself by instantly throwing his weight backwards. 'If I had gone in I don't know how I should have got out again.'

Rubbish thrown outside the door was becoming a hazard: tins, ashes and kitchen waste stuck together in unpleasant icy heaps. Browning found two of Borchgrevink's old skis, fixed a box on top and make a neat small sledge. Abbott and Priestley disinterred the mess with pick and shovel, splinters of icy nastiness flying up into their faces and melting, releasing trapped smells, while Browning dragged loads a couple of hundred yards further off with his sledge. 'As Abbott said today', noted Priestley, 'he, Browning and I make a good working combination. I suggest what work ought to be done; he does it, & B. thinks of ways to make it easier.' Maintaining the buildings, contents and equipment, involved constant effort. Priestley: 'Our domestic arrangements are improving day by day.' On the other hand, their hut seemed worryingly vulnerable to the severe winter storms. After a particularly violent hurricane on 19 June, with the hut shaking and creaking, things tumbling off the shelves, Priestley found pieces of weatherboarding stripped off the outside. 'Methinks that this hut will make no long survival when left to itself down here', he wrote. 'It will be demolished piece-meal until the wind gets a firm hold & then "Goodbye hut".'

Borchgrevink's living hut, intensely cold and ill lit, was generally the men's space, except that now it was doubling as a gym, equipped by Abbott with a couple of rope rings and a punching ball, until the rubber became brittle. Abott made a set of boxing gloves, padding woollen mitts with seaweed quilting sewn outside other mitts, and offered to teach Priestley boxing. The two men sparred by the light of guttering candles, but it was so cold and dark that they could barely see each other through the icy clouds of vapour. Equipment for fencing took longer to achieve: Abbott fashioned sabres from split bamboo and 'two capital tin helmets' made out of old flour tins, worn over a woollen helmet. He and Levick fought, at sabres, on a good stretch of smooth snow just outside the hut, solemn and competitive, on a Sunday in June, at −27° F. Levick: 'I think I am a slightly better fencer than he is.' Abbott: 'I think he is improving.' Then the two men rigged up a line and did high-jumping. Abbott, the navy physical education instructor, and Levick, the navy surgeon specializing in physical health, both weighing around 12½ stone, the two heaviest men in the party, jumping over a rope in the noonday twilight of midwinter, each trying to beat the other.

The existence of Borchgrevink's living hut and store hut was an extraordinary boon, providing somewhere else to go. Even then the multiple functions of the expedition hut added tension to tolerance.

The expedition hut was dining-room, galley and bedroom. It was also the laundry: each man was allocated a day to do his washing, with various methods advocated but the result always tedious hours spent wringing out waterlogged woollen singlets and heavy shirts. It also served as the bathroom: each man with the right to a weekly bath after collecting the ice to melt into water and then setting up the tin bath on the hut floor. Every Sunday it became, briefly, church, and at allocated times each day it was the space in which to relax; most evenings someone volunteered to attend to the almost full-time business of changing the records on the gramophone. It was also a work space. Campbell used the chart table beside his bed. Priestley sat most hours that he had free at the central table, keeping the meteorological log up to date, or his various diaries, or banging out on the typewriter reports and notes, or a revised fair copy of his personal diary. There may have been no escape from the smell of tobacco, but there was no escape either from the peck-peck-peck of Priestley's fingers relentlessly hitting the keys, as he dealt with a permanent state of 'arrears'. Cessation only came out of consideration when someone was ill.

The greatest cause of dissension was temperature. Campbell felt the cold dreadfully and claimed he was unable to write, or work, if it fell too low. 'What he will do during spring sledging', said Levick, 'the Lord only knows.' The cooking stove was too small to heat their hut. With much difficulty and the odd breakage they moved in the much bigger stove from Borchgevink's hut, but getting it fired up took time and ingenuity. 'Everybody was in the best of spirits to-day, while we were labouring under difficulties', Abbott observed, 'so everything went off A.1. & we are still living in hope.' The hut warmed enough for Campbell but was now too hot for everyone else. Levick wanted the hut kept at 35° F, and Campbell wanted it at the 'fearful heat' of 50°, but Priestley said it sometimes got to the 'almost tropical' temperature of 65° and he couldn't work. At the same time constant war raged between Campbell and Levick over ventilation, with Levick insisting on the daily need to open the door and air the living space for about five minutes. Soon, commented Priestley caustically, everyone will be sledging and 'then will live in a draught but without such a range of temperature'.

The acetylene lighting plant was the other great hut irritation. The

Browning stuck his Midwinter Day menu card, designed and illustrated by Campbell, in the back of his diary.

light was either brilliant or increasingly insufficient. Campbell could not stand the smell, and 'comes down heavily on the men whenever there has been the slightest escape. In consequence . . . they have been afraid to get any pressure up on the generators.' Priestley complained that he had to work ten or twelve hours a day reading notes and writing, which strained his eyes and gave him neuralgic headaches. Abbott, Browning and Dickason, as domestics, were responsible for the efficient running of the hut's services; but, as with wives or children, they expressed no preferences about quantity or quality of heat or light.

Routine and order were part of Campbell's method to get through the day, the week, the month. The regulation naval breakfast hour every morning ended with Campbell issuing the orders for the day, followed by the essential winding of the chronometers at nine o'clock. The weekend had its rhythm of Saturday morning scrub-out and Saturday night dinner with toasts to wives and sweethearts, followed by Sunday off, after church. Interspersed were celebrations: everyone's birthday, Campbell's ninth wedding anniversary, even Eton's traditional 'Glorious Fourth', celebrated in Antarctica on 4 June with a bottle of sherry. Midwinter Day on 22 June, the Antarctic Christmas, the central point of the winter, was marked, Campbell thought, with 'great pomp'. His elegant little watercolours of seals, penguins and the *Terra Nova* adorned each man's menu card. He sat at the head of the table, Priestley and Levick to his right, Abbott and Browning to his left, and Dickason at the other end near the cooking, with one string of small paper flags and two sledging flags strung across the table and the washing still hanging from the line, but that couldn't be helped. Browning had edged the bookshelves with the red braid that once decorated the coats of Borchgrevink's sledge dogs, adding a touch of homeliness. They each had a half-pint bottle of champagne and drank the health of everyone at Cape Evans, then dived their hands into a bran dip for little presents provided by Kathleen Scott. Priestley's haul was a packet of pencils (useful for the Met Office, he thought), a set of crayons (useful for those who 'indulge in sketching') and a necklace of green and white beads (usefulness unspecified). Levick showed his photograph album, and there was a general grabbing for the lids of the cracker boxes because they had pictures. Abbott suggested everyone should sing a song and 'some of them' – including Campbell – 'sang in company for the first time; it was great'. Priestley sang the 'Eastern Party sledging song' with 'great style', according to Dickason, 'and altogether we had a very good nights sport enjoyed ourselves immensely, and are now looking forward to our sledging work in the spring.'

To the south, at Amundsen's hut, Framheim, almost buried under snow on the Barrier, Midwinter Day gave way to St Hans's Eve on 23 June, celebrations starting with the inauguration of the sauna and pink, clean, happy bodies in an ice-walled steam room.

At Cape Evans, on a superb still night with 35° of frost and the stars so bright, so crowded in the sky, that they gave enough light to make the night not seem dark, the men sat down to their Midwinter dinner assisted by fifty bottles of Heidsieck 1904 champagne under a heraldic array of sledging flags, with Antarctic images painted on their menu cards by Wilson and a speech by Captain Scott. The speech did not say very much, was uninspired even, but this was Scott's third Antarctic winter and he had a great deal on his mind. At lunch there had been amused readings from the first edition of the 'South Polar Times', edited with assiduous attention by Cherry-Garrard; everyone gathered around Scott at the head of the table 'like a lot of school girls round a teacher', trying to guess who had written what. Wilson had contributed a cartoon on expedition activities in ancient Egyptian style, in which the absent Abbott featured as a builder, all glorious muscles and profile. After dinner Ponting showed lantern slides of the expedition, Oates danced the Lancers with Anton, and the Christmas tree made by Bowers out of a ski-stick and feathers made its entrance, with 'little presents for all of us', said Gran, 'laying aside the distinction between officers and men'. Speeches were required from everyone. 'It is not easy to make such a speech in the competitor's camp', Gran worried, but everyone clapped afterwards. So he thought it must have been all right.

In New Zealand, Harry Pennell had a tracing made of the part of his chart giving the track of *Terra Nova* along the coast that Mawson had planned to cover in his expedition, and he sent it to Mawson with *Terra Nova*'s good wishes and a summary of his conclusions.

And far to the north, in London, Midwinter Day was Midsummer Day, the coronation of George V and Queen Mary, the formal ceremony and pageantry of royalty in London, the high point of this celebratory summer season. Kathleen Scott watched the procession from Admiralty House, and at lunch 'we all drank your health . . .

and tried to imagine your midsummer festivities'. In the Cape Evans hut the King and Queen hung prominently, because Cherry-Garrard, returning to *Terra Nova* after everything for winter quarters had been unloaded, had removed the portraits from the wardroom and skied back, bringing George the naval king and Queen Mary, with her pearls, across the white sea to their new home.

The morning after Midwinter dinner at Cape Adare both Campbell and Levick had fat heads, but alcohol was regulated carefully and there were not many opportunities to indulge. Campbell was making minimal journal entries. They were to the point, as always, but he was eliding dates, occasionally attaching an event to an incorrect date. Levick, too, was ignoring his journal for days at a time, being 'very slack'. He was even late celebrating his thirty-fourth birthday, on 3 July, but this year it did not really feature. A July birthday in England was sunshine, and delicious teas under spreading trees; here at Cape Adare it was darkness, and a freezing wind. At home in England he would be riding his motor bike down country roads. The second week of the thirty-fourth tennis championships at Wimbledon was under way, in a summer of extraordinary heat. Browning had cut out portraits of three society beauties from the illustrated magazines and stuck them at the back of his diary. Here it was every day the same faces, and the same talk. There was no escape.

But it was more difficult than that. Levick told his diary that Priestley could not stand being with Campbell, and that he and Priestley spent time together criticizing Campbell; Levick preferred being with Priestley but, remaining 'outwardly friendly', walked and talked with Campbell. Levick analysed his leader's failings. 'He is not a bad chap', but, and this was serious criticism from Number 2, 'hopelessly out of place as a leader, being much too self-conscious and lacking most sadly in guts.' 'I am, I think,' summarized Levick, 'establishing an ascendancy over Campbell, which has been a good thing in many ways, as I am gradually getting him out of many of his fads.'

By the middle of July a tiff between Levick and Campbell about trimming coal on the ship had escalated. Campbell's face was small and tight. He avoided talking to Levick. He did not look anyone in the eye. Taking the opportunity of Campbell going outside before

135

lunch one day, Levick followed and caught him up. The two men stood on piled pebbles in the dim light and below zero temperatures, between the ice grating on the shore and the great hulk of the cape. Speaking in his role as doctor, Levick told Campbell he was suffering an attack of 'polar ennui'. '[T]o put it plainly, you have got the hump'. Having brought grievances out into the open, and delivered a confident assessment of depressed behaviour, wrapped up in other phrases – 'many a fine chap has had it', 'it's nothing out of the common', 'it's not surprising' – Levick prescribed a tonic 'which will make you feel another man'. All the petty but significant details of lives lived too closely could overwhelm. There was no escape from the pressures of darkness and the long winter. But Priestley in his journal made no comments about Campbell. Campbell mentioned only Levick's general inefficiency, in passing, but little else. The accounts of Campbell and Priestley continued to describe busy, co-operative lives. Stress or distress – neither was mentioned.

During this same half of July, with the darkness of the winter sky pierced by the 'battered half of a crescent . . . dull red in colour', as observed by Dickason, enough light was reflected from the growing moon for Dickason and Abbott to have 'good sport' skiing down the snow slopes. 'The moon was . . . making everything look beautiful', Browning wrote, an alternative light in their sunless world. He did the cooking so Dickason could have a day outside on the 4th. Dickason, physically tough, enjoyed his time away from the galley. The weather was a constant interest to him. He took it as it came, with few complaints, greeting frostbiting winds and extreme cold with a cheerful 'What ho' the <u>noses</u>.'

The usual wind got up from the south on the 7th, bringing the roar of pressure ice from the ocean behind the cape, and blinding drift. In a couple of hours all the snow had blown away, leaving the spaces bare again. It was very cold. Abbott was making linen bags for geological specimens in Borgy's hut, but the scissors, and any other metal he touched, burnt his fingers. Sledging gear needed preparing, and he was working on yet another canvas boat. He was also doing his usual jobs – maintenance on the huts, sledging in ice for water, sledging out rubbish, taking his turn in the galley – and working with Priestley on various ice projects, as well as helping Campbell with the tedious and precise taking of the magnetic dip observations. But in between he walked, ranging far out over the sea ice; he went for a run, did his Swedish exercises, worked in the gym and remembered his mother's birthday. He noticed that a radiant light ran through Venus, newly visible, and he thought, while gazing at the stars, of home and friends on the other side of the world. And he invented a patent nose protector, then cut Browning's hair and made a little paintbrush, using the hair, and a quill from a giant petrel. His journal continued the same outward-facing, enthusiastic, humorous tone it had had from the start of the journey: completely consistent.

Priestley was now over-working, sea ice in the bay having widened the scope for possible scientific activities. His ice notes became copious. He and Campbell tried to install a tide gauge lent from the university in Sydney. Holes were made through the sea ice to take soundings, but they kept closing up. With Browning and Dickason as uncomplaining assistants, Priestley made valiant attempts at marine biology. Any specimen was better than none: all 'collecting' was evidence of work done in Antarctica. But the sea-bed stubbornly refused to yield anything except eight whelks and a worm, found by Campbell and preserved in a bottle. Repeated attempts at fishing were barren. Borchgrevink had been heavily criticized for losing the collections made by the natural history specialist Nicolai Hansen, who had died tragically at Cape Adare in October 1899. Now Priestley couldn't even find any specimens. 'The Biology of the Eastern Party is still, in spite of every effort we have made, nil.' But he found time to write a set-piece statement in his journal, 'in case of any accident during sledging making it impossible for me to do them justice later', acknowledging the three seamen for their willingness to go out of their way to do science, whether they could see any result or not, and for all their ungrudging help.

Priestley was beginning to suffer from another polar complaint, except that it went unrecognized. He had lost his sleep pattern, and was staying up much of the night working at the table, surrounded by the noises of men sleeping, the coughs and snores and restless mumblings. 'I am writing these notes at midnight & still have over four hours of solitude in front of me as I have every night now, so I have plenty of time to meditate on my imperfections.' Then he was sleeping 'all light hours' in bed, surrounded by the action of the day and missing meals. There were compensations. He'd managed to interest himself, and Abbott, in auroras, taking copious notes. One day he hoped to be able to work on some of the physics of whatever · it was that was happening. Now, most evenings, he could catch the brief glory of the southern aurora. Here, so close to the South Magnetic Pole, it was truly magnificent, a performance of virtuosity. Sometimes solo instruments, sometimes the full orchestra of colour, and tempo, and form, white-silver and violet and rich crimson, greens and deep golden yellow, vivid, or subtle; curtains of shimmering light undulating, sudden shifts to flashing searchlights, to unfolding tails of sinuous beauty, to echoes, and reawakening; but always every performance in total soundlessness.

On 21 July, the night after his twenty-fifth birthday (celebrated with tomato soup and a health drink at dinner), Priestley typed up three copies of three or four favourite hymns to use on their sledge journeys on Sundays, or – if they got delayed – to have available to use, until their return 'next year'. The anticipation of the sledging to come was making them all restless. Browning shaved off his whiskers, in preparation, but Dickason was keeping his until the last minute. Priestley thought that they were like 'a hive of bees, before the swarm'. But there was an unexpected pleasure. Everyone had joined together to make Priestley his longed-for sledging flag. The design was his, but Abbott did the sewing and Campbell the decoration, and Levick contributed a precious silk handkerchief. Luckily a St George's cross using the braid from two of Borchgrevink's dog coats looked so nice that Priestley decided not to spoil the effect and to leave adding the Latin motto until he got back home. He and Levick had laboured over the wording. He preferred 'whatever I have I hold' – but 'they say "I hold my own & take thine" is very appropriate given my acquisitive character.'

9

The uncertainty of the ice

27 July–16 August 1911

Us four will have to take as much as possible and get as far
as we can.

Harry Dickason, August, 1911

LEVICK FELT LIKE he used to before an exam. Sledging was getting closer and closer, yet the sun hadn't reappeared, and the
wind was still bitterly cold. After the evening meal had been cleared
on Thursday 27 July, everyone stayed sitting around the table while
Levick gave instructions in basic medicine and surgery, broken arms,
broken legs, actions in case of accidents. Campbell made careful
notes: symptoms of concussion and treatment; what to do for an
operation ('dip knife or instrument in boiling water for 1 minute').
He sketched how to use a hypodermic syringe, noting doses of mor-
phine for a good night's sleep or for an operation.

Everyone was going sledging, which meant leaving the hut empty.
That meant interrupting data collection for science, but exploring
took precedence. Campbell, with Priestley and Abbott, would get as
far west as possible. Levick, leading a support party with Browning
and Dickason, would bring out provisions for a depot, and another
later, as long as conditions were good. Campbell couldn't estimate
daily distances, because he was ignorant of the conditions along their
route, so the length of time their supplies would last could not be
calculated, and no basis for the essential calculations could be established until they started sledging. However, if all went well, everyone
would be back home around the beginning of November, unless –
he used careful words – 'detained by ice-troubles'. If they couldn't
get back, they would 'make the best of things' and live in a snow hut

on seal, waiting until next year's ice was strong enough for them to return, as per Scott's instructions.

It was all very matter-of-fact, except that, with the exception of Priestley, they had never explored while man-hauling a loaded sledge or set up camp after exhausting days in the harness, least of all in winter. Their understanding of how to travel over sea ice was minimal. Winter sledging was harshest of all. Darkness, and cold, had specific disadvantages. A modicum of visibility was necessary to travel over sea ice, and extreme cold was exhausting and slowed actions down. Campbell was a competent skier and had, with his Norwegian experience, a proper respect and some understanding for snow and ice. But, as Levick pointed out, someone would have to come with Browning, Dickason and himself, 'to show us how to look after ourselves'.

Priestley thought both teams would benefit from a trial trip. So it was decided that Campbell, Priestley and Abbott would leave with a fortnight's provisions on 29 July, the first day after the return of the sun – as long as fine weather held. Priestley was feeling relaxed enough not to write final letters to his family. There was always a chance of accidents while working in Antarctica, and this trip shouldn't be any more dangerous than that. But after Levick's medical talk Priestley ran and walked from 10.30 p.m. until 1.00 a.m. south along the sea ice, for 8 miles, then back again, arriving at 3.30 a.m. wet through. He wanted to be 'hard and fit' for the sledge trips. As he walked, he checked for places where in an emergency they could scramble up the cliff from the sea ice, except that out here, alone at night on the sea ice, it was Priestley who was at risk. And, trying to make the switch from night work to day work, he still couldn't sleep.

On Saturday 29 July 1911 the Eastern party's first sledging expedition set off. Campbell, Priestley and Abbott harnessed up, then guided their carefully packed sledge across pressure ice and out on to the sea ice, a difficult surface, salt-flecked and sticky. It was 'desperate hard pulling'. The additional weight of Priestley's geological hammers didn't help. They camped after 10 miles, before Warning Glacier – named by Borchgrevink, because the glacier disappeared from view when a blizzard was on its way. The next morning they were so tired they overslept, and camped after only 6 miles well out on sea ice that was too salty to turn into drinking water, which meant they were miserably thirsty.

On Monday the 31st they glimpsed the returning sun for the first time, a red ball rolling briefly above the horizon at noon; and that afternoon they camped on Duke of York Island at the base of Robertson Bay. Getting across Robertson Bay was the first stage of any journey west. But already their sleeping-bags had frozen. Priestley demonstrated how to bend and pummel the stiff frozen reindeer skin to prise away some of the inside ice layer, but it wouldn't all shake out and on Tuesday morning, 1 August, their sleeping bags as well as their sleeping clothes were wet and sopping. 'One's breath is the trouble,' Campbell reckoned, 'having to sleep with one's head inside. The breath saturates the bag, during the day this turns to ice.'

Part of the misery of winter sledging was lack of sleep, but the little they had been getting was becoming less. The three men sat on their rolled-up, already partly refrozen bags inside their crowded little tent, feeling around for whatever they'd put down, or lost, in the kind of light Priestley called a visible darkness, too cold to take off their mitts but not knowing what they might have got hold of, because hands in mitts can't discriminate. Campbell and Abbott lit up their after-breakfast pipes filled with strong navy tobacco, and Priestley, clammy and shaking with nausea at the smell after a particularly greasy breakfast, pushed outside and vomited.

A hut of rocks had been built on Duke of York Island by Borchgrevink. Campbell, Priestley and Abbott spent the day exploring; but, despite searching, they couldn't find this additional bit of local accommodation. It was snowing, and a soft white layer covered the rocks, filling the gaps between, masking where to put their feet, making geology impossible. The three men were wearing their gaberdine wind-proofed clothes – a loose smock tied around the bottom and neck with that all-purpose cord, lamp wick, and trousers (with no opening) similarly secured. Sewing the back of a wind-helmet on to the smock allowed it to be 'carried as one garment', an approximation to the hood as an integral part of the jacket, Eskimo-style, as used by Amundsen. Snow could be brushed off gaberdine, but snow that landed on clothing made of wool or ordinary cloth caked in minutes, forming a carapace, melting and soaking in, the moment the crystals warmed. Wet jumpers and trousers heavy with their load of absorbed moisture were an extra, miserable hazard of their winter or spring travel, with no chance to dry anything.

They had only poked at the door leading to the west. But, four days into their journey Campbell made the decision to turn for home. The recent snow meant hauling their sledge over the sea ice was even more difficult, and on Wednesday 2 August they only managed to travel a mile an hour. Campbell thought 'we might as well have been pulling over gravel'. Experiences for Campbell were not located within a framework of luck. His interest was the physical realities, his comments generally confined to terse description. But now, with bad weather threatening, they headed off the sea ice and pitched their tent under the ice cliffs, sheltered from the rising wind. Abbott walked up and down, giving Campbell and Priestley first chance to get out of their frozen clothes and into their frozen bags. Then he crawled in to perform the same task, squeezing down between them.

At 9.00 p.m. a terrific din woke them. The wind had changed direction, and furious gusts now punched at their tent, dislodging the blocks they'd piled on the lee-side skirting. Drift was sweeping inside through an ominous gap. Campbell rolled out of his bag, grabbed the skirting of the tent and shouted to the others to do the same – they had minutes only before the tent blew away. Abbott, according to Campbell, had time to crawl outside in a lull, pile more ice blocks on the skirting and then get back in again before the next squall. Priestley said that Abbott had time to force himself into his wind clothes – frozen since he'd taken them off earlier – before crawling outside. But Abbott's story was different: ordered by Campbell, he said, he crawled outside still in his sleeping clothes, into 'the bosom of a howling blizzard – got the shovel & as best as I was able, piled Ice on the skirting. I was blown off my feet once & skidded along the snow.' Luckily he hit the sledge, which helped him find the tent again. Back inside, Priestley lent him a woollen pyjama jacket because his sleeping clothes were now sopping wet. Priestley then instructed Abbott to wedge himself against a section of the tent, where 'within an hour' he heard Abbott snoring.

I was not, however, so fortunate myself, but remained awake all night, holding on to the tent with my head, shoulders and one elbow, and half out of my sleeping-bag most of the time . . . Campbell was also awake for most of the night, and . . . he also was as uncomfortable as could be wished. About 4 a.m. I changed places with Abbott to ease my cramped muscles, but failed to discover the secret which enabled him to sleep, for I was kept awake by sundry blows on the neck delivered by the flapping canvas.

Abbott said that, having 'managed at last to doze off although my head was getting shook about by the bellying of the Tent', he was woken up 'to change places with Mr P, as he could not get any sleep in his billet'. After a struggle they managed to exchange positions.

Mr P said he was no better off in his new position. I was soon dozing again when I was wakened by Lt C asking me to look out for the skirting on his side as well as mine (a bit of a job) I said alright & continued to battle with my side which kept bellying in & flapping violently. Once more I heard a voice: Lt C said I had been asleep – it was a puzzle to me if I was . . . however I continued to keep watch at last the wind eased & we all got to sleep.

Pulling 'for all we were worth' the next morning, Thursday, they struggled a few miles before having to camp. Campbell was determined to get home on Friday the 4th, so they started early, slogging painfully, until finding a sheltered spot to leave their sledge, they slung their sleeping-bags over their shoulders on ski-sticks – uncomfortable and inefficient – and set off like burdened beetles on the final 11 miles.

The three men left at Cape Adare worried what had happened to their companions in the blizzard and decided to organize a search party. But first they walked a little way, in the hope of finding them returning, and met them 3 miles from the hut. Campbell, Priestley and Abbott were treated 'to cigarettes & the latest news (Local). We were all thirsty & drank lots of lime juice, tea, etc. Had a bath & shaved & felt A.1. after a good Dinner.' Each man was weighed. In seven days Campbell had lost 3 lb, Priestley 5 lb and Abbott 9 ¼ lb, leaving him, he recorded, 11 stone 12 ¼ lb. Priestley had a terrific sugar urge, eating raspberry jam by the bottle and bags and bags of toffees.

Campbell had rethought his plans as he trudged along, his canvas waistband pressing against his stomach, the jerk of the heavy sledge behind, monitoring weather and surface, making a succession of repetitive judgements about both. The slow progress was deeply discouraging. They'd been travelling near the coast to enable them to camp on or near land as a safety precaution. On the big journey to the west, Campbell decided, he would have to take the risk and head straight across the sea ice. Most importantly, three men were simply not enough in these conditions of heavy pressure and bad surface. He would have to add a fourth man, and he chose Dickason. Dickason with Levick and Browning had been planned as a supporting team, laying a depot at Smith's Inlet, '70 miles from here', for Campbell's party on their return. Now, as Dickason said, 'Us four will have to take as much as possible and get as far as we can.' Levick and Browning as a two-man team would have to stay generally at the hut, but scientific record-keeping would gain. Browning could deal with the meteorological and other readings, and Levick could get on with his zoological work, which would start with spring.

Given the change in plans, Levick's baptismal first sledging experience could be reduced to a two- or three-day excursion, filming the beauty of Warning Glacier, with its face of striated ice, stripes of glass-green and utter blue. Even then Levick needed a coach and chaperone. Neither Campbell nor Priestley wanted to go, so Campbell dealt with the problem by a gambling word game, which Priestley won. But Priestley realized he'd spelt his word wrong, and 'a hereditary Nonconformist conscience which has frequently given me trouble forced me to own up'. Levick was officially in charge of the party, but he had no experience of leading in these conditions. Priestley had the right to advise, so it was complicated.

The nature of Campbell's leadership was taking time to evolve. The three seamen, when occasion arose, were dealt with according to unyielding rules and stark hierarchy. But within and around that, co-operation could quietly happen. Campbell discussed certain decisions with both officers. He delegated. Levick had competed for the role of actual as opposed to titular leader of the six of them as a group, but in the business of exploring and discovery Campbell had a clear advantage, and it was becoming increasingly obvious that in this context Levick, despite his role as second-in-command, was less of a player and more of a participant. By preference a man of action, Campbell was at last doing what he had come to do. His summers spent in Norway gave him confidence; he had some of his own well-chosen equipment to use; and he was happy to work with Priestley, drawing on his knowledge. Priestley had been given responsibility for sledging preparations, 'as I have had previous experience'.

Abbott's knee had worried him sledging. Back at the hut, running along the ice edge, it gave way. All plans utterly depended on each man's fitness, and Levick ordered Abbott to bed. Levick then left on Tuesday 8 August with Priestley, Browning and Dickason on his trial expedition. 'I am cook, bottle washer, meteorologist, etc. etc. etc.', wrote Campbell, forced into unaccustomed activities, only partially performed. But Campbell couldn't cook and never had. The first day he achieved a pot of tea, the next he tried frying seal's liver. 'Leather!' said Abbott amiably, 'such good exercise masticating it', having got up at 4.00 and 7.30 to stoke the fire, woken Campbell to take the 8.00 a.m. met readings and cleared up after meals. On Thursday, despite serious pain, he cooked breakfast, went out to take the met observations and prepared for the homecoming of the other four.

Competition and co-operation were both essential to success and to survival. Competition defined and maintained status; co-operation was about trading. Competition could push men to their limits, physical and emotional. Co-operation could lead men to find limits they didn't necessarily know were there, or mattered. In these unten-anted spaces the rasping edge of competitiveness could peck away at relationships. Priestley's competitiveness was endemic. He had started a new diary that, unlike his previous diaries, had no mechanism for producing a copy for his family. With the removal of this constraint, like an ever-present moral tutor, Priestley was becoming more open about his feelings. 'L. is accusing me of sneaking his matches but that is an everyday occurence & I am used to.' Each man had to carry his sleeping bag on Levick's practice expedition, and Abbott made carrying slings out of curtain material and white cord. 'I'm proud of the way I carried my bag (the other two were less efficient)', Priestley boasted to himself. But there were benign forms of competition, and a kind of camaraderie of rivalry had developed between him, Dickason and Abbott, each competing over who could observe the most auroras, especially during the unsociable 4.00 a.m. slot. A notebook had already been filled. The notes could end up being of no value, Priestley confided to his journal; but at least they were thorough.

As a sportsman and athlete, Levick competed at every opportunity, but as a doctor he worked generally on the principle of co-operation, sharing his knowledge, giving advice, careful and attentive when his medical skills were needed. The *sine qua non* of the three seamen's selection was their ability to co-operate. Abbott, constantly alert to ways of being helpful, to the requirements of the officers, to the greater good of the expedition, was the best example. On a separate level Abbott, Browning and Dickason co-operated with each other, as friends, but also as a practical way of handling their dual roles of included and excluded.

Anyone reading Borchgrevink's book would know that co-operation had been a scarce resource on his Southern Cross expedition. Deep divisions had scarred relations between Borchgrevink, as leader, and some of his men. The inner circle of British exploring and Antarctic devotees had treated the Southern Cross expedition as unacceptable competition and ignored its achievements. Priestley, Campbell and Levick considered Borchgrevink's book as relevant for fireside pseudo-explorers only, of no use to those (few) men who might come after him, seeking detailed data. And the man wrote like a foreigner; he didn't use English correctly. Now they were here, they were beginning to admit, a little shame-facedly, that there was value in aspects of Borchgrevink's account. The young Australian physicist Louis Bernacchi, subsequently a member of Scott's *Discovery* expedition, had also written about the expedition at Cape Adare, but his book had not been included in Scott's library. Priestley regretted how few books they had that described exploring in Antarctica, but 'we read and reread what we have'.

Abbott's knee continued a problem. On Saturday 12 August 'the

Doctor came & sat by my bed-side after breakfast & all the others gathered round the fire which is near my bed, and we had a very lively conversation on the chances of Capn Scott & Amundsen getting to the pole.' Scott and his three-man Polar party would have an easy time getting up to the polar plateau, they concluded, because all their supplies would be carried for them by the motors, animals and support parties. Their strength intact, they could then dash for the Pole. Amundsen, on the other hand, had a problem. His dogs wouldn't be able to climb the glacier, so he and his men would have to haul their own sledges up – a hard job.

Then Campbell and Levick knocked out their pipes and left the hut with Priestley. Dickason and Browning did the Saturday scrub-up, while Abbott lay in bed, feeling strange because he wasn't helping. 'The final result of our consultation', Abbott wrote in his journal, 'was that it would be a near thing. I say jolly good luck to those who get there whoever they are.'

Scott, at Cape Evans this Saturday, 12 August, was pondering ways to diminish the ponies' suffering from snow-blindness on the polar journey: dyeing their forelocks dark? A sun bonnet? The talk by Oates in the weekly lecture series on horse management on Thursday had inspired much discussion. Then there was the even more serious problem of the ponies' snowshoes. 'Petty Officer Evans has been making trial shoes for Snatcher on vague ideas of our remembrance of the shoes worn for lawn mowing', Scott wrote. The ponies, their numbers reduced after various disasters in March, would drag loads as far as they could before being killed for meat. One of the two ponies returned by Campbell had died, but the other, Jehu, was a useful addition. The dogs would travel some way across the Barrier before turning back, and both motor sledges would get as far as they were capable; then three teams of four men, including the final polar team of four (participants as yet undecided), would tackle the Beardmore Glacier, man-hauling their sledges, with the loads. First one support party, then the other, would turn back, leaving only the Polar party to go forward, the head of an arrow sped onwards by the efforts of ponies, dogs and motors, and the strength and determination of dedicated men.

Clissold, the cook, had taken over two dogs pronounced useless by Meares and trained them. After church on Sunday the 13th Clissold borrowed a lead dog and drove his team of three to Cape Royds, with Gran skiing alongside. Shackleton's hut required some skill to access, but it had become unexpectedly useful as a general store and occasional recreational bolt-hole. Clissold and Gran settled down, made a fire, ate some of Shackleton's delicious food and then brought back a load of 100 lb per dog, in two hours, which Scott noted in his journal as a good performance. Clissold's loot was a ski-sledge and a case of kitchen utensils, Gran's a toboggan and illustrated magazines. Gran observed the way the dogs responded to him as he skied back. 'The dogs are stimulated by the swish of the skis and get the feeling they have a goal to aim at.' For the first time – through this chance opportunity – Gran experienced the co-operation possible between skier and dog. It made him very thoughtful. 'From what I have seen today . . . I believe Amundsen has a very great chance of getting good results with his animals.' The minimum temperature at Cape Evans that day was −40°F.

At Framheim the same Sunday, a minimum of −74.2°F was recorded; the Barrier was much colder than Amundsen had expected. Amundsen's men were working on equipment for the Pole journey, labouring in a range of ice rooms they had dug into the Barrier, cocoons of industry. Sledges, their weight reduced to the least they dared, were being lashed together, and wind-clothing and under-clothing of light flannel were being made on the sewing-machine.

At Cape Adare, Priestley walked north over the sea ice on Monday the 14th, towards the tip of the cape. To his horror he found lanes of open water. Crystals of ice had already formed across the surface, resulting in a thick transparent sludge. The implications for sledging were dire: it would be impossible to force a canvas boat through this kind of surface, but equally impossible to sledge over it. Open water, here, was an 'alarming indication of local instability'. Priestley simply did not trust sea ice. He'd fallen through twice more since the time when the motor sledge sank at Cape Evans. 'I don't want to be an awful example for the next explorer.'

On Tuesday the 15th at breakfast another winter blizzard started, punching drift across the beach, tiny grains of snow hitting exposed skin in sharp stabs of pain. As the wind built, pebbles were scooped up and flung like missiles. The meteorological readings could be done only by crawling on all fours. The ink froze in their fountain pens. Before midnight the wind's speed seemed to double, sweeping down in squalls of terrifying violence. The hut creaked and swayed like something alive, there was an avalanche of objects off the shelves, and the men shivered in their sleeping-bags, alert to the sounds. Priestley, writing in pencil, couldn't convey the force of the wind. The pressure changes with each sudden blast brought acute pain to their ear-drums.

Next morning Dickason went out to do the 8.00 a.m. meteorological readings and came back with startling news. The sea ice had gone. Instead of solid white ice, there was black water. No one could believe it, but each man went out to see the open ocean for himself. Building up during the winter, the sea ice had been three to four feet thick, even thicker in places, stretching for 20 miles. It was a given. The realization that wind could do this was truly shocking. If this ice went, then what ice was safe?

Damage and destruction were everywhere they looked. The wall of stores outside their hut had blown down. Great triangular beams of wood had been lifted and carried along the beach from the roof of Borchgrevink's store house, leaving wild confusion inside and even Priestley's boxes of rocks thrown upside down. Not a trace of snow or grit remained on the beach, scoured to the outlines of its guano-embedded pebbles, in places down to the deep red of newly revealed historic layers. All the dead penguins scattered around since autumn had been swept away. The dried mummies of crabeater seals cemented into last resting places had been driven along by the wind to lodge in new locations.

For Campbell this was the final, cruellest blow. Their journey to the west depended totally on sea ice. All his plans crumbled. He had believed that the ice would be safe until November. The only comfort was that they themselves were safe. If this storm had happened in two weeks' time – given his decisions to sledge straight over the bay – he and Priestley, Abbott and Dickason would undoubtedly have disappeared with the sea ice. '[O]ur hopes of doing a good sledge trip are apparently shattered', wrote Abbott. 'The worst of it is, that as the Ice has broken away after standing so long: if we go away we shall always have the knowledge of the uncertainty of the Ice – but Cede Deo.'

Meteorological instruments were broken, as expected. The tide-gauge, the object of so much painful labour, had of course gone: another layer of failed scientific work. Priestley summarized the impact with accuracy, and some despair.

> My record . . . seems to be a record of failures through no fault of our own. Our plans are all of no avail & will have to be wiped out & a new set made. I could find it in my heart to wish I had not tempted fortune a second time but had been content & gone home . . . My winter has been spent here in work which could have been carried out just as well by any member of the Expedition; I have had no Geology to speak of up to date, & see very little prospect of any in the future.

Disappointment had followed disappointment. For Priestley there was a sense of resignation: 'one cannot help thinking that this is not the last but that fate has other reverses still in store for us.'

At least Borchgrevink now got his due. They had believed that Borchgrevink was wrong when he advised against sledging along the coast. Well, they were the wrong ones. 'Borky will certainly have the laugh of us', wrote Priestley on Saturday the 19th. Everyone was generally depressed: 'the direct result of the sudden quashing of our plans for a useful summer's work.' Now any work they did would not be new because Borchgrevink had forestalled them, and they would not be able to compete with him. The following day, Sunday the 20th, 'we are all still feeling pretty blue', reported Priestley. It was Campbell's thirty-sixth birthday, but the wind blew cold and they stayed inside the hut, six men cooped up together.

The only advantage to the ice breaking up so early that anyone could think of was the hope that birds and mammals might start coming back. That, at least, meant spring, and the beginning of the end of their time here.

10

The damnedest luck

21 August–20 October 1911

Of course I write in ignorance of everything outside our own little circle. I haven't a notion where Campbell is landed, or how he is getting on.

Scott, letter, 28 October 1911

F OR THE FIRST time in over four months, the sun shone brilliantly on Monday 21st August, and everyone could see to climb up to the top of Cape Adare. Only Abbott, his knee still weak, and Browning, cook for the day, stayed down in the hut. Confined by darkness for so long to a triangle of grey shingle and the arbitrary but unpredictable extension of frozen sea, up here on the cape there was visual escape, a kind of freedom, a bird's-eye view. Levick took photographs, Priestley collected rocks, and Campbell and Dickason climbed on up to 2,500 feet. It was possible to see north-west for 100 miles, to where they wanted to be. Squinting into the glare, they tried to work out the state of the sea ice. But it was too difficult to tell.

Below, in the hut, Abbott and Browning did the fortnightly sweep of the chimney. Then Abbott made a dissecting board for Levick, so that he could start dissecting penguins. On the 22nd Levick used the board to examine a penguin he had found dead on top of Cape Adare, explaining the anatomy to Abbott. Levick had discovered his vocation, and it was nothing to do with sledging. Cape Adare had an alternative community. In six or seven weeks it would begin to reassemble, and Levick wanted to be their discoverer, their diarist. His ambition to write a book had found its subject. His avuncular style, shrewd observations and chatty familiarity would fit perfectly with describing the behaviour and habits of the Adélie penguins to the general public. His study would draw on his medical training, powers of observation and inquiring mind, his warm, humane curiosity, his delight in narrative and his newly acquired and vigorously practised skill in photography. He'd always planned to write some notes on the breeding habits of the Adélie penguins at Cape Adare as part of the expedition's scientific work, and so he had been reading everything available. But now Levick was engaged. He had already started a zoological notebook, in which all hands could record anything of interest relating to birds, seals, whales etc., putting their initials. But all, noted Levick, should bear in mind the following:

1. Never write down anything <u>as a fact</u> unless you are <u>absolutely certain</u>. If you are not quite sure, say 'I think I saw' instead of 'I saw,' or 'I think it was' instead of 'It was,' but make it clear whether you are a little doubtful or very doubtful.

2. In observing animals disturb them as little as possible. This especially applies to the arrival of the penguins, as it is most important to allow them to settle down naturally without interference from us, and to the giant petrels, which became wilder last autumn after we hunted them.

3. Notes on the most trivial incidents are often of great value, but only when written with a scrupulous regard to accuracy.

N.B. – Please remember that we have every reason to believe that birds feel pain as much as we do, and that it is well worth half an hour's laborious chase to kill a wounded skua rather than to let it die a slow death.

On the other hand, there was no denying that the return of birds and mammals would mean the joy of fresh food. They couldn't wait to start eating newly laid penguin and skua eggs. Roast penguin, enthused Priestley, was delicious: you couldn't get a more tender or better-tasting bird. They'd just tried last autumn's frozen skua, which tasted like rabbit. Seal was as good as undercut of beef. As for Dickason's steak and kidney pies of seal – they were truly excellent. 'Our chief trouble is not to coax our appetites but to restrain them.'

On Wednesday the 23rd, eight days after the great blizzard, Campbell and Priestley walked together around the beach to discuss possible sledging plans. They came to a decision. Despite what had happened to the sea ice, they would try to achieve their objective of getting west. But, given the uncertainty of the sea ice, they would be very cautious. Every day Campbell and Abbott would ski ahead to check the ice surface, returning to camp at night, and in this way they would all edge forward. The moment they reached any place where the ice had broken right back to the coast, they would turn away. Priestley would do geology, with Dickason helping, and Campbell would do his plane table survey. 'I don't hope for much from the attempt,' Priestley concluded, '& we are perhaps foolish to try it but hope dies hard.'

After dinner on Thursday everyone sat around relaxing while Campbell and Levick told stories about their childhoods. The best bit, Priestley thought, was Campbell describing how he slew his pet rabbit with a croquet mallet for failing to produce offspring, as his brother's rabbit had. He had given his a week to perform, then executed it.

But despite the relaxation of an evening with jokes, Campbell's authority inside the hut was absolute. Priestley, needing more light for his work, had to go through the correct procedure, speaking first to Levick, who asked Campbell for an increase. Abbott, on the other hand, was in the direct line of fire. He had made a leather holster for Campbell's pistol, and little chamois leather bags to protect the precious chronometers so that accurate surveying could be done while sledging. But he suffered a severe reprimand when Campbell, giving the usual 9.00 a.m. order to wind chronometers on Sunday 27 August found that Abbott's chronometer had stopped. Campbell accused him of failing to wind it. There could be no discussion. 'I thought I had wound it nevertheless', Abbott noted.

Campbell was under pressure. A new break-out of sea ice had occurred, leaving just a narrow strip of white to the north of their beach. The sound of surf was unnervingly loud. 'Campbell says he can't see what I have got to write about these days', Priestley confided to his diary on Sunday evening; 'he says he can run his diary for the last week in a few lines, but our cases are different. He is writing an official log while my journal is meant only partially as a record & for my own reading, but mainly as a substitute for my letters home, as there is always a possibility that it may reach home & I may not.'

Priestley listed the advantages of his diary. It was 'accurate in facts, dates & times'; he wrote it up day by day; he wrote it 'to be read by people who knew me intimately & will be able to see further between the lines'; and he had previous experience of diary-writing, so he knew what type of diary would interest himself most – 'so write to please myself'. But Priestley had not included anything about the row this morning with Abbott and the chronometer. Nor had Campbell.

Even though it was Sunday, Priestley had done a little typing. Perhaps, being quiet here at Cape Adare, and always quiet at his parents' home on Sunday, he was reminded of their sitting-room, where everyone gathered together after dinner for hymns, except that the rooms could hardly be more dissimilar – nor (with respect) the company. Why had he not noticed this at Cape Royds? That was a real home to him. But at Royds 'there were more of us' and 'the bustle & work was never suspended to the extent that it is here'.

On Friday 8 September spring sledging, so long anticipated, finally started. All six men left the hut together, with Campbell's party pulling a load like a small truck, a 12-foot sledge lashed on top of their iron-runner 10-footer, and Levick and Browning tugging a 9-foot sledge for a short photographic and geologizing trip. They had tri-alled the iron runners, as prepared for them by Bernard Day, and found them greatly superior to wooden runners.

Abbott left his boots behind. But other things had been left as well: a container of one of their favourite finds from Borchgrevink's hut: chocolate nodules flavoured with lime juice (a wonderful thirst-quencher); also two spoons, and 'the Doctor's pipe'. So Abbott skied back to the hut, 8 miles in one and three-quarter hours – 'Not bad, as ice pressure bad' – and found the hut cold and looking forlorn. After returning, he spent the night in Levick and Browning's tent, the three men in their sleeping-bags smoking and roaring out shanties. The next morning, while Browning crouched over the Primus inside the little tent, shepherding a good steady flame under the cooker for breakfast, Abott and Levick stood outside on the glittering white ice, −25° and the weather fine, with the ethereal beauty of Warning Glacier's ice face as backdrop, and boxed, using their fur mitts: 'fine exercise for a warm up while sledging'.

★

On 8 September at the Bay of Whales, Amundsen started out for the South Pole, restless, worrying about Scott and his motor sledges. If that new technology succeeded, Amundsen knew that his whole journey, however refined his polar techniques, however trained his men and dogs, was meaningless. So he left Framheim, taking nearly ninety dogs and every man except the cook Lindstrom. He couldn't risk waiting. The Pole had to be achieved.

At Cape Evans that day there was a celebratory dinner to welcome a new volume of the 'South Polar Times' – Scott had wanted one more before leaving for the Pole. The Eastern party were remembered. A humorous report described King Victor, 'small, alert and wiry', who ruled, ably and efficiently, a colony 'established somewhere in the Northern part of Victoria Land for the purpose of Exploration', aided by his Doctor, 'slow to move and act, but wise at bottom' with 'a magnificent fund of anecdote' and his 'Rockologist . . . a most retiring but hardworking young man', aided by a 'cheerful and rubicund . . . Abbott' and 'two jesters, Dicko and Brownie'. The dinner also acknowledged the imminent departure of the first sledge party of the season. Teddy Evans, Gran and the 'burly Irishman', Petty Officer Forde, were leaving next morning to find and re-mark Corner Camp on the Barrier, after the winter blizzards. Their sledge was packed and ready down on the ice. 'If you people want to suffer, for heaven's sake, Go!' Scott had said, when they suggested the journey. Forde 'may have a difficult time', noted Gran. 'He has had little opportunity to use skis.'

Sitting at his desk in his den, his companionable pipe held firm between his fingers, faithful 23-year-old naval overcoat folded on his bed, buttons glowing comfortingly, the four gilded stripes of his captaincy gracing the shoulder, and with photographs of Kathleen on the wall, and of his son Peter (whose second birthday was in six days' time), Scott thought about the past winter. The hut had functioned well, with everyone busy. It had been a manageable space, in which he had been able to work on the immense amount of detail underlying his plans for the polar journey. Shackleton's journey had been analysed in detail, with distances, timings and weights carried, all broken down. The central issue for Scott was, as it had always been, how to get sufficient supplies to the right places in time to enable the final party to go forward to the Pole and return. The amounts to be carried – by what and when – had been calculated down to the last nosebag of pony fodder, the quantity of paraffin required to cook food and to melt ice into water and of petrol for that terrible imponderable, the motor sledges. Every arrangement had to take into account the two extremes: the full success of the motors or their complete failure. The weight of camping and ice equipment, gear for the ponies, scientific and navigating instruments, tools, cameras, clothing, sleeping-bags – had all been added up, along with the weights of food, fuel, sledges and each man's personal allowance of 10 lb.

Bowers had checked every figure: Scott considered him the only man capable of grasping and retaining the complexity of the logistics. Bowers had recently lectured on polar clothing, using their polar library and adding in his experience from his recent five weeks' winter journey with Wilson and Cherry-Garrard: all three had endured, according to Scott, 'the hardest conditions on record', attempting to retrieve examples of emperor penguin eggs from Cape Crozier. In addition, Wilson had experimented during the journey with types and quantities of sledge rations: Cherry had eaten up to twelve sledging biscuits a day, Wilson had tried an allowance of 8 oz of butter daily and Bowers had had extra pemmican for lunch. 'It is good', wrote Scott, 'to have arrived at a point where one can run over facts and figures again and again without detecting a flaw or foreseeing a difficulty . . . If the Southern journey comes off, nothing, not even priority at the Pole, can prevent the Expedition ranking as one of the most important that ever entered the Polar regions.'

Spring sledging west of Cape Adare continued for Campbell and his men on and off through September and into October, with maximum effort and minimal gain as small humans toiled among the details of a complex, wild coast, achieving as little as they had assumed they would when they first saw the glaciers, ice falls and rock precipices from *Terra Nova* in February. Campbell, Priestley, Abbott and Dickason crossed diagonally over the sea ice remaining in Robertson Bay to save miles and time, sledging bravely away from the security of land. Campbell made firm decisions, adjusted plans, left food in various depots and then with huge reluctance returned to the hut, before launching another attempt to get towards the undiscovered west. Partly it was the usual problem of logistics: how to carry sufficient supplies to achieve the distances they wanted. Their new member, Dickason, summarized the problem: 'we cannot get along fast enough to counteract for the amount of food we are eating.' Partly it was the difficulty of travelling – relay work, struggling through 'cursed everlasting deep soft snow'; 'doing our best', noted Dickason, but it was desperately disheartening. They discovered bays where they waded through snow lying on the sea ice undisturbed by any winds, waist-deep. Over and over again they achieved only 2 to 3 miles a day. One Sunday 'I turned into my bag without swearing tonight', Dickason wrote, 'the first time this trip, I suppose the hymns had something to do with it as I was turning in whilst singing.' Campbell kept the conventions going. The following Sunday with Priestley and Dickason off geologizing, 'Lt C conducted a small service', reported Abbott; 'he had an audience of one.'

After repeated efforts they reached Cape Wood, that marker point in their minds' maps, 25 miles across the top of Robertson Bay from the tip of Cape Adare as the skua flies. They had got beyond the confines of Robertson Bay, breaking out of their wider prison at last. Campbell decided to sledge across the sea ice, moving in a northwest direction and keeping about 3 miles out from the coast to get easier travelling. But on the evening of 7 October, clearing away snow to pitch their tent, they noticed that the sea ice beneath the snow was dark. Campbell and Priestley had begun changing their clothes before getting into their bags and were discussing their plans when they heard a seal make its eerie wailing call, rising and falling, like a siren, seemingly just beneath their bags. Then Priestley heard what he called a seal's bubbling noise, very close indeed. A seal was swimming in the ocean immediately under their tent. Campbell called to Abbott, waiting outside with Dickason for their chance to get into their sleeping-bags, to get an ice axe and try the thickness. 'The ice all round for a good distance was a brownish colour & looked sodden', noted Abbott; 'it proved to be 8 inches thick – this was a shock, we had to move camp again. While Lt C & Mr P turned out and dressed, Dick & I went in search of better Ice.' After finding something a bit thicker, they camped but hardly slept. Next morning Campbell took a spade and went right in to the shore, digging through deep snow; to find only slush. No ice at all.

If all went well, they were within a day's march of Smith's Inlet, where Scott had hoped the Eastern party might have built their hut and spent the winter. As Dickason said optimistically, Smith's Inlet would be 'nearly half our journey done'. But the ice was impossible and could break up at any time. Also glaciers fronted the sea ice in sheer ice walls: leaving no way to escape up into the mountains. Even if they could get further along the coast – and they might, with luck, reach Cape North – getting back was the problem. Achieving a return, concluded Dickason, 'would be doubtful as with the ice in this condition it is liable to let us through any time or else break up quickly. Finis.' 'A bitter disappointment', wrote Campbell. They would have to turn back. For Priestley, it was

a great and unexpected blow but I see no other way out & we must try to amass as much as possible of scientific matter since the party's work geographically is practically nil. We have had the damnedest luck there is no doubt. I did not sleep last night after we came to the decision and I don't think C did either but the men are quite cheerful as they are over everything.

Terra Nova had first met this coast east of Smith's Inlet on 16 February, after the great storm that blew them north. Eight months later, on Sunday 8 October, in roughly the same area, the sledging party turned back. Campbell decided to travel slowly while he surveyed and Priestley collected rocks. 'We were all fairly tired and very much out of temper with the day and with ourselves', said Priestley, 'though I should say that we all recognised that C could have done nothing else than turn back since the journey would certainly have cost Captain Scott a relief Expedition, though the chances are that we should have been able to last out up the coast ourselves without much hardship.'

Back at the hut, Levick and Browning had been out on various forays taking photographs. They had been experiencing their own version of horror, trapped in their tent by hurricane-force winds as the sea ice worked beneath them, rising and falling, with cracks opening around and the pressure grinding. On returning home, they found the sea ice twisted and heaped by the tremendous winds, and stained dark brown by a layer of basalt grit and penguin guano ripped off the cliff and beach. Dreams of a fortune from centuries of industriously nesting penguins blown in bits out to sea. In circumstances of mutual danger and uncertainty Browning had proved 'a most indefatigable cook and general "bucker up"'. The long-nursed judgement made on the trip to Hut Point now revised, Levick rated Browning a cheerful companion, always thinking of ways to please him with surprise meals. The thoughtful carer of Nigger the cat was now focusing his attention on the doctor. Browning had a potential health problem, having suffered from enteric fever during the Boer War, but Levick acknowledged Browning as 'certainly gifted with brains' and thought he ran the meteorological observations while in the hut 'exceedingly well and intelligently'. Browning had even contributed to the sledging song to celebrate his and Levick's sledging.

Now the Warning Glacier Party (it numbers only two)
    Had their bit of work to do
    But managed to get through
When the camera got frozen up & the light was rather blue
    Things got really very sad
    And the language very bad
    For the surface made them mad
        Though the hut was well in view.
So the Warning glacier party have done their bit of graft
They've sledged all round the coastline glaciers to photograph
Panoramas, ice capped mountains, seal with young as well
And many times they've wished the sledge in H—l
        Well! Well!

Levick had an inventive, science-based approach to personal health and comfort while sledging. He tried rubbing blubber on to his nose to minimize frostbite; and having forgotten to bring his snow goggles, he blacked the upper half of his face with soot from the Primus to reduce the glare.

Most importantly, the Adélie penguins had been arriving since mid-October, walking over the ice or sliding on their bellies, pushing with flippers and feet as they streamed in – long lines of travellers extending unbroken across the sea ice as far as the eye could see. To Levick's astonishment many tackled the arduous climb up the snow-covered steep slopes of the cape to begin building their nests. Hundreds of thousands of them were crowding on to the pebbles, filling the knolls and ridges, until the noise of their greeting and guarding was one continuous wave of sound building in a crescendo, then sinking, then building again. Levick was absorbed in observing, and keeping systematic notes on, what he had decided to call their 'social habits'.

Campbell's party returned to the hut on the afternoon of Friday 20 October, walking in through the gathering sea of penguins, 'All kicking up a row', said Dickason comfortably. The smell of last autumn was back. Levick and Browning were taken completely by surprise by Campbell's return. 'Hut in a great muddle', said Priestley, but everyone celebrated with a good dinner, a drink and a gramophone concert. Dickason had left his diary in the care of Browning, with a note: 'In case I should not return from this sledging trip . . . I entrust this log to the care of F. V. Browning who will cause it to be delivered to my mother, failing her my Brother.' It was good to be home safely. Priestley celebrated with yet another verse for the sledging song to commemorate spring sledging, which 'Thank God! Is over for this year at least'. It was even worse than being seasick, and he couldn't put it more strongly than that.

> Oh! it's fine to go Spring Sledging when the mercury is low,
>> Just on 35 below
>> And your nose begins to go
> When your sleeping bag is sodden & your circulation slow.
>> Then a man's remarks are terse
>> And his answer's just a curse
> Or, if the weather might be worse,
>> At the most but 'yes' or 'No'.

Browning had kept all the meteorological logs and records up to date, collected geological specimens with a geological log and even made ice notes. It was a humbling experience for Priestley. 'He has been invaluable to me . . . what could I want more? There are few men would have done so much.'

On Friday 20 October Amundsen left Framheim the second time for the South Pole, taking only four companions with four sledges and fifty-two dogs. The day was dull and misty, there was a nasty shifty breeze flapping and poking, and Lindstrom, the cook, who considered Fridays unlucky, was worried. Amundsen's first attempt had turned into a complete fiasco, resulting in an unforgiving row and bitterness that continued to erode. Trying too early, with the Barrier relentlessly cold, he and his men had had to return and rethink some of their equipment – their boots were still too tight – and face the implications of the mistake. Four men were bedridden for ten days with badly frostbitten heels; the dogs had to rest their blood-caked paws. Now three men were staying behind at Framheim, besides Lindstrom, the hut's anchor, with instructions from Amundsen to survey and to explore across the Barrier surface to King Edward VII Land.

At Cape Evans on Friday 20 October two teams of men faced each other on the snow-covered sea ice, with goalposts of bamboo marking either end. Ponting wanted to capture a football match on film. Both motor sledges – the first part of Scott's complex departure schedule for the Pole – were almost ready to roll away across the ice. The main Polar party would depart south on 1 November. A small geological party was due to leave for another summer's work in Victoria Land, except that Petty Officer Forde, their all-purpose handyman, was currently out of action, his fingers having been badly frostbitten during Teddy Evans's expedition to Corner Camp. This was deeply annoying to Scott, because there was no replacement. But three games of football had been played at Cape Evans the previous May, and there was just time to create the excitement of another match, to show cinema audiences back home how the men on Scott's expedition relaxed. Scott played centre forward, yelling instructions, endeavouring to get his side winning for the camera. Atkinson, the best of the English players, was meant to score except that Griffith Taylor slipped and Atkinson tripped over him in the general confusion. And Frank Debenham, one of the two geologists set to leave on the geological party but currently keeping goal, hurt his knee so badly that he was confined to bed.

Scott, in command of the Polar party, had been writing sets of instructions to the five men in charge of all the other aspects of the expedition: the ship, the dogs, the Cape Evans hut, the geology party in Victoria Land and Campbell. There were actions for everybody and assumptions made about timing and locations, who would be where, when, and what they should do, or might wish to do, especially during the expedition's second year in Antarctica. Reliant on funds being raised in Britain, Scott could not promise to pay his officers, and the relevant people at Cape Evans had been asked to sign a statement saying that they were willing to forgo any salary. It was a difficult situation. Gran thought that most men nourished the quiet thought that, if Scott got back from the Pole before *Terra Nova* had left, then all plans for another year would be 'thrown overboard and the whole lot of us will set sail for New Zealand'.

Wilson the altruistic, Scott's 'ideal mentor and seconder', the smoother of difficulties, the tactful and trusted go-between, read all the instructions and made a copy of each set. He had been writing in his diary about the journey to come and the inevitable long gaps when attempting to communicate with those dear to him whom he was leaving behind. '[B]y the time I return . . . it will be impossible for me to alter plans however much I may be wanting to return . . . I don't see any other course open to me than to carry through the job I came here for, which was in the main this sledge journey for the Pole.'

In his orders to Pennell, as copied by Wilson, Scott listed the men who were certain to stay in Antarctica and the three men who would definitely leave. He also listed those who might go home on *Terra Nova*, including himself and Wilson – but that depended on when the Polar party returned, the earliest possible date being 15 March 1912, and on letters from home, and whether the mules had been sent. As previously instructed, Pennell was to pick up the geology party at Granite Harbour on the Victoria Land coast, and also Campbell. Having carried out a list of other tasks, 'Should *Fram* not have been heard of, or should public opinion Expect it you might go along barrier and see.'

Scott's instructions to Campbell were based on the assumption that he was 'landed somewhere to the north'. 'I haven't a notion where Campbell is landed, or how he is getting on', Scott wrote to the expedition's agent in New Zealand. 'Of course I write in ignorance of everything outside our own little circle.' But assuming Campbell was somewhere in Antarctica and that Pennell could hand the instructions to him, Scott informed Campbell that he was welcome to stay a second year, if he wished. 'An opportunity offers for the continuation of useful work in all directions.' Given the financial pressures, Campbell could remain where he was only if the work to be done justified the step and food supplies were adequate, and if his party could be relieved in another year's time, and if Levick and Priestley forewent their salaries. (Campbell had already given his up.) If everyone decided to leave on *Terra Nova*, only Priestley (and also Campbell, should he wish) could come on to Cape Evans, but none of the others. But it was also possible that Campbell and his men would be away when *Terra Nova* arrived. 'Being so much in the dark concerning all your movements and so doubtful as to my ability to catch the ship, I am unable to give more definite instructions, but I know that both you and Pennell will make the best of the circumstances, and always deserve my approval of your actions', wrote Scott. 'I hope that all has been well with you,' he concluded, 'and that you have been able to do good work.'

There was not much point to the missive. It was a courteous but rather lacklustre communication from a commander deeply preoccupied with the task on which he was about to embark. Scott's other expedition, planned to run concurrently with his attempt on the Pole and equipped to undertake discovery and science, had come down in the end to this: 'I am sure that you have done everything that circumstances permitted and shall be very eager to see your report.'

Close to departure, Scott had been writing letters dealing with expedition business. To Sir Lewis Beaumont: 'we set out on the southern march tomorrow and of course we realise that the value of all our work depends on its result . . .'. To Kathleen, another long, detailed and loving letter: 'My own darling – I'm charged with love, news & business, and scarce know which to let out first.' Nineteen pages, both sides, in his clear, neat handwriting, issuing instructions, discussing financial matters and his management of the expedition, assuring her he knew how capable she was of handling his affairs – then jotting things down as they came into his head. He was sending a copy of his diary, to use with discretion, as always: 'few people are really safe' – but 'use it to keep friends of Expedition in good humour.' One of the expedition members who had subscribed £1,000 had now offered £3,000; if the necessity arose, it would be called upon: 'he can afford it.' He copied extracts from letters he was sending, so that she would know 'how and why to act' (contemplating his 'wonderful good fortune in possessing' her). The scientific work done was 'really important. It has no direct financial value but will be well understood in the scientific world.' Then, 'As regards myself of course I stand or fall by the Expedition.' But 'as I sit here I am very satisfied . . . I think that it would have been difficult to better the organisation of the party . . . it is all that I desired.'

Then he enclosed a separate letter to her, honest and open, telling her how happy he was to find himself in this position, genuinely to feel a competent leader of his team – and a little surprised. Because this had not been the case. 'I am quite on my feet now, I feel both mentally and physically fit for this work', he wrote, and the important thing was that 'the others know it, and have full confidence in me. But it is a certain fact that it was not so in London or evident until after we reached this spot. The root of the trouble was that I had lost confidence in myself.' As a result things had happened that could have been avoided. But in the main the dangers seemed to have been surmounted. 'Of course all sorts of things may have gone wrong with matters which are not under my control but which are within the limits of my responsibilities such as Campbell's party, the Ship etc – but it is significant of my recovery that I do not allow anxieties to press on me where I deem my actions to have been justified.'

The decks, emotionally, physically and intellectually, were cleared for the Pole. That was the focus. *Terra Nova*, and Campbell's party, were of necessity outside.

11

Penguin summer

21 October 1911–1 January 1912

We are none of us good at disguising our feelings
                    Priestley, December 1911

TO LET
The late inhabitants with much regret
Beg to announce this hut is now to let.
They grieve exceedingly they cannot stay,
But urgent business calls them away.
The hut and furniture, thus on the market,
Remains for anyone who cares to shark it.

The stress was over for the Eastern party. No long journey of exploration was possible. They wouldn't be caught somewhere along the northern Antarctic coast, having to manage until they were picked up some time next year. The short season of light and warmth had begun, the brief concentrated opportunities of summer surrounded them, the sheer energy of living things cramming in their chances to get ashore, to breed and feed. The distant range of mountains enticed, always unattainable but now a guiltless pleasure to contemplate. The simplicity of their lives in their hut here on the beach, among the penguins, the freedom from complications they were about to leave behind, were suddenly poignant. With memories already mellowing, jokes shared, problems managed, Levick's poetry blossomed.

Each time the wind blows plates rain off the shelves,
For, with the hut, we put them up ourselves,
And consequently we're prepared to state
Each plank is split and not a nail's in straight.

The latter dodge was ours, and quite a great one,
(A crooked nail sticks faster than a straight one)
Its all yours for the asking, every splinter,
But, hurry up, it won't last out next winter.

Terra Nova would come for them, if all went well, in the first week of January 1912. In the meantime groups went out on short sledging trips, photographing, geologizing, surveying. Priestley had so much paperwork to get through that he needed 'everyone helping me' – sledging notes from the trip to the west, ice notes, meteorological notes, developing and labelling photographs, labelling rocks. Browning, his arm in a sling, had been annexed by Priestley to sit at the table and make fair copies. A bone from a seal Browning was butchering had scratched him and his glands were enlarged under his left armpit. At the same time Campbell was found to have swollen gums. 'Symptoms are ominous', noted Priestley on 24 October, 'but it is impossible that it should be scurvy as generally understood for we are overeating on fresh meat every day.'

At the end of October, Levick, accompanied by Browning, looked at the rookery of a thousand or so Adélies nesting at Duke of York Island, while Priestley and Dickason climbed up the coastal hills, slipping and sliding over the screes, on up over rock ridges of green quartzite, then a basalt cap, to 3,600 feet. Near the top Priestley slipped and knocked himself unconscious for several seconds. Both men complained about how slippery the surfaces were, how difficult to get a grip, how their feet suffered and hurt. Both were wearing finneskoes, soft fur boots. Priestley's cautious approach to sea ice was well established, but climbing in these conditions involved real risk. While he was away, Abbott made him a pair of trousers out of the curtain material, with green stripes running up and down: 'I do want more clothes', Priestley commented, 'handling cases and rocks have played the deuce with mine.'

Levick was utterly absorbed in his work observing the Adélies, each individual bird as engaging as the next. There was so much to speculate about, to learn. For everyone else penguins were, as always, funny little people. Most human foibles, emotions and failings were ascribed to their new neighbours. The colony just east of their rubbish heap, dubbed Casey's Court and very overcrowded, was full of 'most degenerate and disreputable ruffians'. The men swooped on eggs, describing with annoyance determined penguins attacking their legs as they walked among them, pecking grimly. 'Tiny has just returned from the penguin rookery with eggs for breakfast', Dickason wrote happily during a trip to Duke of York's Island, just after laying started; 'that is what can be called ideal sledging.' Several thousand eggs were collected from nests on the cape, in case they had to stay next year, and boxes full for the men on the ship when it arrived. The hard-won physical resources that had gone into the production of the two eggs per penguin pair were irrelevant, given the desire for fresh food. The reality of the penguin summer was the business of Levick's pioneer study, but there were limits. Getting the meteorological records was arduous enough in bad weather without having penguins to fall over, Priestley reckoned. Determined not to have this portion of the beach encumbered, he evicted those nest builders and egg layers that persisted in claiming their accustomed territory. Late-comers were even invading the immediate precincts of the hut, with penguins climbing the snowbank behind and peering in through the window. The penguins were frightened of the sledge carrying rubbish out and ice back and scattered in a swathe 20–30 yards wide either side, abandoning their nests, when the men rattled it through. Levick was afraid it might alter their breeding habits; Priestley, balancing inconvenience against biology, thought the birds would get used to it.

Priestley, as typist, was the natural choice to put together and edit that proof of English polar activity, the book created and produced *in situ*, or in this case the one-edition-only exclusive, *The Adelie Mail & Cape Adare Times*, of which there were just six copies. Everybody contributed anonymously, with Priestley inserting an editorial voice where he thought necessary, as in an amusing article by Dickason on cooking during spring sledging.

Dickason's account of a typical sledging disaster, dropping one of the precious pots of painfully cooked pemmican (known universally as 'hoosh'), ended with the

contents . . . not wasted, being scraped off the floor with a spoon, and the reindeer hairs which accompanied the hoosh were a welcome variant . . . On asking my companions if they would like tea or cocoa to follow I was told that pemmican was quite enough tonight so I accordingly got on with my own meal . . . (I find it hard to believe this about the refusal of the second course, and I advise my readers to take it with a pinch of salt as we take the pemmican. Ed) When the meal was finished I proceeded to pack up the various things belonging to my department, and in attempting to rise I lifted the floor cloth with me, capsizing the water that was in the outside cooker. The pemmican that was previously spilt had frozen to my trousers.

I could write several paragraphs on the subject of the inconvenience due solely and simply to the low temperatures, and I had even gone so far as to submit some sheets to the Editor, but my respected chief is a strict churchman and he said that while he admired the essay immensely, felt it was incompatible with the politics of the paper to publish illustrated tales, even if true ones. I have not forgotten the blisters on my fingers, the result of grabbing the cooker with my bare hands.
      PRIMUS

Plans were made to explore along the top of Cape Adare, but somehow they dropped away. In the Antarctic lexicon of expeditions summer was the key time to explore and do science. 'Priestley and I are settling down to get as much scientific work as possible done, to try as much as we can at any rate to justify our existence', Levick summarized in his diary on 9 November. 'He and I at least have the satisfaction of knowing that we have done our best, even if that doesn't amount to much.' But, as a party, 'we . . . have undoubtedly hopelessly failed in our object (exploration).'

On 8 November, at the Bay of Whales, three of Amundsen's men – Lieutenant Prestrud as leader and navigator, Johansen (Nansen's companion in his famous trek across the Arctic) and Stubberud (the expedition carpenter) – set out from Framheim with two sledges, fourteen dogs and enough food for six weeks, to explore King Edward VII Land. No depots had been set up, so they couldn't be out for longer. Travelling due east across the Barrier surface to where they expected to find land forming a boundary to the ice, as Scott and others had predicted, they saw only the same flat surfaces stretching on into the far distance. King Edward VII Land was 'Flyaway Land', after all, grumbled Stubberud. It didn't exist. Turning north towards the place where Scott had marked land on his charts in 1902, they travelled for seven days until they were close to the Barrier's dangerous, unpredictable edge. They found the land, as indicated, and by 3 December they had climbed up to a little peak of bare rock, black, worn, with moss growing on its ravaged surfaces, and bits of old birds' nests. It was the first rock they had put their feet on, or touched, in nearly a year. They had all been dreaming of 'great mountain masses in the style of McMurdo Sound, with sunny slopes, penguins by the thousand, seals and all the rest!' But no, there was nothing like that here. They named the rock Scott's Nunatuk – 'nunatuk' being a Scandinavian word that had moved south to the Antarctic, to describe a rocky outcrop or mountain peak sticking up through an ice sheet – and collected specimens, as proof that they had found solid ground. But mostly King Edward VII Land seemed to be an endless expanse of ice and snow, remarkably similar to the rest of the Barrier. A violent spring gale trapped them in their tent for three days and dropped enormous quantities of snow, so they had to stop discovering and ski direct back home across the Barrier ice, travelling 150 miles in eight days.

Amundsen's small party, starting from where Campbell had hoped to set out, had begun filling in the mystery of King Edward VII Land, while Campbell, confined far to the north, was constrained by geography from achieving any of his allocated piece of the unknown.

On 10 November in New Zealand, Harry Pennell wrote to Douglas Mawson with more details of the land he had discovered along the northern coast of Antarctica and the condition of the pack ice, in response to a request for information. 'There is of course not the slightest desire to try and claim our little discovery as a "sphere" or any such thing', Pennell wrote, 'and the sole idea of this letter is to give you all the information I am able to in case it may assist you.' Pennell also included a second letter, concerning a 'delicate' situation he was having to handle, for which he needed Mawson's help. Three (so far) of *Terra Nova*'s men had volunteered for Mawson's expedition, although 'at the same time', Pennell wrote,

> they have signed on for this one for 4 years from June 1910 . . . now they are asking what Captain Scott will think to which I can only point to the agreement and say that they are throwing him over when most in need of help, as the relief of so many (four) will not be all childs play of course . . . I hope you will . . . appreciate the fact that though I have had to persuade them to stay it has been with no idea of ill will to you but loyalty to my chief already I hope on the Beardmore Glacier . . . They all declare they are devoted to Capt. Scott and I cannot believe are really desirous of leaving him in the lurch.

Pennell then laid out Scott's plans for 1912–13:

> they are <u>as far as I know</u>:
>
> 1) If the pole is not reached.
>   Remain at Cape Evans with about 7 others & attack in 1912–13 with men mules & dogs
> 2) If the pole is reached
>   Return himself but land a party of 6 or 8 for useful work somewhere.
>   With things as they are this would now mean on or near K. E. Land.
>   My present instructions are very brief but detailed ones will await me at Granite Harbour or Cape Evans
>
> This ship leaves Dec. 15th.
>
> 1) Pick up Lt Campbell & land him further South
> 2) Pick up Debenham & party at Granite harbour & land him further North
> 3) Procede to Cape Evans & receive instructions as to the mules, the 3rd party (whatever it may be) & the Southern Party.
>   The 1st two have of course also to be picked up again.
> There is no intention of secrecy in our movements; magazine &

newspaper rights are of course guarded as always, but otherwise it is simply a case of not knowing . . .

Whether Capt Scott will find his financial position allows him to leave a party after he himself returns of course I cannot say. But I should think he will be able to. Believe me

yours sincerely

Harry Pennel

At Cape Adare the thaw had started in earnest. The lakes were 2–3 inches deep, the ground swampy and the smell more pungent by the day. Priestley devoted his Sundays to getting on with *The Adelie Mail*.

FOR SALE

A GAS PLANT. Delicate and penetrating aroma. (Carriage free to the first applicant.)

MAKES DARKNESS VISIBLE

Appeals to all the senses in turn . . . When you can't see it you can hear it. When you can't hear it you can SMELL it!

While Priestley was away geologizing, Levick took the chance to do a couple of post-mortems, chloroforming and skinning an emperor penguin on Priestley's conveniently empty bed, and skinning and examining a crabeater seal, balanced on a sledge on the dining-room table.

On Saturday 2 December Dickason thought about how it was twelve months since the ship 'nearly went down with us all after leaving New Zealand'. Significant anniversaries such as this made them think about the ship, and their mail, and how anxious they were to 'try our future somewhere else along the coast'. But the weather was perfect, the air soft yet exhilarating. The sheer joy of just lying on the warm pebbles in the hot sun watching the brash jiggle by in a calm sea and the penguins riding the ice, of listening to the cheep of the newly hatched chicks and all the distant and close sounds of living, meant they were all content. At times like this they remembered their absolute good fortune in being here, in Antarctica.

There were so many penguins, it was impossible to tell how many. But when disaster struck individuals, the men tried to help. Heavy summer snowstorms buried birds up to their beaks, and they dug a few out, becoming puzzled when the freed birds subsequently abandoned their nests. Priestley came across the horrible destruction of a penguin colony buried under an avalanche on 11 December – beaks, flippers, legs, flesh, skin sticking out of discoloured snow. He started work among the injured, mercy-killing the too badly hurt. Campbell called all hands out to help, and they collected bodies for eating, and slew more of the frightfully wounded. For Priestley it was a chastening and educative experience, 'enough to make me more considerate of their feelings in the future'. In spite of avalanches, floods, blizzards, deep snowfalls, leopard seals and killer whales, these marvellous birds managed to continue to flourish. Proximity was bringing awareness. Campbell started systematically exterminating the lithe leopard seals that patrolled the beach-front preying on the departing and approaching birds, watching for their large, almost reptilian heads with wraparound mouths and sharp teeth.

They fed the carcasses to the skuas, in the hope of saving the penguin chicks from the predatory beaks of the birds. Skuas, taking penguin eggs and chicks to feed their young, as they did every summer, were out of favour.

For Levick, with his subjects all around him, his pen fluent, distractions minimal and competition non-existent, his focus and the moment had come together. He had the text of his book *Antarctic Penguins, a Study of Their Social Habits* largely written by the end of December. He was also collecting dead and dried penguins, stones and guano to make an imitation penguin rookery for the British Museum. 'I don't suppose they will have enough birds to carry out his scheme,' said Priestley, 'but if they do, it will be an interesting & amusing feature of the collection.' Priestley, free to accumulate rocks, had amassed hundreds of pounds' weight, as well as picking up some samples of lichen. In general, though, biology continued a failure, 'so unproductive as to be scarcely worth the work put in it'. Dredging produced nothing at all in four hauls but pebbles and seaweed.

Priestley was recognizing in himself a natural bureaucrat – so much so that he thought he might end up in an organization once back in civilization. Before their big sledging journey to the west last September he had packed every specimen, labelled every rock, finished all notes and typed up his diaries into edited versions, with

instructions for what should be done with each package. He continued to keep up to date, unnaturally fortunate, in the abnormal circumstances of this expedition, to have the time and opportunity.
'[M]ine should certainly be one of the best ordered collections in the
show if they get back all right to England.' His journal was even
relaxing into occasional jokes and cartoons. He drew a side-section of
his cubicle as a storage centre, his bed piled with Edgeworth David's
fur coat, rubbish, blanket, dispatch box, wrapping paper, books;
under it were photographs, chocolates, meteorological records,
'proper place for hammers', thigh boots, all lined up. He annotated a
witty diagram of the hut and its immediate environs, with details of
their lives, littered with locations where Levick had lost yet another
piece of Priestley's equipment – 'nailpuller last used by Levick . . .',
'favourite hammer last borrowed by Levick', ice axe, geological
hammer, 'pot of red paint last used by Levick for painting penguins',
and Levick himself, shown lying on his bed, smoking a pipe, tobacco
ash and boxes of matches labelled as scattered on the floor.

For Campbell it was, as it had been from the beginning, a matter
of making the best of a bad job. In many ways Campbell was not a
complex man. He enjoyed sketching, making observant, tender studies of birds, seals and views. He could tell a story wittily and well.
Reserved, even unassuming, he had come through the trials of the
sledging they had experienced as firm but imperturbable, careful,
thorough, naturally in command when it mattered. But now he
relaxed in circumstances not too far removed from his summers in
Norway. He practised shooting, paddled along in the kayak, pipe
firmly gripped between his teeth and muffler wound around his head
turban-style. He did some surveying but didn't over-extend himself.
What he had been able to do, despite deep and continuous frustrations, he had achieved.

For Abbott, Browning and Dickason, hut maintenance over, there
was tidying up and sorting out but otherwise some spare time. They
relaxed together, setting up a miniature rifle range and working on ways
to make new tobacco combinations, to sweeten the strong navy mix.

After church on Sunday 17 December Levick photographed all six
of them outside the hut: the three officers sitting in front and Levick
with the string pulling the camera shutter cunningly hidden under his

hat. Abbott stood straight, his white wool pyjama jacket still spotless, with Browning and Dickason standing alongside, their neat naval beards regrown. Campbell spent the evening pacing the northern icefoot, glass in hand, searching for the ship. 'The sooner she comes', said Priestley, 'the better we shall all be pleased', admitting at the same time that he wanted a full year's meteorological records, so *Terra Nova* could wait until 1 January.

Preparations for their long-awaited sledging expedition on the Victoria Land coast were almost complete. The three seamen had maintained and repaired the sledging gear. Priestley, in charge of sledging food, had weighed out and put all rations in bags, except for that central sledging food, pemmican, which would be done on the ship. The expedition's pemmican, made by Bovril and labelled 'For use in cold regions', came in a tin and had to be shaken out, then divided carefully.

Preparing the food was tedious, but calculating quantities suited Priestley's tidy mind, and he had done it for their spring sledging trip. He and Campbell had already decided on eleven weeks' worth of sledging provisions, for four men; it was easier to work out that way. They didn't know exactly where Pennell would be able to drop them, but Campbell still wanted Wood Bay, north of Mount Melbourne, discovered by Ross in 1841. Borchgrevink had explored Wood Bay on 6 February 1900, and had described enticingly its large pebbly beach and apparent access to the plateau.

Christmas Day 1911 was clear and calm, with brilliant sunshine bringing the temperature above zero. After a couple of hymns in the morning to mark the day Abbott carried the gramophone outside and played some records. Penguins edged up, curious, their heads turning to look out of one eye and then the other, standing still, flippers angled slightly out to reduce heat, then edging away. Priestley took the meteorological observations, changed the barograph and thermograph records, had a quick bout of boxing with Abbott, then together they flensed a leopard sealskin. Dinner was soup, followed by deceased penguin, delicately fried; then came plum pudding and port. They toasted 'absent friends', 'the ship' and 'the Southern party' – all, in all their thoughts. Festivities finished with another open-air gramophone concert, the music spreading thinly. Records they had listened to night after night, marking the end of each day. Ritual and repetition. Both had served them well. The Sunday service, regular mealtimes, the keeping of meteorological records, physical exercise and listening to music all clearly defined areas of allowable companionship.

On Christmas morning *Terra Nova,* heading south, passed the first iceberg, and by dinner there was a fleet of them. 'Fizz and many songs, quite cheery', recorded Bruce. They'd managed to leave Lyttelton on 15 December, despite the hold-up of a fiercely fought dockers' strike in London, as workers turned against uncertain work and minimal pay. To intense relief the ship was hardly leaking. Seven well-trained mules from India were on board, as Scott had requested, and fourteen new dogs. On Christmas Eve Nigger, taunting the dogs, got too close, jumped back and fell overboard; the whaler was lowered, and the small cat, swimming pluckily through the swells, was scooped up and taken to the warmth of the engine room for brandy and a towelling – all in ten minutes, reported Pennell proudly. Stacked waiting for the men in Antarctica were pillowcases full of letters and piles of packages: things to read, eat or wear, carefully wrapped for their multiple journeys. *Terra Nova* was postman, newspaper boy, grocer's delivery cart, ironmonger and ship's chandler, the Army & Navy Stores, the bookshop, the specialist supplier of polar equipment – small slices of things needed or hoped for. But no one on board knew what might have happened here in the south. Eleven months had passed since they left. They'd celebrated Scott on 22 December, the day he hoped to reach the Pole. All going well, the ship should be at Cape Adare in a week, and they could start delivering, and accumulating, news.

On Christmas morning Douglas Mawson's expedition ship, *Aurora,* dragged her anchor in a sudden 3.00 a.m. squall at Macquarie Island, north-west of *Terra Nova*'s position, and briefly ran aground. So they headed out to sea, and turned south towards the Antarctic, leaving men and equipment on shore for a manned signal station – a pioneer radio link. If it worked, the disconnection between what was happening and what people thought might be happening would shrink from months to hours – at least between wherever Mawson built his winter quarters hut, somewhere to the west of Cape North – and Australia.

On the Victoria Land coast the geological party were camped inside Granite Harbour, with Gran's silk sledge flag, the gift of Queen Maud, hung this Christmas day on a cord between bamboos like the washing, with Debenham's marking the University of Sydney, Griffith Taylor's his Cambridge college, and Forde's Irish harp cut out of a specimen bag and sewn on to a piece of green Burberry cloth. Christmas supper was seal steak, fried skua eggs and omelette. Some of the eggs, collected the previous day, contained formed skua chicks, but into the pan they went. Then there was plum pudding and caramels, carried from Cape Evans.

At Cape Evans, across McMurdo Sound, the weather was beautiful this Christmas morning. Simpson had been waiting for a chance to release another of his hydrogen-filled balloons. Bowers had designed a shuttle with miles of black silk thread, running out of a Colman's mustard case, attached to the balloon. At the appropriate moment the silk was meant to break, freeing the recording instruments suspended below the balloon to float to the ground under a parachute also made by Birdie. Simpson had tried two high ascents, and both had failed. Now the right weather had arrived, and Simpson abandoned his role as leader expected to preside over a morale-boosting Christmas dinner. 'I would not lose the opportunity.' Having searched for six hours for his released instruments, he arrived back too tired to enjoy what everyone had left for him. But he was 'very happy'. The balloon ascent had been successful.

The first news of the Polar party had arrived three days earlier, when Bernard Day and Frederick Hooper had walked in exhausted, bringing letters. Simpson noted their 'sorry story' in his diary – the first motor abandoned 20 miles from Hut Point, the second coaxed on about a day's march beyond Corner Camp and then abandoned. Teddy Evans, Lashly, Day and Hooper had hauled as much as they could take from the motors' load to beyond One Ton Depot. Day and Hooper were 'Naturally . . . both very sick with the Barrier and its heavy work,' noted Simpson, 'and both expressed pretty strongly their desire never to see the Barrier again.' The ever-positive Bowers had sent a cheery note about the ponies: 'there is no doubt they are an ill assorted crowd of crocks but they have done splendidly.' There was only enough feed to get the remaining animals as far as the start of the Beardmore Glacier, 'and then they will all have to be shot and used for dog food . . . However that will fit in with the scheme as arranged.' Bowers told Simpson the news he wanted to hear – 'met log going strong' – before ending 'I hope your gadgets are buzzing merrily at Cape Evans.'

Scott had sent a letter to Simpson explaining that he had taken the dog teams on further than intended, with the result that 'the teams may be late returning, unfit for further work or nonexistent'. On their return the dogs had been due to take a load of rations to One Ton Depot, and Scott told Simpson the load must be got out to One Ton 'somehow'. Simpson decided that he would take a party man-hauling the rations. Then, on reflection, he decided he could not go: it would mean stopping his work at the very least for a month, probably more. Now was the best weather for balloon observations; and he alone knew what Scott wished to communicate to the ship's party, when it arrived. Simpson therefore told Day and Hooper that they would have to go back to the Barrier, leaving immediately. They argued for Christmas Day off, but agreed to depart on 26 December, along with Nelson and Clissold: the biologist, the cook, the motor mechanic and the steward, none of whose expedition roles related to Pole-getting, but serving it nevertheless. The only other fresh men at winter quarters were Ponting and Anton. Ponting, unhappy that the weather hadn't been good enough for his photography, intended making the most of the last few weeks before he left on *Terra Nova*; Anton refused to repeat his one experience of sledging. All he wanted was to get away from Antarctica.

Day and Hooper had also brought a brief note from Scott to be sent back to Kathleen:

Lat 81.15 S Nov 24th 1911
Dearest heart
Just a little note from the Barrier to say that I love you!
Animals are not well selected, I knew this in NZ though I didn't tell you . . .

On Christmas Day the first of Scott's support parties was already on its way back. Cherry-Garrard, Wright, Dr Atkinson and Petty Officer Keohane were eating their festive lunch – one stick of chocolate and one and half spoonfuls of raisins – in warm, beautiful weather on the Beardmore Glacier. Christmas Eve had been horrible, with Keohane falling into crevasses eight times within fifteen minutes, and Atkinson going head-first down another. But today they'd found the mid-glacier depot and enjoyed what Cherry-Garrard called a bit of 'rock-snatching' on a moraine. Wright had a piece of white marble with a centimetre-long fossil, and Cherry had some fine specimens: 'every little bit will be of value to someone. After all, they are the farthest South known rocks in the world.' That night for their special dinner they had pemmican with biscuit 'and a good whack of cocoa with ½ lb of Mckellar's plum pudding cooked in it in a bag. Pudding beyond all words', Cherry wrote, 'I feel I could eat sweet things for ever.' Wright, a scientist to the core, noted ('happy but by no means full') that the plum pudding was 1½ cubic inches per man. Somewhere ahead, Meares and Demetri, too tired to mark Christmas, were struggling to get their two teams of hungry, dispirited dogs back across the vast surface of the Barrier. The dogs had travelled 145 miles further south than intended, an extra two weeks.

At the Bay of Whales, Prestrud, Johansen and Stubberud decided Christmas didn't go with constant twenty-four-hour sunshine, but they had a holiday on the 25th, and Lindstrom the cook prepared a banquet of skuas.

Far to the south, but still on the upper reaches of the Beardmore, altitude 8,000 feet, with a fresh southerly wind, two green tents were pegged out on the immensity of white. In each tent were four men enjoying their Christmas meal, deeply tired after a very long march of 15 miles over undulations and several ice falls with crevasses, but knowing that that night they would sleep warmly, because they would have eaten enough: four courses! Pemmican with horse meat and biscuit dust and curry powder and onion powder, then a pannikin of sweetness (cocoa, sugar, more biscuit dust and raisins), then a piece of plum pudding, and another pannikin of cocoa, then five caramels and five pieces of ginger and a biscuit.

During the morning Scott, Wilson, Taff Evans and Oates had looked back. Seeing the other sledge stopped, they knew someone must have fallen in a crevasse, so they waited, getting mighty cold, said Scott. It was Lashly, down to the length of his harness, dangling and spinning inside the wide, icy split until alpine ropes could be organized by Teddy Evans, Bowers and Crean to haul him up again. It was his forty-third birthday. 'Many happy returns', someone said as his head emerged. Lashly's reply was unprintable. They were going well: marching to the limit each day, covering the distances. Their latitude this Christmas evening was 85° 50' S, making the Pole 250 miles away.

Scott, marking the journey towards the Pole with small notes for Kathleen, each carried by a returning party, had been sharing with her, as always, his thoughts about his ghostly pacemaker, Shackleton. From the Beardmore Glacier, on 10 December, carried by Meares and Demetri:

> Just a tiny note to be taken back by the dogs. Things are not so rosy as they might be but we keep our spirits up & say the luck must turn
> So far every turn shows the extraordinary good fortune that Sh had
> This is only to tell you that I find I can keep up with the rest as well as of old (think of you whenever I stretch tired limbs in a very comfortable sleeping bag – Bless you
> C

From latitude 85° S, on 21 December, in a note carried by Wright, Cherry-Garrard, Atkinson and Keohane:

> It's a pity the luck doesn't come our way because every detail of equipment is right – We are miles ahead of Shackleton and can see how pleasantly fortune led him by the hand. Also we begin to see just how & when he began to add to his distances. Between ourselves he never got to 88.23 or within many a mile of it
> It is rather sickening to be up against an imaginary record but all will be well if we can get through to the Pole

★

The day after Christmas, at Cape Adare, everyone except Dickason climbed the steep penguin paths behind the hut to the top of the headland laden with camping gear, pushing past the crowded nest sites, the starbursts of guano indicating meals in and meals out, the scruffy chicks, their grey fluff grubby with spilt food, and blobs of excreta, the noises of protest and dismay as five pairs of boots tramped past. Campbell had ordered a permanent watch for *Terra Nova* to be set up: three teams of one officer and one man on forty-eight-hour look-out duty in a tent overlooking the Ross Sea, starting with Levick and Browning, followed by Priestley and Dickason, then Campbell and Abbott.

Browning used his look-out time to tidy the grave of Nicolai Hansen, Borchgrevink's zoologist, who as he lay dying of an unknown disease in the store hut, aged twenty-eight, had asked to be buried on the lee-side of a boulder he knew, near the head of the cape. The boulder had been carried along by some mighty glacier shaping this land and deposited, a memory of an ancient journey. His companions had laboured to dig and then dynamite out sufficient depth for the body. Browning knelt on the frozen ground, picking out Hansen's name and a cross with small pieces of white quartz and black basalt. Cold preserves. The man was there, wrapped in a Norwegian flag, in a coffin, beneath Browning's careful hands.

On the first day of their look-out duty, Thursday 28 December, Priestley took Dickason 9 miles along the top of the cape, getting almost as far as Warning Glacier and reaching an altitude of 4,300 feet. Priestley complained in his diary about being responsible for the safety of Dickason, 'who like many sailors is not used to working his legs much in this particular way was dead tired long before we got back but he never lagged & only complained from a humorous point of view'. Dickason, who had no nails in his boots and no ice axe, couldn't cross the steeply sloping drifts in safety; he slipped many times, but 'it didn't seem to worry <u>him</u> much'. Priestley had paid for his own ice axe and brought it with him to Antarctica. Campbell had also brought his own. Dickason noted that they took only chocolate on their nine-hour walk. They had nothing to drink and so had to suck ice. After dinner Priestley walked on down the cape to report the journey to Campbell. Ever since the horror of the avalanche,

Priestley had tried to avoid treading too close to the Adélie nests and was proud to get to the bottom without being attacked. Always competitive and alert to detail, he noted in his diary that Abbott and Levick 'both caused more or less havoc amongst the birds' on the way up and were 'severely pecked'.

Some of the skua pairs preying on the penguin colonies were nesting among rocks on top of the cape, their musical calls mournful in the clear air. On the second look-out day Dickason played with two skua chicks – all long legs and fine fluff and incipient, curved little predatory beaks. Priestley thought the skua chicks were 'little rippers' and would have liked one for a pet. He collected another pile of brightly coloured stones for the ship's crew, then signalled in semaphore to Abbott, who was standing on the hut roof – a lot of relaxed nonsense passing from the hut to the tent 'upstairs'.

On New Year's Eve, for old times' sake, Priestley woke everyone at midnight with Caruso. The 'Flower Song' from *Carmen* burst into the silence, underscoring that essential necessity for scientific explorers when locating place with geographical precision and that underpinning of all data-gathering: accurate timekeeping. The new year, 1912, had begun.

12

At last science!

3 January–17 February 1912

The Antarctic teaches us patience if nothing else!

Campbell, 15 January 1912

BROWNING, ON LOOK-OUT duty at the top of Cape Adare, sighted *Terra Nova* on Wednesday 3 January 1912 and hoisted the signal flag, unleashing uproar in the hut, a wild grabbing of things and piling up of possessions. Heavy pack and icebergs held Pennell up, then *Terra Nova* was through, and everyone on board was counting heads on shore. It was the first count in Antarctica: the relief to see six men. Three boats came in, despite a nasty swell, but there was only time to take a few cases before the pack returned with the tide. The next day the bay was still full of ice until in the afternoon, as the tide turned, Pennell got through again. Campbell went aboard in the early evening, leaving, said Levick, 'the rest of us in a fearful rush . . . trying to get as much gear off as we could'.

Pennell was cautious. Robertson Bay had too many hazards and couldn't be trusted. He insisted on departing late in the evening of Thursday 4 January, before everything was aboard. He had negotiated the pack in six days, starting a bit later than Scott last summer, and entering on a different meridian, and he was keen to keep going. Priestley, experienced in the business of departures, had got his boxes of rocks, the typewriter and all his records on board. Campbell tried to make him leave his rocks behind to be collected later, but Priestley knew to move quickly. Levick, a novice, found that his precious sample of lakewater, 'which I most particularly wanted to bring off in order to prepare stained specimens', had to be left behind, 'spoiling my work on the protococci of the lakes'. He had begun working on them the previous July, incubating some in a biscuit tin warmed by a candle. Also left behind were two of the three carefully worked-on leopard sealskins, and all his taxidermist gear. 'It seemed a sinful shame.'

Campbell and his men were on their way south, for their summer sledging trip. They would have five weeks. Not five months, but – at least, in their attempt to salvage their expedition – it was something. The hut, with all the business of nearly a year's living, was abandoned – another layer of human occupation among the penguins, to add to Borchgrevink's.

With the feel of a ship's deck under their feet again, the six men caught up on news, talk, and more talk, glanced at their letters, did whatever business they could fit in and prepared for sledging. Everyone shaved and bathed, except Priestley, who Bruce thought looked 'a weird pirate'. Browning packed up an Adélie penguin skin he'd cured with arsenic soap, sending it with a penguin egg and a skua egg and some local stones to Mr Binmore, a taxidermist in Torquay, to stuff as a memento of Cape Adare. Their sledge meters hadn't been loaded on board – Abbott had left them behind in the rush, according to Priestley – so Davies the carpenter helped make a replacement out of a depth-sounding machine. Distance would now be measured in fathoms, not feet.

On Saturday 6 January *Terra Nova* turned towards the Victoria Land coast, with Mount Melbourne dead ahead: the elegant outline of an extinct volcano, a broad glacier sweeping over its shoulder. But at 8.00 p.m. that bane of their desires, heavy pack, intervened, blocking any chance of landing and exploring Wood Bay. Lumps of ice jostled in the water, filling the spaces, barring their entry, so they headed away, travelling south along the outside edge of the pack for twenty-four hours. As they turned in once more towards the coast on the morning of Monday the 8th, Pennell and Campbell stood together in the crow's nest looking for a way through. But once again the pack seemed to bar all access. Campbell gave up hope. Pennell's next task was to retrieve Griffith Taylor and Debenham, who with Gran and Forde were due to be waiting at Granite Harbour, further down the coast, and bring them north for more geological work. Campbell decided that he would have to stay on board, then land his party at the same time as Griffith Taylor's party, having agreed to explore in different directions. He had waited so long for this chance. Now he would have to accept another compromise. It was so far from what he had hoped.

Suddenly open water appeared behind the ice. *Terra Nova* started pushing and ramming. Campbell and his men began final preparations, knowing that their plans could be aborted. They were in that state of constant uncertainty inherent to being in Antarctica, that divider of personalities, that deliverer of stress – the need to shift between inaction and high activity, decisions made and decisions cancelled, deferred hope and immediate departure. At 6.30 p.m. Priestley was still nailing carefully hoarded spikes into his boots with his geological hammer, 'half a dozen spikes in each'. But late in the evening of Monday the 8th *Terra Nova* got through. At 9.00 p.m., in soft light, she bumped alongside the sea ice at Evans Coves, named after another Evans: not Teddy or Taff, but the formidable Welsh-born New Zealander Captain Frederick Pryce Evans, who, as commander of Shackleton's ship *Nimrod*, had picked up the Magnetic Pole party at Relief Inlet, a few miles down the coast, two years earlier, on 4 February 1909. They were south of Mount Melbourne, not north, as they had hoped. But no matter: it was land.

Getting their things ashore was yet another rush. As on all previous occasions, Campbell had arranged to take emergency supplies for a depot. He had personally seen to every detail, planning two depots: a larger one in case the landing was easy, and a smaller one in case it was at all difficult. The smaller depot was the one actually landed. While the ship's crew played around on the ice, killing penguins for specimens and giving the dogs a run, Campbell, Priestley and Dickason, Levick, Abbott and Browning set off towards land, hauling their two sledges already loaded for their exploring expedition. Pennell and three men from the ship helped, by hauling two sledges loaded with the emergency supplies. There was a mile and a half to get over sea ice, then a stiff pull up a snowdrift on to the ice piedmont. According to Bruce, 'They left some of their stores they had arranged to take behind as it was a good two miles to land.'

Campbell chose a visible place for their depot on an ice cliff covered in rock debris next to a moraine. Abbott, always the man to go the extra mile, returned to the ship with Pennell to obtain their position. Pennell, having picked up the western geological party, would bring them north and land them here at Evans Coves to explore. He would then relieve Campbell and his party, and the geological party, in five and a half weeks' time, on 18 February.

The retrieval of the Eastern party from Cape Adare had happened on *Terra Nova*'s way in to Antarctica this second season – not, as Scott had instructed, on her way out. Campbell had decided on his own initiative to leave Cape Adare and carry out a summer sledging trip on the Victoria Land coast. The time taken to collect him and put his party down again had been as short as possible. But it was well after midnight, and Tuesday 9 January, before the six men had made camp and turned in, having had a last look at the ship steaming away.

Levick, in his tobacco-fuggy tent, read his letters and newspaper cuttings – time on the ship had been too rushed. Campbell in his tent noted happily: 'Night lovely . . . and we are in great hope – scenery lovely.' He had already been lucky, finding a rock with garnets, and a shell. 'At last science!' wrote Priestley. They would sleep for a few hours, then start.

'Pure joy', said Priestley, on the first day of their summer sledging, 9 January. All around them was unexplored land, with rocks everywhere. Campbell, equipped with his own ice axe and *steigeisen* – spikes strapped on to his boots – was keen to achieve a good survey. Priestley was ambitious for geological discoveries. Levick, as expedition photographer, was eager to capture panoramas of the landscapes they would unveil. Campbell had divided the party into two teams. He, Priestley and Dickason would pathfind, with himself and Priestley making the decisions. The balance had shifted with sledging. Levick, as leader of the second team, consisting of himself, Abbott and Browning, was trying hard. Although Abbott had accumulated experience during spring sledging, Levick and Browning were still novices, and Levick had never been able to master navigation. He had, though, listed the equipment allocated to his party in a wallet-sized sledging diary. As well as their sleeping-bags and clothes bags, tent, floorcloth, skis and the all-important matches, they had two small ice axes – not one each, but at least *Terra Nova* had brought a few of these essential pieces of equipment. There was also one spade, and some alpine rope to deal with the mountainous country ahead.

'All snow caps and glaciers', noted Levick. It was grim, but very beautiful, although 'it looks a bit desolate'. By the evening Priestley had already developed his sledging appetite, and acute hunger pangs – 'I have the dickens of a twist', he noted ruefully. At least they had treats from the ship: two legs of mutton and some onions.

Campbell's aim was to work up the glaciers and find a route around Mount Melbourne, getting into the much-desired Wood Bay from the land. He'd left Debenham and Griffith Taylor a note at the depot moraine, outlining his plans to avoid a clash. But the topography was complex. Poking up one glacier after another, each of them bristling with ice falls, the six men plugged on doggedly, falling into crevasses and being jerked out like landed fish.

Very quickly summer sledging delivered its own disadvantages. Levick finished each day with soaked feet. The snow under the tent floorcloth melted, wetting their sleeping bags, making them soggy and clammy. Then a summer blizzard pinned them down in their tents. 'The Antarctic teaches us patience if nothing else! Here we are at the gate, and can't get on', Campbell noted miserably, on 15 January, 'and with our five precious weeks slipping by'. The next day, with snow still whirling outside and Campbell, Priestley and Dickason still in their sleeping-bags, Dickason got his two officers laughing by describing London schoolchildren swarming around to touch him whenever he went out because of the saying 'touch a sailor for luck'. But Priestley couldn't bear it: 'this inaction and lack of work is death to me & I have only a very ordinary share of patience.'

Two days later, on the 18th, the blizzard still blowing, 'I don't mind much where we go so long as I can get some work', Priestley wrote flatly, 'We are all sick of waiting.' The enormous quantities of soft snow that had fallen created new hazards. Thigh-deep drifts hid the boulders beneath, so they stumbled on the slopes of rocks or hit their shins on their hidden sides. They had to relay their sledges, which involved endless standing pulls: 'heartbreaking damned mornings', according to Levick, followed by Priestley's 'wicked afternoons': to everyone 'pure hell'. Goggles impeded their judgement in difficult terrain, but not wearing them resulted in excruciating snow-blindness and days recovering in their tents, which delayed them again.

Priestley continued to take one or two men out with him on all-day reconnaissance trips with minimal food: just a biscuit and a stick of chocolate. Desperately thirsty, he had discovered that shallow bowls sculpted by winds in granite boulders potentially held a precious drink of melted snow. One morning, having pushed the handle of his ice axe into the snow, Priestley stood on its head to reach the top of an eight-foot boulder. As he inserted his neck through a cleft to reach the water, the ice axe gave way. Antarctic death by hanging, except that luckily, he was gripping the edges of the granite bowl.

Everyone hunted for the great treasure, fossils, each with its promise of discovering a plant or creature unknown to science. Priestley wrapped precious specimens in his pyjama jacket, in socks and in mitts. But rocks were heavy and had to be got back to their base camp, so he began making depots.

Part-way through their exploring, a serious problem of misunderstanding between Levick and Campbell over where to rendevous caused a grievous delay. Levick's party had a miserable time waiting, although they celebrated Browning's birthday on the 27th by giving him an empty cigar box and a serenade by Abbott. Uncertain what to do, the three crossed a heavily crevassed area and camped the night of 29 January on a saucer of safety, surrounded by the lids of crevasses that Levick had smashed in, determined to demarcate the only possible area for movement. Neither he nor Browning had any experience of using alpine rope. Browning had only a couple of nails in his boots and slipped constantly. Levick: 'Thank God my party is a cheery one & Abbott and Browning just about as good companions as any man could wish to have'. But he admitted he had got into the habit of very bad language, so unleashing the floodgates of his two Petty Officers' rich, inexhaustible repertoire. Expedition members at the winter quarters hut had characterized Levick as 'slow to move and act, but wise at bottom'. Levick might get lost, or lose things, but he was careful of people.

While Campbell and Levick waited for each other, confused, in the glaciers around Mount Melbourne, King Edward VII Land was at last entered from the sea by members of the Japanese expedition disembarking from their ship the *Kainan-maru* on 23 January. Two of the shore party, having crossed the sea ice and managed to climb up the face of an ice cliff, using crampons, started walking towards the high land. The men, Genzō Nishikawa and Chikasaburō Watanabe, were carrying only a tin of beef and another of condensed milk, some biscuits, a geological hammer, a camera and a wooden post with a record of their journey already written on it. After fourteen hours they arrived at the foot of Scott's Nunatuk – climbed, unknown to them, seven weeks earlier by the Norwegians. As they rested, they heard a tremendous noise behind them and turned to see what they thought looked like thousands of metres of pure white silk suspended half-way across the sky. They jumped back just as a great mass of snow from an avalanche landed, enveloping them in a fog of white snow smoke. But between them and the nunatuk there was a deep crevasse. Gripping the rim, they peered over and heard a wicked wind twisting around in its blue depths; 'stricken by a feeling of desolation', they decided to return to the ship, having first erected the record of their landing, 24 January 1912. It was an extraordinary journey of probably 60 kilometres in thirty hours.

King Edward VII Land had now been broached from the sea, by the Japanese, and across the Barrier, by the Norwegians. This eastern extremity of the great ice shelf did not parallel the majestic landscape at its western end. King Edward VII Land had no smoking volcano, no stately mountains and dramatic ice-free valleys, no rare rocky beaches and hidden coves. It was an austere, ice-gripped unrelenting wilderness.

On the moraines south of Mount Melbourne, Campbell, searching for fossils, made two exciting finds: the trunk and branches of a tree imprinted on a slice of sandstone, and a boulder showing bark from a tree like a pine. By now, 1 February, Campbell had decided to give up trying to ascend the glaciers. Once again the slice of Antarctic map his party had tried to tackle had failed to deliver decent distances. Instead, they would return to the coast and collect rocks and lichens, and survey. It was a cautious move, but sensible, putting them back in the area where they were soon due to be picked up. Priestley decided that there was definitely enough work to keep a scientific party who chose to winter at Evans Coves occupied; 'but I do not want to be a member of it unless I get a chance to go home first.'

Summer sledging was symbolized by a decent growth of beard. A check of progress revealed Campbell with plenty of black hair, but rather spoilt because he had chewed off the end of his moustache. Priestley reckoned his own beard was nondescript; Dickason and Browning had been working at their fine naval versions for some time. Abbott's was represented by a few hairs: with his usual good humour he called them two football teams, eleven a side. Levick, glimpsing his in a melt pool, thought it had a copper tinge, but Priestley said each hair was a deep red fish-hook with the points growing back into the skin. The time of Levick teasing the novice Priestley in the Cape Adare hut was long past. Now Priestley, and Campbell, drew unflattering caricatures of a rotund Levick in their journals.

Nearly back at their depot, the six men stopped to look south along the coast. They could see, 20 miles away, the Drygalski Ice Tongue, that massive glacier extension pushing out into the ocean. West, and behind their backs to the north, the mountains rose clear and glittering. But now they knew the hazards inherent in their elegant forms: the networks of crevasses, the vertiginous ice falls, the deep summer snow, the cracked and seamed surfaces of the glaciers. Further west they could glimpse the straight white line of the inland plateau, that waiting presence they had failed to penetrate. But it was the view to the east that gladdened their hearts. The Ross Sea was blue to the horizon, just a few picturesque pieces of ice riding its surface.

After leaving Campbell, Pennell had found the pack in the Ross Sea unaccountably heavy. *Terra Nova* couldn't get through the ice to Granite Harbour to pick up the geological party, despite four attempts. Breaking through the ice to get into McMurdo Sound was impossible, so the mules and dogs could not be got ashore at Cape Evans. There was no work to be done in the ice. It was a miserable anti-climax to their journey south, an endless business of being caught in the pack, week after week, and struggling to get out again. Loitering in high frustration, Pennell had tried everything. '[S]igns of peevishness everywhere', Bruce wrote on 1 February. 'Every one getting rather fed up with this hanging about.' At least they didn't have Campbell & Co. still on board. Their misery and irritation would have been almost beyond bearing.

For the men waiting in winter quarters at Cape Evans week after miserable week of summer had passed longing for the ship, with her news and fresh faces. Sometimes her masts were sighted across the frozen sea, or smoke from the funnel, but no contact was possible. The famine finally broke on Saturday 3 February, when the dog teams managed to get north across the ice to *Terra Nova*, bringing Atkinson, currently the most senior naval officer at the hut, and Simpson, left in charge of the men at winter quarters. For Simpson the doings of Europe and the rest of the world during the previous twelve months were 'heard in an hour'. Meanwhile everyone on the ship had the pleasure of knowing that all was well at winter quarters. They heard that the eight remaining men of the Polar party had been last seen at latitude 85° S on 22 December, when Atkinson and the three other members of the first support party turned back down the Beardmore Glacier. So Scott could not have reached the South Pole on the longest day of the year, as the ship had celebrated. Nothing had been heard since then, and nothing at all was known about Amundsen. But Bruce thought 'the Pole practically sure'; and since none of Amundsen's depots had been seen on the Beardmore, he was unlikely to have got ahead.

The dog teams carried the letters from *Terra Nova* back across the sea ice to winter quarters, then the parcel post, and the special treat of oranges and apples. Cherry-Garrard did a first sifting of his pillow case of mail, checking copies of *The Times*: 'Half the people one knows seem to come under the Births Marriages and Deaths.' The 'very disappointing' months spent by Campbell and his men at Cape Adare were discussed. Apparently, recorded Cherry-Garrard, they have done practically no sledging; Levick had taken some good photographs; the hut had not weathered the year well. It was considered a very small inventory of achievements. Priestley had sent Simpson a letter with the meteorological records at Cape Adare, but Priestley's estimates of the strength of the winds were difficult to believe.

In Simpson's post there was a letter from his department in India. The department had a small staff of four men, and Simpson read that one was ill, one 'not up to it'. After Scott's lecture on his plans for reaching the Pole last May, it had become obvious that a second winter was inevitable for the expedition. Scott had pointed out that all who stayed must volunteer and would receive no renumeration. 'As for me', Simpson had summarized on 11 June, 'there are no two courses open. It would be sheer folly to neglect the opportunity of a second year's work here . . . my duty clear I told Scott at once.' Scott had been delighted to appoint such a highly qualified man as Simpson to his expedition. 'You know him and his type', he'd written to Kathleen just before leaving for the Pole: 'humble origins and burning for scientific eminence carrying always a simple kindly nature and very narrow views – the very man for the work down here.'

But now Simpson decided that he must leave immediately: 'under the circumstances I must put myself at the disposal of the Government of India . . . to help . . . if I am wanted'. He couldn't think of remaining: there were no 'second thoughts', no point 'crying over spilt milk'. For Simpson there was an opportunity. But that meant there was a 'great deal for me to do' before the ship went north. 'It's hard to leave such work as this in the middle', he wrote later. 'It has taken a year's hard work to get everything going and to learn methods to overcome difficulties, and also to know what to look for. Another years work would go much easier and would give better results, but it is quite out of the question . . . I must get in touch with Simla as soon as possible, so as to be able to return at once if they want me.'

Pennell, having received the large number of instructions left for him by Scott the previous October, had to acknowledge that many could not possibly be carried out. The sea ice was not strong enough to take the weight of sledges loaded with cargo, although at least the mules from India, in good condition after careful attention on their voyage down, could travel across the ice to Cape Evans, and the fourteen new dogs. But, Bruce reckoned, unloading was going to be 'a very long business'. Compared with the previous summer, the sea ice was proving incredibly obstructive this year.

At Evans Coves, Campbell and his men returned to their depot by the moraine exactly four weeks after leaving, on Tuesday 6 February.

Eagerly they looked in their post-box for news from Griffith Taylor and Debenham, only to find the letter Campbell had left for the western geological party untouched. Yet the sea was open, with no sign of pack ice. Very disappointed, they decided that for some unknown reason their friends must have been put ashore further down the coast. Levick 'in his usual happy go lucky way', had left a rucksack with four of Priestley's films on the moraine. As a group, they lost things – a small trail of possessions dropped off sledges, a wind coat, a hammer, a glove – with one of the three seamen usually sent back to look. But the rucksack was too far away to look for, and Priestley had to accept it as an irreplaceable loss.

The next day, Wednesday the 7th, the six of them walked across to what they called the Southern Foothills, where they found a fine beach heaped with old seaweed, and pebbles with dark sand between, and shallow meltwater streams. The higher land was covered in large, rounded boulders of granite and gneiss, as though the scale had been enlarged to a giant's landscape. They had to clamber over or get around each boulder, a bit like the way penguins scrabbled and climbed over rounded rocks that humans could manage easily. On a south-facing slope they found a drift of old snow. Campbell went on up, to take a round of angles for surveying, but the work was unpleasant because an unexpected cold wind was blowing from the west. In that direction the land fell away steeply to an ice plain, its far side bounded by the mouth of a glacier, the Reeves, with a mountain on each side named after Norwegian explorers, Mount Nansen and Mount Larsen, and behind, the plateau. Campbell decided that this must after all be Evans Coves, rather than the place where they had landed and put their depot. Levick saw an emperor penguin and hoped the men hadn't, but they had, and they killed it for fresh meat. Levick was sad: 'we could have done with what we have.'

The day after, Thursday the 8th, the wind blew harder, out of a clear sky. 'Bothersome', said Levick. 'Very galling', said Priestley. A gale, really, blowing hard by the evening, coming from the west, off the continent and down the glacier. They called it the 'infernal cold plateau wind', and it didn't stop. It stripped the pleasure from doing things, bringing at the same time a disturbing sense of summer's end. Priestley examined the dilapidated state of their sledge runners and thought that their equipment was getting worryingly worn out. For the first time he contemplated the possibility that *Terra Nova* mightn't turn up, and that they might have to make their way back down the coast. Levick worried about his boots; they were worn out, and not the right kind for the rocks they were having to cope with.

On Saturday night, 10 February, Campbell decided the moment had come to broach one of their two morale-boosting bottles of the fortified sweet wine Wincarnis. Afterwards Priestley sat alone in his tent 'correcting a couple of months of my Cape Adare diary'. In the second tent the other five had 'what they describe as a naval quack'. But in the end, they all had to get into their bags and get on with the night. Except they all lay awake, wondering what had happened to the geological party, and thinking about what their non-appearance might mean. None of them could get to sleep.

At least Levick made an unexpected happy discovery. Exploring with Abbott and Browning to the southern end of the Southern Foothills on 11 February – and enjoying a competitive sprint with Abbott on the way – they discovered 'a beautiful little cove' with a pebble beach and a small Adélie penguin rookery, with the inevitable skuas in attendance, 'all complete'. Cradled between some of the rocks, they made a second discovery: the mummified bodies of seals. The hair of the skin was fawny-coloured and the desiccated bodies thin but intact; the teeth inside the stretched skin skulls were mostly eroded and diminished by the attrition of wind and cold.

Levick wanted to examine the seals, and to observe a later stage in the summer lives of the adult Adélies and their chicks. His zoological work had been thin. But Campbell and Priestley had already made a decision to explore the Northern Foothills. 'I have to up anchor and join the others,' Levick wrote, 'but shall request to return here at once and spend the rest of my time till the ship arrives on investigating this most interesting find.' Campbell drew Levick a map on the last two pages of his sledging notebook: a considerate little sketch showing *Terra Nova* sailing in the sea, the moraine, Campbell's tent in the Northern Foothills ('position doubtful'), Levick's current camp, and Levick with a body like a rugby ball and a small head on top, kneeling in front of a penguin at the newly discovered rookery. Campbell didn't want another misunderstanding about where to meet.

On Monday 12 February snow fell so heavily that Campbell's party in the Northern Foothills stayed in their bags, 'mostly thinking'. Levick and his men arrived safely and, as there was nothing they could do, got into their bags. The next day Priestley dispatched three penguins for his tent's hoosh, the usual 'grim though necessary murder'. The snow meant Priestley couldn't collect rocks, Levick couldn't take photographs and Campbell couldn't work with the theodolite – so instead Campbell got the three men out on the hill and taught them how to do ski turns. The 14th was fine, so they tried to collect and survey, but a covering of soft snow lay like a deceptive eiderdown over the surface, hiding the jumble of rocks beneath. This meant walking was wretched, every step a potential jar to the knee, a twist to the ankle. But Priestley was positive: 'it is an ideal life we are leading just now but we daren't go away for fear of missing the ship & there is not much to be done in the immediate neighbourhood.' All they wanted to do was to join up with the others and find out what everyone else had been doing. The Eastern party had been alone together, with no respite except four days on *Terra Nova*, since 18 February the previous year. They all needed a change of company.

A visit to Levick's tent called forth Priestley's scathing criticism: 'I have never in my experience seen such an untidy tent as theirs . . .. They have no system and Browning is a very haphazard cook.' But he had to admit that, because of Dickason, the efficiency and smooth functioning of his tent were guaranteed. However, his tent had only one book, *David Copperfield*, and Priestley said he'd read it so thoroughly that he could pass a stiff exam on it. So most of the time they talked over their prospects and possibilities – even more so on the 16th, when snow trapped them all day in their bags.

On Saturday the 17th, with the ship due the next day, they packed up and had a cold pull across the ice back to their moraine depot, sledging in the wind. It was unpleasantly like spring sledging, and they all got frostbitten. At the depot they camped in their old places. Levick, Abbott and Browning tried passing the time debating: should white men box black men for the world championship? Should any man in England be allowed to shoot rabbits on anyone's land? Should bachelors over twenty-eight years old be taxed? One man proposed, one opposed and one arbitrated, taking the roles in turns. Priestley went up the hill to look for the ship. The bay was still open to the horizon. 'Expect her any minute now', he wrote.

Griffith Taylor and his geological party had been ready for *Terra Nova* by 14 January. Their camp, established on the southern side of Granite Harbour on the top of Cape Roberts, was visible out to sea. With a new job starting in Australia, Griffith Taylor had no intention of missing the ship. Several times *Terra Nova* had been sighted across the sea ice, but she couldn't reach them, so Scott's plan for them to go north and explore at Evans Coves couldn't be fulfilled. Leaving a depot at Cape Roberts with one week's provisions, as per Scott's orders, and a letter to Pennell, they started walking home on 5 February. They took only the clothes they were wearing, their instruments and notes: everything else had to be left in the depot. Avoiding the unpredictable sea ice, they climbed a thousand feet up. Very cold and suffering from snow-blindness, they toiled south along the piedmont, with Forde moaning from the pain of his injured fingers, still in awful condition from the frostbite suffered five months earlier. On 7 February they saw, in the distance, the joyous sight of open water beyond the pack ice, which meant, as long as nothing had happened to *Terra Nova* (always a worry), that they could hope to be picked up somewhere. By 15 February they were south of Butter Point, where the Barrier pressed against the coast in a confusion of uncertain sea ice, grounded icebergs, glaciers and moraines. Glancing back, Gran saw – by the merest chance – smoke from *Terra Nova*'s stack. Shouting with joy, they tumbled down a steep slope on to the sea ice to be 'plucked up', as Gran put it. Pennell had just put four sledge-loads of supplies, as per Scott's orders, in a depot at Butter Point. Now he had netted four of his charges.

A blizzard started, and the ship had to dodge about, tumbling and rolling because it was lightly laden, making everyone miserable. The newly rescued, 'wild-looking heavily bearded persons' read old newspapers and heard the news of the others. Gran wasn't surprised to discover how little Campbell and his party had achieved at Cape Adare. They'd experienced exactly the same difficulties as Borchgrevink, he noted succinctly: the mountains were too steep, and the sea ice never quite safe. Gran was interested that five expeditions were in Antarctica this summer – Australian, Japanese, Norwegian, British and German – and that there was no news of the Pole, but 'on board this ship people believe Amundsen has the best prospects. The fact that there was no trace of him at Beardmore suggests to me that he has taken another route. And that is probably best for both parties.' Petty Officer Forde was happy to be back with his old shipmates. Amputation of the top joints of several of his fingers had been averted, and he was on his way home, whatever happened.

On Saturday 17 February, with the wind howling and the snow whirling, *Terra Nova* continued riding out the storm, everyone 'very cold and miserable'. There was no time to get back to the hut at Cape Evans to drop off the geologists, so Pennell headed north, under sail. Six more men were waiting to be picked up, and two days had been lost to the storm. He was due at Evans Coves on Sunday to relieve the Eastern party.

13

Hope deferred maketh the heart sick

18 February–7 March 1912

Bruce was talking to me on the bridge . . . he said that
except for Evans Return Journey he considered . . . that
the ship had had the hardest job of anybody on this
Expedition.

Cherry-Garrard, 26 January 1913

'THIS IS THE day the ship ought to arrive', wrote Campbell,
propped up in his sleeping-bag on Sunday 18 February. He'd
spent more time sitting inside this cocoon of reindeer hide and hair
than he wanted to think about. Another Sunday, but there was no
obligation to hold a service in a tent. 'Blowing a heavy gale all night,
tent poles nearly bent double.' Over the whine and thrum of the
wind he could hear an occasional single mournful honk. Several
moulting Adélies, feathers askew, stood just outside, entirely still,
near to each other but separate.

Priestley began a new diary. On the front page he wrote:

Eastern Party
B. A. E.
Waiting for the Ship
Feb 18th

Later he added a refinement to the address: 'at Hells Gate Moraine
Camp'.

Campbell had put Priestley in charge of preparing the depot
sledges for the ship. Priestley packed one with his geological specimens and oil, one with their spare clothes and the medical kit, and
made a separate depot of food on a third. Then he rigged up a flag,

good and visible. Levick, Abbott and Browning, on look-out duty, moved their tent to a place where they could see down the coast as far as the Drygalski Ice Tongue without having to go outside.

The ship did not come on Sunday, or on Monday or Tuesday. Campbell's entries were brief and terse. 'Blowing like the Devil' (Monday), 'blowing harder' (Tuesday), 'harder than ever' (Wednesday). Slowly but surely the wind was tearing their ageing and worn tents to pieces, chafing holes, bending the bamboo poles almost beyond their bearing. On Wednesday 21 February each tent split. Levick's tent went near the opening, and Abbott had to sew the tear up with his hands bare in the icy wind and clogging drift. Campbell's tent split near the top, but they managed to get a lashing round it. 'Our feelings towards the wind beggar description', Priestley wrote. The wind made him feel helpless, impotent. The worst of a wind was, Priestley thought, you couldn't do anything to it. You couldn't throw stones at it. And it was all made worse by their longing to hear news of the ship, their worries whether everything was all right. Imprisoned in their tents, they were getting less fit, and feeling the cold more. He was suffering attacks of cramp.

The wind eased on Thursday, to be replaced by snow, which continued all Friday the 23rd; but at least they could get out and walk. Food was low, so Browning killed one of the moulting penguins, and Abbott and Dickason tackled a young agile crabeater seal. This one objected: it wasn't the usual supine animal. Abbott and Browning thought its fresh raw blubber tasted like melon; Campbell tried a very small piece and, to his relief, rather liked it.

Their supply of food needed to be controlled and managed. Campbell decided to appoint Priestley in complete charge of all their food – 'In the event of wintering down here, if the ship does not turn up', noted Priestley; 'I hope this will not be necessary for the ship has certainly not been given a chance to pick us up.' It was important to occupy Priestley's youth and high energy, and this time-consuming, meticulous, daily task suited his predeliction to acquire and to order. But most of all, Priestley fretted over what could have happened to the geological party. It seemed to hold the key to the whereabouts of the ship. In particular, Priestley wanted to see his friend Debenham. 'We speculate over and over again. It would be so much nicer if Deb were here as then we could exchange news.' Being anxious about the others helped them avoid thinking about themselves.

Campbell and Levick, as the two senior officers, had already discussed the types of refuge they could reasonably build if they had to. Levick argued for a strong hut built of snow, with the roof made of skis and sledges, the whole lot covered with snow, and Campbell countered with a cave dug out of a snowdrift. Seeing the cave at Cape Evans constructed for Simpson and Wright's magnetic experiments had been useful.

Levick's diary fell silent the day the ship was due. But on Friday the 23rd he began writing again, summarizing the situation: the bitter cold, the tremendous wind and the reasons to be worried. If the ship did not come, and they were not relieved, their means of survival for the winter were sparse. '[W]e have nothing but a few extra sledging provisions with us, & no materials for building a hut, and no fuel and very few matches.' The current thinking of Campbell and Levick himself was to 'try to find a drift to burrow into, and kill enough seals for fuel (blubber) & food to last us till midwinter, when we shall sledge across the sea ice . . . to Cape Evans, 200 miles along to the Southard.' However, everything would probably be all right. The gales had most likely driven the ship north, and she now ought to be on her way here. Hope had to be managed, disappointment corralled, with each man treading his own boundaries of coping, accepting and despairing.

The very next morning, the weather at last calm, Levick as look-out thought he could see *Terra Nova*, a dull black spot on the horizon. The Drygalski Ice Tongue was visible but hazy. Campbell was called to look and reckoned that this was the most likely of all the many sightings so far. It was Saturday the 24th – six days after the ship was due. But, given the tremendous gales, a good time to expect her.

Terra Nova ran into pack ice the day Pennell was due to pick up Campbell's party, Sunday the 18th, so he tied up to a floe and watered ship. There was no point wasting time. In appalling weather he tried to get through seemingly impassable pack all Monday, and again on Tuesday. *Terra Nova* was experiencing her fiercest, heaviest blizzard yet. The storm continued, and the ship drifted north in the pack then drove on in open sea, rolling so heavily that most of the recently embarked geological party were seasick. As the wind eased, they steamed back south, got around the pack and started pushing towards the Drygalski Ice Tongue. Dodging up and down the coast like this, hoping for a way to open through, being stopped by ice, extricating themselves, was a nerve-wracking business. They were using precious coal, which was needed for other priorities: the old problem. By 4 a.m. on Friday the 23rd they were stuck tight in the first evidence of the new winter ice, flat discs of pancake ice. Bruce: 'No amount of driving would move her ahead or astern.' The geological party were horrified to wake and find the ship caught. Gran: 'the prospect of a winter on board, imprisoned in ice, sent shudders through us . . . Campbell . . . will have to tighten his belt . . . perhaps even for months.' All Friday afternoon the ship forced her way south, until caught again in the evening. From the crow's nest they could see open water. If they could only reach it, the way to Campbell was clear. On Saturday 24 February, at 8 a.m., they were right off the end of the Drygalski Ice Tongue. But instead of trying for Evans Coves, their whole effort was now being focused on trying to break the ship free from the ice and escape from the pack. Their 'great fight' to get out lasted until late in the afternoon, with the propeller getting a bad gruelling, according to Bruce. Finally clear, they 'steered away for Cape Evans, leaving Campbell's party for the time, as it was impossible to get near them'.

At Evans Coves, after waiting all Saturday the 24th, the dull black spot seen on the horizon was interpreted as a black shadow on the distant line of pack ice. The sea in the bay was still largely clear of ice. As far as they could tell, there was nothing to stop *Terra Nova* reaching them. So the sighting was just another false alarm. 'Hope deferred maketh the heart sick', wrote Priestley, on Sunday the 25th.

At Cape Evans everyone was anxious. *Terra Nova* – their lifeline – had been gone nine days, with inevitable worries for her safety. Atkinson had left for Hut Point with Demetri and the dogs, in response to a verbal request from Scott for the dog teams to go out to meet the returning Polar party so that their news – 'success or otherwise' – could get to the ship. But the last support party had not yet been heard from, so nothing was known about the Polar party beyond the details dating from 22 December 1911, brought back by the first support party. Gales were constant, snow thick, ice everywhere; deep wind-sculpted drifts almost hid the winter quarters hut, a lonely small building stranded in an overwhelming grey whiteness between the cold ocean and the icy slopes of Mount Erebus.

News arrived at Cape Evans on Friday 23 February. Demetri appeared with the dogs and Tom Crean. Crean told how on 4 January 1912, high on the polar plateau, the last support party had said farewell to the final Polar party, consisting of Scott, Wilson, Oates, Bowers and Petty Officer Evans, with 146 miles to go to the Pole. Scott had unexpectedly added Bowers as a fifth man to his team, leaving Lieutenant Evans, with Crean and Lashly, to get back down the Beardmore and across the Barrier one man short. Teddy Evans had collapsed with scurvy, so Lashly and Crean had dragged him on the sledge. Running out of food, and strength, with Evans desperately ill, Crean had managed to walk the last 35 miles to the hut at Hut Point, where he found, extraordinarily luckily, Atkinson, Demetri and the dog teams. Bad weather had held up their plans to set out across the Barrier to meet Scott, which meant that the dogs had been able to go out and carry Teddy Evans back in, and Atkinson could attend him medically.

Demetri had a letter from Dr Atkinson for Wright:

Dear Silas   22 February
I have just brought Teddy Evans from beyond Corner Camp with a hellish go of Scurvy. Bring with you some few <u>apples</u> <u>oranges</u> and <u>onions</u>
   I want you please to take my team South to meet the last party. If you cannot possibly do so ask Cherry.

Demetri also had a letter from Atkinson to Simpson, as the man Scott had left in charge of Cape Evans, asking 'for Wright to go and take over the dog teams to go south to meet Capt Scott'. As the only doctor, Atkinson now had to look after the sick Teddy Evans until

Terra Nova could collect him from Hut Point and invalid him back to Britain.

Simpson, busy preparing for his own departure to India, had a difficult problem. He had planned to stay in Antarctica a second year, and his decision to pull out left a serious gap. Someone had to take over all his work, and in his view that had to be Wright. Collecting data at set intervals, and managing a number of sophisticated and potentially temperamental instruments, meant being tied to the hut. Wright, however, was pursuing an independent path in ice research. He did not want to be confined indoors, which would be the inevitable result of taking on Simpson's project. Young, energetic and experienced in polar conditions, he was eager to get out and do fieldwork. Simpson, faced with Atkinson's letter asking for Wright to take over the dog teams and sledge south to meet Scott, put the needs of his science first. 'It was not ~~safe~~ convenient for Wright to go for he would be away for probably a month after I had left by the ship', Simpson wrote in his diary on 23 February. Instead, 'I considered that Cherry Garrard would be able to go meet Captain Scott.' He replied to Atkinson but sent both Cherry and Wright to Hut Point 'so that either could go with the dogs'.

Cherry-Garrard knew that it would have to be him. Anxiously he copied the basic diagrams required to navigate into his zoological notebook – the first few pages of which were filled with a numbered list and description of birds killed – and then packed food, rations and gear, collected details of the supplies already at One Ton and listed the news to tell Scott, including the fact that Campbell had been put ashore on the Victoria Land coast with provisions for six weeks. Once, very concerned, Cherry had asked Bill Wilson if not knowing how to navigate mattered. Wilson replied that he would only ever have to do it if the real navigator had gone under.

Charles Wright was one of the 'hardest' of sledgers according to Scott, who had selected him to navigate the first support party back across the Barrier. Short-sighted, but not nearly as bad as Cherry, Wright didn't need to wear glasses for ordinary sledging. Cherry did; but both men experienced virtual blindness when their glasses frosted over while sledging in extreme cold. Cherry had already had one painful experience of Simpson's single-minded attitude to science

when he spent hard weeks building a practice stone hut in preparation for the winter journey to the emperor penguins. But Simpson
had insisted that the hut should be moved, stone by heavy stone,
because he had not realized there would be a blubber fire inside it,
and the smoke would interfere 'with one of his poles collecting the
electric force'.

Simpson's judgement about who should take the dogs out towards
Scott was made entirely in relation to science. On Scott's first expedition, some scientists had been selected on a fairly haphazard basis, and
in certain cases results had been heavily criticized. This time men had
been sought out with professional competence. The practice of science was increasingly professional. Ambitious scientists wished to
manage their own time and resources, with inevitable potential for
conflict. At the heart of the tension between science and exploring
was, and always had been, the allocation of resources. Simpson allocated the resource of Wright away from expedition members – in
particular, the commander – to the needs of science and, in this case,
specifically to the science for which he was responsible, with its com-
mitment to daily data-collecting, and connections to the international
world of meteorological and magnetic work.

Wright kept a diary, in which he generally wrote what he thought.
The month of February 1912 is missing. The record of Wright's feelings and the effect on him of Simpson's decisions are not known.
Cherry's diary, generally full, has no entry for Friday 23 February, the
day Simpson considered him – a man who could not navigate and
had never driven a dog team or experienced being the leader of any
party – as less inconvenient than Wright to send out on to the Barrier
with the dog teams, with autumn approaching.

At Hut Point, 'I'm right in it', Cherry found time to scribble, on
Saturday the 24th, although he was using Atkinson's dates, which
could be one day out. 'I have spent the day in navigation, weights,
and dog training . . . but what one can do one can do & Scott is not
dependent on the dog teams.' Then, leaving for the Barrier on
Monday the 26th, he wrote a positive entry in his small diary: 'Well
I'm off on my own for the first time – first time navigation & 1st time
dog driving with thick weather & strongish head wind & drift – so its
not an easy beginning.' On reaching Corner Camp, 'Dear Sir,'

Cherry wrote in a note left for Captain Scott, 'I very much hope we can get through to One Ton to find you there. Everybody sends their very best wishes to you all, and Demetri and I hope that you have reached the Pole & are all well.'

At Evans Coves on 26 February the Eastern party finished their regular rations, brought ashore for their five-week sledging expedition. With sledges piled ready to go, they were watching anxiously for the ship. Every night, in their two tents, they held a concert, singing whatever came into their heads: a hymn, a music-hall song or a shanty. They couldn't get to sleep, and it helped pass the time. But such heavy amounts of snow fell on the 25th and again on the 26th that the tents were half-buried, and the packed sledges completely buried. The emergency depot of four weeks' sledging food brought ashore from *Terra Nova* had been set aside, in case, as Campbell put it, 'we are down here for a winter in which case we shall want it sledging to Cape Evans in the spring'. Priestley tried to dig through the snow to find the Primus, but all he got was a frostbitten face – so it was dry biscuits and raw blubber for food. They lay in their bags, barely able to move because the thick drifts pressed so heavily against the tent's sides. The unceasing gale forced fine crystals of snow through the pores of the threadbare material, covering everything in brief crusts of white that melted, wetting further the already wet. Blinding drift made it impossible to get outside or see anything. Priestley: 'We can do nothing but lie & think & try to sleep tho none of us are doing much of the latter.'

At midnight on the 28th the wind dropped, almost as though it had been turned off. Dickason decided that 29 February, leap year day, would be their lucky day. The ship would appear. The sea was calm, the view clear, and there was only a thin coating of ice near the shore. They spread their bedding outside to dry – but then the wind gusted, lifting and spinning drift, and in minutes everything was in a frightful state of wetness again.

Campbell and Levick had a sequence of actions planned. 'Although we shan't give up hope for six days, we are starting to prepare for a winter here', Levick noted. With Abbott and Browning he would remain camping at the depot as look-outs; they would also repair the tent, dig out the sledges buried deep in the latest snowdrifts and kill and butcher a seal. Campbell, Priestley and Dickason would take their tent and equipment to the Southern Foothills in order, as Levick put it baldly, to 'select a good snowdrift to make a hole to live in'. Should the ship not appear by 6 March – and the chance was small, because of the pack freezing – then

> we shall conclude that she has gone down, or been injured somehow, as of course she wld never dream of leaving us here for the winter with only 4 weeks provisions, as though we have plenty of seals, they can't know that for certain. However . . . we are only very anxious & have in no way given up hope, believing that the Sthn P have returned very late to Ht Pt & that they are waiting to pick them up before taking us off. Also if the Sthn P are lost, they will naturally wait till the last possible moment for them before coming away.

Bringing the possible loss of Scott and his men, the Southern party, into assumptions about the non-appearance of the ship was a thought to keep private. But digging a hole in a snowdrift – that was getting closer. Climbing the foothills from the beach near Levick's penguins, Priestley saw a couple of snowdrifts and speculated that they 'might do very well for winter quarters if the worst came to the worst'.

Late in the evening of Dickason's hoped-for lucky day, Thursday 29 February, Priestley walked among the pebbles and through trickling water and heaps of old seaweed to the penguin rookery discovered by Levick. The Adélies were still gathered in good numbers, but the sounds of summer had gone and the noises were muted. The birds had nearly finished moulting: they wouldn't be here much longer. Only five seals were on the beach. From the top of the hill they now called Look-Out Hill, Campbell and Dickason saw what they thought was smoke and a black object. Campbell hoped that it was the ship. On every clear day, Priestley remarked dryly, there were two or three false alarms that the ship had been sighted. This time a snowstorm blocked out the view. So there was uncertainty. Again.

As Pennell headed back south on Sunday 25 February after attempting to reach Evans Coves, *Terra Nova* faced the same heavy snow and hard gales that were hitting Campbell and his men in their threadbare tents. But the ship also ran into pancake ice, that precursor of winter freezing. Pennell sent the whaleboat in to Cape Evans a little before midnight, taking the men due to return to the hut. Stumbling ashore through deep snow where this time last year there was almost none, they woke the occupants with the unlooked-for news that all those who wished to leave Antarctica must go on board at once: they had only fifteen minutes to get their things together. *Terra Nova* had been able to spend exactly one period of time at Cape Evans this summer. Now this brief stop threatened to be the last; Pennell could not undertake to communicate with shore again. The weather since the year began had driven their reality with a tough whip hand. Scott's elaborate instructions for Pennell had been impossible to achieve. He hadn't even managed to pick up the six stranded men.

Simpson suddenly found himself 'in a difficulty'. He had sent Wright to Hut Point, so he had no one to leave his instruments with or to do the observations. But, as the man in charge, he had to consult with Pennell. Simpson climbed into the whaleboat, along with Day, whose work was finished now the motors were dead, Anton the Russian jockey, desperate to leave, and Griffith Taylor, whose gear had been packed and ready since last November, so that all he had to do was collect it. None of the occupants left in the hut knew what to do about Simpson's machinery. '[W]e lack technical knowledge here', said Gran, happy to be back in his own space in the hut. 'We do our best, pressing buttons and pulling levers until something happens.'

The next day the gale increased, the wind shrieked, the anchor dragged and most of those on board worked wretchedly hard trying to retrieve it. Pennell talked things over with Simpson and decided to collect Teddy Evans from Hut Point first and then try again to get Campbell. The weather cleared sufficiently for the ship to reach Hut Point just before midnight on the 28th and hoist poor Teddy Evans aboard, wrapped in his sleeping-bag.

Thursday 29 February was calm and clear, allowing cargo to be unloaded at Cape Evans; another task achieved. The last people leaving Antarctica scrambled aboard, including Meares, in charge of dogs, who had suddenly decided to depart, and Clissold the cook, who had recovered from concussion when he fell off an iceberg (where he had been asked to pose by Ponting) but who was now suffering a swollen arm from a poisoned scratch. *Terra Nova* donated Archer, the ship's cook, to Cape Evans, and *Discovery* man Petty Officer Williamson, to replace Forde. 'Everyone dead tired,' wrote Bruce. 'But we've done our work . . . if we can only pick up Campbell now.'

The problem was the lateness of the season. Pennell had experienced the clogging, impenetrable qualities of newly freezing sea ice at the same time the previous year, when he had been much further north. Now, as soon as they left Cape Evans, *Terra Nova* was in the pack, pushing through, then meeting heavier and thicker ice before just managing to get away each time. Fortunately Harry Pennell had turned out to be a natural ice captain.

With Scott still absent, Simpson gone and Evans invalided out, the command of the expedition had fallen on Atkinson, a quiet, thoughtful, conscientious naval surgeon. Atkinson had never exercised command in any capacity, but there was no one else. Campbell, once retrieved, could take over as the senior naval officer. Levick could accompany Evans home as a doctor. With all the departures Priestley would be very useful at Cape Evans. Although Scott had said he would not offer Campbell's three seamen a second year, under the circumstances their energy and enthusiasm might be very welcome. Those who had toiled over the Barrier on behalf of the Polar party were worn and stale. Six, in one sense, fresh men, were waiting to be picked up.

On Friday 1 March *Terra Nova* struggled, stuck, got free and then stuck again in thick, uncompromising pack ice. 'Much anxiety', wrote Bruce, 'but we got her moving.' On Saturday the 2nd 'Campbell's chances of relief are getting woefully small', Bruce wrote. Rationalizing began: Campbell's party had a month's extra provisions on shore, there were plenty of seals, the distance they had to sledge back was only about 200 miles, with three depots in place, two of which they ought to find. Granted, they would have to get to Granite Harbour first, and no one knew if that was possible, but the rest was fairly simple. Assumptions were made: the Eastern party would start travelling in late autumn, as soon as the sea ice formed; the sea ice would hold. During Saturday afternoon the ship began moving towards the Drygalski, and hope was ignited. But by

8.00 p.m. any further attempt was useless. *Terra Nova* turned away, back to Cape Evans for the last time.

In their tent in the Southern Foothills, 'We are all getting fed up with waiting', complained Priestley, 'and are so slack from the underfeeding during the last 12 days bad weather that an ordinary walk of a mile or two makes us tired.' 'If there is still no sign of the ship this morning,' Campbell was writing in his journal, 'I must start killing seals for the winter.' Campbell had no compunction about killing seals. The unexpected issue was the wind. Weddell seals, they all knew from Cape Adare, would not haul themselves out on to the ice if a wind was blowing. Now, as they came to the awful realization that this vile wind they were experiencing might be a constant component of autumn and winter here at Evans Coves, finding and killing seals became a matter of urgency. So on this first day of March 1912 two seals were killed and cut up, and eighteen penguins, '& thus', wrote Priestley, in charge of the commissariat, 'laid the foundation stone of our stock of meat for the winter'. But summarizing the day, as he lay shivering in his bag after dinner, Priestley admitted: 'C is very down today & I was equally so yesterday . . . D is undoubtedly the cheeriest of the party.'

The facts had to be faced. They were highly likely to be marooned, with minimal resources. The potential for catastrophe was real. Campbell and Levick, as naval officers, had assessed the implications, and Priestley had been included in the discussions as, for the purpose, an honorary officer. Certain key strategies needed to be agreed, in advance. Tight discipline would be imposed on the three seamen. The three officers would, in turn, not allow visible differences of opinion to arise between themselves. The previous summer had not been entirely harmonious. That must not be allowed to happen under what would be exceptionally difficult circumstances and intimate, crowded conditions. Perhaps most importantly, a sense of private space had to be created for the seamen. Half of whatever living area they ended up with would be allocated to the men as their mess deck, where they were to have 'free right and privilege to say anything they liked within these territorial limits' – although, of course, it would be impossible for them not to be overheard.

On Saturday 2 March a full gale started blowing, and it blew even harder all Sunday. Campbell's tent ripped badly again. 'We are all miserable & very anxious', wrote Levick, watching the bamboo poles in his tent bowing under the strain. Twelve of the last fifteen days had been spent lying in their bags. The wind was beginning to wind and worm into their very beings. Everything was defined by it: their every movement outside, their every thought about the ship and its safety, or possible harm. The wind had assumed a relentless presence. If anything, it was increasing in ferocity, adding to its repertoire new, short, exceedingly fierce gusts. 'This constant gale . . . is too awful,' wrote Campbell, 'and we have nothing to do but wait for the ship.'

Cherry-Garrard, Demetri and the dogs arrived late on Sunday 3 March at One Ton Depot. First assembled in February 1911, the farthest point they had all reached with the ponies on the depot journey, it was an intensely lonely place, with its small heaps of things that men required in order to survive packed into a mound covered in snow, with a bamboo pole tethered down in four places and a tattered black flag. A blizzard began on the 5th, preventing any travelling until the 7th. The dogs were ravenously eating through their supplies, and there was not enough dog food remaining to try going on further south. Cherry made the decision to stay three more days then start back to Hut Point on the 10th. At night temperatures dropped sharply. Being here, not knowing how far away the Polar party were or when they would come, wracked Cherry's nerves. One night he was so sure he saw the Polar party that he almost started to walk south towards them. Demetri was unaccountably ill. 'It is a very cold wait – waiting & thinking', Cherry wrote.

At Evans Coves, Campbell gave the order to start digging a cave on the slope above Levick's beach on Tuesday 5 March. Standing on the bank of drift snow, they drove the pick in. Levick and Abbott found two more seals and killed them. Next day, the 6th, while Priestley and Browning cooked, guarding the two frayed tents, the others killed ten penguins and worked at digging a shaft down, using Priestley's two short-handled ice axes, the pick-axe and their spade.

On Thursday the 7th, while Priestley and Campbell dug, the others searched for and killed a seal, their sixth. Priestley tried eating large strips of fried blubber for breakfast and thought them excellent. Biscuits and meat fried in the oil from the blubber were equally good, which was a great relief, and 'will mean a lot to us in comfort during the winter'. They hadn't got nearly enough seals. They just had to hope for some calm days, so the animals would appear. The 7th was the last day on which they could expect the ship, 'and she hasn't come', wrote Levick bleakly. 'The last two days have been . . .', and he stopped writing.

Very late on Monday 4 March *Terra Nova*, having finished all jobs possible to do for this season, took Atkinson with Petty Officer Keohane to Hut Point. Atkinson wanted to be at the hut for Scott's return, 'and to tell him that Campbell had had to be left, and to be able to go to their help if Capt Scott wished'. The ship then headed north to make one final effort for Campbell. 'Temperature of 7 degrees F. Wardroom 12 degrees F. Too cold for much writing', recorded Bruce. In the short time since they were last here the ice had thickened, and the conditions worsened. On the 6th they got within 18 miles of the Drygalski Ice Tongue but were then 'hopelessly blocked . . . and only got out with much difficulty & heavy bumping'. This last effort, noted Bruce, 'is really only to make quite certain that we can do nothing, we really know it is futile'. Late on the 6th they gave up.

Terra Nova had experienced a most trying and disappointing season. From the moment they put Campbell and his men ashore for their short summer exploring, 'our luck seemed to be out', Pennell told Kathleen Scott: landing stores at winter quarters had been difficult, the attempt to collect Griffith Taylor had been baulked and now they had been caught four times ('tho it seems more') attempting to retrieve Campbell. 'That is the summary of our exploits this year. Although one does not seem to have done much on paper still it has been a wearying time.'

'[W]e were all heartily glad and considerably relieved,' wrote Simpson, speaking as an escaper, 'when Pennell finally gave up the attempt and set the bow of the ship for New Zealand.'

14

Marooned

10 March–1 April 1912

We had some weary waiting.

Abbott, February, 1913

THE FIRST BIRTHDAY in their new life of straitened rations was Abbott's, on Sunday 10 March. Abbott was probably the hungriest of them all. Two meals a day – seal and a biscuit for breakfast, the same for supper – simply was not enough while doing hard physical labour. But they were all feeling most desperate about the lack of sledging biscuits, those solid 2 oz, palm-sized squares baked to a secret process for the expedition. They could eat six in one go if they had the chance – crunching through the hardness, savouring the joy of biting, chewing, swallowing – but these simple pleasures were now suddenly withdrawn. Their bodies' craving for biscuits was constant, and Priestley allocated one extra to each member of the party, to celebrate Abbott's thirty-second birthday.

The allocation wasn't random. The necessary treats – biscuits, raisins, sugar lumps – had already been set aside, although Priestley suspected a sudden onset of birthdays. He had worked out how much of each type of food they could have, and how often, and had divided their supplies into meals, marking the passage of time with small but significant variations and allocations. Stores were very short, there was no denying, but food was generally in hand, except that with no salt left they were trying to cook their hoosh with salt water. Scavenging along the beach they'd found a sort of white seaweed – 'not bad eating', thought Campbell. The real worry was fresh meat. Whenever the battering wind allowed, they searched for seals, but by the 14th their total of seals was only eleven, with nearly two already eaten. But they'd slaughtered fifty-three more penguins before the newly moulted birds left the rookery.

Dickason and Browning had just solved their second essential – light – by inventing a simple but effective Oxo tin blubber lamp: a few strands of lamp wick or rope suspended from a safety pin across a tin filled with oil melted from seal blubber. It provided 'splendid' light with surprising amounts of heat, and, even better, the pieces of blubber could be eaten after they had given up their oil. The invention of the lamps made everyone feel more cheerful, able to imagine having somewhere proper to live. The lamps would have to be modified to melt their own oil, but that could be done 'when we get into our winter home'.

But the thing that no one could understand – and which made them feel so pessimistic – was the sea. It was entirely free from ice, yet there was no ship. What was stopping her? She must be lost. 'I have not much hope of being picked up now,' Priestley wrote on Wednesday the 13th, '& I don't think the others have either though we don't admit it to each other.' Campbell had his own last day: Friday 15 March. If *Terra Nova* had not come by then, Levick had instructions to leave his look-out camp site on the 16th and bring over his men and tent. This was the final step. Then 'we will all take up our quarters in the hut, or rather ice cave, which is all it is at present.'

Digging had started into the thickest part of the drift, hollowing out the living and sleeping space. The drift size defined how big a hole they would end up with. The maximum length turned out to be 12 feet – the crates the motor sledges had travelled south in had been 16 feet – although they achieved nearly twice the width of a motor crate and a little more height. But it was shelter, their third essential. As they hacked out the ice, they could hear the vile, bitter wind roaring outside. To be protected from it was a most profound relief. Returning to their 'infernally uncomfortable' tents to lie in wet bags covered in snow crystals, listening to the endless racketing, wondering how much longer the fragile cloth protecting them could stand the beating, was a most miserable contrast. It helped to make the prospect of home in a hole in the ice preferable. 'I shall be glad when we can get into our winter quarters', said Priestley. 'At any rate the waiting is very nearly over & we are beginning to get more or less reconciled to our second winter.' And he reverted, briefly, to being a scientist, describing the composition of their drift: the top four feet snow, and under that three or four inches of granular snow soaked in thaw water then frozen. Below that was a slightly irregular boundary line, with layers of grit and seaweed or lake algae, then ice.

Their igloo, or burrow, or hut, or ice-cave − whatever anyone wanted to call it − was where it was, half-way up the slope of a hill, because that was the only place with a thick enough permanent drift. But their possessions were spread between supplies stored at the moraine depot where they had landed, the two tents and various stacks of penguin and seal carcasses. Everything had to be sorted out before the winter. But first, those absolute essentials, their sleeping-bags, cooking equipment and few personal possessions had to be transferred safely from their tents to the cave, over what Campbell tersely described as a 'chaos of big boulders'.

Their local world was changing fast. The companionable beach of summer had become frigid, rigid, losing its life and liveliness. The plateau wind was dictator and constrainer. With the shift to autumn it had established itself, coming always from the same direction, driving everything that happened. The only variables were speed, consistency and occasional absence. Freedom in this place was narrowing down to one thing: freedom from the wind. Its relentless presence swept all surfaces clear. The piedmont was polished blue ice, with no chance for snow to settle. The boulders stood visible on icy ground, unless covered briefly by a snow fall. Campbell noticed that, as the surface of the sea began to freeze, the plateau wind drove the new ice out. It was remarkably lucky that enough snow had accumulated to create a drift where they could live. This was at least something to work at being cheerful about.

Cheerfulness had been noted as a necessary quality from the moment *Terra Nova* left England − a standard by which to select and judge. Cheerfulness countered adversity. It could override exhaustion. It provided bulwarks against loneliness and boredom, against irritation with people and place, repetition and tediousness. The true exponent of cheerfulness potentially did not even experience those counter-productive feelings. Cheerfulness was particularly expected from the men, underpinning all the qualities assumed from those who assist or serve, unquestioning acceptance and obedience, an alertness to the needs of others and a minimizing of one's own, doing whatever was wanted and never complaining. But as a desired quality, cheerfulness extended to every member of the expedition. It was the approach wanted when dealing with going aloft in a blizzard to shovelling coal in temperatures over 100°, from sleeping in hopelessly crowded conditions to butchering seals or putting up a tent in a gale – and perhaps, most of all, to working as a draught animal, hauling a sledge. Beyond all this, there was cheerfulness in the face of crisis such as Campbell and his men were currently facing. And there was cheerfulness when ill, usually a private matter but, given their shared lives, not able to be hidden. It was the optimum, possibly essential, state of mind.

Abbott, Browning and Dickason were exhibiting cheerfulness in impressive quantities. Campbell, as leader, was rather more free from the necessity: the need to manage and make decisions was currently engaging all his attention and abilities. Priestley, facing his third Antarctic winter in five years, alternated between being cheerful as a known and approved state of mind, and being frustrated and fed up. But Levick, to the outside world apparently imperturbable, not a man given to speedy movement or sudden changes of mood or rapid decision-making, was suffering deeply. The way they were living was to him profoundly awful. The way they would have to live was worse. He was dealing with his misery, working through it, but he did not trust himself to make entries in his diary.

Saturday 16 March was the day Campbell decreed for moving out of their tents into the ice-cave, but it was impossible. The wind was blowing too hard to achieve anything.

On Saturday 16 March, Cherry-Garrard struggled in from One Ton Depot to the hut at Hut Point after a horrible journey, with Demetri ill and the dogs thin and frostbitten, to find Atkinson distressed and worried. All contact between the winter quarters hut at Cape Evans and the bare, cold old hut had been severed. Continuing wild storms continually broke up the sea ice. In charge of the expedition, as long as Scott remained absent, Atkinson was facing miserably difficult decisions. Eleven men were missing. Who should he help: Campbell, to the north, or Scott, somewhere to the south? Only four men were available at Hut Point, but Cherry and Demetri were exhausted, and neither could go out immediately again. That left just Atkinson and Patrick Keohane.

Cherry helped Atkinson marshal the arguments. First, the Eastern party. Atkinson had listened to the rationalizing while on board *Terra Nova* during the ship's third futile attempt to relieve Campbell: how Campbell had taken four weeks' emergency food on shore, how he 'must feed on seal, & then come round the coast', using existing depots, travelling on the sea ice or up on the piedmont. It was alarming, noted Cherry, but 'I agree . . . that to try . . . to meet Campbell is useless at present: if we can go N they can come S, & to put two parties there is to double the risk'. Cherry could only 'hope he is . . . on his way round.' Having dealt with Campbell, they started thinking about that most pressing matter: another trip out on to the Barrier to look for Scott, Wilson, Oates, Bowers and Petty Officer Evans. By Sunday the 17th they had decided that Atkinson, taking Keohane, would man-haul a sledge searching out beyond Corner Camp.

In the winter quarters hut at Cape Evans this Sunday Gran noted that it was St Patrick's Day and also Oates's thirty-second birthday.

North of Antarctica, as *Terra Nova* battled through icebergs and snow, the seamen working aloft in the freezing wind, Nigger lost his grip and fell. But no one saw it, and Browning's little cat drowned on Sunday 17 March. Carried on board in Abbott's pocket as a ten-day old kitten, Nigger had survived twenty-one and a half adventurous months, visited Antarctica twice and crossed the wild Southern ocean three times, but he failed on the fourth.

At Evans Coves on Sunday 17 March, Campbell, Priestley and Dickason struck camp and dragged their loaded sledge as far as they could to a depot near the shore. From here to the drift where they had dug out their cave was a mile, a reasonable journey in summer. But getting up the slope over and around the boulders, was increasingly hard. They loaded their worldly goods – sleeping-bags, rucksacks, clothes, cooking things, tools, navigating instruments – on their backs and started walking. The wind increased to gale strength, coming in terrific gusts, knocking them sideways, pushing them around, pausing then rushing back and swiping them off their feet again with their unwieldy loads. A dozen times in three horrible journeys Priestley was thrown to the ground or against the hard granite of the boulders. Dickason, knocked over time after time, hurt his knee and his ankle, and lost his sheath knife. Campbell, thrown across the rocks, lost his compass. Priestley: 'Our tempers have never been so tried during the whole of our life together.'

But by the end of a most awful day they had managed to shift enough gear into the hollowed-out space in the heart of the snowdrift to be able to cook and sleep. To Campbell this start of life in an ice-cave was 'Cold as we have not done the insulation but nice and quiet . . . we can hear the gale roaring outside and it is a great relief to be out of it'. Priestley ate a pint of blubber in great thick slices and felt much better for it. 'A very pleasant hoosh in the new home the first of many equally good I hope and expect, for I don't think there is the slightest chance of the ship coming.' Then 'had some hymns tonight but could not remember many'.

On Monday the 18th, the first day of their cave lives, Priestley, Campbell and Dickason chipped away, enlarging their living space, while outside the gale pounded, and fine crystals of drift worked their way in because they had yet to invent a door. 'Will this wind never stop?' Priestley was still making rhetorical demands. He wanted to fight the wind, but he was impotent. He listed their actions: he'd been out on his storekeeper duties, replenishing the stock of meat and blubber and getting a new tin of biscuits; Dickason had cleared the shaft into the cave; Campbell was 'ill'. The next day, Tuesday the 19th, with the wind at hurricane force, their temporary door blew down, so everything in the cave was covered in drift again. 'Wind not really giving us a chance to do anything', railed Priestley, 'and we are feeling terribly fed up with things.' It made him mad to think about all their possessions and equipment waiting for them on *Terra Nova*; even worse, to imagine them lost, 'along with all my records', if the ship had gone down. That was the worry beyond worries.

Yet poor Levick, Abbott and Browning were out this Tuesday in the middle of the hurricane, struggling against most miserable adversity. The gales had prevented the three men from moving out of their look-out tent near the depot on the day agreed. The hurricane on the 19th meant another day in their bags, watching the tent-poles bend under the strain. Suddenly one snapped, followed by another two, collapsing the tent on top of them, pinning them down. A terrible sensation of panic-inducing suffocation almost overwhelmed them. Their possessions were strewn around the tent, and they weren't wearing their wind clothes, but one by one they struggled out from underneath and got dressed. Browning lay across the three sleeping-bags, holding them down in case the tent suddenly took off, while Abbott and Levick located the collapsed opening and pushed through to try and find somewhere sheltered enough to put up their spare tent. Crawling, because standing in the wind wasn't possible, they could find nowhere and so crawled back in under the wrecked tent. They lay with nothing to eat but raw seal meat and two sticks of chocolate, waiting for a lull in the wind that didn't come, rubbing their chilled feet, hands and faces to keep the circulation going.

A night in these conditions was beyond bearing. The ice-cave was a bit over 2 miles away, but they decided to risk the journey. Crawling around, piling rocks and ice over the fallen tent to protect their irreplaceable sleeping-bags, they set out, moving like crabs on their hands and knees across the worst part, the polished blue ice of the piedmont, with the wind sweeping them sideways and drift swirling so they could barely see, their faces badly frostbitten. Browning's face, said Levick, was an appalling dusky blue, streaked with white patches. They reached the Southern Foothills and huddled together for shelter behind some boulders, completely exhausted with the effort. Then they started again, over and around the boulders, up to the ice-cave.

Inside the cave Campbell, Priestley and Dickason were lying in their bags, Campbell miserably craving biscuits, Dickason his old and favourite pipe (but there wasn't enough tobacco) and Priestley generally fed up, brooding on all his things waiting on *Terra Nova*. Suddenly they heard voices, and their small space was filled with three exhausted, chilled men needing feeding. After that there was nothing for it but try to fit an extra man into each of their sleeping-bags. 'My sleeping mate', said Campbell 'was Levick and I was squashed flat.'

Next day, Wednesday the 20th, the wind eased enough for Levick, Abbott and Browning to go back and bring over their sleeping-bags and possessions. Levick: 'we are now established in the half-finished ice cave', his tentative handwriting revealing his state of mind, 'and are all of us feeling pretty miserable.' The prospect of the winter before them was 'enough to give anyone the hump'. Priestley: 'I am feeling simply famished.'

There had been much general talk in Scott's expedition about enforced winterings on the coast. Campbell had contemplated it as a possible outcome of their big spring sledging trip, if they had managed to get beyond Cape North and been cut off by unstable sea ice. Now, staring at the reality, the looseness of the thinking gaped as theoretical assumptions hit actual necessity. Catching seals and penguins, using their blubber for fuel and light, eating their blubber and flesh – yes. But survival depended on more than the local wildlife. Adélie penguins were available only during spring and summer. Weddell seals were plentiful in spring, much sparser in winter and wouldn't haul out on to the ice when the wind blew. Reduced to an almost exclusive diet of seal meat and blubber, their craving for sweet things and carbohydrates was almost overwhelming. The one biscuit disappeared almost in a moment: crunched up, it sank without a sound and was gone. Salt was essential, but they had enough for emergencies only. They wanted tea, and tobacco. Shelter, assumed to be straightforward, was not. In this place of constant gales and almost no usable snow and ice, shelter required luck and ingenuity. And if they should run out of that apparently simplest of things – matches – they were finished. Five of the six were smokers, so their match use had been heavy. But now light, heat and therefore food depended on their irreplaceable and meagre stocks.

There were plenty of jobs to do and they were well practised at working together on allocated tasks. The inner cave, their living space, still needed extending, and they divided forces, half of them picking at the walls while the other half carried supplies over from the moraine depot – a hard, frostbite-inducing journey. Campbell's nose was already one great painful blister; so was Abbott's. The doorway needed narrowing, so a lintel was made from biscuit boxes on uprights of snow blocks, with a curtain made from a clothes bag. This first day all together as cave residents, 21 March 1912, turned into a red-letter day when Browning saw a seal, killed it and found between thirty-six and forty fish inside it, none of them too digested, and two still not yet dead in its throat. They had three each fried for dinner. The next day for breakfast there would be three more each.

From the start, cooking was divided up into three teams of two. Levick and Priestley went first, 'cook and general servant'. Then Browning and Dickason took over, instituting two immediate improvements: salt-water ice, and the snow-soaked seal's blood from the scene of the kill, which made the most splendid hoosh. The spoon actually stood up in the gravy. Campbell and Abbott were the final pair, Campbell the smallest eater and Abbott the largest, so that would probably balance itself out. Priestley was allowing a double portion of hoosh in the morning and a single hoosh at night, currently one biscuit a day and cocoa from Tuesday to Saturday nights; tea was allowed once a week, on Sunday, with a reboil on Monday. Preparing the meals and cooking took all day. It was so arduous, so tedious and time-consuming that men dreaded their turn; but, critically, all six were sharing the pain. And there was a kind of pleasure watching others toil, knowing the rhythm of the schedule meant the miserable effort was necessary only one day in three.

Salt may have been down to the last emergency tin, but to the smokers tobacco was as serious a lack. The usual substitute, tea leaves, was only available in a severely attenuated form after the Monday night reboil, so they had begun innovating. Currently they were smoking the teak sledge meter, which measured in fathoms not feet, having been part of the depth-sounding machine. Now it was fine shavings, mixed with their naval tobacco. Science, converted to the needs of exploring, ending up serving bodily craving.

Campbell and Priestley were the joint architects of the ice-cave, but everybody innovated. Spaces were excavated on either side of the shaft as safes for meat and blubber. Priestley did the pick work, with a shovel gang to remove the debris. 'We are overcoming obstacles to our comfort every day and indeed these obstacles are useful in that they help us to fill our minds and keep us from brooding about home where they will just be expecting news of the fate of the ship', he wrote. They cut blocks of snow – a better insulator than ice – to

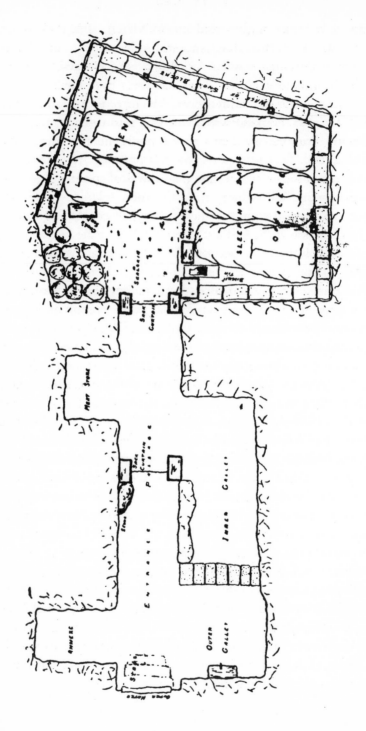

A plan of the ice-cave, drawn by Campbell

line the ice walls, forcing seaweed down the back; then they stopped part-way up, so creating a useful shelf. Half the floor – the side the officers were sleeping on – was covered with pebbles, with a layer of seaweed from the beach on the top and a tent floor cloth over that. The hearth was on the men's side and needed pick-axe work, which meant that the men's insulation of pebbles, seaweed and floor-cloth could not be laid yet, so they were currently much colder in their bags.

Outside, autumn was unrolling and the days shrinking. Priestley remembered that on 23 March 1909 *Nimrod* had arrived in New Zealand, and he had come ashore to the joy of greenness and strangers. Here he was on Saturday 23 March 1912, starting life in a hole in the ice, with five people he already knew too well. After crawling along the passage, negotiating a large granite boulder unavoidably in the way and squeezing under the door lintel into the cave, the galley was immediately on the left, in the corner. It was small, but there was no room for anything more, with Dickason's sleeping-bag next to it. Opposite, in the corner on the right, was Priestley's sleeping-bag, with cases of provisions along the foot, making quite a snug alcove: a kind of recompense for the hard work of being storekeeper 'in absolute charge of rations'. The far corner on the right had Campbell's bag, with Levick between, Abbott opposite him and Browning in the far corner on the left. The total space was about 12 feet by 9 feet, with a maximum height of 5 feet 6 inches. For Abbott, 6 feet tall, standing naturally straight, the missing height was particular misery, but none of them could stand upright. The roof above was hard snow, currently 18 inches thick: enough, they hoped, to withstand the warmth generated by cooking.

But Monday the 25th could be counted a good day. The inside of their hut was finished – at least, all the digging and picking – by sinking the square yard of hearth 6 inches below the floor level, lining it with large flat stones and then insulating the floor on the men's side to bring everything to the same level. The six sleeping-bags now lay on the floor interleaved, like six big maggots in a nest, except that what emerged from each bag each morning was a slowly dirtier, hairier and more disreputable-looking man.

★

On Monday 25 March at Hut Point Cherry-Garrard wrote, 'We are now on the days on which to expect the Pole Party in, pray God I may be right'. He was physically ill and emotionally spent. 'Atch and I look at one another – and he looks and I feel quite haggard with anxiety.' Atkinson thought that the Polar party were unlikely to have scurvy. In comparison he and Cherry were feeling 'quite comfortable' about Campbell. He only needed to 'exercise care'. Cherry listed the Eastern party's advantages: they were fresh and had plenty of seal: Campbell's 'great care was almost a bye word on the ship . . . he discussed the event of shipwreck & also of the ship being unable to get to him with Pennell: & for this reason landed a month's rations as a depot, also discussing the idea of living on seal.' Campbell's virtues as a leader, his caution and forward-thinking, were reaching out a long, unknown hand to ease the worries, and pressure for action, on his fellow expeditioners. Atkinson considered Campbell a man who 'believed in strict discipline and kept it strict'. He thought this would serve him well 'when conditions arose that were adverse'. Cherry repeated the mantra of the clearly visible depots available on his route south. 'Atch was almost sure he saw Campbell's party coming in yesterday afternoon.' The following day, Tuesday, Keohane and Demetri 'thought they saw Campbell's party coming in & we were out on the Point & the sea ice for quite a long time looking for them'.

At the ice-cave the weather on Tuesday the 26th was 'so damnable' that Campbell gave everyone a 'make and mend', a naval day off, with the right to stay inside and sort out personal possessions. Every morning, as he had done at Cape Adare, Campbell gave the orders for the day, followed by the ritual hour of pipe-smoking. Despite minimal space, everyone had to get out of their bags for meals. The naval routines and disciplines ran through their existences like a framework, but inserting itself, cutting through the intention, was the disruption of their bodily functions. Their lives were beginning to revolve around their stomachs, their backsides, their pains and upsets, as their systems tried to cope with the constrained diet. Diarrhoea hit them, and the need suddenly to urinate, sometimes uncontrollable, with subsequent accidents. Then there was the desperate problem of pulling wind clothes on in time to get down the passage when emergency struck, the abject awfulness of failure in the cold, the misery of frostbitten parts of the anatomy and of soiled clothing instantly freezing. At the same time food dreams had started, in all their frustrations, and complexities. Shared misery, waking, and dreaming, truly bringing men together.

'[W]e are settling into our igloo now, and a dismal hole it is too', Levick wrote on Thursday the 28th. But he had started to read aloud in the evening, as a way of bucking everyone up. The choice was Boccaccio's *Decameron* ('a most boring production'), and Dickens's *David Copperfield,* which Priestley already knew almost inside out. On Sunday the 31st, after Campbell had read from the New Testament, they sat in their bags singing hymns, managing to rake up about a dozen, then having a long talk before going to sleep. The insulation of the ice-cave had been improved to the point where they didn't need to get into bed wearing helmets or even finneskoes. Priestley had served out twenty muscatel raisins each. Their plumpness was imaginable still within their dark-brown, flattened wrinkles. Attached by their little woody stalks to the structure of what had once been a bunch of grapes ripening in the sun, with one or maybe two teardrop-shaped tiny stones nestled inside and deliciously sweet, these were their only fruit and the best-tasting of food, unpolluted by blubber, clean and with absolutely no waste: the stones and stalks were eaten or smoked, according to taste. Priestley had decided that muscatels, their supplies boosted by a lucky present he'd unwrapped on *Terra Nova* from his family, would mark the end of each month. Another ritual.

They'd got through their first month. A significant achievement. In his diary Priestley made a laconic entry: '4 pm dinner. Spent a quiet day. Worked a little, loafed a lot.' Being pegged down in a sleeping-bag in a thin tent, with the wind howling, unable to get on and do something, that was misery. Being pegged down in a sleeping-bag in the ice-cave, with the wind securely banished and no requirement beyond managing each day – if that could be called loafing, so much the better.

On 1 April Atkinson and Keohane returned to Hut Point after a brief, futile attempt to help the returning Polar party on the Barrier. They reached no further than Corner Camp, experiencing 'Hellish temperatures and wind'. 'We have got to face it now – the Pole Party will not in all probability ever get back', Cherry concluded. 'And there is no more that we can do.' Immediately he and Atkinson began to worry about the book of the expedition – that core of voyaging and discovery, the need to establish the form of the record, to define the data, to establish traceability, respectability, status. Scott's diary, 'properly edited', would have to be added to by whoever was in charge this year – Atkinson or Campbell. Cherry agreed to act as a kind of official recorder of events.

On 1 April a storm-scarred *Terra Nova* arrived at the first port in New Zealand from which cables could be sent. Pennell went ashore with Drake, the store-keeper. A small launch hovered around the waiting *Terra Nova,* hoping for news. Everyone stared passively down from the decks; all communication had been forbidden. 'Why didn't you get back sooner?' one of the two men in the launch called up, in a derisory tone. 'Amundsen got the Pole in a sardine tin.'

With Bjaaland, Hansen, Hassel, Wisting and sixteen dogs Amundsen had arrived at the South Pole on 15 December 1911, after travelling directly south from the Bay of Whales, avoiding Scott and Shackleton's route, taking risks, finding a vertiginous glacier up through the mountains to the polar plateau, treading new ground all the way. On the empty nothingness of that spot calculated by mathematics and navigation, Amundsen had pitched a small tent dyed bluey-grey, for visibility, placing spare equipment for Scott inside it and a letter to King Haakon of Norway, which he asked Scott to forward. The letter was part of the necessary proof of the achievement that they would announce to the world when they reached Tasmania, all going well, around the end of the first week of March 1912.

To the first members of Scott's expedition to hear it, the news – delivered so casually – was a terrible blow. Simpson, conscious always of the importance to the expedition's credibility of achieving the Pole, considered that the fact that Amundsen had reached it first gave 'the appearance of failure'. At least, Simpson noted, 'whatever else has failed the scientific work has not and that should count for something in the long run.' But regardless of the ultimate verdict, 'there is no doubt that at present we are distinctly under a cloud'.

15

Icy isolation

1 April–31 May 1912

Either we are relieved, or we relieve ourselves.

Campbell, 1912

THE CABLES WITH Antarctic news arrived in London on 2
April. Everyone was anxious to hear about Scott's attempt on
the Pole, but there was nothing more recent than his reports 'from a
hopeful position' on 4 January, with 148 miles still to go across the
high plateau, brought back to winter quarters at Cape Evans by the
last support party. Kathleen Scott received her husband's note of 3
January: 'I think its going to be alright . . .'

The news that the Eastern party had been left to face the Antarctic
winter unprepared needed to be handled with some care.
Assumptions that there could be a problem with Campbell and his
men – renamed the 'Northern Party' by the expedition organizers in
London – were not welcome: it had been clearly laid down that
circumstances such as Campbell now found himself in were manageable. Teddy Evans had nearly died, but he had been returning across
the Barrier, with no fresh food. The six men of Campbell's party
were on the coast, with plenty of access to local animals. Nevertheless
Kathleen Scott needed to have several talks with Mrs Campbell to
persuade her that her husband, Victor, was not in danger. Kathleen
sent on a letter from her brother Wilfred Bruce describing what had
happened. 'I do not feel he was very happy abt Victor and his party',
wrote Mrs Campbell, returning Bruce's letter, 'but I know you & I
will not agree to that point, as you think I am exaggerating the dangers & that I take a morbid view!! But I don't think I do.' Why, for
example, would Pennell have

stretched his orders to such an extent had there been no danger to Victor & his party, because it wd have been better to leave Victor there than to endanger the ship or risk being held up another winter, both of which he did in order to make the . . . last attempt to try and relieve Victor – However there is nothing to be done . . . I'm not fussing more than can be helped. So do not think it – only I shall continue to think what you say others are <u>not</u> thinking & that is that the Northern Party are in a tight place –

In the ice-cave, with uncertainty over their immediate future resolved, Levick was back on an even keel. His role as guardian of the party's physical well-being, on which their morale to an extent pivoted, was central. Getting on with Priestley was important: Priestley controlled the supply of food, but Levick generally managed how it was dealt with. 'Thank God for Priestley,' Levick wrote, 'a fine chap with a sound head on him & I hope we keep as good pals as we are now, for the rest of the time, as I believe the happiness of the party depends very largely on our cooperation in many ways.' On the first day of April, for example, Priestley had dug out two more alcoves in the shaft leading into their cave. He had taken with equanimity a small tragedy: his blubber lamp had thawed the snow block it rested on, tipped over and soaked his rucksack irretrievably with smelly grease. Finally – after examining the powder left in the bottom of a finished tin of biscuits – he reckoned it was part biscuit and the rest granite, paraffin, snow, ice and frozen meat, so there was no point wasting it. To Levick, Priestley seemed a solid source of energy, resourcefulness and practical knowledge.

Levick's greatest concern continued to be bodily malfunctions. Noting symptoms, diagnosing, dispensing medicines, Levick decided that lack of carbohydrates meant the men's urine was too acid: hence the inability to control their urine, wetting their clothes even during sleep. Diarrhoea, he thought, was the result of the salt-water ice they used to cook their hoosh. Campbell downplayed the suffering by understatement: 'B & I suffering from diarrhoea which is most inconvenient this weather.' In truth, getting outside to deal with urgent needs was a grindingly desperate business in the cold and gales. On

Wednesday 3 April, trying to cope out in the snow with the results of a disastrous accident in the middle of the night, Campbell 'got privates & stern frost bitten changing drawers . . . miserable'. '[P]oor chap', he 'came in in a bad way . . . half collapsed.' The next day, after Abbott had collected them from the moraine depot, Campbell served out a selection of new clothes he'd scavenged on *Terra Nova* in January. Browning's attacks of diarrhoea were exhaustingly frequent, and Levick was trying different treatments. Everyone except Priestley was also suffering from repeated painful frostbite. Noses were especially vulnerable, with hardened, peeling knobs forming on the end: 'horny and desquaminating', Levick noted medically. Abbott had a flare up of his old problem, psoriasis, his skin itching miserably. And the filthy dense smoke from the blubber fires inflamed everyone's eyes, resulting in 'stove blindness', or conjunctivitis. Campbell and Browning were trying different ways to get the Oxo tin lamps to melt oil directly from blubber without producing vile smoke, but the cooking fires produced billows.

Good Friday, 5 April, turned out to be a 'grand day'. The wind dropped, so they could leave the cave. The four not on cooking duty collected seaweed to insulate the walls of the cave, and brought back the next allocation of food from the depot. But best of all, with the wind eased, a few seals came up. Campbell and Levick managed to kill and butcher three. Three new carcasses relieved serious anxieties about meat, and blubber for fuel, at least for a while.

On Easter Saturday, despite 'a beastly wind again from the old quarter', they sledged the seal meat up to the cave. Levick asked everyone what they would have to drink and how much, if they had the chance. Abbott said six bottles of Bass beer. Campbell and Dickason chose four pints of stiff chocolate and milk. Priestley wanted a gallon of still lemonade and Browning a pint of tea. Levick preferred a bottle of good red Burgundy, Volnay. Levick's 'great thought' was that the consumption of food 'has become a pleasure of the intellect rather than the gratification of a sense'.

On Easter Sunday, 7 April, 'Tofferino and I spent a very pleasant day over the fires frying & cooking & others in bed except for an abortive walk in the morning because of the blighting wind', noted Priestley. 'All day we entertained the company with a repertoire of songs sacred & profane.' Dinner was a special hoosh of fresh kidney and heart, and a double ration of tea; 'consequently all hands are feeling more reconciled to their lot which to do them justice they generally do about this time of the day.' Campbell then read a chapter from the New Testament and they sang hymns, their weekly 'Sacred concert'. For Priestley, this was 'as near to a church service as we can get'.

Priestley had seized the best bits of the three slaughtered seals – the undercut and the liver – and cached them for the meat they would need when sledging south. Planning for the journey down the coast to Cape Evans had begun as soon as he took over the commissariat. The emergency sledging provisions brought over from the ship were still being kept back, and as well as setting food aside they were also saving clothing. Part of surviving was to plan for leaving. But as a group they already seemed to have spent much of their time planning to leave: waiting to get away from Cape Evans to King Edward VII Land, then managing Cape Adare in anticipation of their precious summer weeks exploring on the coast of Victoria Land. Now, in an ice-cave, they were intent on surviving so that they could get back to where they started, Cape Evans.

In the winter quarters hut at Cape Evans, Easter was a miserable time, with everyone waiting anxiously to hear news of the Polar party. Contact with Hut Point continued cut, as violent storms broke up newly formed winter sea ice. But the ice was beginning to hold. On Wednesday 10 April, Gran, working outside, heard someone shout the long-wished for words 'The polar party's coming'. Gran rushed inside the hut to get the national anthem ready to play on the gramophone as a greeting for Scott. He waited, needle poised, but no one came. Going back outside, he saw in the gloom three figures coated with ice, filthy and bearded. Atkinson, Keohane and Demetri had managed to cross from Hut Point with the dreadful information that the Polar party had not returned. Those at Cape Evans felt the weight of responsibility grip their shoulders and settle into their souls. Their duty, as they now perceived it, must be to find the dead, or at least some kind of proof of what had happened.

But Atkinson had arrived with a different intention. He had read the documents Scott left, including the July 1910 statement to Beaumont that men in Antarctica could live entirely off the land, if not relieved by the ship: an assumption built into Scott's instructions to Campbell. Atkinson, however, had seen the effect of this harshest of places on expedition members. The previous autumn, and now this, he had lived at Hut Point with its smoke, half-darkness and smell of blubber as the great emptiness closed in. Having been out on the Barrier as far as Corner Camp on a last desperate attempt to find the Polar party, Atkinson was certain that Scott and his companions were dead. He 'thinks it is all up with them', noted Wright. That leaden knowledge sat at the centre of Atkinson's being. He did not know where or when or how. On the other hand, Campbell and his men were almost certainly alive. *Terra Nova* might have picked them up on the final voyage out, although Atkinson considered it most unlikely. What could the lives of the six abandoned men be like, facing the winter in an igloo, which seemed to be their only option?

Atkinson, the reluctant but painstaking inheritor of the role of command, could apprehend the dangers facing the marooned men, imagine their feelings: how they must worry about the ship and long for rescue. This winter seemed colder, the weather more extreme, than last. Would they be able to find enough animals to kill? Atkinson was determined to make an effort to help the Eastern party by sledging up the coast. If, as was generally assumed, Campbell was going to wait until the bays froze over and then lead his men down the coast, help would be vital; at the very least, a depot of rations could be left. The coldness was deep, and the sun would soon disappear. The sea ice, as always, was a serious worry. Atkinson now asked the men in the Cape Evans hut to discuss what should be done, but his desire was clear. He wanted volunteers to join him in relieving Campbell.

The general opinion was that 'nothing can have happened to Campbell'. Debenham thought it 'pure risk to go west' but 'quite saw that nothing could not be done'. Others thought all effort should be concentrated on getting out to the Barrier again. Wright, who had just celebrated his twenty-fifth birthday, considered Atkinson 'causelessly alarmed'. Atkinson had been through months of hardship and anxiety; his spirit, Wright thought, was 'pretty well gone'. Any possible trouble Campbell could get into, the relief party were just as likely to experience. More importantly, 'every man will be wanted to go south'. Privately, Wright thought the chances of surviving a journey up the coast to relieve Campbell were low and was entirely against it, but he said nothing and agreed immediately to Atkinson's request for volunteers to help Campbell. Keohane, already exhausted, joined, as did Petty Officer Williamson, recently acquired from *Terra Nova*. As for the impact of his absence on Simpson's work – Wright handed what he could over to Nelson, the biologist.

On Saturday 13 April the relief party set out, man-hauling first to Hut Point, in a biting cold wind. 'Very strange to me to be once more rolled into a fur bag & sleeping on ice', noted Williamson, a strong seaman in the Scott mode, 15 stone. 'The same system still prevails regards sledging just where we knocked off 10 years ago in the "Discovery" so that nothing came amiss to me, as a matter of fact it did not seem as though I had left it for so long a period.' Cherry had been living alone in the hut – 'no place to be alone with the wind howling and the hut creaking', he wrote – and grabbed gratefully at the chance to talk to new faces. It was generally agreed that all the men left at winter quarters, except Williamson, the newcomer, and probably Wright were worn out after their hard experiences on the Barrier, and unfit for sledging.

From Hut Point Atkinson and his small party crossed over the sea ice to the Victoria Land coast, arriving on 20 April at Butter Point, where they depoted two weeks' provisions 'for Mr C & party should they happen to come this way'. Given the conditions they were experiencing, the four men decided to turn back. Williamson listed the arguments. First, the cold was frightful: 'after a hard day's slogging & pulling at our traces & then to turn in to our fur bags not to sleep but to shiver & shake all night & pray for morning to come is not good enough & the party would not last long under these conditions'. Second, the sea ice could not be trusted, and they could not carry sufficient provisions to go the inland route. Third, having seen the conditions, they had concluded that 'Mr C has decided to Winter where he is, in this case he will be all right, but at the same time he will have a very uncomfortable time of it. & I for one do not envy him in the least'. After camping and having some tea they were harnessing up

right: Dickason, assisted by Browning, cooking in the hut at Cape Adare, 1911

below: Harry Dickason, smoking his favourite pipe. In May 1911 Levick took a flashlight portrait of each man sitting on his bed in the Cape Adare hut, surrounded by his personal possessions

Levick's portrait of Campbell shows him working at his chart table, lit by an acetylene lamp and a candle. Campbell's bookshelf and personal photographs are on the wall behind

Priestley in his accustomed position, typing at the central table. Two typewriters were taken to Antarctica on Scott's expedition. The other one was in the winter quarters hut at Cape Evans

Levick's portrait of Abbott sitting on his bed in his corner of the hut, with his personal shelf on the wall behind. The galley is on the left, the stove on the right

Levick about to do a post-mortem. The crabeater seal is balanced on a sledge on the dining-room table. Shelves full of galley equipment line the wall behind, Cape Adare, November 1911

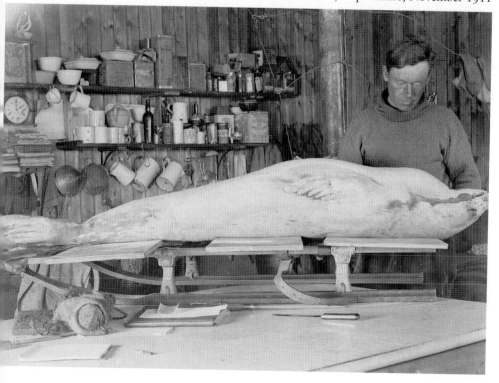

Above: Midwinter dinner, Cape Adare, 22 June 1911. Campbell (at the head of the table) sits between Abbott (on the left) and Priestley. Levick (wearing the party hat) is opposite Browning with Dickason between them. The sledging flags belong to Campbell and Levick

Left: Dickason at the entrance to the Cape Adare hut, carrying the slops bucket, and an ice axe, 1911

Summer sledging, January 1912. Priestley sits on the loaded sledge while Campbell scans ahead with his binoculars. The ropes of the three-man sledge-hauling harness lie on the snow

The two loaded sledges, stopped on the Priestley Glacier. Summer sledging, January 1912

Browning (foreground)
and Abbott resting duri[ng]
summer sledging on the
Boomerang Glacier,
January 1912

Levick, Abbott and
Browning sledged as a
team during the summer
expedition. Levick's
sledging flag hangs abov[e]
the entrance to the tent.
Browning looks out,
Levick sits on the left,
with Abbott on the righ[t]
10 January 1912

right: Abbott (left) and Browning (right) at the entrance to the ice-cave, September 1912

*below:*The interior of the ice-cave drawn in red chalk by Campbell, 21 September 1912. Three biscuit boxes make the entrance. A joint of seal meat and an Adélie penguin hang thawing above the cooking pot, tended by the cook for the day. Priestley sits in his bag on the left, behind the box of stores he controlled

Emerging from the ice-cave, the long journey to winter quarters at Cape Evans ahead of them are Dickason (left), Campbell and Abbott. Photograph taken by Levick, 24 September 1912

Abbott took this photograph of Priestley (left), Levick and Browning as they came out of the ice-cave into spring sunshine on 24 September 1912

when 'Lord, look at that!' Williamson exclaimed. The sea ice at the foot of Butter Point was breaking apart and silently sailing out to sea. Priestley would have shuddered in recognition and memory.

They could not travel up the coast. Campbell and his party could not travel down it. So 'I suppose he will winter', wrote Cherry. Atkinson had tried, however quixotically. The release of no longer having to speculate about what action to take was intense. After struggling through difficult blizzard conditions, the four men arrived back at the Hut Point hut the day the sun disappeared for winter, 23 April, utterly exhausted by 'a very difficult and dangerous trip'. Williamson, despite all, had been expecting to find that the Polar party had returned, but 'they have not . . . no fresh news for us . . . personally I do not know what to think I am half afraid that a great disaster has happened poor fellows'.

The sea ice between Hut Point and Cape Evans was thin and bad. But by 1 May all men plus the two dog teams had managed to cross to Cape Evans, and Hut Point had been abandoned to the winter. Everyone was now gathered together for the first time in their winter quarters, with seven on the mess deck side of the partition, some spare space in their quarters. Six officers on the wardroom side, with sad, empty bunks looking at them.

Cherry-Garrard resumed writing his diary again, comparing life in winter quarters now with the last time he made an entry. 'How different things are . . . Then the ship had just left to pick up Campbell's Party – now they have failed & that party is stranded . . . Then we were just leaving to bring the Polar Party home, & now we know that they will never arrive.' He suspected that when they got back to England 'there will be much discussion & criticism of what has been done here since . . . we knew two parties were adrift'. But he felt 'quite confident that all has been done that could be done'. Sledging at this time of the year was immensely hard, especially for men like themselves who were worn, having just finished a season's sledging. And they discussed it all over again. The constant worries. Eleven of Scott's second expedition were missing, with five dead at least: most now accepted that as certain. The remaining six, they had to believe, were still alive.

★

At the ice-cave life had shaken into a manageable shape. Mornings were probably the worst. Dickason, the guardian of the Primus stove and its precious supply of fuel, cooked breakfast, which was prepared the night before. But they woke with stomachs twisted with hunger, and breakfast barely made an impact before they were suffering gnawing pain again. Priestley's most difficult time was the hour after breakfast, when the others lay smoking in their bags. If he could, he went out into the air. The truth was, they all smelt awful. Personal hygiene didn't bear thinking about. Priestley borrowed Browning's long scissors and hacked at his filthy hair, and cut his beard around his mouth. The only thing they'd sorted out was cleaning their teeth: they used toothpicks made from slivers of bamboo to hook out bits of meat, and wider pieces of soft wood from the Fry's chocolate boxes, their ends chewed to make them pliable, to rub the front of their teeth. The rest of the day depended on weather and jobs. But everyone agreed the evenings, 'rotten day . . . over', were the best. Campbell changed the rules, giving permission for all except the cooks to eat hoosh in their bags. Afterwards there was general conversation, with everyone trying by talking to 'keep thoughts of home away'. Browning told stories about life on a farm, and Campbell told stories about his travels in the navy; Levick would read a chapter or two from one of their few books. But things could trip a man up. For Priestley, singing certain hymns could summon up instant visions of family, which started the worry about his family's worries – the fear of their fears – added to uncertainty about the fate of the ship. Saturday night's concert was less emotive. They roared out anything they could think of, song after song, with Abbott's excellent voice leading, but all three seamen had been in church choirs and Browning had a good memory for music-hall songs. The real significance of the evening meant they had got through another day, with night – and sleep – pushing the time along.

Sleep, however, wasn't all that easy. Someone would need to get up, force on wind clothes, unfasten the door to the passage, then come shuffling back, fasten the door, get out of wind clothes. Abbott, Levick and Priestley, the three biggest, could only fit through the doorway by crawling. The others, slighter, got through by stooping. But whatever their build, shuffling or crawling along the passage, getting around the granite boulder, knocked their shoulders, elbows and knees. Given the bowel problems, some kind of internal 'round-house' was essential, and a small space had been made at the entrance to the passage, only big enough for one, but at least they no longer had to face the raw wind outside. They also now kept a couple of empty gallon oil tins in the cave: one for officers' contributions, one for the men.

Often talking would start. Dickason would have a yarn with Browning, or Campbell would voice early-hours-of-the-morning worries to Levick. Campbell, liable to have a headache or an upset stomach, could be 'a little fratchy'. Lying in his bag next to Campbell, Levick got regular reports on his leader's health, but everyone in the cave could hear the rather self-absorbed details. The talk got on Dickason's nerves in particular. Levick was a snorer, and Browning had a hacking cough. Then someone would need to push out of his bag, struggle to get dressed, grunting with desperation to make it down the passage in time.

Food filled their waking thoughts ('cakes, plum puddings, bread & butter, and biscuits', listed Levick). While they slept, their dreams were mostly filled with food frustration – sitting down to every pos-sible kind of meal, from fish and chips to City banquets, getting ready to eat, only for the food to disappear. Levick and Abbott, the most passive of the party, according to Priestley, managed always to eat their dream meals, which inflicted a real sense of grievance on the other four. But another dream delivered frustration every time. Each man dreamed he was lying awake in the ice-cave, very hungry, when suddenly he remembered there was a shop outside. How stupid to forget! He dreamt the tedious detail of getting dressed, the tiring crawl along the dark tunnel experiencing every bump and turn – and there, behind their snowdrift, was the shop, selling what each longed for, except that it was early closing day. And the shop was always closed.

Levick ordered a week of meals using fresh water and their small supply of salt, to test his theories, and the diarrhoea generally stopped. Getting freshwater ice was easy. They just had to hack at the wall of the 'icery' in the shaft. But lacking salt, they had to go back to col-lecting salt-water ice along the shore, and the 'enemy' appeared again. Nothing could be done, and Levick had to hope their bodies would adjust in time. Here in this place of snow, ice and rocks, the necessities for life turned out to include not only matches and salt, and paper for the roundhouse (another use for the illustrated magazines), but also adequate clothing. They had been away for fifteen months; their wind clothes were summer weight, and their trousers and jackets were rotting and ripping. Their mitts, saturated with blubber and snow, were frozen into the shape of open boxes and barely functioned. The soles of their boots were coming apart from the uppers, exposing their toes to frostbite. The ice coating the inside of their boots never melted, making them tight around the toes. Abbott tried curing sealskin to make moccasins, but nothing worked. Priestley indulged in another joke: they lacked Eskimo wives to chew the leather. And, given the nature of frozen seal and penguin, they needed specialist culinary implements. Sufficient meat had to be hacked somehow off a hard lump of animal to make the hoosh. Whoever was cook's assistant attacked the lump with Priestley's geological hammer and big steel chisel; bits flew off, and splinters of raw meat got caught in clothing, or pulverized scraps landed on the floor. Chips of frayed flesh flew everywhere, but all were collected, as far as possible, since every bit was precious. The meat had to be chopped on the lid of an oil tin box because the smokers, desperate for spills to light their pipes, had whittled away the chopping board.

A year ago they had been building their accommodation at Cape Adare, and collecting birds to eat. Now, in a kind of bitter parody, they were doing it all over again but making an ice-cave, not a spacious hut, and hunting seals and penguins for survival, not as a precautionary addition to a standard diet. They were choking in the smoke from blubber fires, and husbanding single lamps in Oxo tins, not fussing about the fumes from an acetylene plant. They were worrying if the air inside their cave got warm enough to start melting the walls and roof, not arguing over optimum temperatures for working and reading. Last year they had been living in a cut-down version of an English house. Now even the barest essentials of equipment needed to be improvised. But at Cape Adare they'd got accustomed to working together, and practised at solving problems. More importantly, they'd sledged together, experiencing hardship and physical crisis. They'd slept tight in a tent, and got used to sharing minimal space.

Improvements to their icy accommodation continued. They roofed over the passage, constructed an outer door and excavated a second kitchen to try and limit the suffocating filthy fumes, which made their noses stream and their eyes smart and run. The smoke was a constant affliction, filling their small space, this burrow at the end of a tunnel where they lived, slept, ate and cooked, with black soot and greasy droplets. Browning called it a Dorset word, 'smitch'. The once sparkly-white cave ceiling and walls were black, along with everyone's hands and faces. Levick tried an innovation: he broke up bones from the desiccated seals that he'd discovered in the summer and hoped to study, then strewed them across the base of the half oil tin that made their stove, arranging a piece of blubber over the flame so that the oil dripped on to the bones. The result was a clearer flame. Next they pushed a chimney through the roof, but a large crack opened right across their ice ceiling, which was a real worry. The draught from the chimney made the cave too cold at night, so they had to stuff it with a penguin skin wrapped in a scullery cloth before they went to sleep.

But the smoke resulted from blubber, and blubber was the base and centre of their lives. They cooked with it, ate it, relieved their darkness with it. Their world began and ended with blubber. They had to handle it constantly, and the 'dreadful stuff' smeared everything, crept everywhere, pervading 'like a bad smell'. Blubber soaked into their clothes, reducing their ability to keep them warm, and rotted the skin of their reindeer sleeping-bags. At the same time, being able to stomach it was essential. 'I'm taking kindly to blubber now', wrote Levick. 'Our hoosh is like hot cod liver oil with chunks of blubber and seal meat in it; and is very comforting and filling at the price (we haven't had the bill yet).'

Most mornings several figures would emerge through the sack covering the opening to the outside world to do jobs: clearing snow from the shaft leading into the passage, watching hopefully for seals, then scuttling back before getting too frostbitten. On Monday 6 May, during a brief calm, Campbell and Priestley went searching for salt-water ice, walking among places familiar from summer. Light was brief, but there was a benign memory beneath the harsh winter landscape, of skuas and their long-legged chicks running over beach pebbles and trickling melt streams, of the clucks and calls of nesting Adélies, of colours and sunlight. Local places had been colonized with names, pinning down the history of their expedition: Depot Cove, Arrival Bay, Look-Out Hill.

Suddenly Campbell and Priestley saw four tall figures half a mile out on the newly formed sea ice walking towards Arrival Bay, where three months ago they had landed from *Terra Nova*. They stared, thrilled, hardly daring to hope. Yet they had talked so often about the possibility of the ship being caught by the ice to the north in Wood Bay, and of being rescued from that direction. Campbell signalled to Abbott and Levick to come, and Abbott ran down with ice axes. If they weren't men, they were food. Then they saw the flash of yellow on white, the long thin bills lifted high, and knew that the figures were, after all, emperor penguins. Leaping over the tide crack, and getting wet, they gave chase. They had to reach this unexpected bounty before the birds found open water and were lost. The emperors dropped on to their bellies, moving fast over the ice, propelling themselves forward with flippers and feet. Abbott and Priestley felled them. Joined by Levick, who was too out of condition to run, they dragged the birds along on their breasts over the ice; then, bending under the burden, they carried the animals slung like full sacks down their backs, with flippers dangling and jerking as they stumbled around the boulders. The emperors were in superb condition, ready for the business of winter breeding. Two alone equalled the weight of Browning. It was wonderful luck. Monday 6 May went down as a second red-letter day.

The previous evening, sitting in their bags, with the little lamps throwing shifting gleams on to the ice walls and the only sound the sibilant hiss of drift on their roof snowing them in, Priestley had sung the hymn he sang every Sunday:

Day is dying in the west
Heaven is touching earth with rest
Wait and worship while the night
Sets her evening lamp alight
Through all the sky.

Levick, holding his journal close to his blubber lamp, thought the hymn particularly appropriate with the sun just departing for the winter. Their cave was warmer with the layer of snow, probably not that many degrees below freezing: enough, nearly, to thaw their boots out, although the roof now dripped when they cooked. Browning had had a rare day free of the misery of diarrhoea, and everyone, in Levick's view, was feeling 'happy & contented'.

On the morning of Tuesday the 7th, Priestley and Dickason had to tunnel their way through 6 feet depth of drift before they reached daylight. Levick and Browning skinned, gutted and cut up the freshly killed emperors all day, in the bitter cold of the inner galley. Priestley rubbed his windproofs with penguin skin to try and get rid of the grease, but failed: they still stood up by themselves, solid with filth. Campbell, working with Abbott under great difficulties in a space full of meat and carcasses, cooked each member of the party as a treat 'a little steak of emperor breast done as a "filet de Boeuf"' with a 'small piece of fat on top'. The blizzard was blowing so hard that Dickason and Priestley were both blown over, at the entrance to the shaft. Despite this, Priestley recorded that he was 'quite reconciled to our fate'. He had begun to read his last year's diary out aloud after hoosh. Campbell noted that it 'brings everything back to us', and altogether, 'our evenings pass very pleasantly'. They were inseparably bonded, memories of last year adding detail to their long connections. 'The whole party is getting along well together,' Levick thought, 'and our situation has undoubtedly pulled us together as we are all on far better terms than at C. Adair.' Adversity was strengthening them. At the same time Levick and Campbell talked round and round the possibilities of what had happened to the ship, an unavoidably public conversation, with, unspoken, the chance of a disaster in the minds of all three officers. What if they were the expedition's only survivors? It was a strange, frightening thought to mull over in the dark.

The preparation and cooking didn't take so long now. Each joint of meat was being thawed in advance, by suspending it directly from a bamboo near the ceiling, or putting it in a hanging biscuit tin, called the 'oven'. 'The anniversary of my wedding day ten years ago', wrote Campbell on Friday the 10th. 'Served out 10 raisins.' Dickason and Browning, their pairing as mess men strengthening their friendship, lay in their bags 'talking of old times' . The next day, as they were doing the outside jobs – collecting salt-water ice, bringing in the next supply of meat, checking for seals – Campbell, Dickason and Browning saw that the sea ice the emperors had been walking on had already blown out, leaving open water to the horizon. Why didn't the ice stay? Campbell reckoned the season must be exceptional. He couldn't understand it. On the 12th, lying on their bags, Campbell and Levick did a few Swedish exercises. Levick hoped he'd keep it up, 'but one never does'.

On the 13th, with a violent gale blowing, the darkness inside the cave was so intense that the six men overslept until midday. Telling the time was impossible in the dark, and they couldn't waste a match to look at a watch, but keeping track of the days was vital, so Campbell as time-keeper, with Levick as his assistant, invented a system of winding up their watches a certain number of turns to help them estimate the time, before they struck the vital match to check.

On the 15th Levick had an accident in his sleep and wet his clothes – 'it is hard luck' – but told no one. 'C gets into a panic about himself very easily and will be imagining he is going to do the same.' Browning was up every night with diarrhoea, 'poor devil', some-times seven or eight times, but he endured grimly, determined to keep going, to do his share of the jobs. On the 16th, with the weather too bad to get out, everyone except the cooks stayed in their bags suffering smoke and fumes. A rotten day. The next night Levick had another accident in his sleep, and his clothes were soaked again. Again he did not mention it.

Priestley was beginning to prefer lying in bed. He was generally healthy, except that his eyes hurt with the smoke so he didn't want to read. But just being in his bag, letting his mind wander, not both-ering with worries or issues was surprisingly easy to do. Seriously short of seals now, they'd cut their meat allowance back. Better not to try to do much and just lie, and dream. The previous winter, at Cape Adare, he had been restless, striving to achieve a reasonable quantity of science and to improve his physical performance. Here at the ice-cave there was no science that could be done. And to his surprise, without having exercise, without even getting up except briefly, 'we all feel fit'. Levick decided that their present allowance of meat and blubber was 'just about the smallest limit' for keeping up strength with very little work, which was how they were living.

On 17 May came the second (monthly) anniversary 'of the occupation of our dug out'. Abbott suggested a culinary breakthrough: sheep's brains were good to eat, so why not try seal's brain? Priestley picked up his ice axe, walked to the seal depot, chopped off the head of an already butchered seal, levered the frozen brain out of the skull with his chisel, collected the fragments in a tin and threw them into the evening's hoosh. The result was the greatest success of the whole winter. 'Simply perfect', said Campbell. Priestley was keeping all seal bones in a heap, in case they ran out of food and needed to use them for soup. He reckoned their ability to use every possible bit of a seal was unequalled. As for the emperors: the meat and brains had been used for hoosh, the blubber for lamp oil, skin for the cooking stoves and the flippers to brush the floor, and their clothes.

The winds continued to blow, and the snow to drift higher. Life continued to carry on ever deeper inside what Priestley now called 'the warren' or 'the rabbit burrow'. They'd sorted out how to live. Sharing cooking meant two days off out of three. 'I have dreamt the day away again', wrote Priestley on 24 May. 'I could never have imagined that I could have been so contented, even happy in a circumscribed way with nothing to do but just exist, with insufficient to eat & an utter lack of news about anything & anybody I care about.'

The next day, with the snow drifting ever higher and blocking the chimney, the smoke was unbearable so they put out the blubber fire and Dickason heated the dinner hoosh with the Primus, which went out. The lamps went out; a match wouldn't light and nor would another, or a precious third. They'd all complained of headaches but thought they were caused by smitch. In the darkness – with nothing working – suddenly they were out of their bags, and Campbell was driving a spade through the drifts to let some air in. They had been lucky. If it had happened at night, they would have been asphyxiated. They had delayed too long before taking action, and various diary accounts reported who said what to whom, but they'd had a second chance to learn the lesson. Using up the oxygen in the air had occurred once before, to Browning, in Borgy's hut at Cape Adare. Abbott and Campbell dug their way out into a smothering drift, and thickest darkness, to find a bamboo, then climbed up and pushed it down the chimney to create a pathway for air.

They had to find a way of stopping the passage into their burrow being blocked with snow. Abbott and Campbell constructed a hatch with sides made of bits of sealskin and snowblocks, the entrance closed with a sack, half-filled with seaweed, stretched over a bamboo frame.

Cooking creativity continued. Campbell tried stirring the hoosh with a penguin leg minus its meat, and everyone voted it a success. But the cooking area was getting appallingly – unavoidably – filthy. The rituals of cleanliness from Cape Adare couldn't be transferred. Raw meat fell on the tent floor cloth covering the seaweed and pebbles, and in the dark the mess of soot, chips of meat, pieces of sodden seaweed and reindeer hairs from their moulting sleeping-bags, mixed together with blubber, didn't bear thinking about. Their feet lifted after every step with a sickly tearing sound. 'It is just the limit having to worry over the possibility of the meat going wrong in a climate like this,' Priestley wrote, irritated, 'but it is very necessary.' The cook's hands only lost their blackness by handling raw meat and blubber. Levick, with almost everyone now suffering abdominal pains, put up a list of rules on 27 May, including:

> – the meat brought in to be thawed over the fire, should not be put on the floor as hitherto. (This is a mine of filthy blubber, round the fire.)
> – the meat should be used up as it is thawed, and small bits not allowed to accumulate.

'A strenuous day as messmen', Priestley noted at the end of his and Levick's day on cook duty, Wednesday the 29th. Hoosh was a little late, and there was some cat-calling, but all hands were satisfied. While the cocoa was heating, Levick and Priestley sang over twenty verses of 'The Battle Cry of Freedom'. Everyone drank health and happiness to Priestley's mother, in cocoa, with a toast proposed by Campbell and a codicil added by Priestley: 'May she be optimistic about me & may I never again be as much worry to her as I must be at present.' The talk swung to the relief expedition and whether *Terra Nova* was really in trouble, as she must be. 'Time passes quickly and smoothly . . . I am just going to settle down in my bag', Priestley ended, 'and enjoy our mid-weekly stick of chocolate.' The following day, Thursday the 30th, turned out as strenuous. 'The infernal wind blew in gusts', but otherwise it was fine, so Abbott and Levick walked across to the moraine depot and carried back four tins of oil and the medicine chest. Campbell and Priestley brought up a load of meat, blubber, seawater ice, penguins and bones; Priestley went 'an awful cropper in one of the gusts & drove all the breath out of my body. Wonder none of us are not crippled.' But they were provisioned for another fortnight at least. 'We are in high spirits at the good days work', Priestley concluded. And he was learning 'Morse's alphabet' – 'it may be useful some day'.

On Friday the 31st, a day of fearful wind, no one stirred from the cave, except Priestley, who went out for next month's tin of biscuits. Campbell and Priestley managed to collect half a spoonful of cocoa from various articles – the cocoa had been spilt around the middle of the month – and everyone thought it improved the hoosh. Browning and Dickason, sitting in their bags, in inadequate light, were constructing carriers using bamboo and the stripy curtain material left over from the hut at Cape Adare, one for each man on the trip to Cape Evans, in case the sledges had to be abandoned. 'Time slips along & May is gone already', wrote Priestley, sewing patches of curtain material on the knees of his windproof trousers, ripped by crawling along the passage. 'We shall soon be on the march . . . if we are not relieved in July.' The belief that they had not been abandoned, by the ship or by their fellow expeditioners, was vitally important, but the date when a relief party would appear shifted irrevocably forward. Even at Cape Adare they had not set out, on their first brief sledging trip, until 29 July. Here at Evans Coves they were further south. July would be the depth of winter cold, and darkness.

16

Igloo winter

1 June–31 July 1912

Campbell . . . combines the two qualities of action and
calculating in a most peculiar degree and is of all men the
least likely to come to grief by rashness on the one hand
or over cautiousness on the other.

Lieutenant Harry Pennell to Admiral Sir Lewis

Beaumont, 1912

THE SNOWDRIFT ON the hill behind Evans Coves revealed two
indications only of the fetid activity inside: a pipe with a thin
bamboo poking out of the top, rattling in the wind, and a smudge of
rubbish staining the white. Most days someone would emerge into
the 'visible darkness' – the evocative phrase used by Priestley – to
perform a necessary task, collecting provisions from nearby depots or
going down to the shore for seawater ice. But this winter was delivering a double dose of darkness to the six men burrowed into the drift.
Outside, June's full moon was hidden by constant gales and whirling
snow. Inside the cave nothing dented the dark except the brief
smoulderings of smokers' pipes, flames from the cooking and small
circles of yellow from blubber lamps. Day began when the lamps
were lit. Night began by dousing the lamps, bringing a pitch-black
darkness. A more utter darkness it would be impossible to imagine.

They were keeping appropriate times for the two meals, breakfast
and dinner. But dozing and sleeping during the day meant night
could be fitful, and men lay awake in their bags on the floor, listening
to the noises. Everyone wheezed and coughed – the foul smitch was
blamed, but Priestley suspected smoking. Dickason, an addict, had
burnt his mouth smoking wood chips; now he was trying pieces of

his precious hair socks. Campbell was smoking sennegrass – dried sedge brought from Norway to line their finneskoes. Something could be called 'uncomfortable', Levick had decided, only if it was dangerous or painful. Despite the squalor of their surroundings – and they were pretty rough, not to mention cold – on Monday 3 June Levick summoned up one of his positive conclusions: they were all fairly contented or 'at least, not unhappy'. Priestley could see a comic side. If their roof didn't fall in, and if they got through, what revelations they could make 'about the possibility of running cheap Antarctic Expeditions'. On the other hand, they were proud of themselves, with good reason, although this created a kind of conflict. They wanted to be relieved, so that the relieving party could see how well they had done; but at the same time they didn't want to be relieved, preferring, if possible, to 'make a thorough job of the business and relieve ourselves'.

The dominant daily activity remained melting oil from blubber, keeping the fires going and preparing and cooking the two meals. While the messmen worked, the other four watched from their bags. In the Cape Adare hut Campbell had barely known how to make a cup of tea: now he and Abbott were achieving teamwork to be proud of. Browning and Dickason were creative and confident. Priestley and Levick were the singing team, the bag-sitters joining in the choruses: 'Old King Cole', shanties learned on the ship, 'Who Killed Cock Robin'. Cooking and singing were inclusive, putting all participants on an equal footing. As conversations became repetitive and stories heard too many times palled, singing could fill the gaps: there was Levick and Priestley's mess day, the Saturday evening concert and Sunday's sacred concert (with Abbott now contributing the Nunc Dimittis and Te Deum). Except, singing made everyone feel hungrier afterwards.

Levick had invented a new stove, the 'Complex', to replace the long-abused 'Simplex'. It failed, smoking abominably, provoking much mirth among the others. The battered remnant was found, heaved out of the door by Browning and Dickason. Laughing at someone was considered excellent amusement, and no opportunity was missed. But the one subject no one laughed about was the recurring diarrhoea. For Browning it was enough to make him depressed;

and everyone respected and admired his resilience in enduring the most debilitating misery.

On Friday 14 June the wind blew all day, but no one wanted to mend the chimney, so no one did. Browning and Dickason were messmen, which left Campbell, Levick and Priestley lying in a conversational line, and Abbott, alone, opposite. The day passed in great controversies between the three officers about nothing: would fruit cake freeze when sledging? How much chocolate did they leave at Cape Adare? Levick and Campbell had lengthy battles about Imperial politics and national ethics, with the same old questions arising time and time again. The really heated battle was a three-cornered one about the most economical and satisfactory way of eating one's allowance of biscuit. In the evening, with Browning and Dickason back in their bags, the three hands got on with their 'private' sewing; Abbott was particularly neat. But as soon as they finished, noted Priestley, the tents would have to be mended. One tent, used to block the entrance at the beginning of their ice-cave lives, was riddled with pick and shovel holes.

On 14 June, at Cape Evans, a brief lull occurred in the middle of the longest blizzard they had experienced, and each man responsible for a mule got out to exercise his animal. Suddenly the blizzard started again, thick and dark, and several men missed the hut and had to grope their way back. After dinner Atkinson called a meeting of everyone, from both ends of the hut, to explain his views on their future plans, and to hear everyone else's. A choice had to be made, Atkinson explained. They were only thirteen, and their limited forces could not be divided. They could try and relieve Campbell, or they could try and find the Polar party. Two months earlier they had faced the same question, but now the journey south would be looking for five dead men. To the north, a journey would be trying to help six men they hoped were alive. Atkinson pointed out that Campbell's party could have been picked up by the ship, although probably not.

Winter was the greatest danger to the Eastern party. Every day after the end of winter their danger lessened. A relieving party from Cape Evans, given the sea ice, could probably reach Campbell only five weeks ahead of *Terra Nova*. Atkinson then stated his preference:

'the goal of the expedition was the Pole, and its success depended entirely on finding out whether the party had reached it.' There was also a duty to the relatives to obtain news of the fate of the Polar party. All agreed that they should go south, except for Lashly, who would not give his opinion one way or the other. 'Poor fellows it must have been very hard to die and suffer', thought Williamson. For 'Lt C's party we can only hope for the best they have every chance of pulling through but at the same time I should be sorry to have to go through the hunger and hardship they must have had to face, I wish them every luck.'

North, in the ice-cave, every small surprise in their circumscribed world was a major treat. Campbell handed out a new pair of socks each. Levick went through his medicine chest, finding citric acid tablets to mix with water for a drink: 'exquisite', 'a luxury'. Men suddenly remembered their mother's birthdays and celebrated with a special something to eat. Like children, they could barely wait for 'the great day' of the Midwinter feast, on 22 June: the first for four months when they'd go to bed with full bellies. They talked about what they would eat, fondled every detail in their imaginations and, when it at last arrived, started at 6.30 a.m. with breakfast: 'too important to wait any longer − a thick hoosh, 2 penguins seal meat & blubber we also got 4 biscuits & a few raisins', listed Campbell. The day, 'blowing & thick with drift very dark', was spent anticipating the evening hoosh, 'penguin hearts and livers & seal and blubber after 4 sticks of chocolate full whack of sweet cocoa 12 lumps of sugar − 4 citric acid tablets, 2 ginger from the medicine chest a little tobacco and a glass of wincarnis'. It was, everyone agreed, much better than their Midwinter feast the previous year at Cape Adare. Levick tried some verses of doggerel but abandoned getting the lines in order when it became obvious that line 4 needed to be where line 2 currently was:

A gallant explorer was lying
An oxo tin under his head
His comrades around him were sighing
And heartily wished he was dead
As rubbing his stomach he said

Chorus: You could knock me down with a splinter
   I've eaten too much, sad to tell, to tell
   In tasting the joys of midwinter
   Not wisely I fear, but too well.

   Should anyone care to befriend me
   Just toggle me up in my bag, my bag
   But carry me straight, do not bend me . . .

At Cape Evans on Midwinter Day, Cherry-Garrard watched Gran and Williamson decorate the tree with tinsel and twinkling electric lights, thinking of this day last year. Then, 'I did not know what it was to feel the darkness'; now this long, exceptionally harsh winter was getting on his nerves. The sea ice refused to stay in, north of the hut, limiting where they could walk. Hurricanes, gales, blizzards – the Antarctic seemed to be unleashing vile, unending misery. The seven mules had to be exercised. The dogs, chained to a long rope outside with bits of straw on the ground for each, were unutterably miserable. The best thing that had happened was Archer the cook, an older man, good-humoured, who every day cooked them interesting food, tickling their jaded appetites. Crean had lost a stone, Atkinson was not fit, and Debenham had damaged his ankle falling off the top of Ponting's dark-room after returning from the geology trip. Cherry's last edition of the 'South Polar Times' was published, read out to the officers by Atkinson, then handed over to the mess deck. The men had decorated their space for the midwinter feast with red bunting, and several had made sledging flags. After dinner Gran, dressed as a clown, jumped out of Ponting's dark-room and handed out presents, Debenham presented a slide-show, they sang, then went happily to bed. It 'did everyone a lot of good'.

The midwinter feast in the ice-cave was followed by a reduction in their daily food allowance – apart from the good fortune of Browning having another birthday on 27 June (the first had been celebrated on 27 January with Levick and Abbott while lost during summer sledging) and Levick's birthday on 3 July. Priestley: 'we are down to bedrock & have to take another hole in our belts.' Campbell announced a change in their weekly routine: the whole place would be cleared out with a shovel every Wednesday and Saturday, by the three seamen. The following day Campbell, as a reluctant innovator of songs, amazed them all by introducing the Norwegian version of 'Three Blind Mice'. And the day after that, with the wind at only medium strength, they saw a beautiful pale gold and apple-green colour at midday – the first hint of a future dawn, the herald of the sun that would return.

Levick had written another poem, with many verses. 'It is a little in the heroic strain', Priestley decided. They wouldn't therefore adopt it for a sledging song. Notes of criticism were creeping in: 'Levick as usual lost a sock and a mit and got out half an hour later than the rest of us. I have never met his equal at losing things though Abbott runs him pretty close.' And later, clearing out a storehouse, Priestley found his precious missing second ice axe at the base of a snow wall built by Levick, who had unaccountably used it as a foundation. Priestley considered Levick and Abbott the two most passive members of the party, and the least flexible. Both these characteristics, to Priestley, indicated a personality less likely to cope with the stress of the conditions they were living under. It was an assessment that he kept private and alluded to only in generalizations.

Discussions in the cave veered across future plans and old hopes. The possibility of a relief party still beckoned, comforting, seductive: the relief party would come in July or August. Even if they had to start sledging down the coast, they would probably meet it on the way. Behind everything was the inability to come to terms with the non-appearance of the ship. Believing in a relief party was part of believing that the ship was all right. They listed the alternatives. The ship, if wintering on the coast, would send a relief party. If no relief party came, the ship must have been forced to return to New Zealand because of some sort of damage. At a deeper level, a relief party coming to find them meant they had not been forgotten. If their companions at Cape Evans had known that they had been left unprovided for, they would surely have done something. Therefore *Terra Nova* must never have got to Cape Evans with the news of their whereabouts. Because 'if they knew of our predicament they must be very anxious for it is only by chance that we are not in the utmost straits.'

Talk of future sledging down the coast raised the pressing worries of sea ice. The constant wind appeared to have an impact on the sea's ability to freeze. If the sea ice failed, that would significantly increase the time they needed to sledge south, increasing the quantity of sledging supplies they required, and put further pressure on the state of their equipment – clothes, boots and their sledges, already worn out. It was almost inconceivable to have to contemplate crossing glaciers on the journey south, rather than skirting them on sea ice, to have to climb up to the piedmont rather than sledge along the coast on sea ice. Given these complex issues, Priestley thought how content he was to be a slug. 'As long as there are plenty of dreams knocking about I would as soon pass the time that way as any way. It is like having a second though much less real existence.' They were getting habituated. The alternative meant facing leaving, the uncertainty of spring sledging, with all that that involved. They would have to dig deep, dredging up the necessary resources.

But reality was a prodding counterbalance. Their eyes were suffering agonies from smoke. That polar affliction, piles, made life miserable for all, adding to their hardship. Priestley wrote in shorthand about their suffering. 'There has been a falling off in spirits the last few days', noted Levick on 4 June, 'and this morning there being a rather "strained" feeling in the air, I read two chapters aloud to the party after breakfast, which bucked things up a good deal, but only temporarily.' Running seriously low on their stores of frozen meat and blubber, Priestley tried adding Adélie carcasses, roughly chopped, straight into the hoosh – bits of rib, and flipper, and neck. He attacked the sealskin they'd fitted over the outer shaft door, flensing enough blubber from it for two days' hooshes. The fragility of their igloo life was underscored by a second experience of near asphyxiation.

On Wednesday 10 July, a rare fine day, Campbell was out walking and saw a seal; he ran to get Abbott and Browning. They found a bull and a cow – the first seen for three months. It was vital to kill both. Tackling the big bull, Abbott aimed a blow on its nose with his short-handled ice axe, missed, then chased him desperately. They couldn't afford to lose this animal. Jumping on its back, Abbott hit it and 'finally he got him', wrote Campbell, 'in striking one of the seals the knife slipped up his hand & cut three of his fingers badly so I sent him back to the igloo telling him to send Dickason down'. Dickason arrived and worked with Campbell and Browning on the two seals, all delighting in the thickness of their blubber. This was their third red-letter day. 'Great rejoicing this evening', wrote Campbell later. 'Levick & I were messmen so we missed the fun', reported Priestley. 'It was a joyous find,' summarized Levick, 'and we are very thankful, especially for the blubber, of which we were getting very short.'

Levick wrote a sober account of his actions when Abbott arrived, a bit faint, his fur mitt nearly full of blood.

> My hands were filthy & soaked with blubber from the stove, & my fingers stiff with cold, besides which I only had the guttering light of a blubber lamp held by Priestley to aid me. I cleaned off as much blubber as I could from my hands and dressed the cuts with boracic wool & bandages . . . under the circumstances did the best I could, and as the hand was clean and the wounds washed with blood, I thought it better not to poke about the wounds, but to dress them with clean dressings as quickly as possible . . . I shall feel rotten about it if I have missed spotting a broken tendon but really think it would have been risking serious suppuration if I had attempted enlarging the wounds and picking up severed ends of tendons, even if I had been able to find them in this light, owing to the filth of my hands & whole surroundings.

Abbott knew what had happened. His own knife had a handle carefully bound around to prevent his hand slipping. After managing to stab the first seal in the heart, Abbott handed his knife to Campbell, then tackled the second seal with the ice axe, another hard fight. Jumping on its back, he reached out his hand to Campbell for his knife to deliver the necessary stab. In the hurry Campbell handed him Browning's knife. Not noticing in the urgency of stabbing through the thick blubber that he wasn't using his own secure knife, Abbott's hand skidded down the greasy unprotected handle of Browning's knife on to the greasy blade and sliced the base of his three middle fingers on his right hand almost to the bone.

Levick dressed Abbott's fingers in the evening. 'The . . . tendon of the third finger is cut I am sorry to say.' On 14 July Levick made an entry in his rough journal: 'on the 11th inst. I signed an entry in the log for Campbell as a witness, at his request'. He then sealed up the two pages covering the accident with red tape and sealing wax. Whatever Campbell wrote for 11 July in his journal was too heavily crossed out to decipher.

Men of Campbell's background and upbringing could find acknowledging a mistake, however genuine, so difficult that the events surrounding it could quickly blur and a more manageable interpretation emerge, to be believed in and be genuinely convinced by. Being forward-looking and not dwelling on the past – that was considered a virtue. But Campbell was the leader, the sufferer was one of the men and the only witness another seaman, joined almost immediately by the third. What looked like a lack of openess to face what had actually happened now lay unspoken between them. With no reasons reported, two of the mess teams were changed. Close friends Browning and Dickason were broken up, and Browning now worked with Levick. Dickason was paired with Priestley.

On Friday the 12th, another fine day, Browning and Dickason killed two big seals and reported that they'd invented a new and conclusive method of fully killing, rather than half-killing, a seal: stun it as usual, then sever the head completely. Browning: 'if they weren't dead then it wasn't worth trying to kill them.' Priestley felt greatly relieved. They had meat and blubber to last. 'The starvation days are over for the present anyway. I hope our luck has changed.' The snowdrift over the cave was now so deep that Dickason constructed four steps, paved with stone, leading down into the passage. But beyond their drift, across the boulders, the ocean was still dark and open. Ice formed but didn't stay. It was like Cape Adare again, but worse. Priestley tried another joke. 'We are thinking of calling this cave SEAVIEW.'

Priestley spent 20 July, his twenty-sixth birthday, in bed: a whole day off work. A palmist had predicted that he would die in this year, a violent death. Priestley concluded as a scientist that, if he did, it would be nothing other than a coincidence. Levick gave a first aid lecture. On the 21st, his wounds healing well, Abbott resumed his duties one-handed. The blood-soaked bandages had been useful to start the fire in the morning. On the 24th they could see the Drygalski Ice Tongue for the first time since the previous autumn.

The fresh meat and fresh blubber from the newly slaughtered seals tasted delicious. Meals could now be varied, a little, and they were eating more meat. But Levick thought that the increase was causing irritable behaviour and warned everyone to eat less. He was most ashamed with himself for having a row with Priestley ('with whom I have never been on anything but friendly terms with all the winter') and took some medicine 'which I hope will put me in a better frame of mind'. But 'our life is some excuse for being a little irritable at times, however hard one tries to bottle it up.' Outbursts, on the other hand, if allowed to occur, could have serious consequences. Discipline was vital to the efficient functioning of the group. Maintaining a certain level of controlled behaviour was essential. There should be no challenges. Bounds should not be overstepped, despite living so tightly together. Their sense of security depended on it. But Levick was getting desperately tired of being cooped up inside or being harassed by the battering wind outside. Time was hanging heavy. '[O]ne feels inclined to smash the walls of the cave open & get out sometimes.' The 'perfectly damnable winds' were at fault. 'I pity any party if they are making an attempt to meet us at present.'

Levick's boots were now nothing more than sieves for snow; Priestley's were so thin that even with his calloused feet, hardened by repeating blisters, he could feel every rock. Both Dickason's boots collapsed, completely, on 28 July. Their wind clothes, rotten with blubber, tore. But Campbell ordered that, whatever the condition of their current clothing, all spare clothing, and finneskoes, had to be kept for sledging.

At Cape Evans, after weeks of heavy storms and the vilest weather anyone had ever seen, hurricane-force winds blew all night of 27 July, taking out the sea ice again in the bay to the north of the hut. On Sunday the 28th the blizzard was still howling, drift whirling past the door. 'In these conditions our thoughts fly to our comrades north up the coast', Gran wrote in his diary. 'It must be hellish for them with such slender resources. They have scant provisions, and their clothes must be in shreds by now. Let's hope they've been able to kill some seal; otherwise I fear the worst.'

North, in the ice-cave, everyone dreamed, night after night, about the relief party. 'I shall be glad to see them,' Priestley wrote on Monday 29 July, 'for if they don't turn up it will look bad for the safety of the ship.' The old refrain. A small abandoned group of beleaguered men in an ice-cave, constantly populating the coast in their minds. They couldn't be alone, in all this immensity. But it was the middle of winter; the sun had not yet appeared, and they, of all people, knew not to sledge in July. Connections with reality could become tenuous. But it was hope, and hope was part of what kept them going. Relief arriving locally had now been replaced in Levick's mind by a relief expedition from England. The comfort was, it should be leaving England right now, to rescue them in the summer. If it does not come, 'I'll never call the place my country again, but thank goodness there is not much doubt about it.'

On the last day of July Priestley served out the last raisins to the men sitting in their bags, and their last biscuit. He had done his best to make every crumb of biscuit last, assembling broken pieces into jigsaw puzzles of whole biscuits, using choosing games to make certain that allocation was random. The seamen had taken a while to break their habit of deference, always choosing according to rank, which defeated the point. But now, with the apparent failure of sea ice to form, they had to allow for a longer sledging journey than ever anticipated. Going over the Drygalski Ice Tongue rather than around it, perhaps having to travel along the plateau, could involve harsh sledging, which meant they could not leave until the end of September. Rations therefore had to stretch further. Levick had eaten no biscuits for a week as an experiment and thought he suffered no ill consequences. Their cravings for carbohydrate were now much less than they used to be. Priestley set aside a biscuit for 10 August to celebrate the return of the sun, and another for 20 August, to celebrate Campbell's thirty-seventh birthday. Otherwise, all biscuits had to be saved for sledging.

17

Dismal misery

1 August–30 September 1912

Campbell's fate depended on the winter; if he survived it, his chances would improve each day the sun rose higher in the sky.

Tryggve Gran, 16 June 1912

L EVICK WAS TRYING to boost his spirits by removing himself from 'this damned, dismal little hole' of their ice-cave and dreaming of England. He imagined shopping in the tobacco department of the Army & Navy Stores, then 'sitting in the summer house at home smoking my purchases' and having 'gigantic teas' and 'dinners at my club, and breakfast chiefly at home; then thinking of green trees and flowers, pretty girls in summer dresses & all the other things that make life good' and 'the motor bike I'm going to buy myself for a little present for a good boy'. Then, when it all got too much, wanting to 'bust through the walls . . . only theres the beastly thin plateau wind nosing about outside'. Every evening he discussed motor-bike tours with Campbell. They planned routes – at home and abroad – in the minutest detail, including where they would dine and the menu. The other four, all younger and needing to work for their living, had little option but to listen.

On 1 August, to the delight of all, daylight came down the shaft as far as the entrance to the living-cave. They could see the Drygalski Ice Tongue 'shining up', Priestley thought, 'like a plaster of Paris wall'. 'From now on we can look forward to seeing a relief party any day', he wrote. With light returning and their physical horizons stretching, their little world was reconnecting with the larger world. The prospect of the returning sun created its own brand of optimism.

Campbell took Levick out for walks, and Levick's mood lifted. At noon on the 7th the two of them saw a fine glow, which meant the sun was not far below the horizon, 'and the sight of it seemed like life, hope, good food, motor bicycles, and all the many joys of civilization returning to us'.

But the weather remained harsh, and meat was once again tight. On Wednesday the 5th, in foul weather, Priestley had gone digging with a shovel for seal meat under the snow, ice-picking out several sackloads. The flesh had to be prised off in small pieces, and they lost a lot in the process. '[I]ce picks make rough carving utensils and scraps were flying everywhere', Priestley wrote disconsolately. 'I think I smashed one skull to atoms and wasted most of the brain.' Getting the loads to the cave was arduous in the extreme, and he came yet another awful cropper on the slope leading up from the shore, among the mass of granite boulders each blasted into smooth roundness by the incessant wind. Dickason, his helper for the day, lost the sole of his boot. Gone. A total wreck. Priestley: 'We shall all be in the dirt tub soon. . . . it is only a matter of time before the wind & the rocks cause an accident down here.' Supplies were so stretched that he had begun scavenging a layer of sustenance from long-butchered seals. After locating a carcass on the seashore, Priestley chopped the skin with its blubber into squares small enough to carry, then dismembered the skeleton to add to their pile of bones. All supplies were stacked in the ice alcoves – icery, meatery, bonery – excavated off the passage.

Levick's medical responsibilities continued to be onerous. At the end of May he'd been amazed by the party's general fitness: 'after all this forced inactivity and <u>cramped, squalid quarters</u>, I can only regard it as simply wonderful.' On 3 July he'd thought the party 'under their dirt and beards well covered and fit' – and not even pale. But now in August problems were accumulating. Unable to stand upright in the cave, their backs hurt. Browning's diarrhoea had returned with a vengeance. Levick had tried most remedies, but the man was getting thinner. Campbell had suffered a bilious attack. Levick noted that he had expected it for some time. Everyone except poor Browning was badly constipated, most of them with bleeding from their rears, and suffering stomach pains. Levick considered the cause to be the lack of even their meagre ration of biscuits.

Levick reported to Campbell about his party's physical state by private notes passed back and forth. In their shared cave life this was visibly secret information. In reply to a query from Campbell on 8 August, Levick explained that one of Abbott's fingers 'will certainly be no use & will very likely be best amputated: the other two at present doubtful'. If that was the case, Abbott would 'probably have to give up his physical training when he gets back'. He was putting things in the most cheerful light to Abbott, but 'I don't think it is any use telling him this until our little troubles are over!' '[W]as careful not to tell him anything you told me', Campbell wrote back. For Abbott, a man whose physical well-being was central to his sense of self and whose career was now at risk, his dexterity damaged, these were difficult weeks.

Campbell climbed up Look-Out Hill on Saturday the 9th and saw as far as the Ross Sea. They hadn't been singing much, recently, but this Saturday they achieved a concert, really first-class – 'even for us'. On Sunday the 10th their cooking fire made the most fearsome stench, but we 'managed on the whole to preserve our equanimity . . . better than we should have done a few months ago'. They celebrated the sun's official return with a feast, except that they couldn't see it. Priestley exercised his own brand of wry humour: as they were the new arrivals in the Antarctic, it was up to the sun, like the clergyman of the parish at home, 'to visit us first'.

But snow and storms continued. Browning's hand got frostbitten up to the wrist and went ghastly white; getting the circulation going again took a long time. Campbell's nose and cheek were badly frost-bitten through being a 'hard case' and 'foolishly not wearing his wind helmet' while helping Priestley search for a supply of meat he had been saving for the sledging trip south. Campbell reckoned they had shifted a ton of snow before they found it, and shouted the news down the chimney to the cave inhabitants below.

They walked over the piedmont in a strong wind and heavy drift to their first depot by the moraine – renamed Hell's Gate – but found no sign of anything having been visited. They lashed an oil can containing a letter to the flagpole 'in case a relief party turn up'. Finally, on 14 August, Campbell saw the sun 'looking lovely we stood & blinked at each other . . . & then a frozen nose made me return'. The next day he got his whole face badly bitten on a second trip to their original depot, to collect the sledge with the iron runners, but the attempt failed because it was too deeply buried under snow.

They had to be more careful. This longest of long winters was still with them, the challenge still potent to survive all risks and hardships, to manage harsh storms, to negotiate rocks coated in lethal black ice or the slippery, uneven piedmont ice. Overriding everything there was the 'damnable wind all the time'. They'd hated it in the autumn, during their desperate attempts to survive in their tents. Now, six months later, the vile, battering, bitter wind was still here, draining their energy and their will, pushing them over and punishing their exposed skins, making them feel helpless and chilling their bodies. Even their underclothes had holes. To Priestley, the wind seemed to have blown for 180 long winter days without lulling for more than a few hours. There'd been none of the walks for pleasure that they'd managed at Cape Adare: 'our raids for food & necessaries have been one long struggle back & forth', he wrote, because walking with this wind was as bad as walking against it.

Their ice-cave world had been in a kind of stasis, the routine predictable. In a strange way, as Priestley put it, 'we felt as if we were settled here for life'. Now, regardless of the weather conditions, they had to get out and prepare for sledging. But every single action was a struggle: assembling their small bits of equipment, getting their few scattered, worn possessions together, collecting the means to make their sledging journey. Miserably, Priestley wrote: 'we have really had about as unpleasant a six months as is humanly or naturally possible & it is about time we had a rest one way or another.'

The gap between the belief that they would be rescued and the failure of any relief party to appear widened. Yet they still reiterated that 'any day' the relief party would come. There were excited sightings of black specks that could be sledging parties, especially by Abbott: replays of the sightings of *Terra Nova* six months ago. Certain actions had been carried out right at the start of their stay here, relating to undertaking a sledging journey to Cape Evans. They had been seen as a kind of necessary precaution, an insurance policy; now they were converting into concrete plans. Priestley was adjusting: 'we have got so used to talking & thinking of our journey down the coast towards the end of September that we have begun to take the necessity of such a journey for granted.' Levick was honest about the prospect. On the one hand, there was 'relief at getting away from this dismal & squalid life'; on the other hand, 'reluctance at the idea of the bad time we are probably in for'. Obsessively, they all talked about crossing the Drygalski Ice Tongue. As they watched it earlier in the year, clouds of drift had always seemed to whirl above it, indicating bad weather.

On Sunday 18 August, Priestley worked out that it was five months since Levick, Abbott and Browning had battled across to the ice-cave after losing their tent in a blizzard. They'd all had an impossible night, trying to sleep two men in each bag. Then suddenly Priestley thought about Mawson; perhaps because on the South Magnetic Pole expedition Mawson, Mackay and Professor Edgeworth David had all slept uncomfortably together in a three-man bag. And he thought about his friend Frank Wild, who'd been on Shackleton's expedition. Now Wild had joined Mawson's expedition. 'I wonder where he is', Priestley recorded in his diary.

'A most wonderful thing has happened', Campbell wrote on his thirty-seventh birthday, Tuesday 20 August. 'Last night it was blowing hard with open water the wind dropping in the night but fresh again this morning in spite of that good white ice all over the bay! Why it formed in those few hours and not before I can't think. Anyhow I look on it as a good omen.' And he handed out birthday rations to all.

'The end of our igloo provisions is within sight now but so is our stay here please God', wrote Priestley. 'We are much bucked up at the way the sea ice is forming.' But all the following week a strong, cold gale blew continuously and the sea ice was blown out, except for a strip. The gale scooped a hollow in the deep snow on their roof, which they tried to fill, but the wind just scooped it off again. It scooped another hole beside their chimney, with the wind shaping the drift in the way it always did, every year, except that this winter there were men crouched inside. Browning and Abbott had built another attempt at an entrance to the igloo capable of keeping the snow out, a 'regular torpedo boat hatch'. But they were getting vulnerable in their cave. The drip was worse. On the 23rd Dickason and

Abbott had their sleeping-bags and belongings soaked. On the 26th they woke with snow on their faces.

They wanted the Drygalski over, and behind them. The ice tongue was preying on their imaginations, looming as a huge barrier to their march south. In spite of this, there were two more false hopes that the relief party had been seen. Their lives were bumping and jolting. The comparative peace of deep winter had been dislocated by the need to get organized for sledging. Yet it was still as cold, it was still winter, and the wind still blew relentlessly, keeping them in their bags unless they had to go out. They were just as hungry, even filthier. The floor was still in a frightful state. They were still (except Browning, with his own troubles) constipated. The meat they were eating was worryingly rancid, Priestley wrote on the last night of August. There was a bad taste in the hooshes.

In New Zealand, Harry Pennell wrote a long, detailed letter to Sir Lewis Beaumont, who had been authorized by Scott to reassure the public in case of need: 'I have heard . . . that there is considerable anxiety in England as to Campbell's party, and it seems wise to . . . let you know exactly how the facts presented themselves to us last March.' Having described the various attempts made to reach Evans Coves, Pennell laid out the headings under which the shore party's position, if they were not relieved, was assessed:

1. Desperate. Certain or probable disaster if not picked up
2. Journey to headquarters practicable but very dangerous
3. Same as -2- but risks only those of ordinary Autumnal sledging.

The factors determining under which of these headings the shore party's position lay covered ice conditions, nature of coast for sledging, dates when sledging could start, provisions and equipment available, and the health, physique and expert knowledge of the individual members.

You may be sure, Sir, that with the party on shore to be relieved and the ship to be, if possible, kept afloat that the week or so she was in these waters was a time of much heart-burning and viewing and revising of every idea; and in the many times that the situation has . . . since come to mind there has never been any thing to make us think that a wrong line was taken.

That the position was desperate was 'soon dismissed', wrote Pennell, 'as at the worst it would be feasible though uncomfortable to winter at Evans Coves in an igloo'. Concluding that the journey to Cape Evans 'would not be particularly hard and only attended by the ordinary risks of Autumnal sledging', Campbell's position fell into category 3.

Pennell listed Campbell's chief danger as the chance of a shortage of matches. But 'it was a recognised axiom with Campbell . . . that the ship might be wrecked and so he realised, & provided for, the contingency of his being left to his own resources'. Campbell, Pennell recorded, had landed with a depot, organized entirely by himself, with this in mind. Evans Coves had large numbers of seals and penguins, so there was no anxiety about food. Inshore ice would almost certainly freeze early, allowing them to sledge south relatively quickly. There were depots down the coast, which Campbell did not know about – but although welcome, they would not be essential. The party were in the best of health. Their risk of scurvy would be nil, because they were eating plenty of fresh meat; also, Campbell and Priestley were both used to these conditions.

But the greatest factor in their favour, according to Pennell, was Campbell himself, 'who combines the two qualities of action and calculating in a most peculiar degree and is of all men the least likely to come to grief, by rashness on the one hand or over cautiousness on the other'.

On Sunday 1 September, Dickason and Browning went down with acute diarrhoea. Then all were struck down. Campbell, who didn't like seal blubber, was the least affected, but one or other (or sometimes two at once) was shuffling to the roundhouse all night, desperately needy; there was gallows humour ('our small stock of literature is disappearing fast!') but also real suffering, while outside the gales continued. Various theories about causes gave way to the certainty that the biscuit tin in which they thawed their joints contained old bits of decayed meat and blood. Levick 'condemned' it and made regulations, approved by Campbell, about handling meat and the things they used to cut up meat.

At the same time Campbell asked Levick to 'train the party for sledging', so he started them off on exercises that they could do in the cave. No one could stand up straight, so the Swedish drill had to be done kneeling, like some strange form of religion, said Priestley the Methodist, and most of them felt too ill to try. They started preparing their meat rations for sledging, despite the epidemic of diarrhoea. Levick was keeping a daily list of who did what and how often, handing out medicine, limiting their diet, ordering freshwater hooshes according to the tally. 'We chip at the back wall of the cave for fresh ice', noted Priestley, weak from his bad attack and ordered to bed. Levick was particularly concerned for Browning, who was in a fragile state. 'Only two or three weeks more here please God', wrote Priestley on the 8th. 'Our present care is to throw off this diarrhoea & get fit for marching.' But sickness had come at a bad time. Priestley, messman on the 9th, described cutting up frozen meat in a bath of drips from the ceiling with eyes and nose watering from the smitch. He had a raging thirst. The mug of hot water allowed for 'lunch' tasted of blubber, seaweed and penguin, and was full of reindeer hairs. Some of the reindeer sleeping-bags were almost bald. It felt as though they'd been eating hairs all winter.

Tuesday 10 September was a bad day. 'Poor – – broke down this morning', wrote Levick, avoiding any hint of the person's name. 'Said he couldn't eat his hoosh & started to lose his head & generally chuck his hand in.' Campbell and Levick 'both had a go at him & rowed him & then bucked him up generally. He said he was feeling rotten & wouldn't be able to march with us down the coast & a lot of rot like that, but we talked him out of it, & he is comparatively cheerful again tonight. The dismal misery of this dull & filthy hole is beginning to work on us a little, & that's a fact.'

But, leaving the ice-cave meant re-entering the world and its complexity. Their lives in the cave had a kind of simplicity. For Abbott, for example, re-entry meant the reality of his disability. 'Things a bit down at present', wrote Levick next day. Priestley was exhausted from his last attack of illness, Dickason was still ill, and Browning in a bad way: 'I had a yarn with him alone this morning. I am afraid he is getting chronic inflamation of his guts.' Levick condemned the object they used to stir their hoosh. It looked 'suspicious'.

The sledging teams for the journey south, to Cape Evans, had already been decided, each hauling a sledge, with their own tent. The teams were the same as summer sledging: Campbell with Priestley and Dickason, Levick with Abbott and Browning. Now, some time during this difficult period, Browning was 'logged' by Campbell – that is, written down officially in the log-book for committing a misdemeanour, to go on his record. Dickason wrote that it concerned Browning failing to get the hoosh ready by 4.10 p.m. The actual reason appeared to relate to the tent allocated to Levick's sledging party, which Browning, as a member, was meant to be mending but had used to protect his sleeping-bag from leaks coming through the roof. The three seamen on the galley side had taken independent action against getting wet: Dickason, for example, had rigged up a canopy over his bag. But independent action was risky. It could invite a perception of insubordination. The men had to answer to the officers at all times 'in a proper manner': no outbursts or off-hand tone permitted.

An exchange of undated notes between Levick and Campbell dealing with Browning's behaviour revealed the application of naval discipline. 'I am going to have a d'd row with B. tomorrow', Levick wrote to Campbell.

> He has disobeyed me 3 times over the tent & his behaviour tonight simply contemptuous, as in spite of what I said he has not taken in the tent & is simply keeping it out on his bag for bravado, as the drip has ceased . . . I wont trouble you about it as you have put the matter in my hands, but I'll have such a d'd row tomorrow with him that he wont do it again in a hurry I hope.
>
> I propose then, to take the tent away from him, & only let him have it to mend.

Campbell gave his agreement:

I purposely didn't say anything as I want him to take his orders
from you, being your crew

If you do have trouble bring him up before me, but I expect
you will bring him to order yourself without any trouble.

Levick's and Campbell's private notes allowed an outlet for the
potential irritant of sharing their time and space with people not of
their own background, or choosing. Exchanges of 8 and 9 September
criticized the cooking of the seamen, with a snide dig at their explanations for the causes of the diarrhoea. Abbott, Browning and
Dickason had occasional opportunities while working outside for
private talk. Priestley, as always, remained the odd one out, not
having to operate by Navy rules, but equally firmly on the officers'
side of the invisible line. In their small ice-cave, rows were by definition public, but ranks closed in every sense. Rows were left out of
journals and not referred to afterwards. They were part of the inside
life of a small group. Private. Criticisms of each other were generally
handled in the same way. Dickason implied in his diary that 'one of
this party' was a liar, but in carefully coded language. It would not do
to go any further.

The weather relented sufficiently to allow several calm days.
Swedish exercises were continued. Over at the depot moraine
Priestley couldn't find his collection of precious fossils, stored since
the summer, now hidden beneath the snow. Faced by anonymous
level whiteness, he dug frantically, helped by Abbott. Diarrhoea continued, with two or three men being attacked at a time. Levick
considered Browning, a long-time sufferer of enteritis, a separate
problem: 'I wish we had a change of diet to give the poor chap',
Campbell wrote. A new epidemic broke out vigorously half-way
though the month. Given Abbott's injured hand, and the two other
seamen both sick, Campbell repaired sleeping-bags. Sledging rations
continued to be prepared, with fresh meat being cooked and bagged
up, but they didn't have enough. If *Terra Nova* had got through to
Cape Evans last summer, Campbell noted plaintively, 'we may expect
a relief party any time as they will know we are out of food except
seal'.

On the fourth day of Priestley's desperate digging for his geological specimens Campbell suggested excavating somewhere different. Almost immediately their spades hit the rocks. A cache was built of all the specimens, marked with a bamboo and message, just in case a ship called. The sledges had already been dug out, but disappeared under snow in a blizzard. On Saturday the 21st, Abbott and Levick spent the day digging out the sledges again but got caught in another blizzard on the way home and were badly frostbitten. 'We strongly hope to be out of this', wrote Levick, but the next day, after eating fried liver, Priestley, Browning and Dickason all relapsed. 'A damned nuisance,' noted Levick, 'as they were all getting well.' Yesterday's gale had blown all the sea ice out and dropped heavy snow over the land. Inside the ice-cave, sledging gear was being repaired among the sick and suffering. His focus and energy running clear with the prospect of action, Campbell made a detailed drawing of the igloo's interior and a jokey sketch of Priestley in his patched and tattered trousers returning to London, ice axe in one hand and geological hammer in the other, with street urchins sniggering at him. Priestley wrote a note to his father to be left at the moraine depot and ended his ice-cave diary, packing it away. From now on he would use a sledging diary.

On Tuesday 24 September, Levick photographed Campbell with Dickason and Abbott standing among the snow-covered rocks out-side the entrance to the ice-cave in their indescribably filthy clothes, heavy with blubber; and Abbott photographed Levick with Priestley and Browning. A leaving picture, part of convincing themselves they were going. To keep the momentum up, weekly food bags were car-ried to the sledges, stored by the ice-foot and packed on board the 12-footer, with the wooden runners, and the 10-footer with the iron runners. The iron runners had been crucial for sea ice work at Cape Adare. They'd be even more important now – if they found sea ice, as they hoped.

The weather was fine. To Campbell they were ready to start. But Browning was still bad with diarrhoea, and Campbell had to admit they couldn't march until he was better. 'Providentially' an emperor penguin 'strolled up' and was killed, in the hope that Browning would benefit from its meat. Next day, Wednesday the 25th, wind blowing, they stayed inside the cave doing jobs: mending equipment, sorting clothes. 'I hope to leave the igloo tomorrow', Priestley wrote in his new diary, 'once for all I hope'. At least, 'every body appears to be recovering from the last epidemic & I hope that this time it will be for good.' The same day Levick was writing that he and Priestley had begun to think it would be better to wait at least another week before starting: days would be warmer, and the wind would perhaps diminish. However, 'both of us are chipping in willingly & making no demur.' But on Thursday the 26th Dickason was struck down and had to spend the day in bed, feeling worse than he had ever done. Levick decided to write 'Diarrhoea Epidemic Some Points' under eight headings, to show Campbell and Priestley, 'to stop tangential theories about the cause . . . which are apt to cause panic again'.

The weather stepped in. The wind blew too hard to travel. The chance came to kill another seal and, on Saturday the 28th, five emperors. Suddenly, bounty. Now they had extra fresh food, Levick wanted to stay another week. Browning was in a bad way. Levick examined his belly on Saturday the 28th: 'he is feeling generally weak . . . and says he does not feel up to pulling a sledge.' But Campbell was determined to leave. On Sunday the 29th, in slight snow and a raw wind, they packed the sledges with everything except the sleeping-bags and the cookers. The ice-cave was emptying. Browning and Dickason had prepared a pole to set up at the moraine depot, with a cross-piece on top, to attract attention, and a couple of Oxo tins, for notes. A letter written by Campbell dated 21 September 1912 was put in the tin, explaining that the fossil wood must be handled carefully, and summarizing their dates and movements.

On the last day of September, 'Abandoned igloo all v. glad day thick with snow in PM' – Campbell's brief phrases stood in for more happiness than he could write. Trying to travel south, to safety, in autumn had been out of the question. Now it was spring, their first, and essential, opportunity. Browning and Dickason, still ill, stayed in the hut all day, cleaning the cookers, while the other four carried gear down the hill, negotiating the boulders, for the last time. The final packing of the sledges was a slow and tedious job. Campbell had handed out a collection of new clothes. Every man had a vest, a pair of hair socks, four pairs of woollen socks. The rest were divided as fairly as possible – New Zealand sweaters, a pyjama jacket, sleep socks, some wind clothes, thick mitts, winter hats, summer hats. After waiting until the last moment, they changed, with profound pleasure, into what they could of the new.

In the end they didn't get away until after 6.00 p.m. It had been a long day, with thick snow in the afternoon, and they were tired. But Campbell insisted on making a start. So they harnessed up, braced for the weight, divided into their three-man teams: Campbell with Priestley and Dickason, Levick with Browning and Abbott. The new snow made pulling heavy, and they only achieved about a mile, before camping at 8.00 p.m. by the light of half a candle each. Dickason's diarrhoea was very bad in the night. No more journeys along the passage to the roundhouse. Back to exposure to wind and snow. But they were on their way.

Campbell had judged well the man whom he would be relying on most: 'I never expected to look forward to spring sledging,' Priestley wrote that night, 'yet we are as pleased as we can be at getting on the move.' Capable, equable, completely trustworthy, Priestley had become Campbell's right-hand man.

They'd landed at Cape Adare with 30 tons of stuff. They had ended up with just themselves, what they stood up in and two loaded sledges.

18

Drygalski past

1–27 October 1912

The past winter has already begun to seem like a bad
dream, & we are again ordinary mortals.

Levick, 7 October 1912

THE SUN SHONE. The six men were out of the dirt and squalor
of the ice-cave and into a new world, revelling in light and
cleanliness. Almost as wonderful was the sound of silence. The air,
amazingly, was still. No wind buffeted their bodies or filled their
ears. It was the first day of October, and they were truly on their
way. The sledges had to be dragged along one at a time, moving in
stages, with both teams harnessed together, except for Browning,
who was wholly incapacitated, and Dickason, half-crippled with
diarrhoea. But nothing could damped their spirits. They'd seen the
last of Hell's Gate. They were eating their precious sledging rations,
saved since January. Cocoa, sugar, chocolate and biscuits all in the
same meal, with 2¾ pannikins of meat and blubber and some
pemmican – almost too good to be true. Levick considered it a
matter of wonder and pride that even though, having managed 5
miles, they were worn out, they could do a day's work like this 'after
our recent life'.

None of the assessments made by others about the ability of the
Eastern party to cope had taken into account the impact of illness, or
accident, or the implications of reduced or inadequate diet. The significance of even the simplest things was not considered. The Eastern
party, for example, had only one candle left. It had to be saved for
emergencies, given Browning's state, so every evening they had to
camp early. In the mornings their departures were slow, because two

of the six were handicapped: Abbott's three stiff fingers, and Browning's continuing illness, limited their usefulness.

The canvas bands of the harness pressing against their sore stomachs, they heaved the sledges over what they called 'flypaper' snow on Wednesday the 2nd, with Priestley trying a man-hauling joke: 'when I grow up I am going to be a horse.' Stopped by a crevasse wide as a river, they found a snow bridge, roped up and cautiously eased the sledges over the blue abyss. But, blinded by squalls of snow and unable to see where they were going, they camped, having achieved 8½ miles. On the 3rd a blizzard forced them to camp after only 3 miles, tying them to their bags all the next day as well, everything covered in fine drift, 'but we are pretty much hardened to discomfort'. Campbell looked out of his tent early on Saturday the 5th but the blizzard was still blowing so there was 'nothing for it but to coil down in our bags and wait'. At least the rest helped Browning. Restricted by Levick to a diet of raw penguin and no seal or blubber, only slops, the walking exhausted him. And ahead was the Drygalski Ice Tongue, that long glacier extension bounding their southernmost view at Evans Coves: 'no place for invalids'.

But their first important goal was just before the Drygalski: Relief Inlet, where Edgeworth David, Mawson and Mackay had been retrieved by *Nimrod* on their return from the Magnetic Pole. When the blizzard cleared sufficiently, in the afternoon of the 5th, they packed up and got going again, though it was 'heartbreaking & backbreaking work', wrote Priestley. Time had been lost, but it was typical of sledging. As a leader, Campbell didn't complain about days confined in a tent. His approach to weather, snow and ice continued pragmatic. Note them, take the necessary action, then get on. His approach to sickness was equally direct. State it, get help. No secret suffering, no hiding of potentially harmful conditions. Their ice-cave lives had ironed out most bumps of privacy.

The sledges crept forward in the deep layer of soft, wet snow dropped by the blizzard. At the lunch halt on the 6th, Levick's team ate only raw meat. They had developed 'a perfect craving' for it – it was 'the finest possible stuff to sledge on'. Browning was feeling a bit better, so had a snow wash, then Dickason cut his wild, greasy hair, and Browning cut Dickason's. The two friends were separated in different tents. After the tight proximity of the cave, the split into two sledging units had the potential to disrupt. Campbell drew a caricature in his sledging journal of 'Levick after a week's sledging', all bristles and pig-faced. Priestley was already timing their tent against the performance of Levick's in the morning. But laughing at each other was part of their habit of coping, and 'healthy rivalry', to Priestley, was a spur to even greater efforts.

That evening, Sunday 6 October, they camped on the north side of Relief Inlet among small crevasses. They'd managed their first week. The ice-cave was well behind them. An easy snow slope led down to the tide crack, and another led up the other side. Levick considered that everyone was 'improving in health & spirits since leaving our late miserable quarters'. The change to the carefully saved sledging food had done them all good. Browning was even able to do a little pulling, which helped with getting their sledge along. A few seals were lying on the ice. Not needing to kill them was their own version of relief, although with seals about they could always stay here, Campbell reckoned, if they couldn't reach the hut at Cape Evans. Priestley, with Shackleton's expedition always in his head, thought that arriving here today was a strange coincidence because it was on exactly this day in October 1908 that Professor Edgeworth David and the Magnetic Pole party had left Cape Royds to sledge north up this coast. The 'Prof', he thought, 'ought to dream about us tonight'. Edgeworth David's account provided a little information about crossing the Drygalski, and a few details about the journey up the coast. But it wasn't much to go on.

Then they were on to the Drygalski. A series of waves confronted them, each icy undulation divided by ravines with abrupt cliffs or steep snow sides, slippery and wind-blown. Priestley: 'we need decent light' to cross this. But instead, the light deteriorated, dis-torting, merging horizon and sky in milky whiteness, denying perspective. Edging down a slope, with Campbell's sledge in the lead, Priestley suddenly threw himself on the ground, and the sledge jerked to a stop only half a length from a sharp drop. 'Should have taken a bad toss', reported Campbell '& most probably broken ourselves or the sledge – got the other crew to help & pulled sledge on top again & turned E till found a good camping place & then 4.45 camped as light was so treacherous – also D has started his diarrhoea again with all this heavy pulling.' Turning out at 4.00 a.m. the next morning to check the weather, Campbell could barely see the other tent through thick snow. Marching nevertheless, 'light and surface vile', they had a second just-in-time stop on the edge of a cliff, with all six men needed to haul the sledge back up again. Camping that night, Browning's diarrhoea was much worse; but at least Dickason's was at last better.

By Thursday the 10th, the going still heavy, visibility still poor, the work was 'as stiff as ever'. Chewing frozen meat and strips of blubber at the lunch halt, they knew they were getting very weary, and chilled. But part-way through the afternoon the sky briefly cleared, and they could see their first view south. To their joy, the ocean was white to the horizon. The ice was in. Even better, the next moment Dickason suddenly saw Mount Erebus – the shining beauty of the volcano, plainly visible on the horizon. Mount Melbourne was still in sight behind them. The world they had left, linking to the world they were aiming for. Their final worry, getting off the Drygalski, dissolved when they discovered a long snow valley that led them, by stages, on to the sea ice, where they camped in 'great spirits' . They'd done 21 miles since leaving Relief Inlet on the 7th. 'This has been a day we have lived for months', exulted Priestley. All winter the looming barrier of the Drygalski had sat across their projected journey as an obstacle, with the added fear that they would find no sea ice beyond it. All winter, when they'd achieved a difficult job, they'd say – 'Drygalski past!' – ice-cave language for 'problem over'. Now it really was.

Since the start of their sledging, Priestley had kept their provisions next to his sleeping-bag. Now he gave up being general commissariat officer 'and damned glad I am to be rid of it'. The sea ice was in place, so they could stay on the coast and eat seals. They wouldn't need to climb up to the plateau, with its bitter cold and lack of access to essential fresh meat. Priestley handed Levick the stores allocated to his tent for the rest of the journey; Levick could decide now how to divide everything across the days.

A blizzard blew up, so they spent Friday the 11th in their bags until the afternoon, 'not sorry for a rest'. Priestley thought about the journey ahead. Perhaps he could do some geology, but that depended on their speed, which depended on the sea ice surface, and on Browning's health. Hearing an emperor penguin call outside their tent, Priestley woke Campbell. They heard the penguin walk over to the other tent. To their annoyance they heard no sound of slaughter, so Campbell had to get up, kill it with a spade, and together they butchered it in the cold wind. The blood froze and clogged on their knives as they cut the flesh into thin strips to eat, frozen, on the march. 'We as the hunters have collared the heart and liver for our hoosh', wrote Priestley.

In his tent Levick was worrying about Browning: 'I am afraid one can only take a rather serious view of him.' Campbell appeared, to get Abbott to help prepare the sledges for the sea ice. Campbell planned to strap the 12-foot wooden-runner sledge on top of the 10-foot iron-runner sledge, making a high double-decker. Four men would pull on the traces, the other two pull as 'wheelers' one each side, from the rear strut, all six working together in the pattern they'd learned by experience at Robertson Bay. Unpacking the two sledges and then repacking them was very cold work, and Campbell and Abbott got their hands badly frostbitten. Oil tins, crampons, spare boots, moccasins, camera boxes and lenses were stacked on one layer, with the instrument box, two cookers, a bag for each party filled with meat and clothes, the spare tin of biscuits, a box of blubber and emperor meat above. Tents and sleeping-bags were stowed on top of the boxes with the weekly food and biscuit bags. Browning's bedding, which included an extra bag and a sodden blanket, was a heavy added weight.

After depoting all unnecessary clothing, to lighten the weight, they started on Saturday the 12th on the next stage of their journey, achieving their best distance yet, with only one capsize. 'It is as good as a years pay in our pockets', Priestley thought, 'to see the white wall of the Drygalski Ice Barrier behind us, and well behind us.' But the next day, Sunday, their pace slowed. The heavy double-decker ploughed reluctantly through deeply crusted snow, squealing bizarrely 'like a train with all her brakes jammed hard on'. The snow stuck in huge cakes to the runners, then froze as soon as they stopped. Repeated 'standing pulls' were needed to get it started again. Once they crossed the tracks of what they thought was a man on skis, but it was a seal. They were on the longed-for sea ice. But what they had was 'the hardest day yet', according to Priestley, who felt off-colour, as did Campbell. Only 7 miles were achieved. We've still got 'some infernal work in front of us', Priestley was certain.

To Campbell Monday the 14th was 'not such a bad day after all'. But Priestley and Dickason had diarrhoea, Campbell got his nose frostbitten, and although they travelled 10 miles 'hoiking' the sledge over heavy pressure ridges, deeply drifted in soft snow, not more than 7 miles could count as forward journeying. The next day, Tuesday, the sledge could only be moved forward by brute force over heavily distorted ice, heaped in all directions, Browning pulling with his shoulders because he couldn't take the pressure on his stomach. Even finding a flat place to camp was difficult. 'I'm tired of this confounded spring sledging', Priestley wrote despondently. An extra spoonful of cocoa to honour Mrs Campbell's birthday didn't help much, because food was beginning to be a worry again. They'd assumed they would find a succession of seals to live off. But they hadn't seen one since Relief Inlet. And less than half the 10 miles done that day were actually on course. The previous night Priestley had been up with diarrhoea; now it was Campbell's turn to be ill, feeling cold and sick, with cramps and diarrhoea. Levick dosed him in the morning of Wednesday the 16th, then the two of them prospected the route ahead, with a chance to talk. Campbell had decided to decommission the double-decker, given the miserably difficult conditions, so Priestley re-packed the sledges. Each would now have to be relayed separately, which was time-consuming and demoralizing. The day proved 'wearisome' in the extreme; they floundered through high, heavy-pressure ice and deep drifts before finishing up 'quite done', having moved the two sledges possibly 3 miles. Levick was snow-blind, and Campbell said he felt like a bit of chewed string. Everyone was in such a wretched state that Levick decided 'we had better sacrifice one of our two half bottles of brandy tonight, and have a tot all round, which we did'.

Wind, snow and bad light kept them all in their bags on Thursday the 17th, with Campbell happy to rest and remember his son Nigel's birthday. Levick 'served out snow goggles to everyone and advised their use'. Priestley was agitated about food. Only ten days' provisions were left. Reverting to his ice-cave mind-set, he calculated that on half-rations they could last three weeks. If they were squeezed too much, 'we can take things into our own hands & make a bust for it without the sledges'. Next morning, Friday the 18th, he woke with that old familiar hunger pain from the ice-cave, 'a devil of a twist'. But ahead was another day slogging through what turned out to be a massive landscape in which they crawled, and struggled, like dung beetles dragging their burdens. The pressure ridges were 8 to 9 feet high, the snow 4 feet deep. Each sledge had to be relayed, with four men as usual on the traces and a 'wheeler' on either side ready in case of an upset as the sledge skidded and lurched. It was 'infernally heavy work'. Every step was a huge effort. Sometimes they floundered up to their thighs in cloggy snow. Snow squalls swept over them, visibility was poor, the weather enervating and sultry, the temperature rising to possibly above freezing. Priestley rarely commented about the men, but that evening he recorded how they had 'behaved splendidly as usual – Dickason in particular never seemed to have had enough & pulled equally well whether up to his ankles or up to his neck in snow'.

Around 4.00 p.m. the country opened out, and at last from a ridge they got a sight of their next objective: the cliff-like wall of the Nordenskjöld Ice Tongue. It was all taking so much longer than they'd calculated. Levick worried because his tent's provisions were running out. Priestley was concerned, despite having given up the commissariat, because Levick's tent had been using food up faster than they should, and especially their oil. At the same time Levick was worrying that everyone was 'feeling most damnably slack, as if we could hardly drag ourselves along, much less the sledges, but . . . we can't expect to be absolutely fit after our Winter!' Levick believed that fresh meat was essential to stave off scurvy, but there were still no seals in sight.

Campbell drew on his hunting skills. Scanning the sea ice with his glasses, he sighted a lone animal, then set off on skis to follow the seal's tracks to its breathing-hole in the ice. 'We want it badly', said Priestley. These days of hard, slow travel had 'taken a good deal of optimism out of the party'. On the other hand, they shouldn't complain: they could have died already. Then they wouldn't be able to worry about 'starvation to come'.

The next morning, Saturday the 19th, everyone was up at 3.30 a.m., in full daylight, keen to reach the Nordenskjöld. Browning was directed to the seal's hole with an axe and knife and 'a yell soon told us he had been successful'. Levick and Abbott were dispatched with their sledge, to butcher, freeze and pack the meat. Browning pointed out a large cyst on the animal's liver, but Levick passed it as safe to eat. Then he and his men pulled hard for three hours before they caught Campbell's party up, 'with only a ½ minute easy', as Levick plaintively pointed out. But Priestley was irritated that Levick had forgotten to bring the head, so they missed out on brain in their hoosh.

They slogged on, the surface difficult, the wall of the Nordenskjöld apparently only a mile and a half away – yet silver-white, looming huge and suddenly retreating, the miraged ice tongue never got closer. Exasperated, sweat streaming off their faces, they pulled harder than ever until forced to camp, no nearer than they had seemed to be when they started. While they were pitching their tents, the miraged cliffs looked so close that they felt could walk over and collect fresh ice for their cookers. Tired and sunburnt, Levick sat miserably adding up his tent's provisions. Priestley had given him fourteen days' rations of biscuits on the 13th, but six days later he only had eight days' biscuit left, on half-rations. They were not yet half-way home: 'shall have to finish the journey on seal meat I suppose.' The men – as usual, according to Levick – seemed unaware. Browning had cut Abbott's hair the day before, and now the three trimmed each other's beards. On Sunday the 20th everyone trudged on, taciturn, muttering caustic comments and swearing, with the cliffs of the ice tongue dancing and shifting, ever retreating, and tempers frayed almost to the limit. Miscalculating distances in these conditions was deeply demoralizing. The sheer monotony of 'hauling these damned sledges along hour after hour' was rubbing their tolerance raw. After starting at 6.00 a.m. they didn't – finally – reach the ice tongue until 4.00 p.m. Getting to the Nordenskjöld from the Drygalski had taken far longer, and been far harder, than they'd ever imagined: ten weary, tough days.

Fortunately they found a steep snowdrift, which enabled them to clamber up to the top with their gear, then haul up the sledges with alpine rope. They were terribly hungry. Levick wrote worriedly that they would have to 'discard a good deal more gear, & reduce our clothing to the lowest limit'. 'God knows', said Priestley, 'we have no luxuries to dispence with.' But 'I won't leave my records, or specimens, or camera.' Browning was very tired, and Campbell had heartburn. Their stock of food was so low they would be on an 'igloo diet' in a few days. 'We must hope for better surfaces & better marches.'

In Surrey, Admiral Beaumont was writing this day, Sunday 20 October, to Kathleen Scott, enclosing Pennell's letter. It was probably the friends and relatives of those who were with Campbell who had made remarks implying their surprise at the party having been 'abandoned', as they may have put it. But there was nothing in the newspapers, Beaumont assured her. And he had heard no criticism.

Marking their depot on top of the Nordenskjöld with an ice axe, two shovels and an empty red oil can with a message scratched on by Campbell using the point of a knife, 'Party left here 21/10/12 all well making for Cape Evans', the six men crossed the ice tongue in bright calm weather. It was only 4 miles, no crevasses and an easy slope down to a snow-covered plain on the other side. Then they reassembled the double-decker sledge, and pulled until 6.00 p.m. A skua flew over: their first. 'It was only a passing visit', said Priestley, 'so we did not eat him.'

The next objective was 'Depot Island', their first chance to find evidence of other humans on this coast, but Campbell's small-scale Admiralty chart didn't mark the island, so they didn't know where to look. Edgeworth David and Mawson had left specimens here on 1 November 1908, during their slow slog along the sea ice. Beyond was Granite Harbour, where Griffith Taylor and Debenham were meant to have spent the summer geologizing. But they'd never appeared at Evans Coves, so who knew where they had actually been?

Tuesday 22 October was dismal, raw-cold and overcast. The going was exceptionally heavy over horrible pressure. Campbell had an attack of diarrhoea, Browning a relapse, and Levick, leading the man-hauling party, had painful, strained eyes. Sunset was beginning to run into sunrise, and even with an overcast sky the light was harsh and glary. The standing pulls were constant. 'I am looking forward', declared Priestley, 'to a day's sledging without a single – 1, 2, 3, – Heave!' Eager to discover something positive, he scanned ahead through Campbell's glasses and decided a black conical mark was Depot Island. Leaving Browning to rest with Abbott and Dickason – a rare chance for the men to be together – the three officers reconnoitred ahead. But 'hopes of a depot were shattered'. The object was a ridge of ice full of black dust arranged in layers. And so they camped. The following day the weather was equally galling. Campbell, ill all night, felt cold, weak and slack. The standing pulls, and the heaving, shook the invalids up, Priestley thought, and they didn't get much chance to recover. The piggy-backed sledge jerked and slid, swerved and rocked – 'I capsize & innumerable narrow escapes', reported Priestley. At least they killed a seal so had a decent hoosh of brain and liver. Writing in his bag after dinner, the dirty-brown whorls of his finger prints showing where he held the pages down, Priestley noted they were getting low on biscuits, unless they found a depot, or – that underlying hope, and expectation – 'meet a sledge party coming to relieve us'. There were no other options.

At Cape Evans the southern search party was preparing to leave for the Barrier in a week's time. Sledging food was packed and equipment repaired. The mules had pulled their first loads to Hut Point, doing the journey 'splendidly'. The plan was clear. They would search the Barrier for signs of Scott and his four companions, then go as far as the top of Beardmore Glacier. Remembering the horrifying chasms, Atkinson and Cherry-Garrard were convinced that the Polar party were at the bottom of a crevasse. Lashly, on the other hand, thought they had died of scurvy. Cherry, sorrowful, bitter after the unremitting toil of the first summer and autumn and the pain of a miserable winter, was needing to summon all his diminished reserves to face once more going out on the Barrier.

South of the Nordenskjöld Ice Tongue, the sky cleared on Thursday the 24th, the wind dropped, the sun shone, the world was blue and white and sparkling. But all that Campbell, Priestley and Dickason, Levick, Abbott and Browning could think of was the heavy going beneath their trudging feet, the ache in their shoulders, the pain in their bellies: another day's gruelling slog, only this time with the sun grilling their backs. At least there were seals again. A line of picturesque grounded icebergs, lopsided, tilting, provided shelter and access to the water. The females lay on their sides, their pups, small inside their floppy coats, nuzzling for milk, the sound of their bleating like lambs. Skuas pecked at placentas lying on the snow. Here was the coastal larder, as specified in London: an apparently endless supply of meat. Levick had decided that, given their upset systems, they should eat only the choice pieces of a newly killed seal – liver, brain, heart, kidneys, a few slices of undercut – and leave the rest of the animal. Although seal meat suited some of the party very well, he thought their almost purely meat diet, necessarily 'underdone', was having rather a bad effect on others. Given their care during the winter to use every bit of every seal, wasting so much seemed a pity. They'd carried precious pieces of cooked seal meat with them from the ice-cave. Now blood was oozing out of the black slabs, and they threw them away, unappetizing-looking in the bright light and smelling of smitch. At least Levick ordered a bull seal to be killed, instead of a female.

But the six men's yearning was for carbohydrates. Their daily biscuit ration was now down to two each a day, and they feared a return to the miserable constipation they'd suffered in the ice-cave. Dividing the allocation of provisions between the tents hadn't worked. Priestley had taken over control of everyone's food supply again, 'although I have tried to avoid it'. Levick was dosing all except Browning with calomel, a purgative, 'to keep our livers up to the mark'. In the ice-cave, cooking with blubber, they'd managed to include a reasonable amount of liquid. Now, with limited supplies of fuel, they were drinking much less.

That evening, Erebus and Terror clearly visible across the ice-covered Ross Sea, Priestley and Campbell had a long talk about the summer, and what they would find at Cape Evans. They decided 'that we would both prefer to find everyone gone if there was a satisfactory reason to explain them leaving us'. But that would imply trouble to the ship.

Their hardest day's pulling came on Friday the 25th, 7 miles of pure misery that left everyone 'pretty done'. Apart from the exhaustion of man-hauling, Campbell and Dickason had both had a bad night, Browning's back had started to ache and he was feeling sick, and Dickason, who led all day, was now snow-blind. Abbott's name was rarely mentioned on any sick-list; but then, he was barely mentioned at all.

The sun was already hot in a clear sky at 5.00 a.m. next morning, Saturday the 26th. A small island marked on the map near the head of the bay they'd been crossing was tantalizing Priestley. He'd left his skis at Hell's Gate depot but after breakfast Campbell lent him his. Even on the level, 'I've a lot to learn', Priestley admitted, as he skidded down the sides of drifts, fell over and inelegantly achieved the island, where, in his finneskoes, he climbed about searching for signs of Professor Edgeworth David's depot. Poking twelve samples of rocks into a Fry's cocoa tin that he'd brought just in case, he slid back off the island, using his geological hammer to brake, and skied on to where he'd agreed to meet the others, who had gone on ahead. 'Joined up, fairly tired' by noon, he wrote. But he was happy: 'At last geology has begun.' No science had been done by their party for eight months. On this journey Campbell had done no surveying. They had no instruments, not even a thermometer to measure minimum and maximum temperatures. Now, briefly switching roles to become the scientist of the party, Priestley thought he could again begin to feel himself 'useful' to the expedition.

Levick was equally happy. After twenty-seven days out they'd at last hit a good surface. The luxury of just being able to walk along, at nearly 3 miles an hour, feeling only a steady pull on the traces. It was the day he'd waited for, a break from the intolerable, incessant toil of the last few weeks. At 4.00 p.m. they halted for 'seven bell tea'. In the distance were two small islands, and Campbell decided to move on and camp under them: one might turn out to be Depot Island. Approaching, he saw a bamboo, then through his glasses a tin tied to it. But first, the routine of camping had to be got through – tents set up, hoosh prepared, then eaten. All the time Priestley kept looking up at the bamboo. Depots were more than the objects they contained. They were records of what had happened to them, as depots. Would this one be untouched? Might it show that Debenham and Griffith Taylor had visited – or the ship? After all the speculation, 'We shall learn something at last.' At least, 'if noone has been here, I shall be able to get the Prof his specimens myself.'

The meal over, Priestley and Campbell climbed up, opened the tin and found a letter written by Edgeworth David to Shackleton and another to the Commanding Officer of *Nimrod*, which they took to hand to Scott. There were also letters to Edgeworth David's wife, and to Mawson's brother, which Priestley packed away to give to the owners. The depot was intact. No one had been here. So there were no answers to any of their questions. Priestley filled his rucksack with the wrapped and labelled rocks – they would add to the weight of the sledge, he noted, but it couldn't be helped – and 'scrapped' the depot, leaving a message in an oil tin at the foot of the cairn, and (by mistake) a ski-stick. Priestley explored the other island and in long evening light happily collected an Oxo tin of small specimens from erratic gravel in a valley. 'I am more pleased than I can write at finding the depot.'

Campbell, still feeling off-colour, had gone to bed, having talked with Levick about Browning's health. Decisions needed to be made. If only the depot had contained biscuits, wrote Levick, 'instead of stones!' Browning was losing ground steadily and desperately needed carbohydrate. Levick summarized in his sledging notebook: Browning 'is a little down on his luck tho trying to keep up his spirits with his usual pluck.' Possibly he was suffering from Addisons disease, 'but hope it isn't. anyhow I shall soon be able to give him a thorough overhaul thank goodness.' Regarding the rest of the party, Campbell was 'very down on his luck & says he feels very bilious & generally slack. He looks decidedly so. The rest of us are as fit as fleas.'

The next day, Sunday 27 October, after managing to give Browning a ride for one mile of the 12 sledged, they reached Granite Harbour. That evening Levick asked the other tent to hand over some biscuits for Browning, and Priestley agreed to 'sacrifice' a day's ration. Biscuits had become that precious. 'I hope Browning's strength will last out all right', Priestley wrote. 'If it does not we shall have to depot him & the greater part of the gear. . .' Depots could contain provisions, equipment, rocks and, *in extremis*, humans. Then, 'some of us' would 'make a dash in for decent food'. There should be some food at Butter Point. But geologizing would have to go. Even now, Priestley couldn't get out to nearby rocks because his only windproof trousers were torn and he had to mend them.

Campbell walked out over the ice, looking through his glasses for any signs of people, buildings, tents, bamboos . . . anything. But there was nothing. The most difficult part of their journey south was achieved. They had travelled approximately 185 miles. After more than six months' confinement in an ice hole, subsisting on barely sufficient food, weakened by diarrhoea and food poisoning, Browning struggling throughout with chronic illness, and Campbell himself now fighting increasing ill health, they had achieved four weeks of spring sledging. Their provisions had been calculated for a four-week journey, although they were making their food stretch. But today the four weeks were up.

19

Saving themselves

28 October–7 November 1912

> They have had a pretty hard time of it.
> Petty Officer Thomas Williamson, November 1912

TRAVELLING ACROSS THE wide expanse of Granite Harbour on Monday 28 October, no one could see any sign of 'past or present habitation' despite sweeping the place pretty thoroughly with Campbell's glasses. Visibility was excellent. Nearly at the end of October now, the sun burnt their skin, although a cold wind from off the Barrier got up in the afternoon and frostbit their sunburnt noses, inflicting a double dose of pain. Looking west into the bay, Levick admired the blue contortions of a low glacier snout. 'Granite Harbour would be a fine field for a geologist', reckoned Priestley; sadly, there was no time to investigate. With Browning in his present state they had to keep moving. Whenever they took a short spell from sledging, talk was always of the same three well-worn subjects: where the geological party could be, because, obviously, they had never come to Granite Harbour; the chances of having Ross Island to themselves; and – obsessively – the feeds they were going to have, some time not too far in the future.

Food was dominating everyone's thinking. In the ice-cave the six men had managed to survive serious privation, on minimal rations. But they had been lying torpid in their bags for much of the time. Now they were working hard, with all the hunger pangs of intense labour. There was very little left for lunch, and 'the long day is a very hungry one'. Campbell couldn't tolerate blubber in his hoosh, so Dickason and Priestley, sharing his tent, couldn't have any either, and they missed it sorely. Dickason, noted Priestley, 'is the least resigned sufferer and is beginning to get hot under the collar about it'. Levick's tent was better off because Levick and Abbott could have Browning's share of solids. The previous day there had been hundreds of seals at the northern entrance to Granite Harbour. But today, Monday 28 October, there were none. Seals, it seemed, clustered, rather than making themselves available at appropriate intervals for the needy. 'We shall be soon at Butter Point though', wrote Priestley, 'please God.'

The four men pulling out in front on the traces were separated while sledging and so couldn't converse. But Campbell and Priestley could talk across the sledge, and today they discussed summer plans, and even another winter, imagining themselves living at Cape Royds and having a 'very palatial time' – even should they not be relieved – because anything would be palatial 'after the igloo winter'.

That evening, Priestley noted, their camp site was well south of Granite Harbour. To Pennell, to the expedition grandees in London and to the men at Cape Evans, Granite Harbour was the start of the coast that the Eastern party would be able to manage without difficulty. Depots had been laid from here south, although, of course, Campbell didn't know about them. It was a comfortable mantra. But the truth was that the coast the six men had just travelled, from Evans Coves to Granite Harbour, was the bulk of the journey. It was largely unknown, although Mawson, Mackay and Edgeworth David had sledged north along it in late spring and early summer. Even now that they had reached what was considered the known coast, Campbell and his party had no clear idea of exactly where they were in relation to their inadequate chart. They were hauling a loaded double-decker sledge across the sea ice, small dark figures in an enormous landscape of glittering, glaring white.

Having turned out at 4.30 a.m. on Tuesday 29 October, with a thin southerly breeze blowing and the sun already a bright, glary ball, Priestley grumbled to his diary about 'a reform in our domestic economy'. He could only allow a limited amount of food per day, and he wanted to sledge as many hours, and get as far as possible, on that allowance. Time was wasted in the mornings; they were always slow. In the past they'd made this up by cutting out a lunch camp. Now lunch lasted an hour. What with spells, and 'seven bells tea', they were achieving decidedly less than 'a true sledging day'. This morning Campbell announced he wanted a hoosh cooked for lunch, which would use oil and take time. With the weight of commissariat about his shoulders, Priestley was irritated.

The same day, Tuesday 29 October, seven men, seven mules and Wright as navigator left Cape Evans to search for Scott and the Polar party. Atkinson had already gone ahead to Hut Point with the two dog teams, Cherry-Garrard and Demetri. That made eleven men going south, leaving Archer, who had come ashore to cook, and Debenham, his old knee and ankle injuries still a constraint, to look after the Cape Evans hut for the next three months.

Out on the sea ice, beyond Granite Harbour, the Eastern party harnessed up and pulled south for 3 miles. A triangular point of land appeared ahead, protruding out from the piedmont ice. Checking the chart, they decided that it must be Cape Dunlop. Campbell examined the 50-foot-high point through his glasses and saw a bamboo with the remains of a flag attached. At last! Here, surely, they would find news. Making for the land, Campbell and Priestley unharnessed, left Levick with the men and climbed up to search for letters. Attached to the bamboo they found a matchbox with, inside, a letter addressed to Pennell. Campbell opened it. Dated February 1912, it was signed by Griffith Taylor, Debenham, Gran and Forde. So, after all, the geological party had been here. *Terra Nova*, Campbell read, had been sighted from 20 to 27 January, but with neither being able to reach the other, the four men had made a depot and were setting off south over the piedmont. The depot was listed as consisting of spare personal gear, two tins of oil, one of spirits and – in line with Scott's instructions in case they had to come back here – some odd bits of remaining food, such as a couple of cases of biscuits . . . at which point Priestley and Campbell let out such a yell that the others, unable to contain themselves, came rushing up the slope. Searching 'like dogs scratching in the drift', they found a cairn of stones covering the treasure, small bags containing butter, cocoa, tea, sugar, raisins, lard and, joyously, salt. But it was the sheer number of biscuits that overwhelmed them. Crowding around, they put their hands in and ate, and ate. Not to have to nibble, but to crunch, and chew, and do it again, and again, to their heart's content. The long arm of Scott's distant orders, to an Antarctic neophyte, Griffith Taylor: a benediction. Camped by the newly found depot, Priestley celebrated in his diary:

12 noon
Hurrah! Hurrah! Hurrah!
Good news & plenty of biscuits.

Dividing all the food up between the tents, the Eastern party got down to the most enormous feed. Campbell's early morning decision that today he would have a hoosh for lunch was swamped by a feast such as they hadn't had for a year. There was still hoosh, of course, but with cocoa as sweet as they liked, and raisins, and 'lashings of biscuit and butter'. 'I sat for a long time after this little lunch,' wrote Levick, 'with a hunk of butter in one hand and biscuit in the other, biting off alternately first a mouthful of butter then a piece of biscuit, and it was a grand treat.' This was the first fat of any sort except blubber that they'd eaten for ten months. 'Butter is a luxury we never thought of for sledging', wrote Priestley, a little tartly.

Some big questions had been answered. *Terra Nova* had been seen, which removed a big worry from Campbell that his desire to be dropped off at Evans Coves, a change to the ship's orders, might have caused her a problem. But unanswered questions still swarmed around. 'I think the Owner must have got to the Pole', Priestley speculated, '& then made up to fetch us & have been blown out.' Levick still stuck to the theory that *Terra Nova* had got damaged in some way and so had retreated to New Zealand with the Polar party. Finding Griffith Taylor's precious exposed photographic plates in the depot was further proof, to Priestley, that no one was left at Cape Evans. This, as scientific data, would have already been collected, if anyone had been there. The depot also contained Griffith Taylor's 'journal for Captain Scott'. Reading it, Priestley became convinced that they were not, after all, at Cape Dunlop (which, it turned out, was an island rather than a cape). Instead they were at the southern edge of Granite Harbour, at Cape Roberts. Best of all, Griffith Taylor listed a line of depots to come, with locations. 'Without a doubt we are in great riches now after our late circumstances', wrote Levick. There was only one desire left unfulfilled: 'if only they had left a pinch of baccy.'

The place was busy with seals. They were short of fresh meat, a blizzard seemed to be brewing, so a bull was killed and butchered, and the brains, kidney, heart and liver placed on an ice slab to freeze, ready to carry on the sledge. Levick got his clothes soaked with blood carrying the meat back. It was a sober contrast to provisions from containers. Sluggish with food, each man turned into his sleeping-bag, with the joy of reading something new scavenged from the depot. Priestley found a novel, Dickason had *Hamlet*, and Levick read Griffith Taylor's precious volume of Robert Browning's poems. Dinner followed, both tents demolishing another hoosh with more biscuit and lard, including that long-missed drink, tea of proper strength. By the end of the day they'd each eaten fourteen biscuits. Later they were all entertained by watching two bulls fighting fero-ciously, the scene having been set earlier in the day by the killing of the resident bull. Levick's tent decided to eat their whole allocation of sugar, twenty-six lumps each, instead of keeping it, 'so as not to be hungry during the night'. 'Still discussing plans we fell asleep', wrote Campbell. 'What with news from the main party and food (although both were a year old) it was the happiest day since we last saw the ship. I woke in the night, finished my share of the butter and most of the lard, then dosed off again.' 'It is good to live for a day like this today', Priestley thought; 'our troubles are nearly over if we have ordinary luck.'

Wednesday the 30th was another bright, clear, calm day with no blizzard after all. 'I was amused to read that Taylor estimates that the meat of a seal lasts 4 men for 10 meals', Priestley added to his diary as Dickason prepared the breakfast hoosh for their tent. 'At that rate, they will be under the impression that we had to kill about 80 seals to make them last out the eight months. They will expect to find the Antarctic depleted of seals or depleted of us.' It was good to be able to start enjoying their achievement. Their mouths hurt from too many biscuits and the night was wakeful from too much strong tea, but already Levick thought that Campbell and Browning were better on the biscuit diet, and everyone was revelling in the extraordinary luck of the windfall. Perhaps, they decided, they'd better drop to ten biscuits each a day. Levick and Abbott were swallowing Cerebos salt by the teaspoonful, feeding a specific craving. Hooshes in their tent had been cooked with freshwater ice, to help Browning, and they'd eaten no salt for a month.

Campbell and Priestley emptied the Cape Roberts depot of everything except old clothes and the photographic plate changing bag, taking the personal papers and books, specimens of coal and fossil crustacea, and 'a bag of stocks and mits', noted Priestley,' in case we have to winter at Ross Island'. Campbell tied a note to the bamboo to 'explain the looting of the depot'. With oil to spare now, having pitched a tent for lunch, they had hot tea, their first on the journey. They went 'much better in the afternoon in consequence', observed Levick. This was just as well, because they ran into a thick belt of pack ice with badly screwed, jagged pressure. Campbell and Priestley, working as their usual team, reckoned they saved fifty capsizes. One bad lurch pinned Priestley down, but luckily not against an ice crust, or 'I would have broken both legs. I'll try to be more careful, but it's hard to tell when she is going to fall, and the only way is on one or other of us.' Campbell was saved in a second capsize by the fact that the sleeping-bags fell first and pushed him away. Despite the dire conditions, and renewed frostbites to their noses and faces, they still managed 8 miles before camping 3 miles short of what they now knew to be Dunlop Island.

Next morning, 31 October, after several hours of difficult pressure ice, they reached Dunlop Island. From reading Griffith Taylor's report they knew that only six weeks before he left for the Pole Scott had crossed over the sea ice to the Victoria Land coast and visited the island. Priestley collected rocks, while Campbell and Levick searched in vain for signs of Scott's visit. To the south-east, across McMurdo Sound, Mount Erebus was clearly visible and highly active, a column of steam rising high from the crater. Scott's having been here on Dunlop Island gave them the first, tenuous contact since January 1911 with the rest of the expedition members at Cape Evans. Situated at the base of the volcano, the winter quarters hut – indistinguishable, of course, at this distance – had touched their day.

On Friday 1 November – the start of a new month's travelling, spring at its height – Priestley was so happy that he declared it the pleasantest day he had ever spent sledging. Apart from anything else, he could geologize, although the sledge was getting heavier with his rocks. The sea ice surface was uniformly hard and good, the weather perfect, and at 4.00 p.m. they saw a broken bamboo and a cairn – so simple, after what they had been through. It was Griffith Taylor's next depot, just where he said it would be, on Cape Bernacchi. Campbell called a halt for 'seven bell biscuit' (suitably renamed), and the three officers walked up to find nearly a case of the special 'Antarctic' sledging biscuits. Priestley, with an ingrained response to all provisions now, ticked off the sugar (which they were currently out of, again), pemmican (their first), raisins, cocoa and tea: these were all useful, but it was a pity there was no fat, cheese or chocolate. He was pleased about the biscuits, though, because he had already set aside an unopened case for the trip they might do to the old crater of Erebus when they reached Cape Evans.

Priestley was an incorrigible planner. Campbell might be cautious and careful. Also Priestley was acquisitive and competitive, professionally. Levick was competitive, physically. He was also straightforward, fond of the good things in life, sometimes clumsy and forgetful, but caring and reasonably compassionate. Scott hadn't rated Levick. He couldn't see any particular merit in the man. Scott rated most highly those who searched out the extra jobs, did everything asked of them and another layer they found for themselves – such as Bowers, and Cherry-Garrard. Nearly as high in his scale were muscle, strength and bulk, converted in Scott's eye into sledge-hauling capacity: Matonabbee's wives material. On the ship Levick, despite being reputedly immensely strong, had seemed to enjoy most posing for Ponting's camera, by definition an inactive process. Scott's sharp pen had praised Campbell. Priestley, whom he barely knew, had been singled out for one characteristic only: his ability to be extremely seasick. Campbell, a collaborative but firm decision-maker, Levick, a responsible and responsive doctor, and Priestley quiet but affable, driven by a mixture of self-interest and almost schoolboy action. Taken together, they formed an effective, powerful combination of officers. It had worked. It was still working, pairings shifting and aligning according to job and need.

Sledging as a six, as they were now, was particularly successful: Levick the powerhouse, out in front; Abbott, also a powerhouse, a consistent bowman; with Dickason, tough and young, the other bowman. Browning, always eager to take his part and unhappy if he couldn't, fitting in where it best suited him, according to his state of health. Campbell and Priestley, quick-footed, anticipating, trouble-shooting as wheelers, the decision-makers on the road. Man-hauling at its best. Campbell able to draw on his Norwegian knowledge and his skiing skills. Priestley's experience of the business of sledging, camping and generally coping in Antarctica, having been on Shackleton's expedition, proving invaluable. Without it they might never have managed. Yet Priestley had been a last-minute replacement for a geologist who, like all the other scientists on the expedition except Wilson, had never been south.

Campbell and Levick sat on a rock by Griffith Taylor's depot, tucking into a piece of raw pemmican and the undiminished joy of yet another biscuit while Priestley collected. All last summer they had hoped to meet the geological party and fretted at their non-appearance; all autumn and winter they had dreamed they might suddenly appear, as a relief party. Now they knew their friends had got as far as this cape, after leaving Granite Harbour; what had happened beyond that was still unknown.

Piling their spoils on the sledge, they pushed on through pressure ridges in the direction of Butter Point. It was strange to be approaching this much longed-for goal without rushing. Browning and Campbell were already so much better with the new diet. Everyone's lives had changed so fast. Camped on the sea ice, they had 'just had the Royalist feed we have had for a year', wrote Levick. 'I am not ashamed', he went on, squeezed into his reindeer bag, 'to say that I cannot stoop properly to pick anything off the ground – This will sound brutal to the ordinary individual, but to those who have sledged it wont, as only they understand. We little thought, a few days ago, what affluence we should find ourselves in so soon.'

The next morning, Saturday 2 November, they pulled for Butter Point in 'great glee and anticipation'. Leaving the double-decker sledge in the pressure ice with the men, the three officers walked in over the sea ice and found, to their astonishment, a depot filled with

an enormous quantity of stores, a miscellaneous heap of cases including all kinds of foods, and household goods. It was completely
confusing. Looking around, they located a bamboo, broken, then
mended, with a note from Atkinson. Even more confusingly, it had
been written that year, on 14 April 1912, 'stating that he had got as
far as this in his attempt to rescue us but then had to turn back &
giving us directions about how to get to Hut Pt & a warning against
the pressure ice'.

If, before, their imaginations had spun theories, this one piece of
hard evidence spun their minds into conjecture after conjecture,
piling up like the pressure ice they had watched build on their winter
beach at Cape Adare, tumbling back, to pile again in new fantastic
forms. If the ship had taken everyone to New Zealand, what was
Atkinson doing at Butter Point in the autumn? If he was here, why
hadn't they been rescued this spring? And why Atkinson? Campbell
suggested an explanation that seemed to make sense: Atkinson had
moved to Cape Crozier to spend the winter in a smaller hut, ready to
explore in summer, and 'does not think the chances of our being
alive good enough to undertake a journey up the coast'.

But uncertainty was making them feel uneasy. They decided to set
out directly for Cape Evans, sledging straight across McMurdo Sound
on the sea ice. They wanted definite answers. With this decision
made, they concentrated on the food. Levick especially wanted
'luxuries' and selected sweet things they'd been missing: jam, a bag of
sugar, butter and chocolate, a tin of Truemilk. He also took a bottle
of brandy. Since this could be their last night sledging, Levick wanted
a celebration meal, before trying to 'do a bust' the next day and get
the whole way. After achieving 3 miles, they camped on the ice. 'I
have been looking forward for months to my first surfeit of sugar',
wrote Priestley, lying in his bag at 7.00 p.m., feeling uncomfortably
full. But 'we found we could eat very little.' Levick had handed out a
tot of brandy 'to stiffen our digestions'. The truth was that suddenly
all their theories were floating, rootless. Levick: 'we feel most anxious
about things in general & are burning to get in & find out what had
happened.'

But the next morning, Sunday the 3rd, they met a really awful
surface, old pack ice squeezed into ridges, with belts of heavy pressure

– agonizing to walk over in their worn-out finneskoes. Just after midday their iron-runnered sledge collapsed, beyond resuscitation. The sea ice covering McMurdo Sound was not a good place to leave a depot, least of all one containing their precious geological speci-mens and the records of two other parties. But there was no option. After piling everything up, they propped the ruined sledge on end to mark the place in the jumble of ice, like a ghoulish beacon. Packing sleeping-bags, their records and a little food on the remaining sledge with wooden runners, they started again direct for Cape Evans. They were good at getting on with things.

In thirty minutes they were sledging on black, pulpy ice without a speck of snow. Horribly suspicious, Priestley pushed his ski-stick through, and found broken ice and water. Without pausing to speak, they turned and ran back to their abandoned sledge. The sea ice in McMurdo Sound at this time of the year was meant to be reliable. The ice they had run from was very recent – possibly only a week old. Very shocked, they turned south, to get closer to the Barrier. The ice there would be stronger.

Monday 4 November was a day of starting again, from a different place, their overnight camp near the Barrier edge. Campbell with Levick and Browning walked back 9 miles to Butter Point, to fill their rucksacks from 'the great luxury of the good food which some-one has left for us at the depot'. Levick knew that, however anxious they were, the variety was making a difference – most of all, to Browning. The change of diet had worked such wonders with him that 'I can only regard him now as off the sick list'.

Abbott and Dickason, with Priestley walking beside them chat-ting, hauled the wooden-runner sledge back across the sea ice to the depot they'd made the previous day. Dickason and Abbott took the iron runners from the broken 10-foot sledge and fitted them on to their 12-footer. Priestley took the bows off the old sledge for a 'curio', saving small pieces for 'the men'. The re-packed sledge was hauled back to camp, with Priestley taking the chance to sound both men out about whether they would be willing to go on short geological trips this next summer. Campbell had told Priestley that he did not want the men 'to go against their will'. But they both said 'they would like it above all things if we three were the party – I am glad . . . I should like to have a shot for the old crater of Erebus.'

With all their gear once more together, Campbell decided against trying to reach Cape Evans. Instead, they would head for the hut at Hut Point, keeping close to the Barrier edge. Priestley had travelled the route once, in 1908.

On Tuesday 5 November the Eastern party woke early to calm weather with bright sun, and glare. Sledging well, finally on the home run, they saw three black objects moving across the ice: surely they were three men pulling a sledge. 'Campbell and I walked some way to meet them,' wrote Priestley, 'for when we waved they stopped & consulted & we thought it was a sledge party from Cape Crozier coming over to investigate the Butter Point depot.' Campbell told Priestley to semaphore to them, while he looked through his glasses. So Priestley did – the letters he had taught himself in the ice-cave. No result. Suddenly the three men turned. They saw the sheen of their breasts: anticipation shipwrecked, again, on emperor penguins. They had waited so long so see their companions, but it was disappointment once more.

The ice was weak and they had to turn and weave. Spring, and new life, surrounded them: seals and pups lying by the tide cracks, and a great crowd of emperors, shining sleek, at the Barrier's edge. As they walked, they dipped into little cloth bags filled with raisins, figs, chocolate, sugar and raw pemmican, all hung off the sledge like a horizontal Christmas tree 'to keep the wolf off between meals'. Hoosh at 6.00 p.m. was 'ripping', with so many ingredients that Priestley copied down the recipe. His mouth had sores from the unaccustomed food, and his tongue was so swollen that Campbell could barely understand him across the sledge as they marched. Perhaps, volunteered Campbell, after nine months without a wash their ears were at fault. 'Campbell's eyes are so tired as to be practically useless to him', noted Priestley, '& what between my short sight and his blindness we have been a bright pair of pilots to lead a party to safety.' Gentle teasing after a long hard day, like a comfortable old couple.

An hour after midnight, with 7 miles still to do, they decided to camp. Drinking his hot cocoa at 1.30 a.m., Priestley entered the new day, Wednesday 6 November, into his diary: '22 hours work. Ready for bed. We should be in for lunch tomorrow.' He woke after a few hours, 'all the better for the short sleep. We have a short pull to Hut Point & then news I hope.' Their spring sledging from Cape Adare the previous year, despite constant effort, hadn't amounted to much. This, though, was the spring sledging that mattered: home, and survival. They had practically achieved it. But at lunchtime their remaining sledge capsized, with one side collapsing on to the snow. Both sledges had now failed on the home straight. The wind was cold, so they pitched their tents. Levick, Abbott and Browning settled down to hot hoosh and tea, to wait in comfort, while 'the other unit' walked to Hut Point to find another sledge – there was sure to be one – and look for news.

Campbell, Priestley and Dickason arrived at the hut to find it deserted. There were signs that people had been there recently, and signs of dogs, and tethering stakes for the Indian mules, but there 'was no direct news for us'. There was, however, a letter to the commander of the relief ship. Campbell opened it and learned the completely unexpected 'sad news'. How many of the Polar party were missing. Six? Eight? They could not make it out from the letter. 'We are still in a state of suspense', Priestley wrote, 'for we fear for Pennell & Bowers & myself for Day & Oates.' Atkinson, with Wright and the mules, was definitely leading a search party for the bodies. They could infer that Nelson, Cherry-Garrard and Debenham were 'down here', but they didn't know who else.

They located a sledge and were back at their camp by 4.00 p.m. They had news, at last – but such unexpected news. Levick recorded the few details gleaned. 'It seems certain that Capt. Scott, Teddy Evans and Bill were of the party' but 'there is no use in hoping that they have survived the winter.' Priestley thought the best thing that could happen would be 'their bodies are found close here & their records should show that they at least did not give their lives in vain'.

The six of them had been so tightly immersed in their own survival, so detached from the ambition of the rest of the expedition. Levick wrote, almost wonderingly: 'It is difficult to realise suddenly, the bad calamity that must have happened to the Southern Party last year.' Then, on to practicalities. 'There being no other news than that, we are just turning in for some absolutely necessary sleep, and then we are going to shove straight on to Cape Evans, 18 miles off, where we expect to find someone left in charge.' Campbell, thoughtfully, had found some tobacco at Hut Point and brought it back, with a few old rock cakes – memories, particularly for Levick the cake-lover, of times past, and good times to come. They also enjoyed their first fresh vegetable, onions – Amundsen's successfully bringing onions to the Barrier had been noted, and acted on. But for Levick the ongoing question of why no relief party had come for them still pressed. They probably thought at Cape Evans 'that we have shared the same fate, or else that the ship picked us up after all, or some of them would have come out, on the chance of getting to us this spring, and I expect we shall give them a bit of a surprise when we turn up.'

'The pity of it is that three of them are married men', Priestley recorded sorrowfully. But he didn't write his account until the day after finding the letter at Hut Point. 'Yesterday evening I was too upset to write up my diary at all. We were so completely knocked out by the news.' After breakfast on Thursday 7 November, Levick talked to Campbell about the future: 'he is now left head of the Expedition, assuming that Cap. Scott and Teddy Evans are dead, and I am second in command, being Senior N.O.' They depoted the broken sledge, with its contents. Levick would come back to pick it up; given his known navigational difficulties, he made a sketch, noting the bearings in relation to Hut Point and the smoke of Erebus. As befitted a sledging party about to complete a long journey, the six men set off for Cape Evans with due precautions, carrying their sleeping-bags, food and a cooker, as well as their diaries, films and Priestley's best fossil.

The journey was straightforward. The sea ice was firm, the weather continued fine, and they had lunch by the Glacier Tongue, a real return to home territory. By 3.30 in the afternoon they were drawing up to the hut at Cape Evans.

No one was at home. None of the Eastern party knew the hut, except Abbott, who had helped build it. Coming in through the cold porch, the acetylene plant straight ahead, then through into the high, large space, filled with possessions. Other people's lives. The clock was ticking. A fire was burning in the stove. Campbell looked in the dispatch box and found a list of people at the hut. So there were the first facts. One of them sat on a chair – the first time for nearly a year. There was a wall of stores and boxes. Men this side, officers beyond. Not a metaphorical division but an actual one. They had been a team of six, living together for nearly two years. Who sat in which chair now? They had never slept in this place. Whose bed was vacant? Which available? In the far corner, on the left, was Captain Scott's cubby, tidy and neat, with everything in order. Dr Wilson's space next door was equally neat, tidied away. The Polar party had been dead men, here, for a long time. Those living here had had a long time to adjust to it. For Campbell and Levick, Priestley, Abbott, Browning and Dickason the news was raw.

Suddenly they head the barking of dogs, and in walked Debenham and Archer, astonished and overjoyed. Priestley had always focused his longings at Evans Coves, and in the ice-cave, on Debenham, his friend in the geology department at Sydney. There was a particularly poignant joy that it should be Debenham here at the hut. Because the ice was so open, Debenham said, they had given up all hope of seeing any of them this summer. Their best hope was that they had already been relieved by the ship. So there never had been a search party.

In quick succession they got the news. The best was that five men only were dead – not eight, as they had feared. Five good men gone was bad enough, but eight would have been worse. Priestley's greatest relief was to know that Bernard Day was safe. They found out that 'Meares and Ponting have had enough of the Antarctic'. Simpson, they heard, had 'wanted to stay'. Teddy Evans and Forde had been invalided out, and Griffith Taylor had been rather fed up with the Antarctic. They heard about the southern journey, what had happened to the ponies, the dogs, the motors, how the support parties had got on, what Teddy Evans said about the final Polar party as he left them – 'Bowers & Oates weakening a little and looking puffy around the face.'

Terra Nova had landed all their personal gear in February, so they had their clothes, and the letters they'd only had time to glance at, on the way to Evans Coves. They had their first baths for ten months.

They put on clean clothes. They sailed into a sumptuous dinner. They went to bed, in a bed.

'It is hard to realise our comfort and safety now', wrote Levick. 'We are all pretty fit, but after the time we have had, and nearly 6 weeks hard sledging on top of it, it is just about time we had a little comfort & good food, or I think we should have knocked up.'

No one, wrote Campbell, 'can realise what it meant to us to see new faces and to be home after our long winter'.

20

Homewards

8 November 1912–26 January 1913

> I, who had ambition not only to go farther than any other man has been before me, but as far as I think it possible for man to go . . .
>
> Captain James Cook, February 1774

CAMPBELL SAT AT the table in the Cape Evans hut, notebooks and sledging diaries spread open. He needed to begin drawing his charts. Levick sat opposite, his ice-cave journal still exuding the acrid smell of blubber smoke, the pencil entries in his small sledging diary reflecting each long day, writing squeezed on to the page, or untidy with exhaustion. Priestley had already taken over Cherry-Garrard's typewriter. Sitting straight, fingers tapping, just as at Cape Adare, Priestley was working on his most recent journal, turning rough copy into fair copy and then into final typescript in a process of edits, cuts, smoothing, tidying up, changing details when they later proved inaccurate. 'Cape Dunlop' was corrected to Cape Roberts – no point, in his view, retaining a mistake. It was what they'd thought at the time – yes, but they were wrong. Adjustments were made as they got closer to Hut Point, so their approach took account of the concerns they would have had, had they known what they then found out. Priestley added, for example, on 7 November a sentence that had not been in anyone's diary, but an appropriate sentiment: 'If we had arrived a few days ago we would have been able to join in the search party.'

But of course that had been impossible. Looking at themselves, with their clothes off, for the first time down to the skin, they saw pale bodies entirely free of fat, their legs and arms corrugated. Their faces stuck out at the top, burnt, frostbitten, blistered. They looked prematurely aged. Very quickly they developed swollen ankles and legs, with cramps and pains, symptoms worryingly like scurvy, and Levick ordered a seal to be killed, fresh meat for everyone. In truth they were bone-weary. They couldn't do much, even if they wanted to. They wandered around, just being. 'I find our party are not so fit as I thought', admitted Campbell. It was hopeless imagining they could help in the search. Campbell considered taking seal meat 100 miles south on the Barrier and depoting it in case any of the search party coming back had scurvy, and asked Levick's opinion: Levick agreed. Thinking through the practicalities, he advised that the meat would keep all right if packed in ice and buried each night out of the sun.

Levick was developing his negatives, and last summer's exposed plates, very contented with the results. Mostly he was just enjoying the sheer comfort of the hut. The six of them were eating, and eating, to the astonishment and pleasure of Archer and Debenham, putting weight back on remarkably fast. Levick, in particular, was returning to rotundity. But in his heart and mind Levick was more than ready to leave. At the back of his journal he listed the cost of buying the motor bike he had promised himself, adding the costs of licence, number plate, new tyres, another set of carburettors – and drew the machine in all its glory.

Campbell, once more in charge of a hut, reinstated naval routines and got Abbott, Browning and Dickason, just two days after their return, to do a good clear-up and scrub on Saturday the 9th. On Sunday, during Divine Service, they sang for possibly the hundredth time, except with two added voices, 'Praise the Lord ye Heavens Adore Him', because 'it's one of the only hymns Campbell knows', Priestley noted, smiling to himself. The next day, Monday the 11th, Levick, Abbott and Dickason set out for Hut Point to leave a letter from Campbell at the hut for the search party, return the borrowed sledge, then find their old broken sledge, mend it, load it with everything from their depot and bring it back.

The same day, out on the Barrier, Cherry-Garrard, approaching One Ton Depot, thought he saw a tent and was filled with private panic.

'It would be too terrible to find that, though . . . we had done all that we could, if we had done something different we could have saved them.'

Wright, as navigator, always travelled ahead. On Tuesday the 12th, about 11 miles south of One Ton, he saw a small object protruding above the surface off to the right and went across to investigate, not expecting anything of interest. To his great shock it was the top six inches of a tent. The mule drivers didn't understand his signals to stop, but when they did come across, Wright halted men and animals a suitable distance away and they set up camp, avoiding the usual camp noises, waiting for Atkinson and the dog teams. The tent was almost completely covered by two metres of snow, and Gran thought it looked like a boulder in the mountains in winter. When the dog teams arrived, Wright went up to Cherry. Gently: 'It is the tent.'

Atkinson crawled inside and examined the bodies. There were only three: Scott, Wilson and Bowers, lying in their bags. The records were located and retrieved, diaries and journals, letters, exposed films. Some men went in to look; others could not. Atkinson read the lesson from the burial service. They collapsed the fabric of the tent over the bodies, burying them where they were already entombed. The key facts were ascertained. The South Pole had been reached on 17 January 1912. This camp site had been reached on 19 March. The details of illness, then death, of Petty Officer Evans on the Beardmore Glacier, then of Oates, somewhere on the Barrier, south of here, were established.

Gran, standing a little aside, recorded that Tom Crean came up to him and said: 'Sir, permit me to congratulate you. Dr Atkinson has just found Scott's diary, where it is written that our people found the Norwegian flag when they came to the South Pole.'

On Wednesday 13 November, Levick, Abbott and Dickason packed their repaired sledge and hauled it across the sea ice to Cape Evans. Their possessions were finally back where they started. Debenham lined the six men up by the side of the hut for a photograph: Dickason, Abbott, then Browning, relaxed, relieved, then Campbell and Levick with Priestley between. The Eastern party standing together, confident, a team, in front of their sledge. The 10-footer, collapsed and dismembered, had been abandoned on the sea ice in McMurdo Sound, but the 12-footer, re-fitted with the invaluable iron runners, had lasted the distance. It has been the support of all their journeys, west from Cape Adare, north then south, from Evans Coves; buried in winter snows, jerking and skidding and sticking, occasionally capsizing, but bearing their loads. They had succeeded.

'We now', said Campbell, 'settled down to work.' An appropriate narrative was needed, an official account, available when required. Campbell's rough journals and sledging notebooks provided the raw evidence of two and a half years, from the departure of *Terra Nova* in June 1910. Leaving some passages intact, cutting others, deleting comments, smoothing over, Campbell added information or explanations to, or hung summaries off, certain dates, inserting sections of concern, or anticipation, or reasons for action, where they seemed appropriate. Levick, writing out a fair copy of his ice-cave journal, was making a version close to the original, but more flowing, with medical records and some comments removed. But the immediacy of pages written at the time, the diagrams and sketches, the ephemera of daily living, the evidence of physical state in changing handwriting, the paper that had absorbed the smells and grease of the cave, the sledging diaries that had travelled in the pocket sewn to clothing – these were a reality that could not be transferred. Dickason, Browning and Abbott had fair copies of their diaries and notebooks, the clear neat handwriting of their naval training creating attractive journals of record. Priestley was immersed at the typewriter: he had a vast number of notes and records to deal with. The latest rocks also had to be labelled and packed.

While they sat around the table, 'Inexpressible Island' was probably created as the name for the site of their winter igloo. Suitably dramatic, compared with their original name (the 'Southern Foothills'), it resonated with 'Inaccessible Island' offshore from Cape Evans. Once agreed, Inexpressible Island was inserted, retrospectively, into final accounts. As far as their own name was concerned, they were the Eastern party. That, or 'Campbell's party', is how they, and everyone here, referred to them, and the name they used in all their writing. Once the fact that in London they were being called the 'Northern' Party became known, the 'Northern party' went retrospectively into the final accounts, replacing 'Eastern party'. The new title by default diminished the aims of the Eastern party but also helped iron away the failure to achieve most of those aims, making the focus of their activities in the north appear more intentional.

Out on the Barrier the search party continued briefly south, hoping, but failing, to find the body of Oates. By 17 November they were back at One Ton and heading for Hut Point. Plans to achieve some science by surveying and geologizing on and near the Beardmore Glacier – especially pleasing to Wright and Gran – had to be dropped. They must start north 'in search of Lt Campbell's Party' as quickly as possible. But the problems of travelling up the coast on risky sea ice were more acute than ever, with high summer approaching. Also, the winter gales this year had been the worst known, wrenching the sea ice, piling it up in contorted heaps, repeatedly sweeping out the ice north of the winter quarters hut. Wild schemes – according to Cherry-Garrard – to try and reach Campbell by travelling up on the central plateau, then working down to Evans Coves via a glacier, were suggested: 'I think we are all going crazy together', he wrote. But Atkinson was resolute. They didn't know what had happened to Campbell and his men: the Eastern party might all have perished or might have come through the winter but been unable to travel because of sickness, lack of ice or want of gear, or might already have been relieved by the ship. They were ignorant of any facts. Atkinson would have to risk others' lives, perhaps in a useless effort. But they had to try.

Meanwhile, the light was 'rotten' for navigating, and the mules were failing – they wouldn't eat. But then, they were given almost no water. Even if anyone had thought they needed to drink, there wasn't enough fuel.

On Sunday 24 November, Atkinson, Cherry-Garrard and Demetri went on ahead with the dog teams. They pulled in to Hut Point on Monday the 25th to find, on the door, Campbell's letter. It was the most 'unbounded relief'. To Cherry-Garrard it was 'the first real bit of good news since February last . . . how different things seem now!' The pressure to undertake another journey was suddenly and gloriously removed. Continuing straight on to winter quarters, Atkinson and Cherry arrived at 8.00 p.m., to deliver the burden of everything that had been found out beyond One Ton. The joy so long antici-pated by Campbell's party, to see old friends, to share good news, was necessarily muted by the chance of timing, their return colliding with the failure of others to return. But they learned that Scott and his companions had reached the Pole and that Amundsen, as they had surmised he would, achieved it first. Then Atkinson and Cherry lis-tened to the Eastern party's adventures, Cherry writing the details rather flatly in his diary, until two o'clock the next morning. Campbell 'must be a proud man to have led a party safely through such an experience, and they are a fine lot of men, and their seamen are fine fellows'.

The mule party reached Hut Point just after midnight on Wednesday the 27th, to find Atkinson at the hut with Campbell. '[O]h what joy,' wrote Williamson, 'the Dr came rushing out of the hut shaking a bit of paper in his hand we could not quite understand it, but we were not long in suspense for presently we saw Mr Campbell come out. imagine our joy when he told us his party were all safe . . . this is the best bit of news we have had for some time, they have had a pretty hard time of it but thank goodness all is well with them.' Williamson was the only man to have spent any time with Campbell & Co., as they were known on *Terra Nova*. He had seen their disappointment at King Edward VII Land, their frustration at the Bay of Whales, and Cape Adare, their anticipation on reaching Evans Coves.

Having arrived at Cape Evans, the mule party were amazed to see how splendid the six men looked, with 'Dr. Levick . . . the spit image of Henry VIII'. '[W]e were overjoyed to once more meet our old comrades the Eastern Party', wrote Williamson. All together now in the hut, everyone noticed how relaxed and easy Campbell, Priestley, Levick, Dickason, Abbott and Browning were in each other's com-pany, how well they got on, with no obvious divisions.

Priestley thought the story of 'the glorious way in which the Southern Party died' was 'the best news that we could have hoped for under the circumstances'. He approved of the 'incontrovertible proof' of Amundsen's letter to King Haakon of Norway, which had been fortunate to survive the vicissitudes of transport back from the

Pole ('found among bumph', commented Wright). Campbell, who had seen Scott's message to the public, 'says it is a masterpiece'. Priestley briefly let his mind speculate: if '*Terra Nova* had been able to land a party of fresh able-bodied men at Hut Point', the Polar party 'might possibly have been met and saved but it was not to be. Even had the conditions admitted of our being picked up and landed we might have done something.' A collection of rocks dragged on the Polar party's sledge from the Beardmore had been brought back to the hut: 'a great block of iron pyrites in sandstone . . . coal & fossils in quantities', and, Cherry-Garrard enthused, the imprint of a fossilized fern, found only in India, South America and Australia. Among the specimens hauled down the coast by the Eastern party, Priestley's precious imprint of part of a fossil tree was much admired. The specimens retrieved by Campbell and his men included depots left by Edgeworth David and Mawson, during Shackleton's expedition, and by Scott's geologists, led by Griffith Taylor. Heavy rocks, bits of Antarctica, all moved with determination and devotion across the Barrier or along the sea ice. Solid, tangible, relatively unbreakable pieces of data, to take back to England.

For their part, the Eastern party now knew answers to their questions: where everyone had been, when and why things had happened and, more importantly, why they had not. Pieces were now sliding into place, but always, in the background, there was a slight reserve. Apart from Atkinson's determined but futile effort in April, a relief party had not come for them, because it was considered that they could manage. Was there any point in going into the detail of how nearly they hadn't? Bravado, the well-practised cheerfulness, jokiness, making light of things, being tough – the established forms of underplaying – were all doubly required now. They had managed to survive when Captain Scott and Bill Wilson, Titus Oates and Birdie Bowers and Petty Officer Evans had not. The six men 'made light of all their anxious days', said Cherry-Garrard.

Behind and above everything there were Scott's journals. Here was irrefutable evidence of the man, his passionate pursuit of what he wanted, his lining up and attacking of actions, his impulsive decision-taking, his quick judgements on people, his courage and vulnerability, his moodiness and periods of depression, his confidence and losses of confidence: all revealed. Here was his overwhelming desire to achieve the Pole, and the diminishing of hope on the return. Here too was Scott's heightened ability to observe, his continual alertness to science, and his perceptiveness about and eager interest in this part of Antarctica, his special fiefdom. Above all, perhaps, here was his ability to write about it.

In Scott's journals it was possible to read, for example, that in the early spring of 1911 he enjoyed what he made sound like a jolly jaunt up the Victoria Land coast as far as Dunlop Island, experiencing part of the very coast that Campbell and his men had struggled down. Accompanied by the tireless Bowers and his long-term sledging companion Petty Officer Evans, taking Dr Simpson to give him a 'holiday', Scott had achieved a round trip of 152 miles in sixteen days. '[W]e jogged up the coast', Scott had written, collecting rock specimens, including what he thought were veins of copper ore – 'the first find of minerals suggestive of the possibility of working', except that later the geologists identified them as iron pyrites. A section of snapped-off Glacier Tongue was found stranded, with – incongruously – the depot of fodder assembled so conscientiously by the Eastern party on their return from the Bay of Whales still intact. Scott described the coast evocatively – the long, undulating plateau, the mountain ranges behind, the rounded bays, with low ice walls – and observed the various types of sea ice, checking conditions the western geological party would have to deal with. Dunlop Island, where Priestley had collected happily, 'has undoubtedly been under the sea. We found regular terrace beaches with rounded water-worn stones all over it.' Afterwards 'it was easy for us to trace the same terrace formation on the coast.' Then, returning to Cape Evans across the sea ice by a longer than usual route, Scott was caught in a blizzard but marched his party on until forced to camp, tent-bound. Getting going again, he decided to keep marching although he saw another blizzard approaching, 'foolishly hoping it would pass by'. It didn't, and the four men were close to being caught on the ice with no protection, unable to get their tent up. Starting again, despite blistering wind and low temperatures, they staggered into the hut, having taken five days over the crossing and with Simpson's whole face frostbitten.

Scott's confident account when he returned to Cape Evans would have made the journey sound eminently manageable, but he had travelled after a winter in the comfort of the Cape Evans hut. The daily meals on his march, trying out the planned allocation for the southern journey to the Pole, were beyond the Eastern party's wildest dreams in their ice-cave. The four members of Scott's jaunt along the coast ate, daily, a breakfast of pemmican with pea flour, two biscuits, and tea with sugar; for lunch they had three biscuits, 2 oz of butter, tea with sugar and a spoonful of raisins, there was one stick of chocolate for afternoon tea, and a supper of pemmican with onion powder, three biscuits and cocoa with sugar. Eight biscuits a day per man, against the Eastern party's debilitating lack. But to those waiting at Cape Evans it must have seemed that Campbell's party, as long as they had managed the winter, would be able to travel back down this coast without too much difficulty.

And so much action and detail was packed into Scott's journals: excitement, adventure and pleasure, mischance and near disaster, strenuous effort and harsh travelling. To Campbell and his party their own experiences, their accidents and illnesses, their sufferings, their hunger, their battles with wind and blizzard and sea ice, their frustrations, and triumphs and achievements, were just as real, just as intense. But they were now part of the expedition's larger narrative: Rosencrantz and Guildenstern, the supporting cast to a heroic tragedy.

With everyone returned to the hut at Cape Evans, the only desire was to leave Antarctica. Some science was achieved: meteorological data continued to be collected, the magnetic work got through, visits made to Cape Royds. Campbell did a little surveying, Priestley led a group on his planned second ascent of Mount Erebus and spent Christmas in his beloved Cape Royds hut, eating the second tier of his brother Bert's long-travelled, well-aged wedding cake, which had left England in September 1911 and been delivered by *Terra Nova* in February 1912. Another new year began: 1913. Not much work was being done. They read and exercised a bit. The area around the hut was worn and stained with the refuse and use of two years. The random bodies of dog-mangled penguins lay on snow that had not thawed for two years, leaving the black lava beach on which they had first arrived hidden ever since. But mostly they watched for the ship. No one knew when she would come. For Williamson, 'Nothing doing . . . it is about the most d-mnable thing I know of this waiting a day seems like a month.' In Campbell's view, Pennell would expect everyone to be away sledging and so wouldn't come until late – to save coal. Others thought that Pennell would go first to pick up the Eastern party at Evans Coves, and would therefore leave New Zealand early. A range of supplies were available in the winter quarters hut for a third winter, if they were forced to stay here, but very little fuel, so they would have to use blubber. 'We are going on to rations, hoosh morning & night & light meal midday', Cherry-Garrard wrote, flatly, on 17th January. Gran was the one to record the significance of the date: 'it is the anniversary of Scott reaching the Pole.' Campbell, determined to avoid the risk of insufficient fresh meat and blubber, ordered preparations for another winter to begin on Saturday the 18th.

First thing on Saturday a party of men began digging an ice-cave in a drift, while others slaughtered penguins and seals. Then suddenly 'We dropped our tools & gave a mighty yell', wrote Williamson. *Terra Nova* appeared, newly scrubbed, ropes neatly coiled, wardroom decorated, luxuries placed in readiness, bunks with clean sheets. The mail was all sorted, each member's letters 'done up in pillow slips with his name'. The ship gave three cheers. 'We responded but meekly', Williamson noted. Teddy Evans, who had replaced Pennell as Commander, asked through the megaphone 'if we were all well'. Campbell answered 'with the dreadful news', Bruce wrote that night. 'Ships party quite paralysed . . .' The flags were removed, the gala meal put away. But the work of loading and departing had to be got through. *Terra Nova* had not, in fact, called in to Evans Coves on the way south to check on the state of the Eastern party. Instead, carrying out Scott's orders to the Commanding Officer of January 1911, she had entered the pack on an easterly meridian, attempting to reach King Edward VII Land. Ross had been desperately held up by pack ice here in 1842. *Terra Nova* repeated the experience, with tremendous struggles, fights and heavy use of coal.

The day after arriving, on 19 January 1913, the surviving Indian mules and three of the dogs were shot by ship's order. Campbell and Evans sealed up the winter quarters hut, leaving a record, and *Terra*

Nova steamed away from Cape Evans. Two local tasks needed to be achieved: picking up Priestley's Mount Erebus specimens at Cape Royds, then to Hut Point for the carpenter and a party to build a necessary cross to the fallen, a 'pretty stiff' job. Hut Point was stocked with provisions, in case of anyone's need, then locked.

The two remaining tasks were on the way north. A party of five men under Gran, including Dickason and Abbott, retrieved the western geological party's specimens near Cape Roberts, achieving a 17-mile round trip, picking up 300 kg of weight, with the help of a canvas kayak built by Abbott on the ship, Cape Adare-style. The second task was attempting to get into Evans Coves. 'I shall be awfully upset if we don't get our depot', Priestley worried, as they hit heavy pack on Thursday the 23rd and again on the 24th, punching and butting, with the propeller constantly catching on ice, no clear way ahead. For Pennell it was a repeat of his experience the previous year. Landing places in Antarctica needed to be reliable, places both to deliver to and to retrieve from. There was a real fear that Evans Coves would prove too uncertain, and that the attempt to land would be given up. Abandoning their geological records would be 'a great disappointment to Priestley & all the Eastern Party', noted Cherry-Garrard – 'to have spent so many months here for nothing'. But they continued forcing their way through until, running into clear water, they made fast to the solid, slippery sea ice at 3.00 a.m. on the morning of Sunday the 26th. '[R]ather gaunt looking place', Cherry thought, even now, in summer, staring out at the polished ice, swept clear of snow by the incessant wind.

Priestley, with Debenham, Cherry and Gran, fetched the geological specimens. Campbell walked to the igloo with a party including Wilfred Bruce, over the piedmont and up around the boulders. Bruce considered it 'a perfectly marvellous burrow . . . straight down 6 ft, horizontal some 25 ft, and then a chamber . . . Everything jet black & horribly greasy & smelling of blubber.' There wasn't much for a memento, so he took the bamboo hoosh-stirrer. Their lives here were beyond any of his terms of reference. 'These men have probably done a thing no Englishman has ever done, and may well be proud of it', Bruce wrote.

Teddy Evans found it just possible to stand upright in one corner of the 'cheerless hole'; the visit revealed hardship that Campbell 'never would have told'. A good many of the hands paid a visit to 'our "igloo",' said Dickason. Those who did climbed cautiously down the steps, shuffled along the dark tunnel, crawled through the door under the biscuit box lintel and then stood half-upright in the black, noisome inner room, picked up an article of discarded clothing, saturated with blubber, crouched by the cooking hearth, with its bamboo tripod to hold thawing meat, or measured out where six sleeping-bags interleaved on the floor. Then they came back down the hill, negotiating the boulders, shocked and respectful. 'I wish I had seen that igloo: with its black and blubber and beastliness', wrote Cherry-Garrard. 'Those who saw it came back with faces of amazement and admiration.' For Priestley the viewers who mattered most were the men who, during the Eastern party's long months of being marooned, they had imagined, in their repeated conversations, would come to relieve them: the western geological party, and the ship. He was glad they went to the igloo, 'for they will now realize what we have had to put up with during the last winter'.

Campbell, Levick, Priestley, Abbott, Browning and Dickason had saved themselves, as was expected of them. But they had done it by the closest of margins. That was not expected.

On 26 January 1911 Scott had set out to lay the depot on the Barrier which became One Ton. The six men of the Eastern party filed out from *Terra Nova* to wave farewell, happy to be about to start their own expedition. Now, exactly two years later, on 26 January 1913, Campbell & Co. achieved the final task on the Antarctic continent for the British Antarctic Expedition 1910–13: a geological depot retrieved, and a small depot of provisions left, in case anyone should come here in the future and be in need. It was a precaution that ought to be adopted, Williamson thought, for the use of any other party 'who may get stranded along the coast as was our Eastern party of 6 men'.

Terra Nova cast off. The six men watched as the blue ice piedmont, the granite outcrops, the low beach and sloping hill where they had survived their extraordinary winter in a snowdrift among wind-scoured boulders, faded into the distance; they were 'heading homewards'.

No more brilliant thing has ever been accomplished in the history of Arctic or Antarctic exploration.

Lord Curzon, President of the Royal Geographical Society, presenting a gold watch to Lieutenant Victor Campbell, leader of Scott's Northern party, London, May 1913

Acknowledgements

Scott's Last Expedition was published within months of the expedition ship *Terra Nova* arriving back in England in 1913. Volume 1 released the powerful, somewhat edited, journals of Captain Scott, starting in November 1910 and ending with his death in March 1912. Volume 2 recounted what happened to the rest of the expedition: the winter journey to collect emperor penguin eggs, the last year at Cape Evans, the voyages of *Terra Nova*, the geological trips, Campbell's account of his expedition. Scott's journals have been republished many times; Volume 2 of *Scott's Last Expedition* is much less well known.

The London Library's copy of Volume 2 has one handwritten annotation to the text, a rare moment of contact with an anonymous reader. Coming at the end of Griffith Taylor's account of his two geological trips, the annotation reflects an underlying refrain in my research. Griffith Taylor's first trip included Debenham, Wright and Petty Officer Edgar Evans; his second, with Debenham and Gran, had Petty Officer Robert Forde as sledging strong man and general handyman. Griffith Taylor finishes with a rousing acknowledgment of shared experiences: 'What is the best personal result of our sledge journeys? A group of friends who are closer than brothers. Here's luck to my mates – to Debenham, Wright, and Gran!' Someone has added immediately afterwards: 'What about P.O. Forde?'

Resetting the balance has been a driver of my research: to give space to the experiences of others, to listen to the range of voices. In particular, I have tried to bring the aims, and extraordinary achievements, of the six men of Scott's 'other expedition', led by Lieutenant Victor Campbell, back into the main body of the story of what happened in Antarctica a hundred years ago.

Central to the research has been the Scott Polar Research Institute
in Cambridge, with its rich archives. 'To lovers of Polar exploration
and devotees of Polar science, there is one thing above all others
which should give comfort and hope', wrote Raymond Priestley and
Charles Wright in 1922, completing their volume on *Glaciology* for
the British ('Terra Nova') Antarctic Expedition Reports. 'There has
been born at Cambridge . . . the polar Research Institute. . . . As a
repository of records, as a centre of research . . . it should prove
indeed invaluable . . . photographs, diaries, notebooks and other
records . . . will be deposited there . . . the work of discovery . . .
should proceed apace, and the researches of the future be no longer
handicapped.' I have concentrated on the diaries, journals, letters and
other papers held in these archives in Cambridge. All primary sources
referred to in my text are from the Scott Polar Research Institute,
with the exception of those listed as being from The Australian Polar
Collection in the South Australian Museum, where I worked on the
Mawson papers, a document from the Alexander Turnbull Library,
Wellington, and Alexander Smith's letter written on HMS *Erebus*, in
private ownership.

The assistance of all at Scott Polar – the Archivist Naomi Boneham,
the Picture Library Manager Lucy Martin and Hilary Shibata, Mark
Gilbert and Shirley Sawtell – has been greatly appreciated; I am grateful to the Director, Professor Julian Dowdeswell, and the Librarian
and Keeper of Collections, Heather Lane, for my time as a Visiting
Scholar. The British Antarctic Survey prepared the maps, and my
thanks go to Peter Fretwell, Adrian Fox and John Shears. I would
also like to thank Keith Moore, Librarian at the Royal Society, and,
Mark Pharaoh of the South Australian Museum. Wolfson College in
Cambridge provided me – once again – with the space and freedom
to research and write, and I would like to thank Gordon Johnson, the
President, for his hospitality and for the pleasure of being made a
Senior Academic Visitor of the College. The organizations that have
given me the chance to live and work in Antarctica have my con-
tinuing gratitude for benefits that keep delivering, in a multitude of
ways: the United States National Science Foundation Office of Polar
Programs Artists & Writers Program, the Australian Antarctic
Division humanities programme, and the Royal Navy, for time on

HMS *Endurance*. I am grateful for the opportunity provided by the *Kapitan Klebnikov* and Quark Expeditions to land on Inexpressible Island, and to visit the site of the ice-cave.

I would like to thank Julian Dowdeswell, the Director of the Scott Polar Research Institute, University of Cambridge, for permission to publish extracts from manuscripts over which the Institute has rights. I would also like to thank the Scott family, and the Hon. Alexandra Shackleton, for their kind permission to quote from the Scott and Shackleton papers, and the Cardiff Library and Information Service. Every reasonable effort has been made to trace copyright holders, but if there are errors or omissions, John Murray will be pleased to insert the appropriate acknowledgement in any subsequent printings or editions. My sincere thanks go to the families and friends of expedition members who have deposited papers in Cambridge over the years.

To Roland Philipps, managing director of John Murray: thank you for asking me which Antarctic story I wanted to write, for creating the opportunity for this book and for editing it; and thanks to the editorial team, Victoria Murray-Browne, Helen Hawksfield, Matthew Taylor, and to my agent, Caroline Walsh. Most of all, thank you to Richard, my husband, for being so supportive and positive about my repeated absences in Antarctica and Cambridge.

The author and publisher would like to thank the following for permission to reproduce copyright material: British Antarctic Survey, for maps; and David Walton of Bluntisham Books.

The bibliography that follows is a guide only. It lists primary sources used, and a selection from the many books generated by the life and achievements of that complex man Robert Falcon Scott, his two expeditions, some of his companions and the business of exploring Antarctica.

Picture Sources: All photographs and illustrations are from the Scott Polar Research Institute, University of Cambridge, except p. 220, Antarctic Adventure: Scott's Northern Party, Raymond Priestley, C. Hurst & Co, 1974.

Bibliography

SELECTED UNPUBLISHED SOURCES ON THE BRITISH (*TERRA NOVA*) ANTARCTIC EXPEDITION 1910–1913, IN THE SCOTT POLAR RESEARCH INSTITUTE, CAMBRIDGE

Abbott, George, journal, correspondence, sketches

Atkinson, Edward, correspondence

Beaumont, Admiral Sir Lewis, correspondence

Borchgrevink, Carsten, correspondence

Browning, Frank, diary

Bruce, Wilfred, journals, correspondence

Campbell, Victor L. A., journals, workbooks, notebooks, correspondence

Cherry-Garrard, Apsley, diaries, sledging notebook, zoological notebook, notes, correspondence

Darwin, Leonard, correspondence

Day, Bernard, journals

Dickason, Harry, diaries

Evans, Edward R. G. R., correspondence

Fisher, James and Margery, research transcripts and correspondence

Keohane, Patrick, diary, 1911–12

Levick, G. Murray, journals, diary, notebook, correspondence

Mawson, Douglas, correspondence

Papers of the British National Antarctic (*Terra Nova*) Expedition 1910–1913, vols 1–7 (Vols 1 and 2 are also known as 'E. L. Atkinson's Report')

Pennell, Harry, correspondence, notebooks

Priestley, Raymond, journals, diaries, sledging diaries, notes, correspondence, copies of articles

Rennick, Henry, work book, correspondence

Scott, Kathleen, correspondence

Scott, Robert, letter book vol. 1, vol. 2, miscellaneous notes and plans, correspondence

Shackleton, Ernest, correspondence
Simpson, George, diary, 1910–12
'South Polar Times', winter 1912
Terra Nova, logbooks
The Adelie Mail & Cape Adare Times, annotated by Raymond Priestley
Williamson, Thomas, diary, 1912–13

SELECTED UNPUBLISHED SOURCES, THE AUSTRALIAN POLAR COLLECTION, SOUTH AUSTRALIAN MUSEUM

Mawson, Douglas, diaries, correspondence, map

PUBLISHED MEMOIRS, DIARIES, JOURNALS AND ACCOUNTS BY MEMBERS OF THE BRITISH ANTARCTIC EXPEDITION, 1910–1913

Some of the works listed here have appeared in numerous editions. The editions cited here are those to which the Notes (below) relate.

Campbell, Victor, The Wicked Mate: The Antarctic Diary of Victor Campbell, ed. H. G. R. King (Bluntisham Books, Bluntisham, 2001)
Cherry-Garrard, Apsley, The Worst Journey in the World, 2 vols (Chatto and Windus, London, 1937)
Debenham, Frank, In the Antarctic (John Murray, London, 1952)
Debenham, Frank, The Quiet Land: The Diaries of Frank Debenham, ed. June Debenham Black (Bluntisham Books, Bluntisham, 1992)
Evans, Edward R. G. R., South with Scott (Collins, London, 1937)
Gran, Tryggve, The Norwegian with Scott: Tryggve Gran's Antarctic Diary, 1910–1913, ed. G. Hattersley-Smith (HMSO, London, 1984)
Lashly, William, Under Scott's Command: Lashly's Antarctic Diaries, ed. A. R. Ellis (Gollancz, London, 1969)
Levick, G. Murray, Antarctic Penguins: A Study of their Social Habits (Heinemann, London, 1914)
Ponting, Herbert, The Great White South: or, With Scott in the Antarctic (Duckworth, London, 1947)
Priestley, Raymond, Antarctic Adventure: Scott's Northern Party (Fisher Unwin, London, 1904)

Priestley, Raymond, *The Diary of a Vice-Chancellor, University of Melbourne, 1935–1938,* ed. Ronald Ridley (Melbourne University Press, Melbourne, 2002)

Scott, Robert Falcon, *Scott's Last Expedition in Two Volumes,* vol. 1, *Being the Journals of Captain R. F. Scott, R,N., C.V.O.;* vol. 2, *Being the Reports of the Scientific Work Undertaken by Dr E. A. Wilson and the Surviving Members of the Expedition,* arranged by Leonard Huxley, with a preface by Sir Clements R. Markham (Smith, Elder & Co., London, 1913)

Scott, Robert Falcon, *The Diaries of Captain Robert Scott: A Record of the Second Antarctic Expedition, 1910–12,* facsimile edn, 6 vols (UMI, Ann Arbor, 1968)

Scott, Robert Falcon, *Journals: Captain Scott's Last Expedition,* ed. with an introduction and notes by Max Jones (Oxford University Press, Oxford, 2005)

The South Polar Times, vol. 3 (Smith, Elder & Co., London, 1914)

Taylor, Thomas Griffith, *With Scott: The Silver Lining* (Bluntisham Books, Bluntisham, 1997)

Wilson, Edward, *Diary of the 'Terra Nova' Expedition to the Antarctic 1910–1912,* ed. H. G. R. King (Blandford Press, Poole, 1972)

Wright, Charles S., *Silas: The Antarctic Diaries and Memoir of Charles S. Wright,* ed. Colin Bull and Pat Wright (Ohio State University Press, Columbus, 1993)

SELECTED PUBLISHED PAPERS AND REPORTS ON THE EXPEDITION

The scientific results of the British (*Terra Nova*) Antarctic Expedition 1910–13 were published in a series of quarto reports. Of particular interest are 'The Physiography of Robertson Bay and Terra Nova Bay region' (1923), by R. E. Priestley, and 'Natural History of the Adélie Penguin', in *Zoology,* vol. 1 (1915), by G. Murray Levick.

A volume bringing together a range of documents and descriptions was published in 1924 as *British (Terra Nova) Antarctic Expedition, 1910–1913: Miscellaneous Data,* compiled by Colonel H. G. Lyons.

SELECTED ARTICLES ON THE EXPEDITIONS OR BY MEMBERS OF EXPEDITIONS

Articles in *Travel & Exploration: An Illustrated Monthly of Travel, Exploration, Adventure and Sport,* ed. Eustace Reynolds-Ball, vol. 3 (January to June 1910), vol. 4 (July to December 1910)

Reports and articles in the *Geographical Journal*
Priestley, R. E., 'The Psychology of Exploration', *Psyche*, 2 (1921–2)
Priestley, R. E., 'Inexpressible Island', *Nutrition Today* (1969)
SPRI Library pamphlet collection

SELECTED PUBLISHED MEMOIRS AND DIARIES FROM OTHER RELEVANT EXPEDITIONS

Some of the works listed here have appeared in many editions. The editions cited here are those to which the Notes (below) relate.

Amundsen, R., *The South Pole: An Account of the Norwegian Antarctic Expedition in the 'Fram', 1910–1912*, 2 vols (John Murray, London, 1912)

Bernacchi, L., *To the South Polar Regions: Expedition of 1898–1900* (Bluntisham Books, Denton, 1991)

Borchgrevink, C. E., *First on the Antarctic Continent: Being an Account of the British Antarctic Expedition, 1898–1900* (Hurst & Co., London, 1980)

Davis, J. K., *With the 'Aurora' in the Antarctic, 1911–1914* (Bluntisham Books, Bluntisham, 2007)

Hearne, Samuel, *A Journey from Prince of Wales's Fort in Hudson's Bay to the Northern Ocean in the Years 1769, 1770, 1771, and 1772*, [1795] ed. J. B. Tyrrell (Champlain Society, Toronto, 1911)

Kennet, Lady (Kathleen, Lady Scott) *Self-Portrait of an Artist* (John Murray, London, 1949)

Mawson, Douglas, *The Home of the Blizzard*, 2 vols (Hodder & Stoughton, London, 1930)

Mawson, Douglas, *Mawson's Antarctic Diaries*, ed. Fred and Eleanor Jacka (Unwin Hyman, London, 1988)

Ross, Captain Sir James Clark, *A Voyage of Discovery and Research in the Southern and Antarctic Regions during the Years 1839–43*, 2 vols (David & Charles, Newton Abbot, 1969)

Scott, Robert Falcon, *The Voyage of the Discovery* (John Murray, London, 1937)

Shirase, Lieutenant Nobu, *Antarctica: The Japanese South Polar Expedition of 1910–12*, trans. Lara Dagnell and Hilary Shibata (forthcoming)

Wilson, Edward, *Diary of the Discovery Expedition to the Antarctic Regions 1901–1904*, ed. Ann Savours (Blandford Press, Poole, 1966)

SELECTED PUBLISHED SOURCES ON ANTARCTIC EXPEDITIONS, MEMBERS AND HUTS

Ayres, Philip, *Mawson: A Life* (Melbourne University Press, Melbourne, 1999)

Branagan, D., *T. W. Edgeworth David: A Life* (National Library of Australia, Canberra, 2005)

Christie's [catalogues], Exploration and Travel

Conservation Plan, Scott's Hut, Cape Evans (Antarctic Heritage Trust, Christchurch, 2004)

Conservation Plan, Shackleton's Hut, Cape Royds (Antarctic Heritage Trust, Christchurch, 2003)

Conservation Plan, The Historic Huts at Cape Adare (Antarctic Heritage Trust, Christchurch, 2004)

Crane, D., *Scott of the Antarctic: A Life of Courage and Tragedy in the Extreme South* (Harper Collins, London, 2005)

Crawford, Janet, *That First Antarctic Winter: The Story of the Southern Cross Expedition of 1989–1900, as Told in the Diaries of Louis Charles Bernacchi* (South Latitude Research Ltd, Canterbury, 1998)

Fiennes, Ranulph, *Captain Scott* (Hodder and Stoughton, London, 2003)

Fisher, Margery and James, *Shackleton* (Barrie Books, London, 1957)

Flannery, Nancy (ed.), *This Everlasting Silence* (Melbourne University Press, Melbourne, 2005)

Gordon Hayes, J., *Antarctica: A Treatise on the Southern Continent* (Richards Press, London, 1928)

Gregor, G. C., *Swansea's Antarctic Explorer: Edgar Evans, 1876–1912* (Swansea City Council, Swansea, 1995)

Harrowfield, D. L., *Icy Heritage: Historic Sites of the Ross Sea Region* (Antarctic Heritage Trust, Christchurch, 1995)

Huntford, Roland, *Scott and Amundsen* (Hodder and Stoughton, London, 1979)

Huntford, Roland, *Shackleton* (Hodder and Stoughton, London, 1985)

Jones, Max, *The Last Great Quest: Captain Scott's Antarctic Sacrifice* (Oxford University Press, Oxford, 2003)

Lambert, Katherine, *'Hell with a Capital H': An Epic Story of Antarctic Survival* (Pimlico, London, 2002)

Limb, Sue, and Cordingly, Patrick, *Captain Oates: Soldier and Explorer* (Batsford, London, 1982)

Mawson, Paquita, *Mawson of the Antarctic: The Life of Sir Douglas Mawson* (Longman, London, 1964)

Murphy, David Thomas, *German Exploration of the Polar World: A History, 1870–1940* (University of Nebraska Press, Lincoln, 2002)

Nicolson, Juliet, *The Perfect Summer: Dancing into Shadow in 1911* (John Murray, London, 2006)

Pound, R., *Scott of the Antarctic* (Cassell, London, 1966)

Preston, Diana, *A First Rate Tragedy: Captain Scott's Antarctic Expeditions* (Constable, London, 1997)

Quartermaine, L. B., *South to the Pole: The Early History of the Ross Sector, Antarctica* (Oxford University Press, Oxford, 1967)

Riffenburgh, Beau, *Nimrod: Ernest Shackleton and the Extraordinary Story of the 1907–09 British Antarctic Expedition* (Bloomsbury, London, 2004)

Riffenburgh, Beau, *Racing with Death: Douglas Mawson – Antarctic Explorer* (Bloomsbury, London, 2008)

Smith, Michael, *I Am Just Going Outside: Captain Oates' Antarctic Tragedy* (Spellmount Publishers, Staplehurst, 2002)

South: The Race to the Pole (National Maritime Museum, London, 2000)

Thomson, David, *Scott's Men* (Allen Lane, London, 1977)

Wheeler, Sara, *Cherry: A Life of Apsley Cherry-Garrard* (Cape, London, 2001)

Young, Louisa, *A Great Task of Happiness: The Life of Kathleen Scott* (Macmillan, London, 1995)

VISUAL SOURCES

The films and photographs of Herbert Ponting

The drawings and paintings of Edward Wilson

Photographic images and maps in the published scientific reports of the expedition

Photographs, drawings and maps by many members of the expedition held as part of the SPRI Archives and Map Collection and SPRI Picture Library Collection

Among published collections, in particular:

Frozen History: The Legacy of Scott and Shackleton, photographs by Josef and Katherina Hoflehner (Josef Hoflehner, 2003)

SEMINARS AND CONFERENCES

'Scientific Voyaging: Histories and Comparisons', National Maritime Museum and Royal Society, London, 8–10 July 2008

Patrick Collinson, Emeritus Regius Professor of Modern History, seminar, Wolfson College, Cambridge, 14 October 2008

'The Antarctic Treaty Conference', Cumberland Lodge, Windsor, 11 June 2009

Notes

All unpublished sources are in the Scott Polar Research Institute (SPRI) unless otherwise specified.

Abbreviations

BAE Reports: Papers of the British National Antarctic Expedition 1910–13, in 7 volumes

WM: Campbell, Victor, *The Wicked Mate: The Antarctic Diary of Victor Campbell,* ed. H. G. R. King (Bluntisham Books, Bluntisham, 2001)

GJ: Geographical Journal

Gran: Gran, Tryggve, *The Norwegian with Scott: Tryggve Gran's Antarctic Diary 1910–1913,* ed. G. Hattersley-Smith (HMSO, London, 1984)

Scott, *Diaries: The Diaries of Captain Robert Scott: A Record of the Second Antarctic Expedition, 1910–12,* facsimile edn, 6 vols (UMI, Ann Arbor, 1968)

Scott, *Journals: Journals: Captain Scott's Last Expedition,* ed. with an introduction and notes by Max Jones (Oxford University Press, Oxford, 2005)

SLE: Scott's Last Expedition in Two Volumes, vol. 1, *Being the Journals of Captain R. F. Scott, R.N., C.V.O.;* vol. 2, *Being the Reports of the Scientific Work Undertaken by Dr E. A. Wilson and the Surviving Members of the Expedition,* arranged by Leonard Huxley with a preface by Sir Clements R. Markham (Smith, Elder & Co., London, 1913)

Wright, *Silas:* Wright, Charles S., *Silas: The Antarctic Diaries and Memoir of Charles S. Wright,* ed. Colin Bull and Pat Wright (Ohio State University Press, Columbus, 1993)

xix under two headings, Wilfred Bruce, list of names, 29/12/10, and second list, no date, MS 402/1–4

xx 'alas, no longer "Eastern!"', Wilfred Bruce to Kathleen Scott, 27/2/11, MS 1488/2

'going strong', Priestley, January 1911, MS 198

out for an airing, Priestley, 26/1/11, MS 298/14/1; BJ

'good luck party', Priestley, 25/1/11, loc. cit.

2 under their sledge, Priestley, 26/1/11, loc. cit.

'the "amateurs"', Priestley, 25/1/11, loc. cit.

under-used dogs, Raymond Priestley, *The Diary of a Vice-Chancellor: University of Melbourne, 1935–1938*, ed. Ronald Ridley (Melbourne University Press, Melbourne, 2002), p. xv

'off finally', Priestley, 26/1/11, loc. cit.

3 'a success', Raymond Priestley, *Antarctic Adventure: Scott's Northern Party* (Fisher Unwin, London, 1904), pp. 27–31

4 'of the ship', Levick, 29/1/11, MS 1637; D

in their journals, see, for example, Dickason, 26/1/11, MS 1634; DJ; Browning, 26/1/11, MS 870; BJ

yellow and glassy, Gran, p. 216

bone snapped, Sara Wheeler, *Cherry: A Life of Apsley Cherry-Garrard*, (Cape London, 2001) p. 142, p. 315

5 'Last Expedition', see *SLE*

'hindsight bias', see Timothy Garton Ash, '1989 – The Unwritten History', *New York Review of Books* (5–18 November 2009)

'Campbell & Co.', Bruce, 2/2/11, MS 401/1–2

6 'unanswered questions', Nelson Mandela on his own private archive, quoted in *The Guardian* (14 October 2009)

'clay of history', Professor Patrick Collinson, seminar, Wolfson College, Cambridge, October 2008

'need to be heard', ibid.

7 'of the world', cited in Beau Riffenburgh, *Nimrod: Ernest Shackleton and the Extraordinary Story of the 1907–09 British Antarctica Expedition* (Bloomsbury, London, 2004), p. 281

sturdy of leg, see Samuel Hearne, *A Journey from Prince of Wales's Fort in Hudson's Bay to the Northern Ocean in the years 1769, 1770, 1771 and 1772* [1795], ed. J. B. Tyrrell (Champlain Society, Toronto, 1911)

8 sledge dogs, see Nobu Shirase, *Antarctica: The Japanese South Polar Expedition of 1910–12*, trans. Lara Dagnell and Hilary Shibata (forthcoming)

9 'hard won fragments', Professor Joyce Chaplin, keynote address, 'Scientific Voyaging: Histories and Comparisons Conference', London, July 2008

September 1909, 'Antarctic Expedition for 1910', MS 1835; D; BJ

'that achievement', ibid.

'brilliant results', ibid.

10 'can't be done', Kathleen Bruce, MS 1453/3; BJ

11 'Britannia's Barrier', Smith, 10/4/1841, letter written on HMS *Erebus*, 10/4/1841, private collection
named Cape Adare, see Captain James Clark Ross, *A Voyage of Discovery and Research in the Southern and Antarctic Regions during the Years 1839–43*, 2 vols (John Murray, London, 1847; David & Charles, Newton Abbot, 1969)

12 across the ice, see C. E. Borchgrevink, *First on the Antarctic Continent: Being an Account of the British Antarctic Expedition, 1898–1900* (1901; C. Hurst, London, 1980)
'this ice-sheet', Borchgrevink, *First on the Antarctic Continent*, pp. 280–83
bare rock, see Edward Wilson, *Diary of the Discovery Expedition to the Antarctic Regions, 1901–1904*, ed. Ann Savours (Blandford Press, London, 1966), p. 109

13 encompass even more, ibid., p. 110
the journey uncompleted, see correspondence between Scott, Shackleton and Wilson, in Fisher Papers, MS 1456/23/24/26
to the plans, Shackleton, *GJ*, vol. 24, no. 33 (March 1907)
'scientific voyaging', 'Scientific Voyaging' conference

14 mineral resources, Shackleton, *GJ*, vol. 24, no. 33 (March 1907)
former commander, see correspondence in Fisher Papers, loc. cit. For recent detailed discussions, see, for example, D. Crane, *Scott of the Antarctic: A Life of Courage and Tragedy in the Extreme North* (Harper Collins, London, 2005), and Riffenburgh, *Nimrod*
'beyond C. North', Scott to Shackleton, 26/3/07, in Fisher Papers, MS 1456/24
'rigidly adhere to', Shackleton to Scott, 17/5/07, Fisher Papers, loc. cit.

15 'of faith', RS to KS, quoted in David Thomson, *Scott's Men* (Allen Lane, London, 1977), p. 117
letter of agreement, Crane, *Scott of the Antarctic*, p. 390

16 'news came', KS to RS, 17/4/12, MS 1835; BJ, vol. 2
'Scott–Shackleton difficulty', Beaumont to Darwin, 19/6/09, MS 367/1
'that 97 miles', ibid.
'game by you,' 1909, cited in Riffenburgh, *Nimrod*, p. 292

17 'your own', Scott to Shackleton, 1/7/1909, quoted in Margery and James Fisher, *Shackleton* (Barrie Books, London, 1957), p. 256
'McMurdo Sound', Shackleton to Scott, 6/7/09, quoted in Fisher, *Shackleton*, p. 256
'low down ambitions', Wilson to John Fraser, 19/8/09, quoted in Riffenburgh, *Nimrod*, p. 293
'Pole hunting', Beaumont to Darwin, loc. cit.
letter to Darwin, R. Pound, *Scott of the Antarctic* (Cassell, London, 1966) pp. 171–2

18 'breaking new ground', Scott, 'Antarctic Expedition', 15/9/09, loc. cit.
'another nation', 13/9/09, MS 280/28/3; BJ

19 'immediate future', ibid.
'America's confidence', 18/9/09, MS 280/28/3; BJ
final dash, Mawson, abbreviated log, January [1910] in Douglas Mawson, *Mawson's Antarctic Diaries*, ed. Fred and Eleanor Jacka (Unwin Hyman, London, 1988), p. 53
'all the time', Priestley, letter to his brother, mid-1910, in D. Branagan, *T. W. Edgeworth David: A Life* (National Library of Australia, Canberra, 2005), p. 218
continent, see map in Mawson, MAC 11 AAE, The Australian Polar Collection (version as drawn February 1910)

20 'he had not', Mawson, *Mawson's Antarctic Diaries*, p. 53
'the matter', ibid.
'in his socks', Nancy Flannery (ed.), *This Everlasting Silence* (Melbourne University Press, Melbourne, 2005), p. 5

21 'promise nothing', Mawson's Antarctic Diaries, p. 53
'boat reconnaissance', ibid.

22 the unknown coast, see Mawson to Shackleton, letter (date cut off), MS 79 11 AAE, The Australian Polar Collection
'about £70,000', Mawson, *Mawson's Antarctic Diaries*, p. 54
'bless you K' , KS to RS, letter 341, no date, 1835; D:BJ

23 'for the South', Shackleton, 21/2/10, quoted in Fisher, *Shackleton*, p. 257
18 March 1910, Mawson, *Mawson's Antarctic Diaries*, p. 54
'previous expedition', Shackleton to Scott, Fisher Papers, 23/3/07, MS 1456/24

24 'point of view?', Scott to Darwin, 29/3/10, quoted in Fisher, *Shackleton*, p. 258
British contributors, *Appeal for Contributors*, 21 March 1910, enclosed in letter from Beaumont to Scott, 24/3/10, MS 1453/51
letter dated 29 April 1910, Darwin to Shackleton, 29/4/10, MS 79 11 AAE, The Australian Polar Collection. I found the MS letter in Adelaide. The only known version has been a typescript copy held in the SPRI collections, annotated in pencil with an incorrect date (30/6/09)

25 for equipment, 'Shackleton's Contract and Promise', (1910), Omaha/Private/ dated 16 May 1910, MS DM 8DM, The Australian Polar Collection

27 'difficult enterprises', Scott, 'Plans', *GJ*, vol. 36, no. 1
'of such claims', Scott, ibid.
'stores remains', Scott, ibid.
'future occasion', Scott, ibid.

28 'simply immense', Darwin, *GJ*, vol. 36, no. 1
'amongst us', ibid.

29 'can provide', *Travel & Exploration* (March 1910), p. 209

'item for me', Abbott, 8/6/10, MS 1754/1: D
towards Cowes, Abbott, 6-7/6/10, loc. cit.

30 fed it, Browning, 28/8/10, MS 870; BJ
'inseparables', 'South Polar Times', vol. 3, part 3 (October 1911)
religiously inclined, 15/6/10,Wright, *Silas*, p. 8
'special vocation', George Simpson, diary, p. 2, MS 1097/49

31 'live up to it', Wright, *Silas*, 2/10/10

32 tiring task, Atkinson, BAE Reports, MS 280/28, vol. 4
'the hands badly', Simpson, diary, p. 6, MS 1097/49

33 'and throaty style', RS to KS, 28/12/10, MS 1835; D: BJ
'all off', Wright, *Silas*, 31/7/10, p. 13
'quite a sailor', Browning, 28/8/10, MS 870; BJ
the favourite, ibid.
volunteered his services, Abbott, 19/7/10, loc. cit.

34 'it a secret', Abbott, 22/8/10, loc. cit.
'pursue the art', Abbott, 3/8/10, loc. cit.
'sorts of things', Campbell, 17/8/10, MS 1363/1-4:D
'the hornpipe', Abbott, 31/8/10, loc. cit.
'my landing', Campbell, 17/8/10, loc. cit.

35 Barrier surface, results of meeting reported in Campbell's letter to Vera
Campbell, MS 1363/1–4
'loving Coz Vic', Campbell, ibid.

36 Ross Island, see Shackleton to his wife, 26/1/08, quoted in Fisher,
Shackleton, pp. 147–52
'could have landed', Darwin to Scott, 31/06/09, MS 1453/72
proposed expedition, see discussions on *Terra Nova*, 23/12/10

37 'be dangerous', and quotes following, Scott, Statement Supplementary to
the authorised programme of the Expedition, 11 July 1910, MS 761/8/8,
held in the Alexander Turnbull Library, MS – Papers – 0022

38 'Antarctic Regions', ibid.
'number of years', ibid.
a full-rigged ship, Abbott, 20/9/10, loc. cit.
'Edward VII Land', Browning, 30/9/10, loc. cit.

40 'like the natives', 'Outfit and Equipment for the Traveller, Explorer, and
Sportsman, 3: Hints for Travellers in Arctic Regions', *Travel and Exploration*
(March 1910), p. 186
marking the spot, Campbell, MS 1419/3: D
'a day's work', ibid.

41 solve the riddle, Day, 20/12/11, MS 660/1
taking observations, Wright, *Silas*, 2/10/11, p. 28
'for scurvy', Campbell, loc. cit.
'bake bread', Wright, *Silas*, p. 29

42 'block of a man', BAE Reports, MS 280/28/1, p. 13

'the perfect treasure', Scott, *Journals*, 9/1/11
'Antarctica. Amundsen', Gran, p. 14
tell Campbell, on 15/10/11, see Roland Huntford, *Scott and Amundsen* London, 1979 (Hodder and Stoughton), p. 318, p. 572, n.

43   for the Pole, Branagan, *Edgeworth David: A Life*, p. 231
for permission, Branagan, *Edgeworth David*, pp. 226-7
'large Playground', prospectus seen in Tewkesbury Museum
'your enterprise', letter quoted in Paquita Mawson, *Mawson of the Antarctic: The Life of Sir Douglas Mawson* (Longman, London, 1964) p. 43

44   'not get away', ibid., p. 44
'West Antarctica', Gran, p. 14
'him good luck', ibid.

45   'put in store', Abbott, 7/10/10, loc. cit.
'fine fierce lot', Abbott, summary, 8/10/10, loc. cit.
'down the hills', ibid.
frozen Sea of Okhotsk, David Thomson, *Scott's Men* (Allen Lane, London, 1977), p. 152

46   local beauties, Abbott, summary, 1910, loc. cit.
a bit longer, Priestley, 19/12/11, MS 198; BJ
'more comfortable', Priestley, 6/12/11, loc. cit.

47   token wage, Louisa Young, *A Great Task of Happiness: The Life of Kathleen Scott* (Macmillan, London, 1995) p. 110
couldn't be helped, Wilfred Bruce to Kathleen Scott, March 1911, MS 1488/2
'by ponies', Browning, 26/11/10, loc. cit.
weighed a ton, BAE Reports, MS 280/28/1, p. 140

48   board as gifts, Browning, 26/11/10, loc. cit.
jerseys per man, Browning, 29/11/10, loc. cit.
'to our armpits', Browning, see 1-3/12/11, MS 870; BJ
'something solid', Abbott, 3/12/11, MS 1754/1; D
'off your feet', Browning, loc. cit.

49   on the ladder, Wright, *Silas*, p. 45
'their dumb agony', Abbott, summary, loc. cit.
said Teddy Evans, Edward R. G. R. Evans, *South with Scott* (Collins, London, 1921), p. 36
had been worse, Priestley, 6/12/11, loc . cit.
rough work, Browning, 6/12/10, loc. cit.
miserable howl, Abbott, 6/12/10, loc. cit.

50   'horrible slaughter', Cherry-Garrard, 11/12/10, MS 559/18/1-4
'called *ski*', Herbert Ponting, *The Great White South: or, With Scott in the Antarctic* (Duckworth, London, 1947), p. 88
sledging journeys, Thomson, *Scott's Men*, p. 122
would use them, Day, 15/12/10, MS 660/1

51 and violin, Day, 21/12/10, loc. cit.
in January 1908, Priestley, 13/12/11, MS 198; BJ
Eastern party's departure, Priestley, 16/12/11, loc. cit.
'I hate it', Levick, 18/12/10, loc. cit.

52 hard manual labour, RS to KS, 28/12/10, MS 1835; D: BJ
ate it, see, for example, RS to KS, 22/12/10, loc. cit.
300 tons remained, Day, 23/12/11, loc. cit.
in their journals, for the discussions following see entries under 23/12/11
in Day, Gran, Priestley, Cherry-Garrard, loc. cit., and BAE Reports, MS
280/28/1
Edward VII Land, Day, 23/12/11, loc. cit.

53 and his men, Gran, 23/12/10
British newspapers, outlines in *Daily Mail* (18 March 1911), *Sphere* and
Shackleton to RGS; see Mawson, *Mawson's Antarctic Diaries*, p. 54
dead ponies, Gran, 23/12/10, p. 37

54 'about the ship', Levick, 24/12/10, loc. cit.
to each man, Browning, 25/12/10, loc. cit.
cracked metallic voice, Levick, 25/12/10, loc. cit.

55 'another day', Priestley, 26/12/11, MS 198; BJ
'the King', Cherry-Garrard, MS 559/18/1-4
'very trying time', Scott, 26/12/10, *Journals*, p. 49
and destination, Bruce, 29/12/10, MS 402/1-4

57 'old Bug Trap', Henry Rennick, Letters (2) to Daniel Radcliffe, 1910–
1912, MS 1013/5/1-2
'drifting N.W', Bruce, 31/12/11, loc. cit.
spent at sea, Priestley, 30/12/10, loc. cit.
'by the sun', Cherry-Garrard, MS 598/18/1-4

58 'very healthy', Scott to his mother, October 1911, quoted in Pound, *Scott
of the Antarctic*, p. 258,
be at risk, Day, 1/1/11, MS 660/1
'in yr throat', KS to RS, undated latter, MS 1835; D: BJ.
being infectious, in KS to RS, letter written for Christmas Day 1910 and
delivered to RS by Teddy Evans
'cool them down', RS to KS, 1/1/11, MS 1835; D: BJ

59 King Edward's Land, ibid.

60 'to Hut Point', map reproduced in Edward Wilson, *Diary of the Terra Nova,
Expedition to the Antarctic, 1910–1912*, ed. H. G. R. King (Blandford Press,
Poole, 1972), p. 150
'permanently vulgarized', RS to KS, 1/1/11, MS 1835: BJ, vol. 2

61 was breaking, Bruce, 3/1/11, MS 402/1-4
'love you still', RS to KS, 7/1/11, MS 1835; D: BJ
'old place again', Priestley, 3/1/11, MS 198
'go South', ibid.

'King Edward's Land', ibid.

62 '2nd in command', Campbell, '22/1/10' [1911], MS 1363/1–4: D

'tremendous surprise', Priestley, 4/1/11, loc. cit.

'the Skuary', ibid.

'the Ship fast', Abbott, 4/1/11, MS 1754/1; D

'won't be long', Priestley, various verses in MS 198 and MS 298/14/1

63 'one's weary bones', Abbott, 4/1/11, loc. cit.

64 'Oh damn', Priestley, loc. cit.

'rush it across', Campbell, 8/1/11, Campbell, *WM*, p. 36

65 able to move, Priestley, 8/1/11, MS 298/14/1

men who had, BAE Reports, MS 280/28/1

a happy place, RS to KS, 7/1/11, MS 1835; BJ

'a motley crowd', Abbott, 14/1/11, loc. cit.

'relief this is', RS to KS, 14/1/11, MS 1835; BJ

'"The Skuary"', Priestley, 14/1/11, MS 298/14/1

66 ship and shore, Dickason, 16/1/11, MS 1634; D

defects in his diary, Sue Limb and Patrick Cordingley, *Captain Oates: Soldier and Explorer* (Batsford, London, 1982), p. 100

'gentleman he is', Scott, 14-15/1/11; Scott, *Journals*, pp. 89–90

'built animal', Scott, 1/10/11; Scott, *Journals*, p. 293

67 'from a walk', Priestley, 16/1/11, MS 298/14/1

'but the others also', ibid.

68 noted happily, Levick, 16/1/11, MS 1637; D

'or some such people', Priestley, loc. cit.

'flinching at it', Levick, 18/1/11, loc. cit.

'burnished gold', Levick, 19/1/11, loc. cit.

'little holiday', Levick, 20/1/11, loc. cit.

'right moment', Priestley, 21/1/11, loc. cit.

69 'me horribly', Scott, *Journals*, 15/1/11, p. 91

'during blizzards', Scott, 'Sanitary Arrrangements', miscellaneous papers; Scott, *Diaries*, vol. 3

'we expected', Dickason, 22/1/11, MS 1634; D

'luck to them', Priestley, 22/1/11, loc. cit.

70 'to write in', Campbell, '22/1/10' [1911], loc. cit.

'Narrow escape', Dickason, 25/1/11, loc. cit.

'up to his neck', Priestley, 24/1/11, loc. cit.

at its suffering, Scott, *Journals*, 24/1/11, p. 103

'to ourselves', 25/1/11, Priestley, loc. cit.

'so quickly', Browning, 'Thursday', January 1911, MS 870; BJ

71 'all round', Dickason, 26/1/11, loc. cit.

'on the snow', Browning, 26/1/11, loc. cit.

not included, Wilson, *Terra Nova*, 26/1/11

at its loosest, RS to KS, 1/1/11, MS 1835; BJ, vol. 2

'if you can', Pound, *Scott of the Antarctic*, pp. 219–20

detailed orders, Scott, 'Orders to Commanding Officer *Terra Nova*', no date; Scott, *Diaries,* vol. 3

'awfully pleased', Campbell, 30/1/11, MS 1363/1-4: D

73 'sledge it back', Dickason, 27/1/11, loc. cit.

through the head, Branagan, *Edgeworth David*, p. 569

for himself, see Priestley, entry for 27/1/11, loc. cit.

'explored before', Bruce, 27/1/11, MS 402/1-4

74 'definite information', Priestley, 28/1/11, MS 298/14/1

few mementoes, Abbott, 28/1/11, MS 1754/1: D

'left behind', Browning, Saturday, January 1911, loc. cit.

'be land', Levick, 29/1/11, loc. cit.

75 'hard, set floe', 'South Polar Times', August 1902

with the Eastern Party, Scott, miscellaneous papers; Scott, *Diaries,* vol. 3

gooseberries, BAE, Miscellaneous Data, 1924

his notebooks, BAE Reports, vol. 3, MS 280/28/3

76 their hands on, Cherry-Garrard, 19/1/11, MS 559/18/1–4

'attempt a landing', Scott, 'Orders', no date; in Scott, *Diaries*

were brief, Scott, 'Instructions to Leader of Eastern Party'; Scott, *Diaries,* vol. 3

east of Cape Crozier, *SLE*, vol. 2, p. 80

'one long wall of ice', Dickason, 29/1/11, loc. cit.

77 'speed limit', Dickason, 31/1/11, loc. cit.

'or garden Barrier', Priestley, 2/2/11, MS 298/14/1

'compare with this', Bruce to Kathleen Scott, 27/2/11, MS 1488/2

100-foot-high cliffs, Bruce, 2/2/11, MS 402/1-4

'discovered by Capt. Scott', Levick, 3/2/11, loc. cit.

78 withered, Campbell, 3/2/11

gallons of paraffin, Priestley, 3/2/11, loc. cit.

'Barrier or Land', Scott, 'Orders', no date, Scott, *Diaries*

geologist to do, 3/2/11, Levick, loc. cit.

King Edward VII Land, see Priestley, 17/1/08, quoted in Riffenburgh, *Nimrod*, p. 151

79 frighteningly unstable, see, for example, the account in Riffenburgh *Nimrod*, pp. 152–3

'we reported', Priestley, 3/2/11, MS 298/14/1

'edge in 1902', Campbell, *WM*, 3/2/11, p. 43

80 'Shackleton Expedition', Priestley, 3–4/2/11, loc. cit.

pulling on clothes, Priestley, 3–4/2/11, loc. cit.

'heard everywhere', Bruce to KS, 27/2/11, MS 1488/2

'fair race', Priestley, 3–4/2/11, loc. cit.

'all the Winter', Priestley, 3/2/11, loc. cit.

81 'be strained', Bruce, 5/2/11, loc. cit.
    unexpected fashion, Priestley, 4/2/11, loc. cit.
    'breach of faith' and subsequent quotes in this paragraph, Darwin to Shackleton, 29/4/10, loc. cit.

82 'second shore party', R. Amundsen, *The South Pole: An Account of the Norwegian Antarctic Expedition in the 'Fram' 1910–1912*, 2 vols (London), vol. 2, p. 294
    'white hair', Abbott, 4/2/11, MS 1764/1; D
    'very pleased', Browning, 4/2/11, loc. cit.
    better one, Campbell, 3/2/11; Campbell, *WM,* p. 44
    'wonderful day', Levick, 4/2/11, loc. cit.

83 bound for Cape North, Amundsen, *The South Pole*, vol. 1, pp. 203–5
    'South first', Bruce, 27/2/11, loc. cit.
    'Bay of Whales', Campbell, 3/2/11, *WM*, p. 44
    the wall, Nilsen, in Amundsen, *The South Pole*, vol. 2, pp. 287–8
    'wintering there', Campbell, 3/2/11, *WM*, p. 44.
    'running short', ibid.
    'Very disappointed', Campbell to Vera, 11/2/11, 1363/1-4; D

84 'either side', Priestley, 4/2/11, loc. cit.
    'a clear field', Abbott, 4/2/11, MS 175/1; D
    'perfidious Amundsen', Bruce to KS, 27/2/11, MS 1488/2

85 'his best', Levick, 5/2/11, loc. cit.
    'to beat them', Bruce, 5/2/11, loc. cit.
    'each other', Levick, 4/2/11, loc. cit.
    'there first', Priestley, 4/2/11, loc. cit.
    'to us all', Browning, 4/2/11, MS 870: BJ
    'clothing yet', Abbott, 4/2/11, loc. cit.
    'food supplies etc', ibid.

86 'we get there', Abbott, 5/2/11, MS 1570/1
    some geology, Priestley, 5/2/11, loc. cit.
    'to beat Amundsen', Priestley, 7/2/11, loc. cit.
    fall flat after that, Bruce, 7/2/11, loc. cit.

87 underlying land, Amundsen, *The South Pole*, vol. 1, pp. 347–9
    'subjacent land, banks etc.', Amundsen, 'The Norwegian South Polar Expedition', *GJ*, vol. 41 (January 1913), p. 1
    'English sphere', Amundsen, *The South Pole*, vol. 1, p. 2
    the King Edward VII Land coast, Huntford, *Scott and Amundsen* p. 375
    South Atlantic, Amundsen, *The South Pole*, vol. 2, p. 316
    '24 of them', Cherry-Garrard, 5/2/11, MS 559/18/1-4
    'on grub', Cherry-Garrard, 7/2/11, loc. cit.
    'very far', Scott, *Journals*, p. 119

88 'small adventures', Priestley, 8/2/11, loc. cit.
    Bay of Whales, see Cherry-Garrard, summary of report, 23/2/11, loc. cit.

'South door', Cherry-Garrard, 23/2/11, MS 559/18/1–4
'simply glorious', Abbott, 15/2/11, MS 1754/1; D
water the ship, Priestley, 9/2/11, loc. cit.

89   'up to date' , Abbott, 15/2/11, summary, loc. cit.
    'very sad', ibid.
    'a search party', Priestley, 9/2/11, ibid.
    'his feet', Levick, 10/2/11, loc. cit.
    'my temper', ibid.

90   'blown backwards', Browning, 'Thursday', February, loc. cit.

91   remaining third, Scott, 28/12/11, letter 356a, MS 1835; D: BJ
    the gramophone, Levick, 10/2/11, loc. cit.
    'few weeks', Priestley, 21/1/11, loc. cit.
    'a Volunteer', Bruce to KS, 27/2/11, MS 1488/2

92   'almost pitiful', Bruce to KS, March, MS 1488/2
    'our doings', Campbell to Vera, 22/1/11, loc. cit.
    'with snow', Campbell, *WM*, 8/2/11 and 9/2/11, p. 47
    'this year!', Bruce, 9/2/11, loc. cit.

93   'return home', Priestley, 17/2/11, loc. cit.
    of Cape Adare, Campbell, *WM*, 12/2/11, p. 47
    to get back, Dickason, 12/2/11, loc. cit.

94   'stay in our bunks', Bruce, 16/2/11, loc. cit.
    'in this region', *SLE*, vol. 2, p. 81
    50 feet high, Bruce, 15/2/11, loc. cit.
    'that happening', Priestley, 17/2/11, loc. cit.

95   'supply allowed', *SLE*, vol. 2, p. 360
    'pick up somewhere!', Dickason, 17/2/11, loc. cit.
    against it, Campbell, *WM*, 17/2/11, p. 50

96   from the cape, Philip Ayres, *Mawson: A Life* (Melbourne University Press, Melbourne, 1999), p. 35

97   disembarking immediately, Priestley, 18/2/11, MS 298/14/1
    'said so decidedly', Levick [date given as 13 February], loc. cit.
    over probability, Priestley, 18/2/11, loc. cit.

98   'the Eastern Party', Abbott, 18/2/11, loc. cit.
    'glacier ice', Dickason, 18/2/11, loc. cit.
    'admiring the poultry etc.' Priestley, loc. cit.
    'large aviary', Abbott, 18/2/11, loc. cit.

99   meat in hand, Dickason, 2/3/11, loc. cit.

100 last letters home, Browning, 'Monday', February, loc. cit.
    near the window, Abbott, 21/2/11, loc. cit.
    'was quite early', Browning, 'Tuesday', February, loc. cit.
    'Lyttleton once more', Abbott, loc. cit.
    'which had disappeared', Priestley, 20/2/11, loc. cit.
    'North to New Zealand', Campbell, *WM* [18/2/11], p. 50

'along the coast', Scott, *SLE*, vol. 2, p. 81

101 if not impossible, Priestley, 17/2/11, MS 298/14/1

102 'loving Coz Vic', Campbell, 18/2/11, MS 1363/1–4
'bucked up immensely', Bruce to KS, March 1911, MS 1488/2

103 'shall be caught', Bruce to KS, 27/2/11, loc. cit.
were short-handed, Bruce, 20/2/11, loc. cit.
checking the compass, BAE Reports, vol. 1, MS 280/28/1
'smooth as clockwork', Bruce to KS, 27/2/11, loc. cit.

104 pack ice conditions, Scott, 'Orders', no date, in Scott, *Diaries*
'having lost it', Priestley, 20/2/11, loc. cit.
'staggering about', Priestley, 21/2/11, loc. cit.

105 'pretty good doing', Scott, *Journals*, 17/2/11, p. 127

106 'kind of hurrah party', Cherry-Garrard, 17/2/11, loc. cit.
'man of 42', Cherry-Garrard, 22/2/11, loc. cit.
Cherry described: for following quotes see Cherry-Garrard, 23-24/2/11,
holograph diary MS 559/3, and typescript diary MS 559/18/1–4

107 'never touched', Wilson, *Terra Nova*, 22/2/11
'this season', Pennell, *SLE*, vol. 2, p. 361
'Expedition in particular', Bruce, 22/2/11, loc. cit.
'cliffy coast-line', Pennell, loc. cit.

108 'as an ideal day', Scott, 'Plans', *GJ*, vol. 36, no. 1.
'do it again!', Bruce, 26/2/11, loc. cit.

109 agonizing throat, Campbell, *WM*, 3/3/11, p. 53
'An unsavoury mess', Priestley, 27/2/11, loc. cit.
the acetylene plant; see drawing of hut interior, Priestley, after entry for
29/11/11, MS 298/6/4

110 'felt pretty bad', Priestley, 3/3/11, loc. cit.
'the dread scurvy', Levick, 12/3/11, loc. cit.
decomposing material, BAE Reports, MS 281/28/2, p. 11
'having to kill them', Levick, 12/3/11, loc. cit.
impassable for sledging, Levick, 8/3/11, loc. cit.
'absolute prisoners', ibid.

111 sweethearts and wives, Dickason, loc. cit.
'we are jubilant', Bruce to KS, 4/3/11, loc. cit.

112 'all the Party', Abbott, 10/3/11, loc. cit.
'quite fond of him', Levick, 14/3/11, MS 1637; D
'arrival at Lyttleton', Abbott, 15/3/11, loc. cit.
'will be serious', Bruce, 14/3/11, loc. cit.
'damaged somewhere', Bruce to KS, 21/3/11, loc. cit.

113 'want a chorus' and 'stuck to your muzzle', Priestley, 19/3/11, MS
298/14/2
'very apt pupils', Priestley, 21/3/11, MS 298/14/2
'full of trials', Levick, 23/3/11, loc. cit.

'few hours spell', Bruce to KS, 23/3/11, loc. cit.

114 'about people, though', Bruce to KS, 28/3/11, loc. cit.
'there's going to be', ibid.

115 'asleep by 11 P.M.', Campbell, *WM*, 27/3/11, pp. 62–3
'In fact', see entries for 27/3/11 in diaries of Eastern party members

116 'if by myself', Abbott, 31/3/11, loc. cit.
'it is simply grand', ibid.

117 'do it all right!', KS to RS, 12/4/11, letter 363, MS 1853: BJ, vol. 11
'what that was', Mrs Lysaght to Mawson, 26/3/11, MS 79 11AAE, The
Australian Polar Collection
priorities shifted, Shackleton to his wife, Fisher, *Shackleton*, p. 127
'the game better', KS to RS, Pound, *Scott of the Antarctic*, p. 238

118 'from our programme', *GJ*, vol. 37 no. 6
'in advance', Darwin, *GJ*, vol. 37, no. 6

119 'for the south', ibid.
through other ways, Max Jones, *The Last Great Quest: Captain Scott's
Antarctic Sacrifice* (Oxford University Press, Oxford, 2003), p. 75
didn't speak to him, KS to RS, Pound, *Scott of the Antarctic*, p. 239
low-key, L. B. Quartermaine, *South to the Pole: The Early History of the Ross
Sector* (Oxford University Press, Oxford, 1967), pp. 253–4
Scott's expedition, Mawson, *Mawson's Antarctic Diaries*, pp. 55–6. See also
KS to RS, 8/5/11, in Pound, *Scott of the Antarctic*, p. 244
'dislikes you', KS to RS, diary, 24/5/11; Pound, *Scott of the Antarctic*,
p. 245

120 'any other direction', Markham, *GJ*, vol. 36, no. 1
'could be imagined', Mawson, *Mawson's Antarctic Diaries*, p. 55

121 'went to bed', Priestley, sledging song, 4th verse, 18/4/11 (in diary after
22/4/11), MS 298/14/2
'as hard as nails', Levick, 4/6/11, loc. cit.

122 haphazard manner, Priestley, 12/7/11, MS 298/6/4
'very devout', Priestley, 13/5/11, MS 298/14/2
'awfully pleased', Priestley, 6/1/11, MS 198
'the same strain' and subsequent quotes in this paragraph, Levick, 6/4/11,
loc. cit.

123 'living and messing', Levick, 6/4/11, loc. cit.
'losing their heads', ibid.
owners' requirements, Levick, 8/3/11, loc. cit.
'winter months', Levick, 12/3/11, loc. cit.

124 'lacking in guts', Levick, 6/4/11, loc. cit.
'overstepped the mark', ibid.

125 'unpleasantness arising', ibid.
'question altogether' and subsequent quotes in this paragraph, Priestley,
16/4/11, 298/14/2

126 'another person', Levick, 20/4/11, loc. cit.
had personalities, Levick, 25/4/1, loc. cit.
'curled our hair', Priestley, 18/4/11, loc. cit.
'coast journey', Priestley, 13/5/11, loc. cit.

127 penetrate the interior, Borchgrevink, *First on the Antarctic*, pp. iv–v

128 not exaggerated, see Levick and Priestley, entries for 5/5/11, 7/5/11, 9/5/11, 2/8/11 and 16/8/11
of the ocean, Browning, 22/5/11, loc. cit.
by Browning, Dickason, 17/5/11, loc. cit.; see also Levick, 24 /5/11, loc. cit.
'I am responsible', Priestley, 2/6/11, loc. cit.

129 'future existence?', Priestley, 18/5/11, loc. cit.
in the galley, Levick, 15/4/11, loc. cit.
'"You blighter!"', Dickason, 14/6/11, loc. cit.
'out again', Abbott, 22/7/11, loc. cit.

130 make it easier, Priestley, 14/6/11 and 15/6/11, loc. cit.
'day by day', ibid.
'"Good bye hut", Priestley, 19/6/12, loc. cit.
'than he is', Levick, 11/6/11, loc. cit.
'is improving', Abbott, 16 /6/11, loc. cit.

131 'only knows', Levick, 4/6/11, loc. cit.
'living in hope', Abbott, 30/5/11, loc. cit.
he couldn't work, Priestley, 2/7/11, loc. cit.; Levick 4/6/11, loc. cit.

132 'range of temperature', Priestley, 2/7/11, loc. cit.
'the generators', Priestley, 18/8/11, loc. cit.

133 they had pictures, Priestley, 22/6/11, loc. cit.
'it was great', Abbott, 22/6/11, loc. cit.
'in the spring', Dickason, 22/6/11, loc. cit.

134 'round a teacher', Cherry-Garrard, 23/6/11, MS 559/18/1
and profile, reproduced in Thomas Griffith Taylor, *With Scott: The Silver Lining* (Bluntisham Books, Bluntisham, 1997), opp. p. 266
'competitor's camp', Gran, 22/6/11
his conclusions, Pennell to Mawson, 27/6/11 C: Pennell MS 182 AAE, The Australian Polar Collection

135 'midsummer festivities', Pound, *Scott of the Antarctic*, p. 246
'very slack', Levick, 24/6/11, loc. cit.
'of his fads', Levick, 2/7/11, loc. cit.

136 'another man', Levick, 15/7/11 and 18/7/11, loc. cit.
'in colour', Dickason, 1/7/11, loc. cit.
'look beautiful', Browning, loc. cit.
'the <u>noses</u>' , Dickason, 26/5/11, loc. cit.

137 'have made, nil', Priestley, 12/7/11, loc. cit.
'justice later', Priestley, see 2/6/11, MS 298/14/2

his sleep pattern, Priestley, 7/7/11, 11/7/11, loc. cit.

138 'my imperfections', Priestley, 9/7/11, MS 298/14/2
'before the swarm', Priestley, 20/7/22, MS 298/6/4
'acquisitive character', Priestley, 21/7/22, loc. cit.

139 'as we can', Dickason, 5/8/11, loc. cit.
closer and closer, Levick, 24/6/11, loc. cit.
for an operation, Campbell, see MS 280/8/2; BJ

140 'look after ourselves', Levick, 7/8/11, loc. cit.
'hard and fit', Priestley, 27/7/11, loc. cit.
'desperate hard pulling', Campbell, *WM*, 29/7/11

141 'turns to ice', Campbell, *WM*, 1/8/11, p. 75
'carried as one garment', BAE Reports, MS 280/28/2 and B(TN) AE
1910–1913, *Miscellaneous Data* compiled by Colonel H. G. Lyons, 1924

142 'over gravel', Campbell, 2/8/11, *WM*, p. 78
next squall, ibid.
sopping wet, Abbott, see detailed account, 2/8/11, loc. cit.

143 'flapping canvas', Priestley, *Antarctic Adventure*, pp. 129–31
'to sleep', Abbott, loc. cit.
'after a good Dinner', Abbott, 3–4/8/11, loc. cit.

144 'as we can', Dickason, 5/8/11, loc. cit.
'to own up', Priestley, 6/8/11, MS 298/6/4

145 'previous experience', Priestley, 12/7/11, MS 298/6/4
'meteorologist, etc. etc. etc.', Campbell, 8/8/11, *WM*, p. 79
of the other four, Abbott, 8–10/8/11, loc. cit.
for his family, Priestley, 12/7/11, MS 290/6/4
'I am used to', Priestley, 11/8/11, MS 298/6/4

146 boasted to himself, Priestley, 7/8/11, loc. cit.
were thorough, Priestley, 25/8/11, loc. cit.
at Cape Adare, see L. Bernacchi, *To the South Polar Regions: Expedition of
1898–1900* (Bluntisham Books, Denton, 1991)
'what we have', Priestley, 30/8/11, loc. cit.

147 'whoever they are', Abbott, 12/8/11, loc. cit.
'lawn mowing', Scott, *Journals,* 11/8/11, p. 266
members of the shore party, see Scott, 'The Southern Journey 1911-1912',
8/5/11, in 'South Polar Times', MS 505/5

148 a good performance, Scott, 14/8/11, *Journals*, p. 267
'with his animals', Gran, 13/8/11, p. 117
−40°F., Wright, *Silas*, p. 157
'the next explorer', Priestley, 14/8/11, MS 298/6/4

150 'Cede Deo', Abbott, 16/8/11, loc. cit.
'in the future', Priestley, 16/8/11, loc. cit.
'store for us', Priestley, 16/8/11, loc. cit.
compete with him, Priestley, 19/8/11, loc. cit.

151 'is getting on', Scott to Kinsey, 28/10/11, Pound, *Scott of the Antarctic*, p. 256

difficult to tell, Campbell, *WM*, 21/8/11, p. 81

anatomy to Abbott, Abbott, 22/8/11, loc. cit.

152 'a slow death', Levick, as noted in Priestley, 21/8/11, MS 298/6/4

'to restrain them', Priestley, 23/8/11, loc. cit.

153 'hope dies hard', Priestley, 23/8/11, loc. cit.

for an increase, Priestley, 18/8/11, loc. cit.

'it nevertheless', Abbott, 27/8/11, loc. cit.

of their beach, Levick, 25/8/11, loc. cit.; Dickason, 25/8/11, loc. cit.

'I may not' and subsequent quotes in this paragraph, Priestley, 27/8/11, loc. cit.

154 roaring out shanties, Abbott, 8/9/11, loc. cit.

'while sledging', Abbott, 9/9/11, loc. cit.

155 'Dicko and Brownie', from 'Celebrities Who Live in Glass Houses', *South Polar Times*, vol. 3, part 3, October 1911, in Scott, *Diaries*, n. p.

'burly Irishman', Griffith Taylor, *With Scott: The Silver Lining*, p. 410

suggested the journey, Gran, 6/9/11, pp. 122–3

'to use skis', ibid.

weights carried, see Scott, 'The Southern Journey, Lecture in Winter Quarters Hut', 8/5/11, MS 505/1

156 of 10 lb, see Scott, 'The Plan of the Southern Journey', 13/9/11, MS 505/5

'conditions on record', Scott, 2/8/11; Scott, *Journals*, p. 255.

'entered the Polar regions', Scott, 10/9/11; Scott, *Journals*, p. 255–6

157 'we are eating', Dickason, 14/9/11, loc. cit.

'whilst singing', Dickason, 17/9/11, loc. cit.

'audience of one', in Priestley, 24/9/12, loc. cit.

try the thickness, Campbell, *WM*, 7/10/11, p. 94

158 search of better ice, Abbott, 7/10/11, loc. cit.

'up quickly. Finis', Dickason, 7/10/11, loc. cit.

'are over everything', Priestley, 8/10/11. loc. cit.

'without much hardship', Priestley, long summary, 8/10/11, 298/6/4

159 cliff and beach, Levick, 17/9/11, loc. cit.

' "bucker up" ', Levick, quoted in Katherine Lambert, *Hell with a Capital H: An Epic Story of Antarctic Survival* (Pimlico, London, 2002), p. 90

'and intelligently', ibid., p. 91

the sledging song, noted by Priestley, 25/10/11, MS 298/6/4

reduce the glare, Levick, 13/10/11, loc. cit.

160 'social habits', Levick's book, published in 1914, *Antarctic Penguins: A Study of their Social Habits*. Part 1 covered 'the Fasting Period' and Part 2 the 'Domestic Life of the Adélie Penguin'

'kicking up a row', Dickason, 20/11/11, loc. cit.

'this year at least', Priestley, 21/10/11, loc. cit.

'At the most but "yes" or "No."', ibid.

161 'done so much', ibid.

and to explore, Amundsen, *The South Pole*, vol. 2, p. 204

Victoria Land, and Campbell, see Evans, *South with Scott*, pp. 144–65

162 'for New Zealand', Gran, 20/10/11, p. 136

'ideal mentor and seconder', BAE Reports, MS 280/28/1–2

copy of each set, Wilson, *Terra Nova*, 22/10/11; see MS 280/28/1

'for the Pole', Wilson, 17/10/11, loc. cit.

orders to Pennell, Scott's instructions to Pennell, vol. 3, BAE 1910-13 (a), Plans

163 'barrier and see', Scott's instructions for Commanding Officer, *Terra Nova*, see 280/28/1

'our own little circle', Scott to Kinsey, 28/10/11, Pound, *Scott of the Antarctic*, p. 256

'in all directions', instructions to Lieutenant Victor Campbell, see 280/28/1

'to see your report', ibid.

'to let out first', RS to KS, letter 366a, 11/10/1911, MS 1853; BJ vol. 11

164 'fit for this work', RS to KS, ibid.

165 'our feelings', Priestley, 6/12/11, MS 298/6/4; BJ

'shark it', by 'Bluebell' (pseudonym for Levick), *The Adelie Mail & Cape Adare Times*, p. 19, MS GB15, 'Adelie Mail'

166 'next winter', ibid.

'helping me', Priestley, 22/10/11, loc. cit.

'every day', Priestley, 24/10/11, loc. cit.

'with mine', ibid.

167 'ideal sledging', Dickason, 8/11/11, MS 1634; D

'encumbered', Priestley, 22/10/11, 5/11/11, loc. cit.

used to it, Priestley, 22/10/11, loc. cit.

168 'my bare hands', 'PRIMUS', Dickason, 'Our Cooking Column', *The Adelie Mail & Cape Adare Times*, pp. 15–18

'our object (exploration)', Levick, 9/11/11, loc. cit.

169 'all the rest!', Lieutenant K. Prestrud, in Amundsen, *The South Pole*, vol. 2, p. 245

'may assist you', Pennell to Mawson, 10/11/11, C: Pennell, MS 182 AAE, The Australian Polar Collection

a second letter, ibid.

171 'Harry Pennel', ibid.

'can SMELL it!', Priestley, *Adelie Mail & Cape Adare Times*, p. 2

dining-room table, Priestley, 17/11/11, loc. cit.

'leaving New Zealand', Dickason, 2/12/11, loc. cit.

'along the coast', ibid.

all hands out, 11/12/11, ibid.; Campbell, *WM*, 12/12/12, p. 104

172 'in the future', Priestley, 11/12/11, loc. cit.
'of the collection', Priestley, 30/11/11, loc. cit.
'put in it', Priestley, 19/12/11, loc. cit.
'pebbles and seaweed', Priestley, 13/12/11, loc. cit.

173 'right to England', Priestley, 5/11/11, loc. cit.
'all lined up', Priestley, 29/11/11, loc. cit.
on the floor, ibid.

174 beards regrown, Priestley, 17/12/11, loc. cit.
'all be pleased', ibid., and Priestley, 20/12/11, loc. cit.
all rations in bags, Priestley, 25/12/11, MS 298/6/5; BJ
for four men, Priestley, 19/12/11, MS 298/6/4; BJ
gramophone concert, Dickason, 25/12/11, loc. cit.

175 'quite cheery', Bruce, 25/12/11, MS 402/1–4
Pennell, *SLE*, vol. 2, p. 374
out to sea, J. K. Davis, *With the 'Aurora' in the Antarctic, 1911–1914* (Bluntisham Books, Bluntisham, 2007) pp. 21–2

176 made by Birdie, Cherry-Garrard, 25/4/11, MS 559/18/1–4
had been successful, Simpson diaries, 'Summary' 31/12/11, MS 1097/49

177 'the Barrier again', ibid.
'at Cape Evans', Bowers to Simpson, no date, MS 704/4
'or nonexistent', Scott to Simpson, 24/11/11

177 'Lat 81.15', ibid.
Nelson and Clissold, account of these decisions in Simpson, loc. cit.
back to Kathleen, RS to KS, 24/11/11, MS 1853; BJ, vol. 2

178 'in the world', Cherry-Garrard, 25/12/11, MS 559/18/1–4
'things for ever', ibid.
inches per man, Wright, *Silas*, 25/12/11, p. 225
extra two weeks, Scott, *Journals*, p. 499, n.; also Atkinson, MS 280/28/2, vol. 2, p. iv

179 cold, said Scott, Scott, *Journals*, 25/12/11
on 10 December, RS to KS, 10/12/11, MS 1853; BJ, vol. 2
on 21 December, RS to KS, 21/12/11, loc. cit.

180 careful hands, Janet Crawford, *That First Antarctic Winter: The Story of the Southern Cross Expedition of 1898–1900 as Told in the Diaries of Louis Charles Bernacchi* (South Latitude Research Ltd, Canterbury, 1998), p. 158
'point of view', Priestley, 28/12/11, MS 298/6/5: BJ
'severely pecked', Priestley, 28/12/11, ibid.

182 'if nothing else!', Campbell, *WM*, 15/1/12, p. 115
of possessions, Dickason, 3/1/12, MS 1634; D
see six men, Bruce, 3/1/12, loc. cit.
'we could', Levick, 4/1/12, loc. cit.
everything was aboard, Bruce, 4/1/12, loc. cit.

183 'a sinful shame', Levick, loc. cit.

'a weird pirate', Bruce, 6/1/12, loc. cit.

according to Priestley, Priestley, 8/1/12, loc. cit.

184 'dozen spikes in each', ibid.

one actually landed, Pennell, MS 14; also Campbell, *WM*, 8/1/12, p. 112;
Levick, 10/1/12, MS 1637

dogs a run, Priestley, 8/1/12, MS 1097/4

'two miles to land', Bruce, 8/1/12, loc. cit.

next to a moraine, Priestley, 8/1/12, MS 1097/4

obtain their position, Dickason, 8/1/12, MS 1634; D

185 on 18 February, Campbell, *WM*, 8/1/12

steaming away, Dickason, 8/1/12, loc. cit.

'scenery lovely', Campbell, 8/1/12, MS 280/8/1

'At last science!', Priestley, 8/1/12, loc. cit.

country ahead, Levick, 9/1/12, MS 1423/1

186 'a bit desolate', Levick, 13/1/12, loc. cit.

'dickens of a twist', Priestley, 9/1/12, loc. cit.

'weeks slipping by', Campbell, *WM*, 15/1/12, p. 115

'death to me', Priestley, 16/1/12, loc. cit.

'sick of waiting', Priestley, 18/1/12, loc. cit.

'heartbreaking damned mornings', Levick, 23/1/12, MS 1637

'pure hell', Priestley, 23/1/12, MS 1097/4

187 the granite bowl, Priestley, 20/1/12, loc. cit.

by Abbott, Levick, 27/1/12, MS 1637; D and MS 1423/1

'wish to have', Levick, 17/1/11, MS 1637: D

inexhaustible repertoire, Levick, 3/2/12, loc. cit.

'wise at bottom', 'South Polar Times', vol. 3, October 1911; Scott, *Diaries*,
vol. 4, n.p.

188 in thirty hours, see Shirase, *Antarctica: The Japanese South Polar Expedition of
1910–12*

like a pine, Campbell, 1/2/12, MS 280/8/1

189 'to go home first', Priestley, 2/2/12, loc. cit.

eleven a side, Priestley, 3/2/12, loc. cit.

190 'this hanging about', Bruce, 1/2/12, loc. cit.

'heard in an hour', Simpson, 3/2/12, MS 1097/49; also MS 704/1–4

'the Pole practically sure', Bruce, 3/2/12, loc. cit.

'Births, Marriages and Deaths', Cherry-Garrard, 3/2/12, MS 559/18/1–4

inventory of achievements, Cherry-Garrard, 4–5/2/12, loc. cit.

191 'not up to it', Simpson, 6 /2/12, loc. cit.

'Scott at once', 11/6/11, loc. cit.

'work down here', RS to KS, letter 366, Oct 1911, MS 1853; BJ, vol. 2

'if I am wanted', Simpson, 6/2/12, loc. cit.

'if they want me', Simpson, 18/2/11, loc. cit.

be carried out, Bruce, 3/2/12, MS 402/1–4
'very long business', Bruce, 8/2/12, loc. cit.
192 'happy go lucky way', Priestley, 6/2/12, loc. cit.
'what we have', Levick, 7/2/12, MS 1423/1; D
'Bothersome', Levick, 8/3/12, loc. cit.
193 'naval quack', Priestley, 10/2/12, loc. cit.
'all complete', Levick, 11/2/12, loc. cit.
'most interesting find', ibid.
discovered rookery, ibid.
194 'grim though necessary murder', Priestley, 13/2/12, MS 1097/4
ski turns, Campbell, *WM*, 13/2/12
'immediate neighbourhood', Priestley, 14/2/12, loc. cit.
'haphazard cook', ibid.
the roles in turns, Levick, 16/2/12, MS 1637
195 'any minute now', Priestley, 17/2/11, loc. cit.
'plucked up', Gran, 15/2/11
'bearded persons', Bruce, 15/2/12, loc. cit.
196 'both parties', Gran, 15/2/12 and 16/2/12
197 'this Expedition', Cherry-Garrard, 26/1/13, MS 559/18/1–4
'ought to arrive', and subsequent quote, Campbell, 18/2/12, MS 280/8/1
new diary, Priestley, MS 1097/4
198 'harder than ever', Campbell, 19–21/2/12, MS 280/8/1
'beggar description', Priestley, 22/2/12, loc. cit.
attacks of cramp, ibid.
all their food, Priestley, 23/2/12, loc. cit.
199 'exchange news', ibid.
on her way here, Levick, 23/2/12, MS 1423/1
200 'ahead or astern', Bruce, 23/2/12, MS 402/1–4
'even for months', Gran, 23/2/12, p. 173
'to get near them', Bruce, 24/2/12, loc. cit.
line of pack ice, Campbell, 24/2/12, MS 280/8/1
201 to the ship, see BAE Reports, MS 280/28, p. xi
'ask Cherry', 22/2/12, MS 1178/1–2; D
'meet Capt Scott', Simpson, 23/2/12, MS 704/1–4; MS 1097/49
202 'to go to meet Captain Scott', ibid.
'with the dogs', ibid.
zoological notebook, Cherry-Garrard, MS 559/7; 135
had gone under, Cherry-Garrard, 15/6/11, MS 559/18/1–4
203 'the electric force', Cherry-Garrard, 8/5/11, loc. cit.
'dog teams', Cherry-Garrard, 24/2/12, MS 559/7; 135
'easy beginning', Cherry-Garrard, 26/2/12, loc. cit.
204 'are all well', Cherry-Garrard to Scott, 26/2/11, MS 559/11; BJ
'in the spring', Campbell, 25/2/12 and 26/2/12, MS 280/8/1

'of the latter', Priestley, 27/2/12, loc. cit.

wetness again, Priestley, 29/2/12, loc. cit.

'a winter here', and subsequent quotes in this paragraph, Levick, 29/3/12, MS 1423/1

205 'before coming away', Levick, 29/2/12, loc. cit.

'to the worst', Priestley, 29/2/12, loc. cit.

206 'in a difficulty', Simpson, 25/2/12, loc. cit.

'until something happens', Gran, 26/2/12, p. 176

207 poisoned scratch, Cherry-Garrard, 18/2/12, loc. cit.

'pick up Campbell now', Bruce, 29/2/12, loc. cit.

'we got her moving', Bruce, 2/3/12, loc. cit.

fairly simple, ibid.

208 'makes us tired', Priestley, 1/3/12, MS 1097/4

'for the winter', Campbell, 1/3/12, loc. cit.

'cheeriest of the party', Priestley, 1/3/12, loc. cit.

an honorary officer, see Raymond Priestley, 'The Psychology of Exploration', *Psyche*, 2 (1921–2), pp. 18–28

'territorial limits', ibid.

209 'very anxious', Levick, 3/3/12, MS 1423/1

'is too awful', Campbell, 4/3/12, loc. cit.

'waiting & thinking', Cherry-Garrard, 8/3/12, loc. cit.

Tuesday 5 March, Campbell, 5/3/12, loc. cit.

210 'during the winter', Priestley, 7/3/12, loc. cit.

'days have been', Levick, 7/3/12, MS 1423/1

'if Capt Scott wished', Simpson, 4/3/12, loc. cit.

'for much writing', Bruce, 4/3/12, loc. cit.

'know it is futile', Bruce, 6/3/12, loc. cit.

'a wearying time', Pennell to KS, 'northbound march', 1488/2

'for New Zealand', Simpson, no date, loc. cit.

211 'weary waiting', Abbott, letter, 2/2/13, MS 1965: D

for the expedition, BAE Reports, MS 280/28/1, vol. 1, 'Formation of the Expedition'

of the party, Priestley, 10/3/12, MS 1097/4

salt water, Campbell, 15/3/12, MS 280/8/1

'not bad eating', Campbell, 16/3/12, loc. cit.

212 'our winter home', Priestley, 8/3/12, loc. cit.

'to each other', Priestley, 13/3/12, loc. cit.

'at present', Campbell, *WM*, 15/3/12, p. 127

213 'second winter', Priestley, 15/3/12, loc. cit.

then ice, ibid.

214 and worried, Cherry-Garrard, 18/3/12 and 19/3/12, MS 559/7; 135

215 'round the coast', and subsequent quotes in this paragraph, Cherry-Garrard, 16/3/12, loc. cit.

cat drowned, Griffith Taylor, *With Scott*, p. 428

216 lost his compass, Priestley, 17/3/12, loc. cit.
'life together,' ibid.
'out of it', Campbell, 18/3/12, loc. cit.
'remember many', Priestley, 17/3/12, loc. cit.
'never stop?', Priestley, 18/3/12, loc. cit.
had gone down, Priestley, 19/3/12, loc. cit.

217 circulation going, see Levick, 19/3/12 and 20/3/12, MS 1423/1
to the ice-cave, ibid.
'squashed flat', Campbell, 19/3/12, MS 280/8/1

218 'pretty miserable', Levick, 20/3/12, loc. cit.
'simply famished', Priestley, 20/3/12, loc. cit.

219 in its throat, Priestley, 21/3/12, loc. cit.
naval tobacco, Priestley, 23/3/12, loc. cit.
meat and blubber, Priestley, 30/3/12, loc. cit.
'fate of the ship', Priestley, 23/3/12, loc. cit.

220 'height of 5 feet 6 inches, Abbott, MS 1965; D

221 'living on seal', Cherry-Garrard, 25/3/12, MS 559/7; 135
'that were adverse', BAE Reports, MS 280/28/1
'yesterday afternoon', Cherry-Garrard, 25/3/12, loc. cit.
'looking for them', Cherry-Garrard, 26/3/12, loc. cit.

222 personal possessions, Campbell, 26/3/12, MS 280/8/1
'hole it is too', Levick, 28/3/12, MS 1637; D

223 'loafed a lot', Priestley, 31/3/12, MS 10974; BJ
'temperatures and wind', Wright, *Silas*, p. 268
'that we can do', Cherry-Garrard, 2/4/12, MS 559/7; 135
Atkinson or Campbell, Cherry-Garrard, 3/4/12, loc. cit.
'in a sardine tin', Griffith Taylor, *With Scott*, p. 434

224 'under a cloud', Simpson, April 1913, MS 1097/49

225 'to be alright', RS to KS, 3/1/12, loc. cit.
'Victor and his party', Mrs Campbell to KS, MS 1453/59; D

226 'in many ways', Levick, 1/4/12, MS 1423/2; BJ
'this weather', Campbell, 26/3/12, MS 280/8/1; BJ

227 'half collapsed', Levick, 3/4/12, loc. cit.
psoriasis, Levick, 26/4/12, loc. cit.
conjunctivitis, Levick, 15/4/12, loc. cit.
'from the old quarter', Levick, 6/4/12, loc. cit.
'of a sense', Levick, 1/4/12, loc. cit.

228 'we can get', Priestley, 7/4/12, MS 1097/4
'polar party's coming', Gran, p. 187
what had happened, ibid.

229 'up with them', Wright, *Silas*, 11/4/12, p. 268
'happened to Campbell', Cherry-Garrard, 16/4/12, loc. cit.

'not be done', Cherry-Garrard, ibid.

'causelessly alarmed', Wright, *Silas*, 11/4/12, p. 268

230 'to go south', ibid.

Nelson, the biologist, *SLE*, vol. 2, p. 314

'long a period', Williamson, 14/4/12, MS 774/2

'hut creaking', Cherry-Garrard, 11/4/12, loc. cit.

'in the least', Williamson, 20/4/12, loc. cit.

231 'look at that!' Atkinson, *SLE*, vol. 2, p. 314

'he will winter', Cherry-Garrard, 23/4/12, loc. cit.

'and dangerous trip', Cherry-Garrard, 23/4/12, loc. cit; see also Cherry-Garrard, 'Copy of Atkinson's Diary of Western Trip', MS 559/7; 135

'poor fellows', Williamson, 23/4/12, loc. cit.

season's sledging, Cherry-Garrard, 2/5/12, loc. cit.

232 around his mouth, Priestley, 14/4/12, loc. cit.

'rotten day . . . over', Levick, 12/4/12, MS 1423/2; BJ

'of home away', Priestley, 2/4/12, loc. cit.

on a farm, Priestley, 3/4/12, loc. cit.

233 Dickason's nerves, Dickason, 30/5/12; Lambert, '*Hell with a Capital H*', p. 134

'butter, and biscuits', Levick, 12/5/12, loc. cit.

always closed, see Priestley, 'The Psychology of Exploration', pp. 27–8

appeared again, Priestley, 18/4/12, loc. cit.

235 constructed an outer door, Levick, 21/4/12, 23/4/12, MS 1423/2; BJ

a clearer flame, Levick, 26/4/12, loc. cit.

'bill yet', Levick, 4/5/12, loc. cit.

236 winter breeding, see Priestley, 6/5/12, loc. cit.; Levick 7/5/12, loc. cit.; Campbell 6/5/12, MS 280/8/1

237 'happy & contented', Levick, 6/5/12, loc. cit.

with filth, Priestley, 6/5/12, loc. cit.

'of fat on top', Priestley, 7/5/12, loc. cit.

'back to us', Campbell, 7/5/12, loc. cit.

'at C. Adair', Levick, 4/5/12, loc. cit.

only survivors?, Levick, 12/5/12, loc. cit.

near the ceiling, Priestley, 9/5/12, loc. cit.

'10 raisins', Campbell, 10/5/12, loc. cit.

238 'old times', Dickason, 10/5/12, MS 1065; MJ

'never does', Levick, 12/5/12, loc. cit.

'do the same', Levick, 17/5/12, loc. cit.

'poor devil', Levick, 15/5/12, loc. cit.

did not mention it, Levick, 17/5/12, loc. cit.

and dream, Priestley, 16/5/12, loc. cit.

'feel fit', Priestley, 22/5/12, loc. cit.

239 'smallest limit', Levick, 28/5/12, loc. cit.

'our dug out', Campbell, 17/5/12, loc. cit.

seal's brain, Priestley, 17/5/12, loc. cit.

their clothes, Priestley, 18/5/12, loc. cit.

'care about', Priestley, 24/5/12, loc. cit.

240 pathway for air, Priestley, loc. cit.; Levick, loc. cit.; Campbell, *WM*; see entries for 25/5/12

bamboo frame, Campbell, 27/5/12, MS 280/8/1

tearing sound, Priestley, 2/6/12, MS 298/14/3

'very necessary', Priestley, 28/5/12, loc. cit.

'to accumulate', Levick, 27/5/12

'as mess men', Priestley, 29/5/12

'at present', ibid.

241 'useful some day', Priestley, 30/5/12, loc. cit.

improved the hoosh, Priestley, 31/5/12, loc. cit.

'in July', ibid.

242 'on the other', Pennell to Sir Lewis Beaumont, no date, 1912, from 'Elmslie Bay, The Sounds, NZ', MS 14 P

wood chips, Dickason, 7/5/12, loc. cit.

243 hair socks, Priestley, 21/6/12, MS 238/14/3

'not unhappy', Levick, 3/6/12, MS 1423/1

'Antarctic Expeditions', Priestley, 6/6/12, loc. cit.

'relieve ourselves', Priestley, 5/6/12, loc. cit.

hungrier afterwards, Priestley, 14/7/12, MS 298/14/3

among the others, Priestley, 6/6/12, loc. cit.

244 of biscuit, Priestley, 14/6/12, loc. cit.; Campbell, 14/6/12; Levick, 14/6/12

everyone else's, Cherry-Garrard, 14/6/12, MS 559/18/4; Gran, 16/6/12, p. 202

245 'reached it', Gran, 16/6/12, p. 202

or the other, Cherry-Garrard, 14/6/12, loc. cit.

'every luck', Williamson, 14/6/12, loc. cit.

full bellies, Priestley, 18/6/12, MS 298/14/3

'of wincarnis', Campbell, MS 280/8/1

246 'do not bend me', Levick, written in back of MS 1423/2

'the darkness', Cherry-Garrard, 22/6/12, MS 559/18/1-4

unutterably miserable, BAE Reports, MS 280/28/2

geology trip, Cherry-Garrard, 14/4/12, MS 559/7; 135

'lot of good', BAE Reports, MS 280/28/2

'in our belts', Priestley, 23/6/12, MS 298/14/3

247 and Saturday, Priestley, 27/6/12, loc. cit.

sledging song, Priestley, 23/6/12, loc. cit.

'pretty close', Priestley, 21/6/12, loc. cit.

'utmost straits', Priestley, 4/7/12, loc. cit.

248 'real existence', Priestley, 30/6/12, MS 298/14/3
'but only temporarily', Levick, 4/7/11, MS 1423/2
days' hooshes, Priestley, 6/7/12, loc. cit.
near asphyxiation, Priestley, 7/7/12, loc. cit.
'Dickason down', Campbell, 10/7/12, MS 280/8/1; BJ

249 'rejoicing this evening', ibid.
'missed the fun', Priestley, 10/7/12, MS 298/14/3
'very short', Levick, MS 1423/2
'surroundings', ibid.
the bone, Priestley, see *Antarctic Adventure*, p. 317
'sorry to say', Levick, 11/7/12, loc. cit.

250 'at his request', Levick, 14/7/12, loc. cit.
to decipher, Campbell, 11/7/12, loc. cit.
'kill them', Browning, 12/7/12, loc. cit.
'luck has changed', Priestley, 12/7/12, MS 298/14/3
'SEAVIEW', Priestley, 10/8/12, loc. cit.
a coincidence, Priestley, 19/7/12, loc. cit.

251 'bottle it up', Levick, 28/7/12, loc. cit.
'at present', Levick, 27/7/12, loc. cit.

252 'safety, of the ship', Priestley, 29/7/12, MS 298/14/3
'doubt about it', Levick, 30/7/12, MS 1423/2
used to be, Levick, 2/8/12, loc. cit.
for sledging, Priestley, 22/7/12, loc. cit.

253 'in the sky', Gran, 16/6/12, reporting Atkinson on 14 June, p. 202
'about outside', Levick, 7/8/12, MS 1423/2
'plaster of Paris wall', Priestley, 1/8/12, MS 298/14/3
'party any day', ibid.

254 'to us', Levick, 2/8/12, loc. cit.
'of the brain', Priestley, 5/8/12, loc. cit.
in the extreme, Priestley, 2/6/12, loc. cit.
'down here', Priestley, 5/8/12, loc. cit.
'simply wonderful', Levick, 30/5/12, loc. cit.
'and fit', Levick, 3/7/12, loc. cit.
stomach pains, Levick, 14/8/12, loc. cit.

255 'you told me', notes between Levick and Campbell, 8/8/12, written in MS 1423/2
'even for us', Levick, 10/8/12, loc. cit.
'months ago', Priestley, 10/8/12, loc. cit.
'us first', Priestley, 13/8/12, loc. cit.
'wind helmet', Campbell, 12/8/12, loc. cit.
Hell's Gate, Priestley, 15/8/12, loc. cit.
'turn up', Campbell, 13/8/12, loc. cit.
'me return', Campbell, 14/8/12, loc. cit.

256 'all the time', Levick, 2/8/12, loc. cit.
against it, Priestley, 15/8/12, loc. cit.
'for life', Priestley, 10/9/12, loc. cit.
'or another', Priestley, 15/8/12, loc. cit.
'any day', Priestley, 1/8/12, loc. cit.

257 'for granted', Priestley, 12/8/12, loc. cit.
'in for', Levick, 14/8/12, loc. cit.
'good omen', Campbell, 20/8/12, loc. cit.

258 their faces, Priestley, 26/8/12, loc. cit.
march south, Campbell, 20/8/12, loc. cit.
had been seen, Priestley, 28/8/12, loc. cit.

259 'on the other', Pennell to Beaumont, MS 14, no date
desperately needy, Levick, 5/9/12, loc. cit.
disappearing fast!, Levick, 6/9/12, loc. cit.

260 cut up meat, Levick, 3/9/12, loc. cit.
'for sledging', Levick, 4/9/12, loc. cit.
'for marching', Priestley, 8/9/12, loc. cit.
'that's a fact', Levick, 10/9/12, MS 1423/2

261 still ill, Levick, 14/9/12, loc. cit.
'of his guts', Levick, 11/9/12, loc. cit.
'suspicious', Levick, 14/9/12, loc. cit.
by 4.10 p.m., Dickason, in Lambert, *Hell with a Capital 'H'*, p. 134
over his bag, Priestley, 13/9/12

262 'without any trouble', date not given, Levick, MS 1423/2; BJ
diarrhoea, ibid.
'of this party', no date, quoted in Lambert, *Hell with a Capital 'H'*, p. 134
'poor chap', Campbell, 14/9/12, MS 280/8/1
'except seal', ibid.

263 'damned nuisance', Levick, 22/9/12, loc. cit.
Priestley and Browning, Levick, 24/9/12, loc. cit.
from its meat, Campbell, 24/9/12, loc. cit.; Levick, 24/9/12, loc. cit.

264 'all I hope', Priestley, 25/9/12, MS 1097/4
'no demur', Levick, 25/9/12, loc. cit.
'panic again', Levick, 27/9/12, loc. cit.
another week, ibid.
'a sledge', Levick, 28/9/12, loc. cit.
'snow in PM', Campbell, 30/9/12, MS 280/8/2; BJ

265 summer hats, Campbell, lists, MS 280/8/1
'on the move', Priestley, 30/9/12, MS 1097/4
right-hand man, see Atkinson, 'Careers of Members', BAE Papers, vol. 1,
MS 280/28/1

266 'ordinary mortals', Levick, 7/10/12, MS 1423/1
with diarrhoea, Priestley, 1/10/12, MS 1097/4

'our recent life', Levick, 1/10/12, loc. cit.

267 'a horse', Priestley, 2/10/12, loc. cit.
'to discomfort', Priestley, 4/10/12, loc. cit.
'bags and wait', Campbell, *WM*, 5/10/12, p. 157
'no place for invalids', Priestley, 3/10/12, loc. cit.
'backbreaking work', Priestley, 5/10/12, loc. cit.
'to sledge on', Levick, 6/10/12, loc. cit.
cut Dickason's, Priestley, 6/10/12, loc. cit.

268 and pig-faced, Campbell, no date, MS 280/8/2; BJ
greater efforts, Priestley, 'Psychology of Exploration', p. 18
them all good, Levick, 7/10/12, loc. cit.
'about us tonight', Priestley, 6/10/12, loc. cit.
sharp drop, Levick, 8/10/12, loc. cit.

269 'heavy pulling', Campbell, 8/10/12, loc. cit.
'stiff as ever', Priestley, 10/10/12, loc. cit.
'great spirits', Levick, 10/10/12, loc. cit.
'rid of it', Priestley, 10/10/12, loc. cit.
'for a rest', Campbell, 11/10/12, loc. cit.

270 'our hoosh', Priestley, 11/10/12, loc. cit.
'view of him', Levick, 11/10/12, loc. cit.
the rear strut, Priestley, 12/10/12, loc. cit.
added weight, Priestley, 13/10/12, loc. cit.
'behind us', Priestley, 12/10/12, loc. cit.
'jammed hard on', Priestley, 13/10/12, loc. cit.

271 'hardest day yet', ibid.
'bad day after all', Campbell, 14/10/12, loc. cit.
'spring sledging', Priestley, 15/10/12, loc. cit.
'wearisome', Campbell, 16/10/12, loc. cit.
'quite done', Levick, 16/10/12, loc. cit.
'which we did', Campbell, 16/10/12, ibid

272 'advised their use', Levick, 17/10/12, loc. cit.
'without the sledges', Priestley, 17/10/12, loc. cit.
'heavy work', Priestley, 18/10/12, loc. cit.
'in snow', ibid.
'our Winter!', Levick, 18/10/12, loc. cit.

273 'starvation to come', Priestley, 18/10/12, loc. cit.
'been successful', Campbell, 19/10/12, loc. cit.
'minute easy', Levick, 19/10/12, loc. cit.
'I suppose', ibid.
'hour after hour', Levick, 20/10/12, loc. cit.

274 'lowest limit', Levick, ibid
'better marches', Priestley, 20/10/12, loc. cit.
heard no criticism, Beaumont to Mrs Scott, 20/10/12, MS 2/15

'making for Cape Evans', Priestley, 21/10/12, loc. cit.
'did not eat him', Priestley, 22/10/12, MS 1097/4

275 '1, 2, 3, – Heave!', Priestley, 22/10/12, loc. cit.
'were shattered', ibid.
to recover, Priestley, 23/10/12, loc. cit.
'to relieve us', ibid.
on the Barrier, Cherry-Garrard, 4/10/12, 9/10/12, MS 559/9

276 bad effect on others, Levick, 24/10/12, loc. cit.
smelling of smitch, Priestley, 24/10/12, loc. cit.
'tried to avoid it', ibid.
'to the mark', Priestley, 26/10/12, loc. cit.
'them leaving us', Priestley, 24/10/12, loc. cit.

277 snow-blind, Priestley, 25/10/12, op, cit.
'geology has begun', Priestley, 26/10/12, loc. cit.
last few weeks, Levick, 26/10/12, loc. cit.

278 'specimens myself', Priestley, 26/10/12, loc. cit.
'finding the depot', ibid.
his sledging notebook, Levick, 26/10/12, loc. cit.

279 'decent food', Priestley, 27/10/12, loc. cit

280 'time of it', Williamson, 27/11/12, MS 774/2
'present habitation', Priestley, 28/10/12, loc. cit.
'very hungry one', ibid.

281 'collar about it', ibid.
'please God', ibid.
'igloo winter', ibid.
'domestic economy', Priestley, 29/10/12, loc. cit.

282 'in the drift', Cherry-Garrard, 26/11/12, MS 559/18/4

283 'plenty of biscuits', Priestley, 29/10/12, loc. cit.
'a grand treat', Levick, 29/10/12, loc. cit.
'for sledging', Priestley, 29/10/12, loc. cit.
'blown out', ibid.
Polar party, Levick, 29/10/12, loc. cit.

284 'late circumstances', ibid.
into his sleeping-bag, Campbell, *WM*, 29/10/12
fourteen biscuits, Cherry-Garrard, 26/11/12, loc. cit.
'dosed off again', Campbell, *WM*, 29/10/12
'ordinary luck', Priestley, 29/10/12, loc. cit.
'depleted of us', Priestley, 30/10/12, loc. cit.

285 specific craving, Levick, 30/10/12, loc. cit.
'winter at Ross Island', Priestley, 30/10/12, loc. cit.
'of the depot', ibid.
'in consequence', Levick, 30/10/12, loc. cit.
'other of us', Priestley, 30/10/12, loc. cit.

Scott's visit, Priestley, 31/10/12, loc. cit.
286 about the biscuits, Priestley, 1/11/12, loc. cit.
287 'for a year', Levick, 1/11/12, loc. cit.
'glee and anticipation', Priestley, 2/11/12, loc. cit.
288 'pressure ice', ibid.
'up the coast', ibid.
'do a bust', Levick, 2/11/12, loc. cit.
'our digestions', Priestley, 2/11/12, loc. cit.
'had happened', Levick, 2/11/12, loc. cit.
289 'the depot', Levick, 4/11/12, loc. cit.
'the sick list', ibid.
290 'of Erebus', Priestley, 4/11/12, loc. cit.
'Butter Point depot', Priestley, 5/11/12, loc. cit.
'between meals', ibid.
'to safety', ibid.
291 'lunch tomorrow', Priestley, 6/11/12, loc. cit.
'news I hope', ibid.
'the other unit', Levick, 6/11/12, loc. cit.
'news for us', Priestley, 6/11/12, loc. cit.
'sad news', Campbell, *WM*, 6/11/12
'Day & Oates', Priestley, 6/11/12, loc. cit.
'the winter', Levick, 6/11/12, loc. cit.
'in vain', Priestley, 6/11/12, loc. cit.
292 'last year', Levick, 6/11/12, loc. cit.
'we turn up', ibid.
'by the news', Priestley, 7/11/12, loc. cit. (also in typescript 1097/4)
'Senior N.O.', Levick, 7/11/12, loc. cit.
smoke of Erebus, ibid.
293 relieved by the ship, Priestley, 9/11/12, MS 1097/4; BJ
have been worse, ibid.
'of the Antarctic', ibid.
'wanted to stay', ibid.
'around the face', Levick, 7/11/12, loc. cit.
294 'knocked up', ibid.
'our long winter', Campbell, *WM*, 7/11/12, p. 169
295 'man to go', James Cook, *The Journals of Captain Cook on His Voyages of Discovery*, ed., J. C. Beaglehole (Boydell Press, Woodbridge, 1999), p. 322
'search party', Priestley, 7/11/12, MS 1097/4
296 'as I thought', Campbell, *WM*, 8/11/12, p. 170
out of the sun, Levick, 9/11/12, MS 1423/1
all its glory, Levick, see back of loc. cit.
297 'could have saved them', Cherry-Garrard, 11/11/12, MS 559/18/1–4
'It is the tent', Cherry-Garrard, 12/11/12, loc. cit.

'to the South Pole', Gran, 12/11/12, p. 216

298 'down to work', Campbell, *WM*, 15–24/11/12, p. 130

into final accounts, see Priestley, B(TN)AE, 'Physiography of Robertson Bay and Terra Nova Bay Region', 1923, p. 53

299 appear more intentional, see Campbell's account, 'Narrative of the Northern Party', in *SLE*, vol. 11, pp. 79 and ff. Campbell gives 25/1/11 as the date for the departure of Scott's depot party – not the correct date, 26/1/11.

'Campbell's Party', Williamson, 13/11/12, MS 774/2; Cherry-Garrard, 15/11/12, loc. cit.

'crazy together', Cherry-Garrard, 17/11/12, loc. cit.

they had to try, Atkinson, 'The Search for the Polar Party', MS 280/28, pp vii–viii

'rotten for navigating', Wright, *Silas*, 18/11/12, p. 349

'unbounded relief', Atkinson, 24/11/12, loc. cit.

'seem now!', Cherry-Garrard, 25/11/12, loc. cit.

300 'are fine fellows', Cherry-Garrard, 26/11/12, MS 559/18/4

'well with them', Williamson, 27/11/12, MS 774/2

'Henry VIII', Gran, 28/11/12, p. 221

'of the Eastern Party', Williamson, 28/11/12, MS 774/2

'under the circumstances', Priestley, 25/11/12, MS 1097/4

'incontrovertible proof', ibid.

301 'among bumph', Wright, *Silas*, 17/11/12, p. 349

'a masterpiece', Priestley, 27/11/12, loc. cit.

'done something', ibid.

India, South America and Australia, Cherry-Garrard, 28/11/12, MS 559/18/4

'anxious days', Cherry-Garrard, 25/11/12, loc. cit.

302 'up the coast', and subsequent quotes in this paragraph, Scott, *Journals*, pp. 287–9

iron pyrites, Atkinson, 'Spring Journey up Coast, 1911', Part 1, MS 280 28/1–2ER

over the crossing, Scott, *Journals*, pp. 289–90

303 cocoa with sugar, see Simpson, diary, September 1911, MS 1097/47

304 'seems like a month', Williamson, 17/1/13, MS 774/2

New Zealand early, Cherry-Garrard, 12/1/13, MS 559/18/4

'light meal midday', Cherry-Garrard, 17/12/12, loc. cit.

'the Pole', Gran, 17/12/12, p. 232

'with his name', *SLE*, vol. 2, p. 394

'but meekly', Williamson, 18/1/13, loc. cit.

'quite paralysed', Bruce, 18/1/13, MS 402/1–4

heavy use of coal, see Pennell's account, *SLE*, vol. 11, pp. 389–94

by ship's order, Cherry-Garrard, 26/1/13, MS 559/18/4

305 'pretty stiff' job, Bruce, 21/1/13, MS 402/1–4
'get our depot', Priestley, no date, MS 1097/4
'for nothing', Cherry-Garrard, 24/1/13, MS 559/18/4
'gaunt looking place', Cherry-Garrard, 26/1/13, MS 559/11
'smelling of blubber', Bruce, 26/1/13, MS 402/1–4
'proud of it', ibid.

306 'never would have told', Evans, *SLE*, vol. 2, p. 402
'our "igloo"', Dickason, 26/1/13, MS 1634; D
'and admiration', Apsley Cherry-Garrard, *The Worst Journey in the World*, 2
vols (Chatto and Windus, London, 1937) p. 570
'last winter', Priestley, 'January 1913', MS 1097/4
'Eastern party of 6 men', Williamson, 4/1/13, loc. cit.
'heading homewards', Cherry-Garrard, 26/1/13, MS 559/11

307 'Antarctic exploration', Lord Curzon, *GJ*, vol. 43 (July 1913), p. 90

Index

Abbott, Petty Officer George Percy ('Tiny'): in Eastern party, xx, xxii, 4, 39; makes will, 29; qualities, 29–30; on outward voyage, 32–4, 38; on final refit of *Terra Nova* in New Zealand, 45; learns pony management, 45; on dogs and ponies in storm on *Terra Nova*, 49; learns Russian, 50; on choice of winter quarters, 62; lands at winter quarters, 63; on Scott's shaving, 65; falls in ice, 70, 129; takes material from Shackleton's hut, 74; lands at Balloon Bight, 78; on Norwegians' clothing, 85; prefers dogs to ponies, 85; carries Campbell's report to Scott, 88; saved from fall into sea, 89; life and activities at Cape Adare, 97–8, 100, 109, 111, 126, 130–1, 133, 136–7, 173; helps build hut at Cape Adare, 104, 111–12, 116; celebrates birthdays, 111–12, 211; falls ill, 112; status, 123; makes canoe, 127; sledging, 127; Levick teaches photography, 128; Dickason bakes pie for, 129; competes with Levick, 130; and rubbish disposal, 130, 137; skiing by night, 136; makes notes on auroras, 138; sews Priestley's sledging flag, 138; on sledging expeditions, 139–43, 153, 156–7; loses weight sledging, 144; knee trouble, 145–7, 151; competes and co-operates, 146; makes dissecting board for Levick, 151; reprimanded by Campbell for not winding chronometer, 153–4; retrieves forgotten items on sledging expedition, 154; makes trousers for Priestley, 166; collects fresh eggs, 167; photographed, 174; plays gramophone outside, 174; on lookout for *Terra Nova*, 180, 198; pecked by penguins, 181; on second season sledging expedition, 184–5, 204; serenades Browning on birthday, 187; beard, 189; in discussions with colleagues, 194; kills seals, 198, 209, 248; repairs Levick's damaged tent, 198; eating and appetite, 211, 219, 233; cheerfulness, 214; takes kitten on board *Terra Nova*, 215; works in hurricane, 216; makes way to ice-cave at Evans Coves, 217; nose frostbitten, 218; singing, 232; spends second winter in ice-cave,

232–4, 237, 239, 241, 257–8, 306; kills emperor penguins, 236; cooking, 237, 239, 243; and ventilation problem in ice-cave, 239–40; Priestley on, 247; injures hand, 249–50, 255, 260, 262, 267; and disciplinary matters, 262; photographs ice-cave party, 263; prepares for sledging journey away from ice-cave, 263; on journey from ice-cave to Cape Evans, 270, 273, 276, 291; little-mentioned, 277; swallows salt, 285; sledging powers, 287; rebuilds sledge, 289; reaches hut at Cape Evans, 292; cleans hut at Cape Evans, 296; retrieves broken sledge, 296–7; diary, 298; at ease with companions, 300; retrieves geological specimens near Cape Roberts, 305
Adare, Cape: Ross finds and names, 11; Borchgrevink at, 12, 195; Mawson plans to leave party at, 20, 43–4, 117–18; Shackleton plans to explore, 23; *Terra Nova* explores, 53; Campbell's Eastern party approaches and establishes base at, 93, 95–101, 107–11, 118, 195; hut built, 104, 108–9; isolation, 110; scientific observations, 110; gale damage, 112–13; and advance of winter, 121; life at, 122–33, 135–7, 180, 234; hierarchy and discipline, 123–4; winter storms, 127–8, 149; rubbish disposal, 129–30, 137; temperature and lighting in hut, 131–2; celebrations, 133; instruments lost, 150; and return of sun, 151; plans to explore abandoned, 168; summer thaw, 171; hut abandoned, 183
Adélie Land, 27
Adélie Mail & Cape Adare Times, The, 167, 171
Adélie penguins, 54, 59, 61, 68, 74, 98–9, 151, 160, 166–7, 193, 205
Admiralty Mountains, 97
amateurism: as British ethos, 90
Amundsen, Roald: leaves for Antarctic, 42; in Bay of Whales (Framheim), 80, 82–5, 88; aims to reach South Pole, 81–3, 86, 107, 147, 196; employs dogs, 85–6, 88, 148, 155; on structure of Barrier, 86–7; Scott learns of presence, 105–7; presence in Antarctica reported to London, 116; Darwin regrets not being informed of

plans, 119; celebrates Midwinter, 134; dress, 141; journey to Pole, 155, 161, 190; reaches South Pole, 224, 297, 300; message to King Haakon on success at Pole, 300

Antarctic expeditions (1897–1912), xxiii–xxiv

Antarctica: lack of life, 8–9; unexplored, 11; appeal to explorers, 13, 18–19; hardships in, 25; unpredictable, 76; shortage of landing spaces, 96

Archer, Walter William, xxii, 65, 207, 282, 293, 296

Armytage, Bertram, 61, 72

Arrival Bay, 236

Atkinson, Dr Edward L. ('Atch'): in Western party, xxi; joins expedition, 31; on storm out of New Zealand, 49; attacks Campbell, 54; first sight of Victoria Land, 57; finds new tapeworm, 69; on Pennell's command, 103; brings mail bag to Safety Camp, 106; anti-scurvy measures, 110; football-playing, 161–2; returns with Scott's support party, 178–9; meets *Terra Nova* on return to Antarctic, 190; treats Teddy Evans for scurvy, 201; takes command of expedition, 207, 214–15, 229; taken to Hut Point on *Terra Nova*, 210; attempts relief of Scott's party, 215; at Hut Point with Cherry-Garrard, 222; on Campbell's leadership qualities, 222; returns to Hut Point with Keohane, 223; returns to Cape Evans to overwinter, 228, 244; and fate of polar party, 229; tries to relieve Eastern party, 229–31, 244; decides whether to search for Scott or Campbell in summer, 244–5; health, 246; fears fate of Scott's party, 275; leads search party for Scott, 282, 291, 297, 299–301; leaves note at Butter Point, 288; finds Scott's tent and bodies, 297; meets Campbell on return, 300

Aurora (ship), 175

auroras, 138, 146

Australia: Scott in, 42; financial support for Scott, 43–4

Baily, Petty Officer, 56

Balloon Bight (Balloon Inlet; Barrier Inlet), 35–6, 51, 77–9, 83, 87, 105

Beardmore glacier, 85, 178, 190, 196, 275, 299

Beaumont, Admiral Sir Lewis, 16, 37, 104, 114, 119, 229, 258, 274

Belgica (ship), 44

Bernacchi, Cape, 286

Bernacchi, Louis, 146

Binmore (Torquay taxidermist), 183

Borchgrevink, Carsten: base and hut at Cape Adare, 11–12, 95–100, 104, 107–8, 110–11, 127, 130–1, 195; uses inlets in Barrier, 36, 79; names Cape Tennyson, 62; uses dogs, 79; uses kayak, 127; on winter storms, 127–8; loses natural history specimens, 137; names Warning Glacier, 140; builds rock hut on Duke of York Island, 141; on

co-operation and divisions, 146; advises against sledging along coast, 150; explores Wood Bay, 174; *First on the Antarctic Continent*, 12, 74, 146

Bowers, Lieut Henry R. ('Birdie'): in Western party, xx; death with Scott, 4, 301; qualities, 42, 286; and coal supply for *Terra Nova*, 52; lands supplies at winter quarters, 63; takes ponies to Hut Point, 105; Christmas celebrations, 134; checks Scott's figures for polar journey, 156; winter journey with Wilson and Cherry-Garrard, 156; and balloon equipment, 176; and ponies on polar journey, 177; helps rescue Lashly from crevasse, 179; on journey to Pole, 201, 293, 302; body found, 297

Brissenden, Leading Stoker Robert, xxii

Britannia's Barrier, 11–12

British Antarctic Expedition (*Terra Nova* expedition; 1910–13): Scott leads, xix; and Scott's death, 5; scientific objectives, 23

Brocklehurst, (Sir) Philip Lee, 72, 74

Browning, Petty Officer Frank V. ('Rings'): in Eastern party, xx, xxii, 4, 39, 71; cares for ship's cat, 29–30, 33, 47, 215; joins *Terra Nova*, 29–30; qualities, 30; instructed by Edgar Evans, 38; in New Zealand, 47–8; on pumping out *Terra Nova*, 48; exhausted by sledging competition, 63; breaks in pony, 65–6; and Scott's farewell to Eastern party, 70; takes material from Shackleton's hut, 74; lists supplies, 75; meets Amundsen in Bay of Whales, 82; on Amundsen's presence in Antarctic, 85; delays Levick on ski trip, 89–91; at Cape Adare, 97–8, 109, 116, 126, 129, 133, 135, 173; learns to read instruments and keeps meteorological records, 113, 128, 144, 160; attempts to catch fish, 115; status, 123; invents alarm device, 128; learns photography from Priestley, 128; and rubbish disposal, 130; takes over cooking, 136, 151, 159, 194; assists Priestley, 137; shaves off whiskers, 138; and sledging expeditions, 139–40, 145, 154, 158–9, 204; remains at Cape Adare hut with Levick, 144; competes and co-operates, 146; reported in 'South Polar Times', 155; practises photography, 158; contributes to sledging song, 159; makes copies of Priestley's notes, 166; photographed, 174; on lookout for *Terra Nova*, 180, 182, 198; leaves Cape Adare, 183; later sledging expedition, 184; birthdays, 187, 246; beard, 189; kills penguin, 198; at Evans Coves, 204, 209; invents lamp, 212; cheerfulness, 214; works in hurricane, 216; makes way to ice-cave at Evans Coves, 217; kills seals, 219, 248, 250, 273; life in ice-cave at Evans Coves, 219, 232–3, 235, 237–8, 241, 243–4, 257, 306; diarrhoea, 227, 238, 243–4, 254, 258–64, 266–7, 269–70, 274; near asphyxiation at

Browning, Petty Officer Frank V. *(continued)*
Cape Adare, 239; cooking, 243; paired
with Levick, 250; hand frostbitten, 255;
logged for misdemeanour, 261–2; cuts
companions' hair, 267, 273; on journey to
Cape Evans, 274, 276, 278–9, 289, 291;
backache, 277; decline, 278–9; improves
after new diet, 284, 287, 289; sledging, 287;
cleans hut at Cape Evans, 296;
photographed at Cape Evans, 297; diary,
298; at ease with companions, 300
Bruce, Wilfred M.: in ship's party, xx, xxii; on
Eastern party, 5; joins Scott in New
Zealand, 47; on board *Terra Nova*, 55, 94,
112–14, 210; lists parties, 55–7; at Butter
Point, 73; on bleakness of King Edward
VII Land, 77; writes to sister Katherine, 77,
84, 92, 112, 114; encounters *Fram*, 80–1,
86; on Norwegians in Antarctica, 84;
unloads pony fodder, 88; saves Abbott
from fall into sea, 89; position in
expedition, 91; journal, 92; at Cape Adare,
100; on Campbell's unhappiness at Cape
Adare, 102; praises Pennell, 103; makes
land on *Terra Nova*, 107; on *Terra Nova*'s
escaping ice trap, 111; celebrates Christmas
on *Terra Nova*, 175; and Campbell's later
sledging expedition, 184; believes Scott
reaches Pole, 190; on unloading difficulties
from *Terra Nova*, 191; on *Terra Nova*'s
entrapment in ice, 200; on picking up
parties, 207; on leaving Campbell for
second winter, 225; visits Evans Coves on
Terra Nova, 305
Burton, Petty Officer, 56
Butter Point, 72, 195, 230, 279, 281, 287–9

Campbell, Cape, 61
Campbell, Lil (Victor's wife), 92, 225, 271
Campbell, Nigel, 271
Campbell, Lieut. Victor L. Arbuthnot ('the
wicked mate'): in Eastern party, xx, xxii, 5,
21, 23, 38–9, 55, 70–2, 75; leads scientific
team, xxi, 41; and Scott's departure, 3–4;
authority, 31; on outward voyage, 34; and
proposed landing in Antarctica, 34–6;
writes to cousin Vera, 34–5, 62, 70, 83,
101; selects landing party, 38–9; and care of
ponies, 40–1; told of Amundsen's departure
for Antarctic, 42; spots iceberg from *Terra
Nova*, 49; provisions for prospecting trip at
Balloon Bight, 51; appropriates matches,
54; learns sledge-hauling, 62–3; unloads at
winter quarters, 62, 64–6; deprived of good
ponies, 66; hears supposed shouting, 68;
kills seals, 68, 129, 208, 227, 248–9; snow-
blindness, 69; commands *Terra Nova*, 71–2,
74–5, 85–6, 88, 93–4; at Butter Point, 73;
288–9; seeks landing on King Edward VII
Land, 76–8; on disappearance of Balloon
Bight, 79; meets *Fram* and Amundsen in
Bay of Whales, 80, 82–4; survey of King

Edward VII Land, 81; writes report for
Scott, 88; character, 92, 173; departs for
Robertson Bay, 92, 100, 124,
135, 153, 189, 298; and coal shortage on
Terra Nova, 93; forced to land and winter at
Cape Adare, 95–8, 100–1, 104, 107; on
Terra Nova's departure for New Zealand,
100; orders *Terra Nova* to relieve Eastern
party at beginning of summer 1912, 101;
and building of hut, 108–9; scientific
observations at Cape Adare, 110, 113, 115,
137; life at Cape Adare, 115–16, 125, 131,
133; Markham praises achievements, 120;
disagreements with Priestley, 122–3, 135;
leadership, behaviour and discipline,
122–4, 133, 144–5, 153, 222, 251, 267, 296;
smoking, 122, 141, 242; relations with
Levick, 123–4, 135–6; plans and undertakes
sledging explorations, 127, 139–44, 152–4,
156–8, 160, 174; sensitivity to cold, 131;
Christmas celebrations, 135; decorates
Priestley's sledging flag, 138; makes notes
on medical care, 139; loses weight sledging,
144; attempts cooking, 145; and
disappearance of sea ice, 149; thirty-sixth
birthday, 150; tells stories of childhood,
153; reported in 'South Polar Times', 155;
conducts religious services, 157, 228; turns
back from sledging expedition, 158, 160;
foregoes salary, 163; Scott's final written
instructions to, 163, 229; swollen gums,
166; fails to explore King Edward VII
Land, 169; orders permanent watch for
returning *Terra Nova*, 180; and return of
Terra Nova to Cape Adare, 182–4; second
season sledging expedition, 184–6, 191–4,
204–5; finds fossil tree remains, 188; grows
beard, 189; awaits arrival of *Terra Nova*,
197–8; favours snow cave for refuge, 199;
Terra Nova attempts to retrieve, 207–8,
210, 215; stranded at Evans Coves, 208–10;
on edible seaweed, 211; and non-arrival of
Terra Nova, 212; constructs and moves into
ice-cave at Evans Coves, 213–17, 219, 222,
225, 232–3, 235, 237–9, 243–54, 258–9,
262; and cheerfulness, 214; loses compass
when blown over by wind, 216; nose and
face frostbitten, 218, 255–6; cooking and
eating, 219, 237, 240, 243; suffers diarrhoea
and frozen parts, 226–7; Atkinson aims to
relieve, 229–30; finds and kills emperor
penguins, 236; and ventilation problem in
ice-cave, 239–40; Pennell praises, 242, 259;
and Abbott's injured hand, 249–50, 255;
thirty-seventh birthday, 252, 257; imagines
life on return to England, 253; bilious
attack, 254; Pennell writes to Beaumont on
plight of, 258–9; logs Browning for
misdemeanour, 261; prepares for sledging
journey away from ice-cave, 263; sketches
ice-cave, 263; and diarrhoea epidemic, 264;
leaves ice-cave for Cape Evans, 264; on

journey from ice-cave, 267–89, 291–2; sketches Levick sledging, 268; kills emperor penguin, 270; illness on journey, 271, 274–5, 277–9, 284; reaches depot at Cape Roberts, 282–5; qualities, 286; health improves, 287; changes direction for Hut Point, 290; eye trouble, 290; finds tobacco, 292; reaches Cape Evans, 293, 295, 300; photographed at Cape Evans, 297; narrative of expedition, 298; at ease with companions, 300; admires Scott's message to public, 301; scientific achievements, 301; surveying at Cape Evans, 303; prepares for third winter, 304; returns to Evans Coves on *Terra Nova*, 305–6

cheerfulness: as desired quality, 213–14

Cheetham, Boatswain Alfred B., xxii, 65, 103

Cherry-Garrard, Apsley ('Cherry'): in Western party, xxi; departs on expedition, 30; on outward voyage, 33; on killing of seals, 50; first sight of Victoria Land, 57; seasickness, 57; and ponies, 87; sleeps through blizzard, 87; cooking, 106; sledges with Scott, 106; edits 'South Polar Times', 134, 246; hangs royal portraits in Cape Evans hut, 135; journey with Bowers and Wilson, 156; returns with Scott's support party, 178–9; receives mail from *Terra Nova*, 190; Simpson sends to Hut Point, 202–4, 209; wears spectacles, 202; diary, 203, 231; at One Ton Depot, 209; reaches Hut Point, 214, 222, 230; on difficulty of relieving Campbell, 215; pessimism over polar party, 224; as recorder of expedition events, 224; on Atkinson's attempt to reach Campbell, 231; overwinters at Cape Evans, 246; fears fate of Scott's party, 275; in search party for Campbell, 282, 291, 296, 299–300; Scott esteems, 286; on discovery of fossilised plant, 301; on food, 304; and attempts to enter Evans Coves to retrieve geological specimens, 305; on visit to ice-cave at Evans Coves, 306

Christchurch, New Zealand, 43

Christmas: celebrations, 54–5, 133–4, 174–6, 178

Clissold, Thomas, xxi, 148, 177, 206

competition and co-operation, 145–6

Copp, Petty Officer, 56

Corner Camp, 80, 84, 87, 106, 155, 161, 223

crabeater seals, 149, 198

Crean, Petty Officer Thomas, xxi, 39, 54, 179, 201, 246, 297

Crozier, Cape, 59–62, 156, 288

Daily Mail, 18, 23, 119

Daily Telegraph, 19

Darwin, Major Leonard, 16–17, 23–5, 28, 44, 81–2, 118–19

David, Professor T. W. Edgeworth: reaches magnetic South Pole with Mawson, 38, 73, 257; arranges Australian grant for Scott, 43;

provides clothes for Priestley, 46, 115, 173; Priestley works with in Sydney, 53; in Shackleton's hut at Cape Royds, 66, 268; picked up at Relief Inlet, 267; leaves specimens at Depot Island, 274, 277–8, 301; sledges along coast, 281

Davies, Francis: works ashore, xxii; and final refit of *Terra Nova* in New Zealand, 45; builds hut for winter quarters, 63; at Cape Adare, 97–8; makeshift repairs on *Terra Nova*, 114; makes sledge-meters, 183

Day, Bernard C.: in Western party, xxi; as motor mechanic, 46, 64; admires skis, 50; and Scott's instructions on secrecy, 58; at Ross Island, 59; provides runners for sledges, 74, 154; carries letters from polar party, 176; returns to Barrier, 177; re-embarks on *Terra Nova*, 206; not in final Polar party, 293

Debenham, Frank ('Deb'): in Far Western party, xxi; joins Scott, 43; four-man geological party sets off, 72–3; and British amateurism, 90; member of second geological party, 161–2; injures knee playing football, 162; sledge flag, 176; *Terra Nova* to pick up at Granite Harbour, 183; due to be relocated, 183, 185–6; Priestley's anxiety over, 198–9; on Atkinson's proposed relief of Campbell's party, 229; damages ankle, 246; searched for at Granite Harbour, 274; depot found at Cape Roberts, 282; left at Cape Evans, 282, 291, 296; meets Campbell's party at Cape Evans, 293; photographs Campbell's party, 297; retrieves geological specimens at Evans Coves, 305

Depot Island, 274, 277–8

Dickason, Seaman Harry ('Dick'): in Eastern party, xx, xxii, 39, 71; and Scott's departure, 4; joins *Terra Nova*, 29; on Eastern party ponies, 65, 69; on Abbott's fall, 70; on Scott's farewell to Eastern party, 70; at Butter Point, 73; on appearance of Barrier, 76; on *Terra Nova*'s character, 77; in Robertson Bay, 95; at Cape Adare, 97–9, 105, 109–10, 126, 173; cooking and domestic duties, 105, 116, 129, 152, 232, 239, 243, 284; learns to read instruments, 113, 128; attempts to catch fish, 115; status, 123; skiing in winter, 136; assists Priestley, 137; beard, 138, 174, 189; and sledging expeditions, 139–40, 144–5, 156–8; competes and co-operates, 146; reports sea ice gone, 149; reported in 'South Polar Times', 155; on penguins, 160; climbing on coastal cliffs, 166; article on cooking during sledging, 167–8; on gathering fresh eggs, 167; photographed, 174; climbing at Cape Adare, 180–1; on lookout for *Terra Nova*, 180; on second season sledging expedition, 184, 185, 186, 204–5; efficiency, 194; attempts to kill crabeater

Dickason, Seaman Harry *(continued)*
seal, 198; invents lamp, 212; spends second
winter in ice-cave at Evans Coves, 212,
215–17, 219, 232–3, 237–9, 241, 243–4,
248, 306; cheerfulness, 214; blown over
carrying goods, 216; smoking, 242; kills
seals, 248, 250; paired with Priestley, 250;
boots disintegrate, 251, 254; diarrhoea, 259,
261, 263–6, 269, 277; and disciplinary
matters, 262; on sledging journey from ice-
cave to Cape Evans, 266, 267, 272, 280,
284, 286, 289, 291; Priestley praises, 272;
snow-blindness, 277; misses blubber in
hoosh, 280–1; reading, 284; sledging
ability, 287; rebuilds sledge, 289; cleans hut
at Cape Evans, 296; retrieves broken
sledge, 296–7; diary, 298; at ease with
companions, 300; retrieves geological
specimens near Cape Roberts, 305
Discovery (ship), 12, 14, 21, 53, 59
dogs: on Antarctic expeditions, 1–2, 148; on
board *Terra Nova*, 47; Amundsen employs,
85–6, 88, 155, 224, 247–8; Scott takes on
polar journey, 177–8; shot at expedition's
end, 304
Drake, Francis, xxii, 114, 224
dress, 46, 115, 142–3, 264–5
Drygalski Ice Tongue, 189, 198–200, 210, 250,
252–3, 257–8, 267–70
Duke of York Island, 141, 166–7
Dunlop Island (Cape), 282, 285, 302

Eastern party (or Northern party): composition
and designation, xix–xxiv, 38, 55–6, 298–9;
in Scott's plans, 27, 34–6, 52–3, 59;
scientific role, xix, 41; supplies and
equipment, 42, 75–6; ponies, 65–6, 69, 88;
departs, 70–2, 74–6; in Bay of Whales,
80–4; and survey of King Edward VII
Land, 81; as separate expedition, 82, 88,
95–6; leaves for Robertson Bay, 92; at
Cape Adare, 100–1; first sledging
expedition, 140–1; described at Cape
Evans, 155; relaxes in summer, 165; awaits
arrival of *Terra Nova*, 194, 197; spends
second winter at Evans Coves, 208–10,
213–21, 225, 232–52; assessment of dangers
to, 222, 225–6, 229; plans survival and
return to Cape Evans, 228; Atkinson
attempts to reach and relieve, 229–31;
prepares to sledge from ice-cave to Cape
Evans, 260–1; sledging journey from ice-
cave to Cape Evans, 266–90; reaches base
at Cape Evans, 292–4, 300; learns fate of
polar party, 293; physical condition on
return, 295–6; account of expedition,
298–9; Atkinson to search for, 299; reserve
over lack of relief effort, 301; scientific
achievements, 301; *see also* Campbell,
Lieut. Victor L. Arbuthnot
emperor penguins, 59–60, 156, 192, 236, 264,
270

Erebus, Mount, 11, 17, 59, 201, 269, 276, 285,
290, 303
Evans, Cape: Scott's winter quarters at, xix;
Scott renames, 62; hut established at, 63–5,
69, 91; Eastern party return to, 73–4, 88,
292; *Terra Nova* attempts to reach, 84,
189–90; *Terra Nova* reaches, 206, 304;
ponies and mules at, 65–6, 86, 88, 244;
Midwinter celebrations at, 134;
temperature at, 148; football match at, 161;
Christmas at, 176; and Campbell's plans to
sledge to/from Evans Coves, 256–7, 207,
215, 256–7; life at (winter 1912), 228, 231,
244, 251; Eastern party's sledge journey to/
from Evans Coves, 266–90; southern
search party leaves from, 275, 282; Eastern
party at, 292–5, 300, 303; departure of
expedition from, 305
Evans, Petty Officer Edgar ('Taff'): in Western
party, xxi, 39; Priestley talks with, 2, 4;
death with Scott, 4, 297, 301; on outward
voyage, 38; at Butter Point, 73; makes
snow-shoes for ponies, 147; on journey to
Pole, 179, 201, 302
Evans, Lieut. R. G. R. ('Teddy'): in
Western party, xx; joins Scott's expedition,
21, 30; on outward voyage, 33–4; leaves
New Zealand, 48; on dead ponies aboard
Terra Nova, 49; chooses winter quarters, 62;
in charge of supplies ashore, 63; takes over
weakest ponies, 105–6; departs on sledge
journey, 155, 161; on journey to Pole, 176;
returns from Scott's polar party, 201;
seriously ill with scurvy, 201–2, 225; taken
on board *Terra Nova*, 206; rumoured death
with polar party, 291–3; commands *Terra
Nova*, 304; visits Evans Coves ice-cave on
Terra Nova, 305
Evans, Captain Frederick Pryce, 184
Evans Coves: *Terra Nova* at, 184–5, 196; *Terra
Nova* fails to reach, 198, 200, 207, 210;
decision to prepare for winter at, 199,
204–5, 208; ice-cave (igloo) dug, 209;
Eastern party occupies winter ice-cave,
213–21, 226–8, 232–59; ventilation
problems, 239–40; light returns (summer
1912), 253–6; Eastern party leaves, 264–5;
Terra Nova party visit and inspect ice-cave,
305–6

food: Christmas, 133–4, 174–6, 178; from local
fauna, 152, 166; carried on sledging
expeditions, 156–7; preparation, 174;
Priestley given complete charge of, 198,
211, 226, 228, 240, 248, 250, 252, 254,
257–8, 276, 282, 286; craving for, 211, 218,
223, 227, 233, 245, 276, 280; on sledging
journey from ice-cave to Cape Evans, 266,
268–9; cache found at Cape Roberts,
282–3; *see also* penguins; seals
Forde, Petty Officer Robert: in Western party,
xxi; departs on sledge journey, 155; fingers

frostbitten, 161, 195–6; sledge flag, 176; at Granite Harbour, 183; picked up by *Terra Nova*, 196; leaves Cape Evans, 207; leaves message at Cape Roberts, 282; invalided out, 293

fossils: search for, 187–8, 262, 301

Fram (ship): leaves for Antarctic, 42, 44; *Terra Nova* meets in Bay of Whales, 80, 82–3; sails for oceanographic work in South Atlantic, 87

Framheim (hut), 82, 87, 134, 148, 155, 161

frostbite, 161, 195–6, 218, 227, 255

Gaussberg, 20, 23

George V, King: coronation, 134–5

Gerof, Demetri: in Western party, xxi, 178, 206; in New Zealand, 45; on journey with Cherry-Garrard, 209, 214, 222; returns to Cape Evans, 228; in search party for Campbell, 282, 285, 299

giant petrels, 104, 121

Glacier Tongue, 70–1, 88, 89, 302

Gran, Tryggve: in Western party, xxi; joins expedition, 31; photograph with Campbell, 34; and Amundsen's departure for Antarctic, 42, 44; claims to see iceberg from *Terra Nova*, 49; teaches skiing to expedition members, 50; skiing accident, 69; status, 90–1; at One Ton Camp, 105; at Christmas celebrations, 134; skis alongside Clissold to Cape Royds, 148; departs on sledge journey, 155; on expected return to New Zealand, 162; sledge flag, 176; at Granite Harbour, 183; spots *Terra Nova*, 195; in trapped *Terra Nova*, 200; at Cape Evans, 206, 215, 246, 251; and Atkinson's party's return to Cape Evans, 228; on Midwinter Day (1912), 246; leaves message at Cape Roberts, 282; congratulated on Norwegians reaching Pole, 297; on Beardmore Glacier, 299; records anniversary of Scott's reaching Pole, 304; retrieves specimens near Cape Roberts, 305

Granite Harbour, 7, 162, 176, 189, 195, 274, 280–2

Haakon VII, King of Norway, 91, 224, 300

Haig, Major-General Sir Douglas (*later* 1st Earl), 71

Hansen, Nicolai, 137, 180

Heald, Petty Officer, 56

Hearne, Samuel, 7–8

Hell's Gate (moraine), 255, 266

hierarchy and discipline, 123–4, 144

Hooper, Frederick, xxi, 176–7

Hut Point, 59–60, 62, 69, 88–90, 106, 200, 202–3, 206, 209–10, 222–3, 230–1, 282, 290–2, 305

hymn-singing, 115, 228, 236

Inexpressible Island: as name for sight of ice-cave (igloo), 298

Japanese expedition: departs for Antarctica, 114; enters King Edward VII Land, 187–8

Johansen, Hjalmar, 168, 178

Journal of the Royal Geographical Society, 13, 119

Joyce, Ernest, 67

Kainan-maru (ship), 43, 187

Keohane, Petty Officer Patrick, xxi, 178–9, 210, 215, 222–3, 228, 230

killer whales, 23, 172

King Edward VII Land: Scott names, xx, 12; Shackleton plans to explore, 13–14; Scott plans to explore, 17–18, 21, 27, 35–6, 41, 52–3, 59; Campbell draws map of, 34; Eastern party aims for, 70–2; Shackleton attempts to reach, 71; Eastern party fails to find landing place, 76–8, 83, 86, 92; Norwegians explore, 168–9, 188; Japanese expedition enters, 187–8; *Terra Nova* tries to reach, 304

Knowles, Seaman, 57

Larsen, Mount, 192

Lashly, Chief Stoker William, xxi, 39, 176, 179, 201, 245, 275

Leese, Petty Officer, 56

leopard seals, 172

Levick, Dr George Murray ('the Old Sport' or 'Tofferino'): in Eastern party, xxii, 38, 74; and Scott's departure, 4; diary, 6, 67, 123, 135, 199; on outward voyage, 32; as party zoologist and photographer, 41; chafes at ship life, 51; accumulates secret stores, 54; learns sledge-hauling, 62–3; collects ballast for *Terra Nova*, 66; grows beard, 68, 189; kills seals for food, 68, 72, 209, 227; snow-blindness, 69, 237; on attempted landing on King Edward VII Land, 77; lands at Balloon Bight, 78; visits Amundsen's camp, 82; on race with Amundsen, 85; delayed on ski trip with Browning, 89–91; view of Browning, 89, 159; Bruce on, 92; sick on *Terra Nova*, 93; advises staying at Cape Adare, 97; unloads at Cape Adare, 98; photography, 100, 110–11, 113, 190, 263, 296; at Cape Adare, 104, 133; shoots giant petrels, 105; and building of Cape Adare hut, 108–9; and provisioning with birds and penguins, 110; and Abbott's illness, 112; poems, 113, 137, 165, 245; hymn-singing, 115; loses objects, 115, 192; praises Priestley, 121, 226; conciliates between Campbell and Priestley, 122–3, 125–6, 135; smoking, 122; plans novel, 123–4; relations with Campbell, 123–4, 135–6; teaches Abbott photography, 128; offers outside work to Dickason, 129; fencing and competing with Abbott, 130; on temperature control in hut, 131; Christmas celebrations, 135; thirty-fourth birthday, 135; and Priestley's sledging flag motto, 138; lectures on medical matters

Levick, Dr George Murray *(continued)*
and treatment, 139; and preparations for sledging expedition, 139–40; first trial sledging excursion, 144–5; remains at Cape Adare hut with Browning, 144; zoological work, 144, 193; and Campbell's leadership, 146; competes and co-operates, 146; studies Adélie penguin, 151–2, 160, 166–7; instructions on scientific method, 152; tells stories of childhood, 153; on sledging expedition, 154, 158–9; reported in 'South Polar Times', 155; personal health and comfort techniques, 159; asked to forego salary, 163; scientific work, 168, 171–2, 182; Priestley describes and sketches, 173; on lookout for *Terra Nova*, 180, 198–9, 212; pecked by penguins, 181; and return of *Terra Nova* to Antarctica, 182, 185; leaves behind specimens, 183; fails to master navigation, 185; on second season sledging expedition, 185–6, 192–4, 204–5; misunderstanding with Campbell over rendezvous, 187; boots wear out, 193; finds sheltered cove with seals and penguins, 193; tent damaged by wind, 198; favours strong snow hut, 199; accompanies sick Evans home, 207; stranded at Evans Coves, 208–10; suffering, 214; works in hurricane, 216; makes way to ice-cave at Evans Coves, 217–18; cooking at Evans Coves, 219; reads to companions, 222, 232; spends second winter in ice-cave at Evans Coves, 223, 226, 232–3, 237–41, 243–5, 251, 254, 257, 306; on men's bodily malfunctions, 226; improves lamps, 235; kills emperor penguins, 236; rules on meat, 240; singing, 240, 243, 245; birthday, 246; Priestley on, 247; paired with Browning, 250; row with Priestley, 251; hopes for relief expedition from England, 252; imagines being in England, 253; and men's deteriorating health, 254–5; welcomes returning light (summer 1912), 254; on prospective journey to Cape Evans, 257; on tainted food, 260; trains companions with physical exercises, 260; and Browning's misdemeanour, 261–2; on Browning's diarrhoea, 262, 270; prepares for sledging journey away from ice-cave, 263–4; notes on diarrhoea epidemic, 264; on journey from ice-cave to Cape Evans, 266, 268, 271–4, 276–8, 280–2, 284–5, 288–9, 291; takes charge of food supplies, 269, 272–4; eye trouble, 271, 274–5; on eating seal meat, 276; enjoys food found at depot at Cape Roberts, 283–4; swallows salt, 285; qualities, 286; sledging ability, 287; selects sweet foods at Butter Point, 288; learns of fate of polar party, 291; speculates on lack of relief party, 292; at Cape Evans, 295; and physical condition of party on return, 296; plans to buy

motorcycle, 296; retrieves broken sledge, 296–7; writes account of expedition, 298; appearance, 300; at ease with companions, 300; *Antarctic Penguins, a Study of Their Social Habits*, 172
Lillie, Dennis G., xxii, 80
Lindstrom, Henrik, 161, 178
Lysaght, Gerald, 22, 117
Lyttelton, New Zealand, 43–8

Mackay, Dr Alistair: accompanies Mawson to magnetic South Pole, 38, 73, 257, 267, 281
McCarthy, Petty Officer, 56
McDonald, Petty Officer, 56
McGillion, Petty Officer, 56
McKenzie, Petty Officer, 56
McLeod, Seaman, 57
McMurdo Sound (Bay), 11–12, 16–18, 44, 288–9; ice sea, 60, 189, 289
Macquarie Island, 175–6
magnetic South Pole, 19, 20, 38, 78, 257
Mandela, Nelson, 6
Markham, Sir Clements, 119
Mary, Queen of George V, 134–5
Mather, Petty Officer, 56
Matonabbee (Chipewyan chief), 7–8
Mawson, Douglas: meets Scott, 19–21; plans independent Antarctic expedition, 21–2, 27, 36, 43–4, 53, 81, 119; alliance with Shackleton, 22–3, 25; fund-raising, 22, 117, 119; lives off seals on 1908–9 expedition, 38; reaches magnetic South Pole, 38, 73; letters to Scott, 43–4; prospecting in outback, 43; in Shackleton's hut, 66; at Butter Point, 73; wishes to land at Cape Adare, 96; addresses Royal Geographical Society, 117–18; anger on learning of Campbell at Cape Adare, 117, 119; frustrated in London, 120; Pennell sends tracing of *Terra Nova* route to, 134; writes re plans, 169; sails for Antarctic on *Aurora*, 175; sleeps in three-man bag, 257; picked up at Relief Inlet, 267; leaves specimens at Depot Island, 274; sledging at Granite Harbour, 281; Campbell recovers deposited specimens, 301
Meares, Cecil H.: in Western party, xxi; acquires ponies in Siberia, 45, 47; sings own composition, 54; at Hut Point, 69; mocks *Terra Nova*, 76; sledges with Scott, 106; returns from Barrier, 178; taken on board *Terra Nova*, 206; tired of Antarctic, 293
Melbourne, Australia, 42–3
Melbourne, Mount, 183–4, 186, 188, 269
Midwinter celebrations, 134, 246
motors: Scott's plans for, 10, 64; abandoned by Scott, 176
mules: arrive from India, 191; employed, 275, 300; refuse to eat, 299; shot at expedition's end, 304
Murray, James, 67

Nansen, Mount, 192

Neale, Petty Officer, 56

Nelson, Edward W. ('Marie'), xxi, 177, 230, 291

New Zealand: *Terra Nova* takes on coal and stores in, 37, 42, 52; Abbott in, 45; population, 47; *Terra Nova* leaves, 48, 55, 171, 304; Priestley, in, 67; *Terra Nova* delivers mail to, 72; *Terra Nova* returns to, 100–1, 111, 114, 210, 224, 247, 283, 288; mutton from, 109; land connection to Antarctica, 118; Pennell in, 134, 169, 224, 258; Scott writes to agent in, 163, *Nimrod* in, 221; *see also* Lyttelton

Nigger (cat), 29–30, 33, 47, 86, 159, 175; drowned, 215

Nilsen, Lieut. Thorvald, 80, 82–3

Nimrod (ship), 21–2, 49, 66–7, 78–9, 221, 267

Nishikawa, Genzō, 188

Nordenskjöld Ice Tongue, 272–4

North, Cape, 11, 13, 14, 20, 23, 27, 53, 94, 158

North Pole, 9, 10, 81, 83, 85

Northern Foothills, 193–4

Northern party *see* Eastern party

Oates, Captain Lawrence E. G. ('Titus'): in Western party, xxi; death with Scott, 4, 297; joins expedition, 30–1; on managing ponies, 40, 45, 47, 66, 87, 147; attacks Campbell, 54; allocates two ponies to Eastern party, 65; requests mules to replace ponies, 71; at One Ton Camp, 105; dances at Christmas, 134; on journey to Pole, 201, 293; thirty-second birthday, 215; search for body, 299

Omelchenko, Anton L.: in Western party, xxi; brings ponies to Scott in New Zealand, 45; at Cape Evans, 88, 177, 201; dances with Oates, 134

One Ton Depot, 105, 209, 296–7, 306

Parsons, Petty Officer, 56

Paton, Petty Officer, 56

Patterson's Inlet, Stewart Island, 114

penguins: at Cape Adare, 97, 121; as food source, 152, 208–9, 212, 263, 270; rescued by Eastern party members, 171–2; *see also* emperor penguins

Pennell, Lieut. Harry L. L.: takes over command of *Terra Nova*, xxii, 71, 95, 103–4, 107–8; birthday celebrations, 53; on nature of King Edward VII Land, 77; visits Amundsen's camp, 82; exploring and discoveries, 107–8; navigates through ice, 108, 205, 207; return voyage to New Zealand, 114; holds press conference in Christchurch, New Zealand, 119; achievements, 120; sends details of *Terra Nova*'s track to Mawson, 134, 169; Scott writes orders for, 162–3, 191, 206; outlines Scott's plan to Mawson, 170; on rescue of

ship's cat, 175; returns to Antarctica, 182–4, 189; unable to land through ice, 189–90; picks up Griffith Taylor's party, 195; attempts to relieve Eastern party at Evans Coves, 196, 199, 225; on frustrations of second season, 210; arrives in New Zealand (April 1912), 224; praises Campbell, 242; writes to Beaumont from New Zealand on plight of Campbell's party, 258–9, 274; and Eastern party at Granite Harbour, 281; Griffith Taylor's party leaves message for at Cape Roberts, 282; collects party at end of expedition, 304

ponies: characteristics, 1–2, 9; care of, 40, 47–8; arrive in New Zealand, 45; deaths on *Terra Nova*, 49; landed at Cape Evans, 62, 88; Eastern party acquires two, 65–6, 69, 86; mishaps, 70–1; affected by blizzard, 87; deaths, 106; snow-blindness, 147

Ponting, Herbert G.: in Western party, xxi, 177; cinematographs Scott's departure across ice, 1; and Gran's skis, 50; films at winter quarters, 63, 69; at Butter Point, 73; shows lantern slides at Christmas, 134; films football match on ice, 161; last few weeks, 177; tired of Antarctic, 293

Prestrud, Lieut Kristian, 168, 178

Priestley, Bert: wedding cake, 303

Priestley, Raymond: in Eastern party, xx, xxii, 64, 70; witnesses Scott's departure across sea ice, 1–4; journal/diary, 2–3, 6, 124, 126, 153–4, 173, 180, 189, 193, 223, 263; role as geologist, 2; as member of Shackleton's 1907–9 expedition, 2, 4, 43, 46, 61, 65, 72, 78, 221; on Mawson, 19; joins Scott, 43, 46; dress, 46, 115, 166, 173; seasickness on *Terra Nova*, 49, 57; on pack ice in Ross Sea, 51; and Mawson's proposed expedition, 53; acquires secret stores, 54; at Ross Island, 59, 62; and search for landing place, 60–2; composes songs, 62–4, 121, 126, 160; instructs colleagues in sledge-hauling, 62; falls through ice, 65, 148; collects ballast for *Terra Nova*, 66; geological and scientific work, 66, 86, 112, 115, 121–2, 128, 131, 137–8, 153, 158, 168, 172–3, 174, 185, 187–8, 262, 277–8, 286, 289–90, 302; revisits Shackleton's hut, 66–8; on killing seals, 68; on guiding ponies, 70; at Butter Point, 72–3; takes equipment from Shackleton's hut, 73–4; takes Borchgrevink's book, 74; on appearance of King Edward VII Land, 77; lands at Balloon Bight, 78; in Bay of Whales, 79; on Amundsen in Antarctic, 80, 86; entertains men from *Fram*, 82–3; on nature of Norwegians, 84; carries Campbell's report to Scott, 88; on Levick, 91; Bruce on, 92; brings magazines from Shackleton's hut, 93; and coal shortage, 94; and search for winter base, 94; advises

Priestley, Raymond (continued)
staying at Cape Adare, 97; at Cape Adare, 98, 100, 104, 111, 116, 131–3, 149; and provisioning with birds and penguins, 104–5, 110, 194; and building of Cape Adare hut, 108–9; gives book to Abbott, 111; copies Levick's poem, 113; teaches Browning and Dickason to use intruments, 113; boredom and isolation, 121–2; Levick praises, 121, 226; relations with Campbell, 122–3, 125, 135; status and relations with colleagues, 122–4; sledging experience, 127, 132, 140, 145; teaches Browning photography, 128; on subjects of discussion, 129; and rubbish disposal, 130; loses sleep pattern, 137–8, 140; acquires sledging flag, 138; on sledging expeditions, 139–42, 144, 146, 156–8; loses weight sledging, 144; competitiveness, 145; on loss of instruments and records through wind, 150; plans sledging expeditions with Campbell, 152–3; requests more light, 153; reported in 'South Polar Times', 155; praises Browning's record-keeping, 161; asked to forego salary, 163; on Campbell's suspected scurvy, 166; knocked unconscious, 166; paperwork, 166; edits Adelie Mail, 167, 171; on penguin behaviour, 167; finds and helps injured penguins, 172; awaits and prepares for return of Terra Nova, 174, 180, 197, 200, 208, 295; prepares food for sledging expedition, 174; plays gramophone for New Year (1912), 181; loads rocks and records on to Terra Nova, 182; beard, 183, 189; adds spikes to boots, 184; on second season sledging expedition, 185–8, 192–3, 204–5; near-hanging in ice, 187; sends meteorological records to Simpson, 190; films lost by Levick, 192; spends second winter in ice-cave at Evans Coves, 192, 209, 215–17, 219, 227, 234–5, 237–44, 246–53, 255–7; manages and allocates food, 198, 211, 226, 228, 240, 248, 250, 252, 254, 257–8, 272, 275–6, 282, 286; at Cape Evans, 207, 209–10, 295; in discussion on danger of being marooned at Evans Coves, 208; moves to winter quarters, 212; cheerfulness and frustration, 214; blown over carrying goods, 216; shares out muscatel raisins, 223; anxiety over family, 232; and personal hygiene, 232; hymn-singing, 236; cooks seal brains, 239; singing, 240, 243; birthday, 250; paired with Dickason, 250; row with Levick, 251; on incessant wind, 256; exhaustion from illness, 260–1, 263; on Levick's physical exercises, 260; supports officers, 262; on leaving ice-cave, 264–5, 267; as Campbell's right-hand man, 265; on journey from ice-cave, 267–78, 280–92; gives up commissariat, 269; diarrhoea, 271; reaches Edgeworth David's depot, 277–8; skiing, 277; misses blubber in hoosh, 280; finds food and objects in depot at Cape Roberts, 283, 285; qualities, 286; Scott on, 286; sledging ability, 287; on eating sugar, 288; mouth and tongue swollen, 290; on fate of polar party, 292; meets Debenham on reaching Cape Evans, 293; types up journal and record, 295, 298; photographed at Cape Evans, 297; at ease with companions, 300; finds fossil, 301; climbs Mount Erebus, 303; on return visit to ice-cave at Evans Coves, 306; Antarctic Adventure, 3

Reeves glacier, 192
Relief Inlet, 184, 267–9
Rennick, Lieut Henry E. de P., xxii, 34, 57
Roberts, Cape, 195, 283–5, 295
Robertson, John, 11
Robertson Bay, 53, 72, 81, 85, 92, 95, 111, 141, 156–7, 182
Ross, Captain James Clark, 6, 11–12, 87, 304
Ross Island: Shackleton lands on, 14–15, 17; Scott reaches, 59–62, 76
Ross Sea: pack ice in, 49
Royal Geographical Society, 16–17, 22, 24–6, 36, 117–19; see also Beaumont, Admiral Sir Lewis; Darwin, Major Leonard
Royal Society, 22
Royds, Cape, 59–62, 66, 70, 74, 148, 154, 303, 305

Safety Camp, 105–6
science: Shackleton includes, 13–14; Scott's plans for, 17–18, 26, 28, 119–20; Mawson's plans, 20, 22, 96, 118; on Terra Nova, 30, 32, 41, 51–2, 83, 86; geologists recruited, 43; at Cape Evans, 63, 176–7, 191, 202–3, 206, 298, 303; geological expeditions in Victoria Land, 72–3, 276, 283, 285; difficulties on Barrier, 78; Eastern party's plans, 101; Wilson's views of advantages of Cape Adare, 107; science tackled at Cape Adare, 110, 112–13, 115, 121–2, 128, 137–9, 144, 146, 150, 158, 166, 168, 171–2, 182–3, 195; in Antarctica, 118–19; Levick studies penguins, 151, 160, 166–7, 172; rules for zoological notebook, 152; Scott's assessment of expedition scientific work, 164; on Eastern party's summer sledging, 185–8, 193; at ice-cave, 213, 238, 277; Simpson's assessment of, 224; on Eastern party's journey to Cape Evans, 277–9; plans for search party to achieve, 299; rocks collected, 301; Scott's report of finding copper ore, 302; Terra Nova collects specimens on way out of Antarctica, 305–6
Scott, Kathleen (née Bruce): confidence in Scott's reaching South Pole, 10; on Scott's reaction to Shackleton's plans, 15; Mawson meets, 21–2; in South Africa and New

Zealand with Scott, 34, 45; sews name-tags on men's clothing, 48; letters from Scott, 51, 58, 60–1, 65, 163, 177, 224; brother Wilfred writes to, 77, 84, 92, 112, 114; chooses curtain material, 109; writes to Scott, 114, 116; attends Mawson's RGS lecture, 119; provides presents for men's Christmas, 133; watches coronation procession, 134; Scott makes note for on polar journey, 179; letter from Pennell, 210; reassures Mrs Campbell of Victor's safety, 225; Beaumont writes to, enclosing Pennell's letter, 274; at Dunlop Island, 285

Scott, (Sir) Peter, 114, 155

Scott, Captain Robert Falcon: on British Antarctic Expedition (1910), xix–xx ; in Western party, xx; sets out across sea ice, 1–3; takes sledge dogs and ponies, 2; death, 3–5, 292, 301; aims to reach South Pole, 9, 12–13, 17, 26, 71, 80–1, 108, 147, 302; on transporting loads, 9–10; as leader of 1901–4 expedition, 10, 12; claims regional exclusiveness, 13–15, 23–5; rivalry with Shackleton, 14–17, 22–4, 36, 119; scientific objectives, 17–18, 23; plans route to Pole, 18; meets Mawson, 19–21, 27; funding, 24, 45, 63, 162, 164; speech to Royal Geographical Society, 25–8; organises expedition, 26; takes command of *Terra Nova* in South Africa, 33–4; revises plans for landing Eastern party, 34–6; on risk to *Terra Nova* of being trapped in ice, 37; announces landing party, 38; and Mawson's planned expedition, 43–4; leaves New Zealand, 48; plots course through pack ice, 50; on maintaining secrecy, 58; smoking, 58; chooses winter quarters, 60–3; revisits Hut Point, 69; on sanitary arrangements, 69; says farewell to Eastern party, 70; criticises Shackleton's early attempt to reach King Edward VII Land, 71; orders to Campbell to find winter quarters, 76, 83; and partition of territories and aims, 81–2; unaware of Amundsen's presence, 86; on condition of ponies, 87; and discipline, 91; and Campbell's winter base, 94; orders to Pennell on commanding *Terra Nova*, 95, 100, 104; and Eastern party at Cape Adare, 100–1; Campbell reports to on Amundsen's presence, 105–7; depot-laying, 105; rescues dogs from crevasse, 106; expedition supported by RGS, 119–20; Midwinter celebrations, 134; on organisation of expedition and journey to Pole, 147, 155–6; on journey to Pole, 161, 179, 201; writes instructions before polar departure, 162–3, 206; final letters to Kathleen, 163–4, 177; and King Edward VII Land, 169; Pennell describes plans to Mawson, 170–1; takes dogs further south, 177; Atkinson seeks with Keohane, 215; Amundsen leaves equipment for at South Pole, 224; journals

and account of expedition, 224, 301–3; notes on living off land, 229; feared dead, 231; search party plans to look for, 275; view of Levick, 286; Campbell's party learns of fate, 291–2; reaches Pole, 297, 300; tent and body found, 297; message to public, 301; qualities, 301

Scott's Nunatuk, 169, 188

seals: as food source, 37, 38, 129, 140, 152, 208–9, 211–12, 219, 227, 239, 248, 264, 273, 275, 284, 376

Shackleton, Sir Ernest: leads Antarctic expedition (1907–9) 1–2, 10, 13–16, 18, 78–9; with Scott on 1901–4 expedition, 10; balloon ascent, 12, 14; regional constraints and partition of territories, 14–15, 24, 82; Scott's resentment of and rivalry with, 14–17, 22–4, 36, 119, 179; and Mawson's proposed expedition, 21–3, 25, 27, 44, 53, 119; financing and funds, 22–3; proposes to lead, 22–3, 36; lecture tour in America, 23, 25; fails to find Balloon Bight, 36; and Scott's recruitment of Priestley, 43; at Ross Island, 59–60, 65, 148; Scott's party finds hut, 66–7; at Cape Royds, 70; attempts to reach King Edward VII Land, 71; commercial interests, 73; Lysaght supports, 117; attends Mawson's RGS lecture, 118; Scott analyses journey to Pole, 155, 179

Simpson, George C. ('Sunny Jim'): in Western party, xxi; on Cherry-Garrard, 30; on outward voyage, 32; makes ice-cave, 74; releases balloons, 176; learns of Scott's polar journey, 177; at Cape Evans, 190; scientific work, 190, 230; decides to return to India, 191, 202; and arrival of Pennell at Cape Evans, 206; on board *Terra Nova* for return to New Zealand, 210; learns of Amundsen's reaching Pole, 224; journey with Scott, 302

skuas, 109, 152, 172, 181

sleep: difficulties, 127–8, 140–1, 143

Smith, Alexander, 11

Smith's Inlet, 94, 144, 158

South Africa: *Terra Nova* in, 33–4, 38

'South Polar Times', 134, 155, 246

South Pole: race for, 15–16, 18–19, 26, 71–2, 84, 86, 108, 147; Amundsen sets off for, 155, 161; Scott departs for, 161; Amundsen reaches, 224, 297, 300; Scott reaches, 297, 300

Southern Cross expedition, 146

Southern Foothills, 192, 205, 208

Stewart Island, 112, 114, 116

Stubberud, Jorgen, 168–9, 178

Taylor, Thomas Griffith ('Griff'): in Far Western party, xxi; joins Scott, 43; leader of a four-man geological party, 72–3; and British amateurism, 90; football-playing, 162; sledge flag, 176; leader of second geological party at Granite Harbour, 183,

Taylor, Thomas Griffith (continued)
196, 210, 274; and Campbell's second
season expedition, 186, 192; re-embarks on
Terra Nova, 206; and Depot Island, 278;
leaves message and photographs at Cape
Roberts, 282–5; depot at Cape Bernacchi,
286–7; tired of Antarctic, 293; geological
work, 301
temperature (indoor): control and dissension
over, 131
temperature (outdoor): extreme low, 148
Tennyson, Alfred, Lord: cape named for, 62
Terra Nova (ship): personnel, xix–xxii; Scott
leaves, 1; refitted for expedition, 25;
reconnoitring role and activities, 27, 36,
53, 61, 72, 107–8, 118; sails for Antarctic,
28–30; on outward voyage, 32–3, 38; risk
of being trapped in ice, 37; final refit in
New Zealand, 43, 45–7; encounters storm
out of New Zealand, 48–9; enters and
clears ice, 50–1, 54, 57, 207; coal
consumption, 52, 93–4; plans to explore
unknown coast, 52–3, 72, 104; Christmas
aboard, 54–5; at Ross Island, 61–2; moves
to Glacier Tongue, 70; Campbell
commands, 71, 85–6, 88; Pennell takes
over command, 71, 95, 103–4; meets Fram
in Bay of Whales, 80–3; lands at Cape
Adare, 96, 99–100; sails for New Zealand
under Pennell, 100, 111–14; discovers new
coast, 107–8, 120; Campbell orders to
relieve at beginning of summer, 101;
escapes being trapped in ice, 111; Scott's
instructions for return, 163; plans to pick
up Eastern party, 166, 199–200; some crew
volunteer for Mawson's expedition, 170;
Eastern party awaits return, 174, 197–8;
returns to Antactica, 175, 182, 189; and
Griffith Taylor's party, 183, 195, 210;
penetrates ice on return trip, 184, 205–6;
makes contact with Cape Evans party, 190;
at Cape Evans, 206–8; picks up parties,
206–7; at Hut Point, 210; returns to New
Zealand (March–April 1912), 210, 215,
224; fails to collect Campbell's party, 212,
240–1, 247; lands Eastern party gear, 293;
arrives at Cape Evans to pick up returning
men, 304
Terror (ship), 11
Terror, Mount, 11, 276
thirst, 141
Times, The: on British aim to reach South
Pole, 18
tobacco: quantity of, 47; shortage, 219

Victoria Land, xix, 11–12, 14, 57, 72, 161, 174,
183, 185

Warning Glacier, 140, 144, 154
Watanabe, Chikasaburō, 188
Webb, Seaman, 56
Weddell seals: killed for food, 38, 41, 68, 208
weight loss (human), 144
Western party: composition, xx–xxi, 55–6;
designated, xix
Whales, Bay of, 36, 79–84, 86, 106, 114, 116,
155, 178
Wild, Frank, 67, 257
Williams, Petty Officer, 56
Williamson, Petty Officer Thomas S.: joins
shore party, xxii, 207; Priestley talks with,
2; falls through ice, 64; volunteers for
Atkinson's party to relieve Campbell,
230–1; on fate of polar party, 245; at
Cape Evans, 246; and Campbell's
successful return, 300; and arrival of Terra
Nova at Cape Evans, 304; on supplying
depot of provisions for future expeditions,
306
Wilson, Dr Edward Adrian ('Uncle Bill'): in
Western party, xxi; sets off across ice, 1–2;
death with Scott, 4, 301; with Scott on
1902–3 expedition, 10; attempts to cross
Barrier, 12; and Scott's rivalry with
Shackleton, 14; turns against Shackleton,
17; Mawson dislikes, 21; and Cherry-
Garrard, 30; bird-skinning, 34; leaves New
Zealand, 48; qualities, 48; skins seals, 50;
reaches Ross Island, 59; plans possible
route to Pole, 60; chooses winter quarters,
62; describes Adélie penguins, 68; makes
farewells to Eastern party, 70–1; sledges
with Scott, 106; Midwinter celebrations,
134; journey with Bowers and Cherry-
Garrard, 156; copies Scott's instructions,
162; diary, 162; on journey to Pole, 179,
201; scientific concerns, 202–3, 287; body
found, 297
women: as beasts of burden, 7–8
Wood, Cape, 157
Wood Bay, 97, 101–2, 174, 183, 186
Wright, Charles S. ('Silas'): in Western party,
xxi; on Campbell, 31; qualities, 32; on
Levick, 41; at Butter Point, 73–4; and
British amateurism, 90; returns with Scott's
support party, 177, 179; at Cape Evans,
201; short-sightedness, 202; takes over
Simpson's work, 202–3, 206; diary, 203; on
Atkinson's proposed relief of Campbell's
party, 229–30; on fate of polar party, 229;
leads search party for Scott, 282, 291, 297;
on Beardmore Glacier, 299; on
Amundsen's message to King Haakon,
301